Psycho... Theories of RELIGION

Psychological Theories of RELIGION

JAMES FORSYTH

University of Ottawa

Upper Saddle River, New Jersey 07458

Library of Congress Cataloging-in-Publication Data

FORSYTH, JAMES [date].
  Psychological theories of religion / JAMES FORSYTH
    p. cm.
  Includes index.
  ISBN 0-13-048068-1
  1. Psychology, Religious—History—20th century. I. Title.
  BL53 .F615   2003
  200'.1'9—dc21   2002070938

VP, Editorial Director: *Charlyce Jones Owen*
Acquisitions Editor: *Ross Miller*
Assistant Editor: *Wendy Yurash*
Editorial Assistant: *Carla Worner*
Editorial/Production Supervision: *Joanne Riker*
Prepress and Manufacturing Buyer: *Brian Mackey*
Director of Marketing: *Beth Gillett Mejia*
Marketing Manager: *Chris Ruel*
Marketing Assistant: *Scott Rich*
Cover Art Director: *Jayne Conte*
Cover Designer: *Bruce Kenselaar*

This book was set in 10/12 Palatino by East End Publishing Services, Inc.
and was printed and bound by Courier Companies, Inc. The cover was
printed by Phoenix Color Corp.

Acknowledgments and credits begin on page xiii, which constitutes
a continuation of the copyright page.

© 2003 by Pearson Education, Inc.
Upper Saddle River, New Jersey 07458

Printed in the United States of America

10 9 8 7 6 5 4 3 2 1

ISBN 0-13-048068-1

Pearson Education LTD., *London*
Pearson Education Australia PTY, Limited, *Sydney*
Pearson Education Singapore, Pte. Ltd
Pearson Education North Asia Ltd, *Hong Kong*
Pearson Education Canada, Ltd., *Toronto*
Pearson Educación de Mexico, S.A. de C.V.
Pearson Education—Japan, *Tokyo*
Pearson Education Malaysia, Pte. Ltd
Pearson Education, *Upper Saddle River, New Jersey*

CONTENTS

PREFACE   ix

ACKNOWLEDGMENTS   xiii

I. SIGMUND FREUD

Religion and the Father Complex   1

Life   3
Theory of Personality   7
Theory of Religion   16
Evaluation   28
Suggested Readings   46
Notes   47

II. C.G. JUNG

Religion and Archetype   51

Life   52
Theory of Personality   59
Theory of Religion   68
Evaluation   88
Suggested Readings   98
Notes   99

III. WILLIAM JAMES

Religion and Temperament   103

Life   105
Philosophical Context   110
James' Psychology of Religion   115
Evaluation   127
Suggested Readings   131
Notes   131

IV. ERICH FROMM

Religion and Humanism   135

Life   137
Theory of Personality   142
Theory of Religion   149
Evaluation   157
Suggested Readings   161
Notes   162

V. GORDON ALLPORT

Religion and Personality   165

Life   167
Theory of Personality   171
Theory of Religion   176
Evaluation   188
Suggested Readings   192
Notes   192

VI. ABRAHAM MASLOW

Religion and Self-Actualization 195

Life 197
Theory of Personality 203
Theory of Religion 209
Evaluation 217
Suggested Readings 220
Notes 220

VII. VIKTOR FRANKL

Religion and Self-Transcendence 223

Life 225
Theory of Personality 227
Theory of Religion 232
Evaluation 238
Suggested Readings 243
Notes 243

APPENDIX

Questions and Answers 245

I. What Is Religion? 245
II. What Is the Psychological Source or
Root of Religion? 246
III. What Is the Psychological Value of
Religion? 247
IV. What Is Religious Experience? 249

INDEX 251

PREFACE

The title of this book suggests that religion is a phenomenon that can be studied psychologically. It is also true that religion cannot be reduced to a merely psychological phenomenon nor its meaning exhausted through psychological understanding. Since religion deals with transcendence, that is, with what transcends or lies beyond our ordinary life experience, it lies—at least in this respect—beyond the scope of psychological analysis. What then does the psychologist of religion study? The traditional answer is "religious experience." As this term suggests, the subject matter of the psychology of religion is the human side of religion, that is, religion as it is experienced by the human subject. Thus, while psychologists cannot study God as an ontological reality (since this lies beyond the scope of psychology), they can study the image of God existing in the mind of the believer; while they cannot judge the validity of the believer's faith, they can study the psychological roots and consequences of that faith; while they cannot study the transcendent object of religion, they can study the religious personality whose faith makes God, to use Jung's phrase, "psychologically real."

Even as a human reality, however, religion is a many-faceted phenomenon. To speak of religion as a psychological phenomenon is to speak of only one aspect of this human side of religion. Accordingly, the psychology of religion is only one discipline within the field of religious studies. When we speak of the human side of religion, we are speaking of the human relationship and response to the transcendent realities of religion (God, revelation, afterlife, etc.). Such a response suggests that human personality has a "religious" dimension to which religious realities correspond or certain needs to which religion provides an answer and which, therefore, make religion meaningful. One of the preoccupations of the psychological theorists surveyed in this book is to locate and describe this religious dimension of personality and thereby account psychologically for the phenomenon of religion. In a preliminary way, however, it should be pointed out that, in its human aspect, religion is rooted in the desire for *self-transcendence*. This fundamental human desire has sometimes been described as the quality of "more" or the human desire to go beyond the limitations of one's everyday life and consciousness. What it amounts to is a desire for a new level of existence which transcends the limitations of one's present existence.

It is easy to see how such a desire can translate into a desire for an afterlife, for life after death which is not merely an extension of one's present life but a qualitatively different life. The great religions, however, also speak of the possibility of a transformation of one's present existence. The desire for self-transcendence is frequently expressed in images which transform the hoped for transcendent level of existence into a place, whether an afterlife in heaven or an earthly utopia. The fact that this is a fundamental *human* desire is illustrated by the fact that it finds expression in both religious and secular forms. A church congregation singing a hymn about the joys of heaven where all the troubles of this life are left behind, is expressing the same fundamental desire as is found in a secular song such as "Over the Rainbow" with its dreams of a place where "the clouds are far behind me" and "troubles melt like lemon drops."

When religion speaks of salvation or enlightenment, these words become meaningful only in the context of the limited and incomplete nature of our human existence. These limitations are experienced at three levels: as the limitations of human consciousness; as the limitations imposed by the individuality and uniqueness of the human person; as the limited and fragmented state of our knowledge—our failure to grasp the ultimate meaning and destiny of our human existence. Accordingly, the human desire for self-transcendence, whether expressed in a religious or a secular way, takes the form of the pursuit of three basic values.

1. *Integrity or wholeness.* This is the pursuit of an altered or expanded state of consciousness, a deeper and wider experience of the self. Jung's concept of the "self" and William James' discussion of the "wider self" point to the fact that one's total self cannot be identified with the narrow limits of ego-consciousness. The religious injunction "know thyself" refers to the wider or deeper self beyond the limits of our everyday consciousness.

2. *Community.* The self also transcends itself by overcoming its individuality through bonds of love and solidarity with others. As Erich Fromm emphasizes, the price of our individuality and uniqueness is a sense of isolation and alienation from others. While religion has frequently appealed to those who are socially alienated or marginalized, it also speaks to the kind of "existential" alienation which is the inevitable consequence of human existence.

3. *Ultimacy.* This refers to the attempt to put life into some kind of ultimate context, to discover its ultimate meaning and destiny. Gordon Allport speaks of religion as a search for "complete knowledge" and "unfissioned truth," while Viktor Frankl defines it as a search for "ultimate meaning."

These three aspects of the human desire for self-transcendence are reflected in the traditional concerns of religion: personal transformation, the creation of community, and ultimate meaning and destiny.

The psychology of religion—as one might expect—focuses mainly on the experience of personal transformation or the quest for wholeness. At the same time, it is interested in the psychological source, meaning, and value of all three forms of self-transcendence in their religious expression. It is, however, only one way of studying the phenomenon of religion. Since religion is a multifaceted phenomenon, it may be studied from a number of different perspectives. Consequently, religious study uses the methods of a number of disciplines—history, anthropology, philosophy, sociology, and psychology—to come to a fuller understanding of the phenomenon of religion. A complete understanding of religion cannot be rendered by any one of these disciplines. Religion is both a psychological and a sociological phenomenon; both a philosophical and a historical phenomenon. The psychology of religion studies the psychological dynamics underlying religious beliefs, attitudes, and behavior. The result is a variety of psychological understandings of religious phenomena. Thus, in the theories of religion discussed in this book, the psychological interpretations of religion run the gamut from Freud's pathological "obsessional neurosis" to Frankl's humanly fulfilling "search for ultimate meaning." Since, however, psychology deals with human experience, all these theories have this in common: They attempt to uncover the psychological meaning of religion, that is, the human experience behind religious language. The optimal result of this is to restore some kind of experiential meaning to terms such as "God," "sin," "grace," "salvation," and so on, words which have become meaningless to many religious believers.

The purpose of this book is to provide the student of religion with an introduction to the psychology of religion by reviewing seven psychological theories of religion: those of Sigmund Freud, C.G. Jung, William James, Erich Fromm, Gordon Allport, Abraham Maslow, and Viktor Frankl. These theorists have been chosen for the following reasons:

1. They represent the seminal thinkers or classical theories in the field of psychology of religion. Later developments in the field (e.g. those deriving from object-relations theory, archetypal psychology, or transpersonal psychology) represent developments of their original formulations.
2. Given the seminal nature of the work of these theorists, it is reasonable to suggest that the study of the psychology of religion should begin with an examination of their thought.
3. Though many others have made valuable contributions to the psychological study of religion, our survey restricts itself to those who have offered a more or less comprehensive theory of personality and, therefore, of the religious personality.

4. The views of these seven theorists on religion are deduced from varying schools of personality theory—psychoanalytic, archetypal, humanistic and existential—and, therefore, offer us ways of understanding religion in the context of differing modes of human self-understanding.

In examining each of these psychological theories of religion, the following format has been followed. A brief introduction and biographical sketch of the theorist is followed by an outline of his theory of personality and his theory of religion. Finally, an evaluation of the theorist's contributions to the psychological study of religion is attempted. The purpose of this evaluation is not to present an exhaustive critical review or pronounce any kind of final judgment, but to discuss the theorist's influence on the field, to point out some developments from and reactions to the theory, and to raise certain questions with a view to stimulating the reader's own critical response. It is also hoped that this format will help the reader to appreciate the extent to which each theory is not only derived from the theorist's personality theory but also influenced by his personal life experience.

I am grateful to the following Prentice Hall reviewers who's comments were helpful in preparing the manuscript: Ronald G. Ribble, University of Texas, San Antonio and David Wulff, Wheaton College.

James Forsyth

ACKNOWLEDGMENTS

Sigmund Freud © Copyrights, The Institute of Psycho-Analysis and The Hogarth Press for permission to quote from *The Standard Edition of the Complete Psychological Works of Sigmund Freud* translated and edited by James Strachey. Reprinted by permission of the Random House Group Ltd.

The Standard Edition of the Complete Psychological Works of Sigmund Freud volumes. 4, 11, 14, 19 translated and edited by James Strachey. ©Basic Books, HarperCollins Publishers.

The Standard Edition of the Complete Psychological Works of Sigmund Freud volumes. 13, 18, 20, 21 (Civilisation and its Discontents/The Future of an Illusion) translated and edited by James Strachey. © W W Norton Company.

The Standard Edition of the Complete Psychological Works of Sigmund Freud volume 21 (Moses and Monotheism) translated and edited by James Strachey. © Knopf, Random House, Inc.

Collected Works of C.G. Jung, Bollingen Series XX, tr. R.F.C. Hull. Copyright © 1977 by Princeton University Press. Reprinted by permission of Princeton University Press.

Memories, Dreams and Reflections by C.G. Jung, edited by Aniela Jaffe, translated by Richard and Clara Winston. Translation copyright © 1961, 1962, 1963 and renewed 1989, 1990, 1991 by Random House, Inc. Used by permission of Pantheon Books, a division of Random House, Inc.

The Varieties of Religious Experience by William James. © 1961 by Macmillan Publishing Company, Inc. Reprinted with the permission of Scribner, an imprint of Simon & Schuster Adult Publishing Group.

Psychoanalysis and Religion by Erich Fromm. © 1950 by Yale University Press. Reprinted with permission.

Religions, Values, and Peak-Experiences by Abraham Maslow. (Columbus: Ohio State University Press, 1964). The author is grateful to Ann Maslow Kaplan for permission to quote from this source.

I. SIGMUND FREUD

Religion and the Father Complex

Sigmund Freud (1856–1939)
National Library of Medicine.

Psychoanalysis has been such a pervasive force in the intellectual and cultural life of the twentieth century that it seems strangely fitting that the beginning of the century should coincide with the publication of Freud's *The Interpretation of Dreams* (1900). Psychoanalysis is sometimes said to have been born in 1895 when Freud, together with Josef Breuer, published *Studies on Hysteria*. By his own account, however, Freud begins to use the word "psychoanalysis" only in the following year with his formulation of the theory of repression, "the cornerstone on which the whole structure of psychoanalysis rests."[1] Up to this point, Freud had relied on the method of hypnosis (the effect of which was dramatic but short-lived) to help the patient recover "forgotten" memories, and the cathartic release of the associated emotions provided relief—albeit temporary—from hysterical symptoms. The theory of repression provided an answer to the question of why the patient could recall

1

certain events and emotions only when a particular technique such as hypnosis was applied. Repression was seen as the source of inner conflict and the resulting neurotic symptoms.

> The theory of repression became the foundation-stone of our understanding of the neuroses. A different view had now to be taken of the task of therapy. Its aim was no longer to "abreact" an affect which had got on to the wrong lines but to uncover repressions and replace them by acts of judgment which might result either in the acceptance or in the rejection of what had formerly been repudiated. I showed my recognition of the new situation by no longer calling my method of investigation and treatment catharsis but psychoanalysis.[2]

Here in a nutshell, was the psychoanalytic method: Unlock repression, thereby bringing into consciousness the repressed memory of the traumatic event, and then reevaluate the event through a conscious, rational "act of judgment." The repressed material had been repressed precisely because it had "in some way or other been digressive; it had been either alarming or painful or shameful by the standards of the subject's [conscious] personality."[3] One way of unlocking repression was through the interpretation of the patient's dreams, for Freud asserted that "a dream is the (disguised) fulfilment of a (repressed) wish."[4] In dreams repressed material (events, impulses, wishes) reappear in disguised and symbolic form. But dreams are not peculiar to those suffering from pathological conditions, for indeed, everyone dreams. Consequently, Freud believed that with the interpretation of dreams, psychoanalysis became not just a branch of psychopathology but a general science of the mind.

> Previously psychoanalysis had only been concerned with solving pathological phenomena.... But when it came to dreams, it was no longer dealing with a pathological symptom, but with a phenomenon of normal mental life which might occur in any healthy person. If dreams turned out to be constructed like symptoms, if their explanation required the same assumptions.... then psychoanalysis was no longer a subsidiary science in the field of psychopathology, it was rather the foundation for a new and deeper science of the mind which would be equally indispensable for the understanding of the normal. Its postulates and findings could be carried over to other regions of mental happening; a path lay open to it that led far afield, into spheres of universal interest.[5]

In other words, psychoanalysis could be used as an interpretive tool to investigate the psychological roots not only of mental illness but also of humanity's "cultural problems" including the problems of religion. Indeed, Freud himself seems to have been of the opinion that his investigations into the origins of religion and morality "have perhaps awakened more public sympathy than psychoanalysis itself."[6]

Life

Sigmund Freud was born on May 6, 1856, at Freiberg in Moravia. His father, Jacob Freud, was a Jewish wool merchant who, because of difficult economic circumstances for which anti-Semitic elements blamed Jewish merchants, moved his family out of Freiberg, finally settling in Vienna when Freud was 4 years old. This city was his home from 1860 to 1938 when, because of the Nazi occupation of Austria, he moved to London where he spent the last 15 months of his life. The configuration of Freud's family was unusual. His father was a 40-year-old widower with two grown-up sons when he married Freud's mother, Amalie Nathansohn, a young woman 20 years younger than Jacob. Moreover, one of Freud's half-brothers was already married with a son of his own so that Freud was born an uncle. After Sigmund, the firstborn, seven other children were born to Jacob and Amalie.

Freud's childhood includes a network of relationships which seem to be significant for his future development. The relationship with his mother was very close. Amalie was convinced of her son's future greatness and organized family life to some extent around his needs and studies. He was allowed to eat his dinner in his room so as not to lose study time, and the piano was removed because he insisted that his sister's practicing interfered with his concentration. In later life Freud wondered whether these assumptions about his future greatness could have been "the source of my thirst for grandeur?"[7] It was precisely this desire to be famous and recognized and to find a place in history which seems to have complicated many of Freud's professional relationships. From his father Freud seems to have derived a sense of his Jewish and biblical legacy (though Jacob seems to have been liberal and free thinking) and a sensitivity to anti-Semitism. When Freud was about 12, his father recounted an incident prior to Sigmund's birth in which, while walking in the street, he encountered a Gentile who knocked Jacob's new fur hat into the mud and shouted, "Jew! Get off the pavement!" When asked how he reacted Jacob replied, "I went into the roadway and picked up my hat." This passivity on his father's part toward anti-Semitic hostility caused Freud to feel shame for his father. Throughout his life Freud remained sensitive to anti-Semitism (of which apparently, there was no lack in Vienna), and this sensitivity seems to have been a motivating factor in his choice of C.G. Jung, a Gentile, as his "crown prince" and heir apparent in the leadership of the psychoanalytic movement. Vincent Brome reflects on the possibility that Freud's choice of Jung as his successor was motivated by a desire to defuse the anti-Semitism directed at the predominantly Jewish membership of the Vienna Psychoanalytical Society. Brome concludes that "the whole theme of anti-

Semitism was to play a part in his relations with Jung, and Freud never really escaped, for the rest of his life, from early anti-semitic bitterness and suspicions."[8] Brome also suggests that in his adult relationships "Freud played out with a number of people... his love-hate relationship with his father."[9] Freud himself, however, linked "what is neurotic, but also what is intense in all my friendships" to his relationships with his nephew John and his younger brother Julius. John was his first playmate and "companion of my misdeeds."[10] In this relationship he finds a psychological root of the ambivalence that was to mark so many of his adult friendships for "we loved each other and fought with each other, and this childhood relationship... had a determining influence on all my subsequent relations with contemporaries. Since that time my nephew John has had many reincarnations... unalterably fixed as it was in my unconscious memory." The effect of this unconscious memory seems to have been an emotional need to have "an intimate friend and a hated enemy" who frequently "have come together in a single individual."[11] At the birth of his younger brother Julius, Freud experienced the usual sibling rivalry and admitted that he wished his little brother would die. Julius' death at the age of 8 months (when Freud was just 19 months) "left the germ of [self-]reproaches in me."[12] This lingering sense of guilt seemed to remain with Freud into adulthood.

In Freud's self-analysis the "prime originator" of his neuroses was "an ugly, elderly but clever woman who told me a great deal about God Almighty and hell and who instilled in me a high opinion of my own capacities."[13] This is a reference to the Catholic nanny who was employed in the Freud household in Freiberg and who took care of Freud until he was two and a half, at which point she was dismissed for stealing money and encouraging young Sigmund to steal. In a letter to Wilhelm Fliess in 1897 Freud makes reference to this and links it to his current feelings of inadequacy as a therapist for just as this woman who "complained because I was clumsy and unable to do anything ... got money from me for her bad treatment, so today I get money for the bad treatment of my patients."[14] Much has been made of the influence of this nanny on Freud's religious thinking and attitudes. She was a Catholic who regularly took the little boy to Sunday mass with her, thus introducing him to Catholic ritual and to her own brand of Christianity preoccupied, as it was, with hell and damnation. J.N. Isbister has suggested that this experience, together with a lifelong experience of the anti-Semitism of Vienna's Catholic establishment, "gave Freud an enduring aversion to Christianity" and was a possible factor in his negative assessment of religion as a "universal obsessional neurosis."[15] Others see in Freud's attitude to religion and to Christianity in particular an ambivalence rather than a simple aversion.[16] This interpretation gains credibility when we consider the fact that while some of Freud's writings (those explicitly dealing with religion) constitute a refutation of religion, his reflections on the human condition (in terms of the conflict of Eros and the death instinct) seem to ask the ultimate religious question:

Can life triumph over death? Whatever the truth of the matter might be, it seems clear that Freud's views on religion have emotional as well as intellectual roots. Some would view this as subjectivity, others as genius.

Though he did not feel "any particular predilection for the career of a doctor,"[17] Freud entered the University of Vienna in 1873 as a medical student. His first love at this point, however, seems to have been science, and the taking of his medical degree was postponed until 1881 due to a six-year hiatus at the physiological laboratory of Ernst Brucke. Practical financial considerations led him to give up theoretical work in favor of a career as a physician, and he became a resident physician at the Vienna General Hospital in 1882. His primary interest was in cerebral anatomy and neurology and in 1885 he was appointed university lecturer in neuropathology. A critical turning point in Freud's life was the few months he spent in 1885-1886 studying under Jean Martin Charcot at the Salpetriere Hospital for Nervous Diseases in Paris. Charcot's interest was in the treatment of hysteria through hypnotism, which he seems to have regarded as nothing more than a branch of neuropathology. For Freud, however, it proved to be the beginning of a gradual shifting of his interest from neuropathology to psychopathology. In 1886 he married his fiancée, Martha Bernays, and set up a private practice in Vienna specializing in nervous diseases. Between 1888 and 1895 Freud worked, in collaboration with Josef Breuer, on the treatment of hysteria through the method of inducing cathartic recall of traumatic events by hypnosis. This collaboration produced *Studies on Hysteria* in 1895. From 1893, however, Freud's views began to differ from those of Breuer, and his espousal of the theories of repression and of the sexual aetiology of the neuroses was the beginning of the development of the psychoanalytic technique and theory. At the turn of the century, Freud published *The Interpretation of Dreams* and *The Psychopathology of Everyday Life* and, with these publications, the focus of psychoanalysis included not only pathological states but normal mental life as well. Hence Freud's interest, later in his career, in issues of culture, religion, and morality.

This development of his own psychoanalytic theory seems to have been significant for Freud as a person in at least three ways. First, his ideas represent for him that "certain degree of independence of judgment" which was the one redeeming consequence of the isolation and alienation he felt because of his Jewishness and the unorthodox nature of his theory.[18] Second, the application of psychoanalytic theory to social and cultural issues seems to represent a rediscovery and reaffirmation of the sense of identity he intuited as an adolescent when, as he tells us, his curiosity was directed "more towards human concerns than towards natural objects."[19] Thus, his interest, in the latter part of his career, in cultural and religious topics is considered as a phase of "regressive development," that is, a return to his earliest and most fundamental concerns. In the light of this, his early interest in physiology, anatomy, neurology, and even psychotherapy take on the appearance of a "detour" away from his true vocation.

My interest, after making a lifelong detour through the natural sciences, medicine and psychotherapy, returned to the cultural problems which had fascinated me long before, when I was a youth scarcely old enough for thinking.[20]

Third, Freud's desire for the fame and recognition that goes with being the sole creator of an original scientific theory seems to have led to the deterioration of several personal and professional friendships. Of his break with Breuer he said, "The development of psychoanalysis afterwards cost me his friendship. It was not easy for me to pay such a price, but I could not escape it."[21]

A similar type of breakup was to occur with several of his most gifted followers and disciples. The seemingly tolerant Freud seems to have been threatened by any of his disciples who developed original ideas which called for any modification of his own psychoanalytic theory. Vincent Brome remarks:

When someone put forth a proposition which seriously disturbed his own views, he first found it hard to accept and then became uneasy at this threat to the scientific temple he had so painfully built with his own hands. Thus his tolerance was qualified by insecurity.... [22]

This insecurity, which seems to have fueled his desire for recognition as an original scientific thinker, along with the ambivalence which he felt in his personal relationships—his need to have "an intimate friend and a hated enemy"—and which he himself explains as rooted in infantile relationships, seems to have been at the root of several such breakups, notably those with Alfred Adler in 1911 and Carl G. Jung in 1913.

It could be said that both Adler and Jung, in their theoretical formulations, found themselves outside the confines of strict Freudian psychoanalysis by reason of their refusal to assign the same importance to sexuality in human motivation and in the aetiology of the neuroses that Freud did. On the subject of Freud's insistence of the primacy of sexuality in human motivation, Jung has said:

There was no mistaking the fact that Freud was emotionally involved in his sexual theory to an extraordinary degree. When he spoke of it, his tone became urgent, almost anxious, and all signs of his normally critical and skeptical manner vanished.[23]

On one occasion Jung reports that Freud said to him, "my dear Jung, promise me never to abandon the sexual theory. That is the most essential thing of all. You see we must make a dogma of it, an unshakable bulwark."[24] It seemed to Jung that Freud, who saw religion and its dogmas as the adversary of science, was turning his own scientific hypothesis into "an article of faith for all time."

Whatever the emotional roots of Freud's sexual theory might have been, the rejection of the primacy of sexual motivation in human behavior by both Adler and Jung led to an irreparable break with Freud. Each man went on to develop his own theory and method of psychotherapy. In Adler's "individual psychology" the dominance of the sex drive is replaced by the aggressive "will to power." The Oedipus complex, for Adler, was not explained in terms of the child's sexual attachment to mother but as the phenomenon of the pampered child whose attachment to mother (including sexual attachment) is an attempt to maintain power over the mother. Jung saw the incestuous sexual wish as itself symbolic of a deeper desire—the desire for rebirth, which was seen as a religious or spiritual need. This kind of thinking represented for Freud the very kind of "occultism" against which he wanted to build an "unshakable bulwark" by making his sexual theory a dogma.

The picture which emerges from the facts of Freud's life is that of a complex figure. Scientific rigor and concern for truth are mingled with ambivalent feelings, infantile fixations, insecurity, and the overdriven quality of his desire for fame and recognition. His biographer, Ernest Jones, reported that, on board the ship taking him to America in 1909, Freud found his cabin steward reading *The Psychopathology of Everyday Life*. Most authors would be pleasantly surprised and perhaps inwardly flattered by such a discovery. To Freud, however, it was "an incident that gave him the first idea that he might be famous."[25] The popularity and durability of the theories of both Adler and Jung—"the two heretics"—lends a certain irony to Freud's claim that "both of these attempts against psychoanalysis have blown over without doing any harm."[26] It is also significant that he thinks of them only in terms of the possible threat they might pose to psychoanalysis. On the other hand, Freud and his theory have also survived, and even a brief review of that theory, which we shall now undertake, reveals a profound contribution to human self-understanding and a view of the human condition which goes far beyond the "pansexualism" of which it is often accused. Much of this theoretical writing—including *The Ego and the Id, The Future of an Illusion, Civilization and Its Discontents, Moses and Monotheism,* and *An Outline of Psychoanalysis*—was completed during the last 16 years of his life when Freud was in constant pain from an incurable cancer of the jaw and from the debilitating operations to treat it. While we may challenge Freud's theoretical formulations and speculate about his possible neurotic fixations, his personal courage seems to be beyond question.

Theory of Personality

Critics of Freud have sometimes referred to his understanding of human personality as "mechanistic." This criticism is based on a reading of Freud as the creator of a dynamic psychology which was based on the application of the principle of the conservation of energy to the human mind and to human personality. At the same time, it must be remembered that the notion of the transformation and conservation of energy was merely a theoretical model for the understanding of mental and emotional phenomena and does not exhaust the meaning of Freud's theory. Bruno Bettelheim has argued that this reading of Freud is one-sided, concentrating on an early stage of Freud's thought, when his interests were scientific and medical, and disregarding the more mature formulations of his theory, which were more humanistic and more concerned with human and cultural problems.[27] In this brief overview of Freudian theory the emphasis will be on this humanistic and cultural aspect in both his instinct theory and his theory of culture. It is this aspect which gives Freudian theory an enduring relevance to religious thought. Freud may have been an "unrepentant atheist" with "an enduring aversion to Christianity," but his theorizing, as we shall see, was an attempt to come to grips with the tragic dimension of life, which is also a central concern of religion.

The two discoveries of Freud which are most basic to his theory of personality and which, at the same time, aroused the greatest opposition when first introduced are (1) the concept of the unconscious, the contention that mental processes are largely unconscious and that conscious processes of the mind are isolated parts of the whole psychic entity; and (2) the theory that human instinctual life—particularly that of the sex instinct—plays a basic and predominant role not only in the aetiology of nervous and mental disorders but also in human cultural and social achievements. Freud himself viewed the discoveries of psychoanalysis as the most recent of three great attacks by science on humanity's "naive self-love." The first was the discovery by Copernicus that our earth was not the center of the universe; the second was Darwin's biological theory of evolution, which deprived the human animal of the privilege of having been specially created; and the third is the psychoanalytic theory of personality, which reveals to us that we are not even masters of our own inner life and that we are subject to motives and impulses of which we are unconscious.

It is this theory of personality which must be considered carefully in assessing Freud's significance for religion and not just his ideas about religion as such. What he says about religion and the religious personality is rooted in and derived from what he says about human personality.

Theory of Instincts

The concept of instinct is basic to Freudian theory in the sense that instincts are conceived of as the starting point or basis of human behavior. The aim of all human activity, even the most cultural or artistic, is ultimately the satisfaction of primary instinctual drives (sex and aggression). The gratification of an instinctual drive involves the discharge of psychic energy and the reduction of tension which accompanies that discharge. The object of the instinct is that object or person through which the aim of the instinct is achieved, and the instinct is the psychological wish for or drive toward the appropriate object for the reduction of biologically rooted tension. In other words, the instinctual aim of reducing tension is "conservative" in that it seeks to maintain a state of equilibrium or to return the organism continually to a tensionless or quiescent state (homeostasis) by finding suitable objects upon which to expend the psychic energy represented by the instincts. Thus life is a continuous cycle of instinctual need—resulting tension—discharge of instinctual energy on an appropriate object— reduction of tension. With renewed buildup of tension the cycle begins again.

The finding of a suitable object for the satisfaction of instinctual impulses is the work of the psychic apparatus—the theoretical construct of id, ego, and superego—which Freud used to describe psychic operations. The id is the unconscious reservoir of psychic energy or instinctual needs which seeks direct satisfaction, if not in the real world, then in the world of fantasy, dreams, and wish fulfillment, because it does not distinguish between fantasy and reality. Freud describes the instincts as "the forces we assume to exist behind the tensions caused by the needs of the id."[28] But real satisfaction cannot be found in the realm of fantasy, and so it becomes the task of the ego—that part of the psychic apparatus which is closest to the external world of reality and includes one's conscious, thinking processes—to find the appropriate instinctual object in the real world. The ego decides how an instinct is to be realistically satisfied. It must therefore calculate the consequences of any given way of gratifying an instinctual wish and must sometimes inhibit the impulses of the id because of perceived dangers to the organism in the real world. Of the id and the ego Freud remarks:

> No such purpose as that of keeping itself alive or of protecting itself from dangers by means of anxiety can be attributed to the id. That is the task of the ego, whose business is also to discover the most favourable and least perilous method of obtaining satisfaction, taking the external world into account.[29]

The ego acts as a buffer zone between the impulses of the id and the real world (the source of satisfaction) "and endeavours by means of experimental actions to calculate the consequences of the course of action proposed."[30] Whereas the ego inhibits the impulses of the id for realistic reasons, the superego, which represents the internalized rules and ideals and prohibitions of parents and society, inhibits the id for moralistic reasons. In the language of psychoanalysis, the id operates on the pleasure principle, the ego on the reality principle, and the superego on the principle of right and wrong. The superego, as we shall see later, begins to develop in the oedipal stage of growth when the child begins to "introject" or internalize parental commands and prohibitions.

But even the ego has an unconscious function, that of repression. There are certain possibilities of satisfaction or impulses toward certain objects (cathexes) which must be "ruled out" or repressed by the ego—not permitted to become conscious because of realistic, social, or moral considerations. When this occurs, a substitute object must be found toward which the energy of the instinct can be "displaced." If the substitute object is considered morally or culturally superior to or more socially acceptable than the primary (repressed) object, psychoanalysts speak of "sublimation" rather than displacement. Sublimation "consists in the instinct's directing itself towards an aim other than, and remote from, that of sexual satisfaction."[31]

For Freud, this process accounts for the diversity of interests among people as well as advances in science, culture, the arts, and religion, for these pursuits represent sublimations of more primitive instincts. Thus we do not speak of an artistic or religious "instinct" for it is not an instinct in its own right, but a sublimation of a more primary instinct. An instinct which is deflected in this way toward a substitute object is partially frustrated, that is, in regard to its primary aim, and is therefore described by Freud as "aim-inhibited." This obtains "in cases where a certain advance has been permitted in the direction of satisfaction and then an inhibition or deflection has occurred. We may suppose that even in such cases a partial satisfaction is achieved."[32] Later theorists such as Allport and Frankl will criticize this view of human motivation on the grounds that it tends to rob art, culture, and religion—the very things which make life rich and meaningful—of any intrinsic value. These human pursuits are seen as mere sublimations of primary instincts and therefore substitute objects.

The development of Freud's instinct theory can be traced in the successive formulations by which he attempted to identify those primary instincts which are the fundamental motivating forces in human personality. It must be remembered that Freud was committed to a dualistic and conflictual model of human personality in which the human person is seen as torn between conflicting drives or instincts. In the first formulation of this theory, the conflicting instincts are identified as the sex instinct and the "ego-instincts." These are seen as two qualitatively different drives and the distinction is based on that between hunger (the aim of which is self-preservation) and love (the aim of which is preservation of the species).

The ego-instincts are "instincts which aim at preserving the individual" and include self-preservation, self-affirmation, aggression, and mastery. The sex instinct, on the other hand, is the "instinct which strives after objects" and its chief function is the preservation of the species. The term "libido" was used to denote the energy only of the sex instinct for the ego-instincts "have no libidinal purpose."[33] Freud finds support for his distinction between ego-instincts and sex instincts in biology, which assigns to sexuality a function (procreation) that transcends the individual. In relation to the ego, therefore, sexuality may be seen in two ways: first, as serving the needs of the ego by way of sexual satisfaction; second, as serving a purpose which goes beyond the individual ego and its satisfaction and in the achieving of which purpose "the individual organism is looked upon as a transitory and perishable appendage to the quasi-immortal germ plasm bequeathed to him by the race."[34]

A reformulation of the instinct theory followed the publication of Freud's essay "On Narcissism" in 1914. Here he proposed that in infancy the libido is first directed toward one's own ego. This discovery led him temporarily to abandon the idea of a conflict between two qualitatively different instincts (sex and ego) and to speak of an undifferentiated libido which could be directed either toward oneself or toward a loved object. Variations of the infant's primary narcissism are expressed as ego-libido (love of self) as opposed to object-libido (love of others). Here the distinction is not based on the polarity of two qualitatively different instincts but on the polarity of cathexes or object choices of the undifferentiated libido.

The problem with these first two formulations was that they did not satisfy Freud's intuitive conviction regarding the duality of human personality in the sense that the poles of the conflict as described in each formulation were not true opposites. Both the sex instinct and object-libido were seen as expressions of Eros, the love instinct; but by the same token the self-preservative ego-instincts and ego-libido seemed, to Freud, to be simply narcissistic forms of Eros. This does not express a true duality of opposites and Freud remarks: "Nevertheless, there still remained in me a kind of conviction, for which I was not as yet able to find reasons, that the instincts could not all be of the same kind."[35] It was necessary to find the real antithesis of Eros, an instinct the aim of which was not self-love but self-destruction. Freud's answer to this question was his concept of the death instinct or death wish which he advanced in *Beyond the Pleasure Principle* in 1920. In this work he bases the hypothesis of the death instinct upon a number of clinical observations which led him to suspect that there was something "beyond the pleasure principle" at work in one's psychic mechanism. These observations included the phenomena of repression, which turns the possibility of pleasure into a source of unpleasure, of children's play which is characterized by compulsive repetition, even of unpleasant experiences and of the process of "transference" in therapy by which a patient acts out or repeats unpleasant repressed experiences in his or her relationship with the psychoanalyst.

All of this revealed to Freud the existence of "something that seems more primitive, more elementary, more instinctual than the pleasure principle which it over-rides."[36] This more primitive apparatus is the tendency, Freud argued, of all organic life to restore an earlier state of things, that is, to return to an inorganic state. The death instinct would then represent the psychological expression of this tendency inherent in every living organism. "We may suppose," Freud argued, "that its final aim is to lead what is living into an inorganic state. For this reason we also call it the *Death Instinct*."[37] Freud also refers to this instinct as the "destructive instinct," for he theorized that the original desire for one's death comes into conflict with one's narcissism or self-love. Under the influence of narcissism, the death instinct is deflected outward and takes the form of aggression toward others. In other words, the death instinct becomes observable in the aggressive ego-instincts.

At the same time, in order to preserve a true duality, it was necessary to expand the meaning of Eros so that it becomes the real antithesis of death. Up to this point Eros as the "love instinct" had been identified with the sex instinct. As such it was not the true opposite of death since it operated according to the same "Nirvana principle" as the death instinct, in the sense that the aim of every sexual impulse was the reduction of tension and ultimately that state of complete quiescence, which coincides with the aim of the death instinct. Consequently, at this stage in the development of his instinct theory, Freud could assert that "the aim of life [Eros] is death." Eros, then, in this final formulation, goes beyond sexuality in its meaning and becomes the life instinct which resists death because it does not participate in the conservative nature of instinctual life.

In the end, the most fundamental distinction that Freud makes between Eros (the life instinct) and the death instinct is that Eros is a unifying principle while the death instinct is divisive and destructive.

> I drew the conclusion that, besides the instinct to preserve living substance and to join it into ever larger units, there must exist another, contrary instinct seeking to dissolve those units and to bring them back to their primaeval, inorganic state. That is to say, as well as Eros there was an instinct of death.[38]

It should be pointed out at this point that Freud's hypothesis about the conflict of two basic instincts—a unifying life instinct and a divisive and destructive death instinct which dominate human existence—has not been widely accepted even among psychoanalysts. It is frequently rejected or ignored on the grounds that it is "unscientific." Erich Fromm has referred to it as an "unproved speculation." In this regard, two things should be kept in mind.

First, when Freud speaks in this way, he seems to be speaking from a position beyond strict psychological theory. When he speaks of the conflict of Eros and death, we cannot even be sure that he is still speaking of instincts in any technical meaning of that term. It is as if he "ontologizes" them, turning them into objective forces which seem to dominate human existence. It would be best to regard this "unproved speculation," therefore, as an intuitive insight rather than a scientific finding. Freud himself implies as much in the tentative language he uses. He describes his hypothesis of Eros and death as "a kind of conviction for which I was not as yet able to find reasons." Therefore he put forward his views "only tentatively"; nevertheless, "in the course of time they have gained such a hold upon me that I can no longer think in any other way."[39] And finally, he admits that his theory of the two basic instincts was arrived at "after long hesitancies and vacillations."[40]

When we say that Eros and death dominate human existence, we imply that these are pervasive drives which operate at every level of human life. On the biological level, the function of the Eros is to form individual cells into a living organism while the function of the death instinct is to dissolve the unity of the multicellular organism so that it returns to an inorganic state in death. On the psychological level, Eros operates through the sex instinct which unites two people into a psychological unity and assures the continuance of the life of the species, while the death instinct is operative in the ego-instincts which dissolve the unity between individuals through mechanisms of self-affirmation, aggression, and mastery. On the social level Eros is operative in the process of civilization, the purpose of which, Freud states, is "to combine single human individuals, and after that families, then races, peoples and nations into one great unity, the unity of mankind."[41] The death instinct, on the other hand, creates barriers to civilized social life such as war, racism, prejudice, and aggression. Humanity's need to repress death in the form of aggression so that it may live according to life instinct is the basis of Freud's theory of civilization or culture.[42]

Theory of Culture

In his essay *Civilization and Its Discontents* (1930), Freud defines civilization or culture as "the whole sum of the achievements and the regulations which distinguish our lives from those of our animal ancestors and which serve two purposes—namely to protect men against nature and to adjust their mutual relations."[43] Civilization thus appears as humanity's way of dealing with that reality which interferes with its pursuit of happiness according to the pleasure principle. This reality presents a twofold obstacle to human happiness: the forces of nature (including our own biological decay) and the hostility and aggression which infect human relationships. Civilization, therefore, tries to control the forces of nature through science and technology and to regulate human relationship through its legal, religious, and cultural systems. It might be said, then, that the origin of civilization lies in the conflict between pleasure and reality—the pleasure (happiness) we seek and the reality we encounter which presents obstacles to that happiness.

At a deeper level, however, Freud locates the origin of civilization in the conflict between Eros and the death instinct. We have seen that, under the force of one's narcissism, the death instinct is deflected outward and takes the form of aggression toward others. It is this aggression—the externalized death instinct—which militates against the possibility of happiness in human relationships and accounts for the "social sources of distress." The task of civilization then becomes the removal of this source of unhappiness through the repression of human aggression and hostility. Civilization's goal is to promote the conditions necessary for the triumph of Eros over the death instinct by repressing the death instinct in the form of aggression. But it must be remembered that the Eros-death conflict is biologically rooted in individual human nature. Hence the repression of aggression is ultimately not carried out for the sake of civilization. Rather, we create civilization in order to carry out on ourselves the repression which is necessary not because of civilization but because of the conditions of individual human nature. In this regard, it is significant that Freud does not say that Eros serves civilization but that "civilization is a process in the service of Eros."[44] The conflict, therefore, between the individual driven to seek instinctual gratification and a civilization which demands instinctual renunciation in the interest of communal life would appear to be a secondary phenomenon since it is rooted in the deeper conflict of Eros and death within each individual.

In its attempt to resolve the conflict, civilization represses aggression by replacing the individual rule of the strongest with the rule of a united number and its demand for instinctual renunciation sets up a tension between civilization and its values and the demands of individual life.

> This replacement of the power of the individual by the power of a community constitutes the decisive step of civilization. The essence of it lies in the fact that the members of the community restrict themselves in their possibilities of satisfaction, whereas the individual knew no such restrictions.[45]

Freud poses the question as to whether a form of civilization could be achieved which would find some kind of accommodation between the claims of the individual and the cultural demands of the group "or whether this conflict is irreconcilable."[46] He tends to be pessimistic about this possibility because of his theoretical position that the conflict—and therefore the source of tragedy—is rooted in individual human nature and not in social and cultural institutions. There is something, therefore, inevitable about the discontent of the civilized person because the discontent is rooted in the conflict within his own human nature and cannot, therefore, be eliminated by reforming the conditions of social life.

This notion of the inevitability of discontent in civilized life gives Freud's theory a tragic quality. For this reason Erich Fromm has referred to Freud's theory as not sufficiently "radical" in the sense of not calling for radical political and social reform. It could be argued, however, that a theory which locates the source of tragedy within unchanging human nature rather than changing and reformable social institutions is, for that very reason, more radical. Bruno Bettelheim has taken issue with those translators and followers of Freud who have glossed over his insistence on the tragic dimension of human existence and have denied Freud's basic proposition that culture cannot be had without uneasiness and discontent. In doing so they leave the impression that

Freud was critical of a civilization which brought about discontent with life and that psychoanalysis believes in the possibility of a civilization without discontent. "Such a notion," he argues, "is childish and narcissistic, completely contrary to what Freud had in mind."[47]

This tragic view of human existence becomes evident in Freud's discussion of the dynamics of civilization. We have seen that what civilization ultimately seeks to accomplish is the triumph of Eros—the life instinct—over the death instinct. Toward this end, it does two things. First, it sublimates sexuality, directing its energy away from direct sexual gratification and toward "aim-inhibited" ties of friendship. It does this by imposing an organization on sexual love directing its energy into genital, heterosexual, and monogamous channels. This has two consequences. First, sexual love becomes aim-inhibited love or friendship, thus establishing a bond among people which runs contrary to their natural aggressiveness. Freud felt that such an aim-inhibited, libidinal bond among people was necessary to hold a society together. Practical considerations of necessity were not sufficient to overcome our natural aggressiveness. Second, the organization of sexual life has the effect of subtracting energy from sexuality and directing it toward work and cultural pursuits to the obvious benefit of civilization.

The second tactic used by civilization in the service of Eros is the repression of the death instinct in the form of aggression and destructiveness. Aggression is the organism's own death instinct deflected outward toward others. Under the influences of civilization's repressions, however, aggression is internalized again and directed toward one's own ego. In the process of the individual's internalizing of society's restrictions on aggression, the energy of the aggression is taken over by the superego (conscience) and is experienced as guilt, which Freud describes as "the tension between the harsh superego and the ego that is subjected to it." In this way, he maintains, the death instinct in the form of aggression "is introjected, internalized; it is, in point of fact, sent back to where it came from—that is, it is directed towards his own ego." It is thus through the process of internalization which creates the superego that civilization gains control over the individual's aggressive impulse not only by external coercion but also "by weakening and disarming it and by setting up an agency within him to watch over it, like a garrison in a conquered city."[48] This internalization of aggression first takes place during the oedipal stage of growth at which time the child begins to introject or internalize the commands and prohibitions of the parent who represents the extraneous authority of culture. After internalization the authority of the parent becomes the authority of the superego (the child issues commands and prohibitions to himself), and, therefore, the aggressive impulses toward the parent as external authority and obstacle to his wishes is now directed toward himself and experienced as guilt.

This sense of guilt is subsequently reinforced in wider forms of communal life beyond the family (church, school, social life) so that the authority of the parent becomes the authority of civilization whose rules are to be internalized. Here then is the source of Freud's tragic view of human existence, for the process of civilization seems to be self-defeating. In order to bring about the triumph of life (Eros) over death, civilization represses the death instinct by repressing its external expression as aggression. This results in the internalizing of aggression and its redirection toward one's own ego so that it is now experienced as guilt. Thus, by some kind of tragic irony, the death instinct continues to dominate human existence (in conflict with Eros) in the form of guilt which Freud saw as a derivative of the death instinct.

Civilization, Freud argues, pursues the goal of Eros—the unity of all humanity—but it can do so only through the guilt-producing repression of aggression. Thus "it can only achieve this aim through an ever-increasing reinforcement of the sense of guilt."[49] This guilt is the source of the discontent we feel in civilized society and, for Freud, "the price we pay for our advance in civilization is a loss of happiness through the heightening of the sense of guilt."[50] And since guilt is an expression of the death instinct, then, in some sense, the experience of guilt is an experience of death, a "death" we experience precisely as the result of our pursuit of life through the process of civilization. Civilization, in Freud's view, represents "the struggle for life of the human species."[51] Paradoxically this struggle results in the experience of death in the form of guilt. Or, as Paul Ricoeur has observed, "Culture comes upon the scene as the great enterprise of making life prevail against death" but in the end "civilization kills us to make us live."[52]

Theory of Religion

In describing the human condition in terms of the struggle between life (Eros) and death and in raising the question, "Can life triumph over death?" Freud was asking one of the most fundamental questions of human existence. It is a question, in fact, which seems to carry him beyond any narrowly conceived scope of psychology, since it is also a philosophical and religious question. In the hands of a theorist more favorably disposed to religion, this kind of theorizing might have led to the conclusion that the central problem faced by humanity was ultimately a religious one. If Freud had a concept of "healthy" religion, it would have been derived from this analysis of human existence in terms of the struggle between life (Eros) and death. When Freud examined religion, however, it was not as a student of the essence of religion, but religion as it is practiced by the average person. Here he found not an engagement in this struggle between life and death but an escape from it. After describing the evolution of civilization as the struggle between Eros and Death he adds: "and it is this battle of the giants that our nurse-maids try to appease with their lullaby about Heaven."[53] In his own words, he was concerned "much less with the deepest sources of the religious feeling than with what the common man understands by his religion," which he nevertheless regards as "the only religion which ought to bear that name." He then goes on to describe this religion in terms of abject submission to and dependence on God which is "patently infantile" and "foreign to reality."[54]

Freud's theory of religion can be examined under three aspects: (1) religious belief as an illusion (2) religious practice as an obsessional neurosis and (3) the proposed historical evidence for this interpretation.

Religion as Illusion

We have seen that civilization pursues its goal of Eros by repressing the aggressive instinct and sublimating the sex instinct. These two tactics are complementary: one aims at repressing the "primary mutual hostility of human beings"; the other aims at replacing that hostility with "aim-inhibited" bonds of love and friendship. Freud writes:

> Civilization has to use its utmost efforts in order to set limits to man's aggressive instincts and to hold the manifestation of them in check by psychical reaction formations. Hence, therefore the use of methods intended to incite people into identifications and aim-inhibited relationships of love, hence the restriction upon sexual life, and hence too the ideal commandment to love one's neighbour as oneself—a commandment which is really justified by the fact that nothing else runs so strongly counter to the original nature of man.[55]

It is this "original nature of man" which finds itself in tension with the restrictions imposed by civilization, for civilization imposes on the individual a certain degree of renunciation of his or her natural sexual and aggressive instincts. This demand for instinctual renunciation runs into opposition from what Freud calls the remains of the individual's "original personality which is still untamed by civilization."[56]

Freud sees civilization as having the function of alleviating human suffering and unhappiness, which is seen as having a threefold source: the forces of nature, the biological decay of our bodies, and the aggression and hostility which mar human relationships. Our response to the first two of these is to mitigate human suffering as much as possible, but ultimately to resign ourselves to the inevitable. Regarding the third, however, we try to control and regulate human relationships through the religious and cultural systems of civilization. Hence civilization's imposition of instinctual renunciation through sexual restrictions and the repression of aggression. But this instinctual renunciation does not come easily since, as Freud argues, "every individual is virtually an enemy of civilization." Why is this so? Because the "masses are lazy and unintelligent; they have no love for instinctual renunciation" and because "men are not spontaneously fond of work and... arguments are of no avail against their passions."[57] Hence, in Freud's view, the need for a certain degree of coercion in civilized society. However, when we consider how limited has been civilization's success in regulating human relationships through instinctual renunciation, "a suspicion dawns on us that here, too, a piece of unconquerable nature may be behind—this time a piece of our own psychical constitution."[58]

Among the "mental assets" of civilization Freud lists morality and religion. Morality, for Freud, was a product of the socialization process. Beginning at the oedipal stage of childhood, an individual begins to develop a superego or conscience through the internalizing of the commands, prohibitions, and values of parents and then of society. As previously noted, the effect of such internalizing is that the individual begins to issue these commands and prohibitions to himself or herself. The external authority of civilization is replaced, to some extent, by the internal authority of the superego, thus lessening the need for external coercion. Morality thus turns people from opponents of civilization into its vehicles. Religion assists this process by promoting belief in a God who, in addition to being a loving and protecting father, like any other father makes demands upon us through his commandments. These demands include the cultural demands for instinctual renunciation. Religion thus becomes an agent of civilization in demanding instinctual renunciation through divine prohibitions. In this way civilization's precepts are reinforced by being seen as having a divine origin. The very things commanded and forbidden by civilization (killing, injury, theft, etc.) are commanded and forbidden by God.

How is this possible? Freud explains that this happens because of the sense of helplessness and dependency that we feel not only in childhood but also in adulthood. In adulthood we outgrow most of the fears and anxieties of childhood only to be confronted by a new set of fears and anxieties for we are still subject to the forces of the environment, both human and natural, from without and the insecurities that come from within. The child, Freud argues, turns first to its mother, the first love object, for protection against "all the undefined dangers which threaten it in the external world—its first protection against anxiety." This function of loving protector, however, is soon taken over by the father. But if feelings of helplessness, dependency, and anxiety continue into adulthood, so does the need for a loving, protecting father in the face of the fears and anxieties of adulthood. This need is projected onto God, who becomes the surrogate or substitute father.

> When the growing individual finds that he is destined to remain a child forever, that he can never do without protection against strange superior powers, he lends those powers the features belonging to the figure of his father; he creates for himself the gods whom he dreads, whom he seeks to propitiate, and whom he nevertheless entrusts with his own protection. Thus his longing for a father is a motive identical with his need for protection against the consequences of his human weakness.[59]

Thus, in Freud's view, the reaction to this continuing need for a loving, protecting father is "the formation of religion." But notice that the relationship with this substitute father is marked by ambivalence for the loving, protecting father is also someone "whom he dreads, whom he seeks to propitiate." For Freud, this is so because the ambivalent feelings of the child toward the father at the oedipal stage—love and admiration linked with fear and hostility—are projected onto the relationship with God, since the father/God who loves and protects also commands.

Religious belief in God, then, is seen by Freud as a renewal of the infantile state of helplessness. Hence it is regressive. It is also an illusion since it is based on wish fulfillment rather than on objective evidence. In other words, we believe in God not because there is any objective, rational evidence to support such a belief, but because we want to have a God, that is, a father figure who will protect us against the harsh realities and conflicts of life. For Freud, this acquiescence in human helplessness, insignificance, and impotence is not the attitude of a truly religious person who would be more inclined to actively seek a remedy for these human problems.

> Critics persist in describing as "deeply religious" anyone who admits to a sense of man's insignificance and impotence in the face of the universe, although what constitutes the essence of the religious attitude is not this feeling but only the next step after it, the reaction to it which seeks a remedy for it. The man who goes no further, but humbly acquiesces in the small part which human beings play in the great world— such a man is, on the contrary, irreligious in the truest sense of the word.[60]

Even for those who reject this analysis of religion, it does demonstrate the distorting role that wish fulfillment can play in religious belief.

It must also be pointed out that when Freud designates religious belief as an illusion, he is not saying that such belief is necessarily false, that is, that it is a *delusion*. A belief is an illusion, he explains, "when a wish fulfillment is a prominent factor in its motivation, and in doing so we disregard its relations to reality."[61] Thus Freud's proposition about religious belief is not in itself a refutation of that belief but an identification of what he believes to be the psychological/emotional mechanism that is operative in the motivation of beliefs which may or may not be objectively true. As for the objective truth of religious beliefs, Freud remarks, "Of the reality value of most of them we cannot judge; just as they cannot be proved, so they cannot be refuted."[62]

It could be argued, therefore, that in speaking of religious belief as an illusion, Freud's main interest was not in refuting religion. The demise of religion seems to be something he takes for granted. His more urgent concern seems to be the separating of morality from religion. When religion reinforces cultural demands for instinctual renunciation, he argues, by adding divine sanctions to them, then these demands are seen as ultimately coming from

God. Thus when people stop believing in God and lose their respect for religion they will also lose their respect for cultural commands and prohibitions, that is, for morality. There are, for example, very good practical and rational reasons for civilization's prohibition of murder. In attributing this prohibition to God, "we are investing the cultural prohibition with a quite special solemnity, but at the same time we risk making its observance dependent on belief in God." And when this divine sanction is added to less serious prohibitions whose moral quality is more relative and which are more clearly cultural in origin, then "the halo often looks far from becoming." It would be far better, Freud argues, "if we were to leave God out altogether and honestly admit the purely human origin of all the regulations and precepts of civilization."[63] In other words, cultural demands must be dissociated from God and religion and presented as the rational requirements of civilization independent of belief in God. This would be Freud's answer to the question of whether moral teaching should have a religious foundation.

Religion as Obsessional Neurosis

When Freud comes to speak of religion as an obsessional neurosis, religious observance appears to be an expression of death rather than life. In this view, religion is seen as rooted in guilt feelings and, as we have seen, guilt is a derivative of the death instinct. Religion as an obsessional neurosis originates in the ambivalent feelings characteristic of neuroses. The child first experiences these ambivalent feelings during the oedipal stage of growth, at which time his love and admiration for his father as ideal and protector is mingled with hostility toward that same father who is seen also as an obstacle standing in the way of his sexual desire for his mother.(The obvious one-sidedness of this theory, the result of its being based on the male child's ambivalence toward the father and the father-son sexual rivalry, will be discussed later in this chapter). In Freudian theory, the oedipal stage is the phallic stage of sexual development. At this point the mother becomes the son's first love object, which, for Freud, meant sexual love. This sexual desire for mother brings the boy into conflict and rivalry with the father for mother's love. The result is the aforementioned ambivalence and the desire on the part of the child to kill the father and have mother to himself. These two wishes correspond to the two crimes of King Oedipus in the Greek myth and in the play of Sophocles (parricide and incest). Hence the name given to this complex of feelings by Freud. What Oedipus did unwittingly—kill his father and marry his mother—is what the little boy wants to do, also unwittingly, that is, unconsciously. The ambivalence toward father is guilt-producing since the son cannot go on hating the one he loves and admires without feeling guilty. And the fact that it is merely a wish does not eliminate the guilt, for the superego punishes even for evil wishes. Moreover, because the hostility or aggression is a derivative of the death instinct, the ambivalence expresses the conflict of Eros and death.

Whether one has killed one's father or has abstained from doing so is not really the decisive thing. One is bound to feel guilty in either case, for the sense of guilt is an expression of the conflict due to ambivalence, of the eternal struggle between Eros and the instinct of destruction or death.[64]

This "eternal struggle" accounts for "the fatal inevitability of the sense of guilt."[65]

In the normal resolution of the Oedipus complex, the child represses his sexual desire for mother so that his attachment to mother now becomes "aim-inhibited" tender affection. This repression is facilitated by the fact that, at the same time, the boy *identifies* himself with the father. This involves "the introjection of the object [the father] into the ego." This taking of the father into himself has two aspects. The father is introjected or internalized first as loved and admired, and this is the basis of child's ego-ideal and second, as the hated obstacle to his wishes and source of commands and prohibitions, which becomes the basis for the formation of conscience or superego. It is through this introjection of the father's commands and prohibitions—including the incest taboo on his sexual desire for mother—that the child is able to overcome his ambivalent feelings toward the father. If the source of command and prohibitions is no longer the father but his own superego, then, since the father is no longer the obstacle to his wishes, the father can be loved and admired without the admixture of hostility and resultant guilt. If, however, the child, for whatever reason, fails to outgrow his ambivalence in this way, feelings of hostility and therefore a lingering sense of guilt continue to dominate the relationship with the father. Thus when the image of the father is projected onto God as surrogate father, the hostility and the resulting guilt feelings are incorporated into the religious relationship with God.

In this way, religion becomes, for Freud, an obsessional neurosis or what today would be called an obsessive-compulsive neurosis. In the case of religion, the obsessive aspect would be the unconscious hostility toward the father God which constantly tries to break into consciousness and produces feelings of guilt at the conscious level. The compulsive aspect would be religious observance—prayer, worship, ritual. Just as compulsive hand washing might be the ritual by which the neurotic manages the guilt feelings which result from unconscious obsessions (impulses, thoughts, memories, etc.), so religious ritual, in this view, is seen as a way of managing the guilt feelings associated with the believer's unconscious hostility toward God. Thus the outward display of love and reverence masks an unconscious ambivalence. It was in his 1907 essay "Obsessive Acts and Religious Practices" that Freud first proposed such a parallel between religious ritual and the features of an obsessional neurosis. His conclusion at that time was that, because of these correspondences, "one might venture to regard the obsessional neurosis as a pathological counterpart, to describe this neurosis as a private religious system, and religion as a universal obsessional neurosis."[66] Both, he maintained, originated in repressed instinctual impulses with this difference: In the neurosis the repressed instinct was sexual while in religion the repressed instinct was "of egoistic origin." In his subsequent writings, Freud identified this egoistic origin as the ambivalent feelings toward the father/God and tried to trace the historical roots of that ambivalence as we shall now see.

Historical Foundation

To this point, Freud's account of religion refers only to the *ontogenesis* of religion, that is, an interpretation of the phenomenon of religion in the context of individual development. In this regard, Freud sees religious belief and practice as originating in the "longing for the father" and in the ambivalent feelings toward one's father and the resulting guilt which arise during the oedipal phase of childhood. It is the relationship with the father which is critical for the development of religion. As Robert Bocock concludes, "Psychoanalysis finds, in work with individuals, that their notion of God, and their relations with God, parallels their notion of, and relations with, their father."[67] In speaking thus, Freud is answering the ontogenetic question: What are the conditions of individual psychological development which account for religious belief and behavior?

In two works in particular—*Totem and Taboo* (1913) and *Moses and Monotheism* (1939)—Freud addresses the further question of the *phylogenesis* of religion, that is, the question of the origin of religion not in terms of individual development but in terms of racial development. The phylogenetic question then would be "What are the conditions of the history and development of the human race which account for the phenomenon of religion?" In asking this question Freud wanted to establish an historical foundation for the psychological truth underlying the phenomenon of religion. If he could point to an event or series of events in the history or prehistory of the race which would account for the seeming inevitability and universality of the feelings of ambivalence and guilt upon which religion is based (the psychological truth), then religion could be seen as evidence not of theological truth (the existence of God) but of an historical truth. The phylogenetic problem was to find the historical truth that would substantiate the psychological truth which Freud believed accounted for the phenomenon of religion in individual development.

Freud's search for this historical truth really amounts to an interpretation of history based on his already existing psychoanalytic theory. This approach is justified by the hypothesis that there is a concordance between individual and racial psychology. Accordingly in the case of an individual, the memory of an early traumatic experience can be repressed and then reappear later in life in the form of a neurosis (including the "obsessional neurosis" of religion). In the life of humanity, religion represents a similar case of the "return of the repressed" for, as Freud maintains, "in the group too an impression of the past is retained in unconscious memory traces."[68] Freud's hypothesis, then, concerning the origin of religion may be stated as follows: In individual life the Oedipus complex is the source of ambivalence and guilt which find expression in the neuroses, including religion. In a similar way, humanity, in its prehistory, underwent an experience analogous to the Oedipus complex, which accounts for the origin of religion. Conversely, the individual's oedipal experience is a reliving of the primeval event.

In support of this hypothesis, Freud, in *Totem and Taboo*, attempted to locate that oedipal experience in humanity's prehistory or, in his own words, "to reconstruct the ancient situation from which these consequences followed."[69] In doing so he makes use of data and "theoretical reflections" supplied by anthropologists and ethnologists of his time—most notably Charles Darwin, J.J. Atkinson, and W. Robertson Smith. Twenty-six years later, in *Moses and Monotheism*, he admits that his espousal of certain anthropological theories was based on the fact that they provided him with "valuable points of contact with the psychological material of analysis and suggestions for the use of it," that is, they facilitated his psychoanalytic interpretation of history. For this reason he defends his continued use of Robertson Smith's theories on totemism which by then had been generally rejected by scholars because "I had a right to take out of ethnological literature what I might need for the work of analysis."[70] In any event, the reconstruction of the prehistoric life of humanity which emerges from Freud's selective use of data runs as follows: In prehistoric times human beings lived in small hordes each of which was governed by a despotic father who ruled by brute force and who appropriated all the females of the tribe for his own sexual purposes. Consequently, the younger males were belabored, killed, or driven into exile. In time, however, the exiled sons rebelled against this oppression, killed the father, and consumed his body. Through this rebellion the patriarchal system was brought to an end and replaced by a matriarchy, and the primal horde ruled by the primal father was replaced by a totemistic brother clan. But the father was not merely an object of hatred, he was also loved and admired by the sons, who hoped to acquire his strength by eating his flesh. Because of this, their act of rebellion was followed by remorse and guilt, and in the brother clan certain restrictions were observed to prevent its repetition.

In the first place, instead of the father, a certain animal was declared the totem. The totem animal took the place of the dead father in that it was regarded as the ancestor and protecting spirit of the clan, and no one was allowed to kill it or eat its flesh. On the other hand, a yearly totem feast was held at which the totem animal was killed and eaten. The prohibition against killing the totem animal combined with the yearly ritual killing and eating of it (a reenactment of the original crime) suggests to Freud that the totem was a surrogate for the murdered father. Onto the totem were projected the ambivalent feelings of love and hostility of the sons toward the father—the same ambivalent feelings experienced by every child toward his father in Freud's view.

Psychoanalysis has revealed that the totem animal is in reality a substitute for the father; and this tallies with the contradictory fact that, though the killing of the animal is as a rule forbidden, yet its killing is a festive occasion and with the fact that it is killed and yet mourned. The ambivalent emotional attitude, which to this day characterizes the father-complex in our children and which often persists into adult life, seems to extend to the totem animal in its capacity as substitute of the father.[71]

In time the totem animal is replaced by the gods of classical antiquity and finally by the one God of monotheism who is, like the totem animal, a father-substitute. Totemism, therefore, is seen as the origin of religion since it represents the first instance of projecting ambivalent feelings toward the father onto a superior being and the first way of atoning for the guilt which resulted from those feelings and from the crime of parricide.

Totemic religion arose from the filial sense of guilt, in an attempt to allay feeling and to appease the father by deferred obedience to him. All later religions are seen to be attempts at solving the same problem... and are reactions to the same great event with which civilization began and which, since it occurred, has not allowed mankind a moment's rest.[72]

In this way, Freud argues, the killing of the primal father and the resulting totemistic religion has had "a determining influence on the nature of religion."[73]

The second great prohibition of totemism was the "incest taboo" by which the brothers bound themselves not to have sexual intercourse with or marry any woman of the same clan and to marry only a woman of another clan (exogamy). This seems to have served two purposes: First, it created a certain equality among the brothers by preventing any one of them from usurping the position of the murdered father and appropriating all the women of the clan by force. If none of the brothers could have any of the women, no one of them could have them all. Second, by renouncing the women for whose sake they had killed the father, the sons were atoning for their killing of the father by what Freud calls "deferred obedience." Thus the restriction formerly imposed upon them by the father's presence they now imposed upon themselves.

For Freud, then, the significance of totemism with its "two principal ordinances" would seem to be threefold. First, it represents the origin of religion for it determines the character of all subsequent religion as Freud sees it, that is, the projection of ambivalent feelings toward the father onto a divine father-substitute and the expiation of the guilt resulting from ambivalence. Second, totemism represents the historical root of the Oedipus complex in the sense that, in the Oedipal experience, the child, by reason of his sexual desire for the mother and hostility toward the father, repeats—if only in fantasy—the crime of the sons against the primal father and experiences the same guilt.

Freud points out that the two fundamental taboos of totemism correspond to the two repressed wishes of the Oedipus Complex.

> If the totem animal is the father, then the two principal ordinances of totemism, the two taboo prohibitions which constitute its core—not to kill the animal and not to have sexual relations with a woman of the same totem—coincide in content with the two crimes of Oedipus, who killed his father and married his mother, as well as with the two primal wishes of children, the insufficient repression or re-awakening of which forms the nucleus of perhaps every psychoneurosis.[74]

From this similarity Freud suggests the probability that "the totemic system was a product of the conditions involved in the Oedipus complex."[75]

This brings us to the third significant point about totemism for, if it represents the historical root of the Oedipus complex, it thereby represents the origin not only of religion but also of law, morality, and civilization. Freud argues that "the beginnings of religion, morals, society and art converge in the Oedipus Complex."[76] We have seen that, in Freud's theory of civilization, social organization is based on instinctual renunciation, that is, on the renunciation of sexual and aggressive impulses. Such instinctual renunciation makes possible social organization, the investing of energy in work and cultural pursuits, and the development of conscience and morality. Freud sees the first instance of this in the two great taboos of totemism by which the sons of the primal father place restrictions on their aggressive impulses (the prohibition against killing the totem animal) and their sexual impulses (the incest taboo). Totemism, Freud states, as the "earliest form of a religion which we recognize, carries with it, as indispensable constituents of its system, a number of commands and prohibitions which have no other significance, of course, than as instinctual renunciations."[77] With the killing of the primal father and the appearance of the totemistic brother clan, Freud suggests that the brothers entered into a form of social contract by which "the first form of social organization came about with a renunciation of instinct, a recognition of mutual obligations; the introduction of definite institutions pronounced inviolable (holy)—that is to say, the beginnings of morality and justice."[78]

In *Moses and Monotheism*, Freud proposes an analogy between the killing of the primal father and the traumatic experience which is at the core of a neurosis. The memory of the trauma is repressed but reappears later in the form of neurotic symptoms. In the same way, the killing of the primal father—humanity's "original sin"—acts as a repressed memory which reappears in the form of a neurosis, that is, the religious illusion. It is in the context of this analogy that Freud accounts for the monotheistic character of Judaism and Christianity. Monotheism, he argues, represents a "return of the repressed," that is, the return to humanity's consciousness of a repressed memory of a traumatic event. What humanity remembers in this case is the fact "that they once possessed a primal father and killed him...."[79] The unconscious memory of this event is what Freud calls humanity's "archaic heritage." In the neurosis of an individual the "return of the repressed" in the form of neurotic symptoms is frequently occasioned by the occurrence of an event which is similar in content to the original traumatic event. The symptoms exhibited by neurotics as a reaction to the reappearance of this repressed material may take the form of a positive compulsion to repeat the trauma or a negative inhibition or phobia but in either case "we may recognize in their condition a direct expression of their fixation to an early portion of their past."[80]

This theory of neurosis is then applied to the history of the Jewish people—in particular the history of the exodus from Egypt under the leadership of Moses—to explain the monotheism of Judaism as an example of the "return of the repressed." Citing the research of scholars such as J.H. Breasted, Edward Meyer, and Ernst Seelin, he proposes the twofold hypothesis that (1) Moses was not a Hebrew but an Egyptian and (2) after the exodus from Egypt the Jews rebelled against Moses' leadership and killed him. In Freud's argument this murder of Moses by his people is "an important link between the forgotten event of primaeval times and its later emergence in the form of the monotheist religions."[81] This reconstructed history of Moses and the Israelites would read as follows: During the Eighteenth Dynasty in the fourteenth century B.C. the priests of the sun god at Heliopolis introduced the idea of one universal god (monotheism). The worship of this god—Aton—was embraced and promoted by the Pharaoh Akhenaton (who had changed his name from Amenhotep). Akhenaton made the Aton religion the state religion and imposed it on his people. The old polytheism with its emphasis on ritual magical thought and belief in a life after death gave way to a pure religion of joy in Aton's creation and the ethical injunction to practice truth and justice. This, Freud notes, was "the first and perhaps clearest case of a monotheist religion in human history."[82] This monotheistic religion, however, was abandoned under the reign of Akhenaton's successors and in 1350 B.C. the Eighteenth Dynasty came to an end.

Only this much of the story is historically established. Therefore, Freud suggests, "and now our hypothetical sequel begins."[83] The hypothesis is that the Moses of the Exodus story was in fact an Egyptian and a disciple of Akhenaton and the Aton religion. When this monotheistic religion was discarded by the Egyptians, Moses introduced the Jews to the Aton religion and the custom of circumcision. At some point between the exodus from Egypt and their taking possession of the land of Canaan, the Jews rebelled against Moses, killed him, and rejected the Aton religion he had imposed on them. Also during this time the Jews who were leaving Egypt united with nearby tribes related to them and accepted, under the influence of Arabian Midianites a new religion which involved the worship of the volcano-god Jahweh. This new God was of a completely different character from Aton. Whereas Aton was a symbol of peace, truth, and justice, Jahweh was harsh, vindictive and punitive. Freud argues that the Moses who, according to the biblical account, introduces the Jews to the worship of Jahweh and is described as the son-in-law of a Midianite priest is in fact a different person from the Moses who led them out of Egypt and who had imposed the Aton religion on them. For the sake of continuity, however, the biblical account identifies them as the same person.

Why was it necessary to identify these two men as the same person? Because, Freud argues, "in the course of time the God Jahweh lost his own characteristics and grew more and more to resemble the old God of Moses, the Aton."[84] The account identifies the Egyptian Moses and the Midianite Moses as one and the same person because in fact Aton and Jahweh became the same god. This is explained as due to the fact that the followers of the original Moses (whom Freud identifies with the "Levites" of the biblical account) and later the prophets kept alive the concept of the one god Aton in such a way that his attributes came to be assigned to Jahweh. Thus Jahweh becomes no longer a vindictive tribal god but the one universal god who disdains ceremonial and sacrifice and asks only for belief in him and a life of truth and justice. Why this return to monotheism took place is explained by Freud in terms of the theory of neurosis and the return of the repressed. The killing of Moses and the resulting guilt was the event which reawakened the memory of the original trauma—the killing of the primal father. The monotheistic worship of Jahweh represents the return of the repressed memory of that event though in disguised form just as the neurotic symptom is a distorted memory of the original trauma.

Freud proposes that, with St. Paul and Christianity, the primeval source of this guilt is identified as "original sin", but the fact that the original crime was the killing of the deified father is attested to by the fact that atonement can be made only by the death of the Son of God. This son, the "leader of the brother horde," sacrifices himself, but in the process becomes deified himself and thereby takes the place of the Father God.

Thus Christianity becomes a Son religion whereas Judaism had been a Father religion. In this way, Freud believes, the ambivalence which is at the heart of religion is expressed, for the son sacrifices himself to the Father but ends by usurping the place of the Father, "just as every son had hoped to do in primaeval times."[85] Freud concludes:

> What is certainly of decisive importance, however, is the awakening of the forgotten memory trace by a recent real repetition of the event. The murder of Moses was a repetition of this kind and later, the supposed judicial murder of Christ: so that these events come into the foreground as causes. It seems as though the genesis of monotheism could not do without these occurrences.[86]

With this quotation we are returned to Freud's original proposition about belief in God. It is an illusion based on wish fulfillment and cannot be sustained by objective rational arguments. Its emotional basis is in fact the ambivalence and guilt associated with a neurosis and therefore can be brought to expression only through some triggering event such as the death of Moses or of Christ, which recalls the crime against the primeval father.

Evaluation

Critical reflection and reaction has raised the following questions about the Freudian interpretation of religion. At first glance these questions might appear to arise from a religious desire to refute Freud's negative analysis of religion. They are, however, questions that belong to any objective assessment of Freudian theory and summarize reaction to that theory from both theological and scientific sources.

Is It Reductionist?

Does Freud reduce the phenomenon of religion to a purely psychological phenomenon, that is, one that is entirely explained in terms of the psychological processes of wish fulfillment, ambivalence, and guilt? Even the alleged historical data that Freud brings to bear on his interpretation of religious phenomena seem to be reconstructed in such a way as to reflect the dynamics of the Oedipus complex. The content of religious belief and devotion—God, the sacred, transcendence—is seen as the "exalted father," that is, as an imaginary figure created through projection of the human father figure. God is a product of wish fulfillment, the "longing for the father." Onto this substitute father figure are transferred the feelings of ambivalence and guilt which characterized the Oedipus complex of one's childhood. This process is similar to the "transference," which is an essential feature of psychoanalytic therapy by which the patient projects onto the analyst childhood feelings toward the parental figure which had been repressed. The neurotic behavior of the patient is explained with reference to repressed childhood feelings. In like manner, religious phenomena are explained with reference to repressed childhood feelings toward the father. And these repressed feelings are inevitably feelings of hostility which come into conflict with one's conscious religious feelings of love and devotion and are thus guilt-producing.

One can easily understand why genuinely religious people would find this interpretation of religion, in terms of the dynamics of neurotic behavior, reductionist and inadequate as a comprehensive theory of religion. This does not in itself constitute a refutation of Freud's theory or demonstrate it to be without value for understanding the religious personality. To be sure, there are canonized saints who seem to exhibit the repression, ambivalence, and guilt of which Freud speaks. On the other hand, it is difficult to dismiss deeply religious people such as Mother Teresa and Martin Luther King, Jr. as immature and neurotic. Even from a scientific point of view, to explain such a complex and varied a phenomenon as religion in terms of a single psychological dynamic is to invite the charge of reductionism. Freud partially responds to this charge by explaining that religion cannot derive from or be explained in terms of a single source or origin. Psychoanalysis, he argues, seeks, as in duty bound, to gain recognition for one of the sources of religion (i.e., in the dynamics of the Oedipus complex). However, he adds, "that does not mean it is claiming either that that source is the only one or that it occupies first place among the contributory factors."[87] He concludes that for a comprehensive understanding of the complex phenomenon of religion the findings of psychoanalysis should be synthesized with the findings from other fields of research. In this statement at least, Freud concurs with the aims of contemporary religious studies which seek to bring various fields of research—history, psychology, sociology, and so on—to bear on an understanding of the phenomenon of religion. Nevertheless, in *Moses and Monotheism*, he states that he never doubted that religious phenomena were to be understood *only* on the model of the neurotic symptoms of the individual which represent the return of the repressed memory of a childhood trauma. In the case of religion, what returns is humanity's repressed memory of important happenings in the primeval history of the human family (the killing of the primal father and its aftermath). It is their origin in repression and guilt which explains the "obsessive character" of religious practices. Accordingly, they "are effective on human beings by force of the historical truth of their content."[88]

It is difficult to synthesize these two statements. Is religion a complex phenomenon which can be understood only through the insights of various areas of research, or is the psychoanalytic theory of neurosis sufficient in itself? We have seen that Freud looks to history and anthropology to corroborate his psychoanalytic interpretation of religion, but the result seems to be a psychoanalytic reconstruction of human history on the model of the Oedipus complex. It is certainly legitimate to explain religion in terms of the psychological dynamics underlying religious belief and practices, for, whatever else it might be, religion is certainly a psychological phenomenon. But is it nothing more? Furthermore, as a psychological phenomenon, is it to be understood solely in terms of the *pathological* dynamics by which Freud categorizes it? Giving Freud the benefit of the doubt, we might state his position as follows:(1) Psychoanalysis is only one of many areas of research which contribute to an understanding of religion. (2) The psychoanalytic contribution to the study of religion reveals it to be a pathological phenomenon of mental life.

Unlike some later theorists, Freud does not have a concept of "healthy" religion (except, perhaps, implicitly in his theory of personality). As far as his explicit writings on religion are concerned, religion as such is regressive, infantile, and neurotic. While this may not be adequate as an interpretation of the complex phenomenon of religion, that is, as a *psychology of religion*, it nevertheless represents a *psychopathology of religion* which has proved useful in accounting for neurotic distortions of religion.

In the end, Freudian theory has been found significant for an understanding of religion in at least three different ways. As a psychology of religion (religion as infantile, regressive, and obsessional), it has understandably drawn a defensive reaction from religious and theological sources. As a psychopathology of religion, it has been found helpful in identifying the neurotic sources of unhealthy religion and the influence of wish fulfillment on religious belief. As a theory of personality—especially the analysis of human existence as the struggle between Eros and death—it provides a psychological anthropology—an understanding of the human condition—which may be put in dialogue with the corresponding religious view of human existence. A comparison of Freudian and religious answers to the question "Can life triumph over death?" may prove more fruitful than the polemics which mar the debate over Freud's explicit theory of religion. In the end, what Freud says about human personality and the human condition may have more religious significance than what he says about God and religion.

Is It Unscientific?

The term "unscientific" has been applied not only to Freud's theory of religion but also to some aspects of his theory of personality. This is true especially of his delineation of the tragic dimension of human existence, that is, in his vision of human existence as the "eternal struggle" between Eros (the life instinct) and the destructive and divisive death instinct. As we have already observed, it could be argued that in describing human existence as a struggle between life and death, Freud was approaching a religious understanding of human existence; that in asking the question "Can life triumph over death?" he was asking a religious question; and that in describing the process of human civilization as an attempt to bring about that triumph, he was speaking of a religious enterprise. There is certainly an analogy between this analysis of the tragic dimension of human existence and the religious vision of a humanity in need of redemption. Some critics, however, including, it would seem, most contemporary psychoanalysts, dismiss the concept of the death instinct as either unscientific or irrelevant. As for the "unscientific" character of this concept, which Erich Fromm called an "unproved speculation," it has already been noted that Freud did not advance it as a proven scientific fact. He speaks of the Eros/death theory as being more in the nature of an intuitive insight, a conclusion arrived at "after long hesitancies and vacillations"[89] and "a kind of conviction for which I was not as yet able to find reasons," but a conviction which became so strong that he could "no longer think in any other way."[90]

As for the charge that the Eros/death conflict is an irrelevant concept, this may be true within the confines of psychoanalytic therapy. As already noted, however, Freud was going beyond psychoanalysis in this narrow sense when he pointed in this way to the ultimate source of the instinctual conflict dealt with in therapy. When he speaks at this level he is not merely proposing a method of treating neuroses; he is using psychoanalytic theory to explore the meaning of the cultural, artistic, and religious aspects of human existence. Freud believed that this function of psychoanalysis was perhaps more valuable than its psychotherapeutic aims. What is perceived, therefore, as irrelevant to the therapeutic process may indeed be relevant to an understanding of the human condition. One of the functions of religion is to be a source of hope in the face of the kind of tragic dimension of human existence that Freud delineates. Consequently, those who have revised Freud's theory of the Eros/death conflict were engaged in an essentially "religious" enterprise, since they were trying to find a way out of the pessimism of Freud's tragic analysis of the human condition and thereby offer hope in the midst of this tragedy. That pessimism stems from Freud's contention that the cultural enterprise of bringing about the triumph of life over death is self-defeating in that culture's repression of the death instinct in the form of aggression has the effect of reinstating it in the form of guilt. Redemptive religions seem to accept the inevitability of guilt and the tragic quality of human existence and respond with a promise of redemption from guilt which is seen as having a liberating and transforming effect on the believer.

The alternative to this religious response is to offer a more optimistic view of the human condition. This is what the humanistic revisers of Freudian theory have done. They reject the notion of a biologically rooted dualism of Eros versus death which locates the source of repression, guilt, and tragedy within the individual. In its place they propose a dualism which is rooted in environmental and historical conditions and which, therefore, locates the source of guilt and tragedy outside the individual. Thus the answer lies not primarily in the transformation of the individual but of the environment or of society. Erich Fromm,[91] Herbert Marcuse[92] and Norman O. Brown,[93] use different theoretical formulations, but all have contended that humanity's hope for the future lies primarily in the removal of the social sources of repression. This debate over the relative merits of changing the individual or transforming social structures is ongoing today. Freud's solution is unequivocal: The problem ultimately lies within the individual since the conflict between Eros and death takes place within the individual psyche.

Freud's theory of religion is also said to rest on an unscientific foundation in that his investigations into the historical roots of religion in *Totem and Taboo* and of Judeo-Christian monotheism in *Moses and Monotheism* are speculations based on faulty historical and anthropological data. Regarding Freud's theory of the primal horde, S.G.F. Brandon contends that "his reconstruction of this primeval drama had the sanction of no archaeological or anthropological evidence; however, its novel interpretation of the sex instinct as the source of religion caused much excitement and gave it a publicity it did not deserve on scientific grounds."[94]

Speaking of the same theory, Eli Sagan states: "What is certain is that Freud had absolutely no evidence of such an event or events, and, therefore, no matter what he imagined it was, it was definitely a made-up story."[95]

As valid as these criticisms are, they do not, in themselves, invalidate Freud's theory of religion. Freud's theory of the primal horde represented an attempt to construct an historical foundation for his psychoanalytic interpretation of religion, to explain the universality of the Oedipus complex and therefore of religion. Both the Oedipus complex and religion were seen as the result of unconscious memory traces of a prehistoric event and, therefore, as a repetition or reenactment of that event in the life of the individual. In other words, the ontogenesis of religion is explained as the repetition of the phylogenetic event through the mechanism of some kind of racial memory. But is the literal, historical truth of the primal horde theory essential to Freud's theory of religion? Perhaps there is an analogy here to the Christian doctrine of original sin, which is also linked to a prehistoric "event"—the fall of Adam and Eve. The "primeval drama" of the primal horde serves the same purpose as an explanation of the origin of religion as does the story of Adam and Eve—their sin and expulsion from the garden of Eden—in explaining the reality and universality of sin and guilt. For Christianity, every individual, in some sense, repeats the sin of Adam; for Freud, every individual relives, in the oedipal experience, the experience of the primal horde. The recognition of the Adam and Eve story as an ahistorical myth rather than an historical event does not in itself invalidate the doctrine of original sin. The doctrine is not about something that happened in the past; it is a statement about human existence. The mythical terms in which the doctrine is expressed serve to emphasize the universality of sin and guilt in human existence. In raising the question of the truth or falsity of this doctrine, therefore, we are not asking whether the story of Adam and Eve is historical but whether the doctrine conveys a truth about human existence.

This is the same type of question that we would address to any psychological theory: Does it convey a truth about human existence? Does it explain the observable facts? Does it make sense out of our human experience? In assessing Freudian theory, this is a more important question than the question of the historical truth of the primal horde theory. Would it not be possible to read this theory as a myth which gives expression to what is perceived as a truth of human existence—the universality and inevitability of the oedipal experience and therefore of religion—and not as an explanation in terms of historical causality? If so, then the question of the *historical* truth of the primal horde theory would be no more relevant to the question of the validity of Freud's theory of religion than is the question of the historical truth of the Adam and Eve story to the question of validity of the Christian doctrine of original sin. As with that doctrine, Freud's theory of religion must be evaluated on how well it explains and makes sense of our human experience.

Is It Prejudiced?

In 1958 Gregory Zilboorg made the following remark about Freud's theory of religion: "Be it remembered that by 'psychology of religion' Freud did not understand human psychological processes by means of which religious belief might come to expression, but rather the refutation of religious faith."[96] This raises the question of whether Freud's psychological theory of religion is a justification or rationalization of his preconceived ideas about religion, that is, his personal atheism, or whether his atheism is the result of his psychological investigation of the roots of religious belief and practice. However one answers this question, it seems fair to counter Zilboorg's criticism with the observation that, whatever the strengths or weaknesses of Freud's psychology of religion might be, it is quite clearly a theory of the "human psychological processes by means of which religious belief might come to expression." Those psychological processes, however, are seen as pathological and hence the refutation of religion, within the confines of the theory itself, is inevitable.

For James Jones, Freud's atheism was less a refutation of religion than a presupposition he brings to the study of religion. In proposing a new approach to the psychoanalytic study of religion, Jones begins by stating: "An heir of the Enlightenment, Freud assumed that atheism was normative and religion was but a vestige of the childhood of humankind."[97] This statement (the truth of which seems evident from a reading of *The Future of an Illusion*) again raises the question of the possible relationship between the negative evaluation of religion in Freud's psychoanalytic interpretation and his personal atheism. Was his atheism a conclusion of his analysis of religious phenomena or was his assumption that "atheism was normative" the foundation of his theory of religion? Strictly speaking, one could argue that neither of these statements is true since atheism as such—the denial of the reality of God—is not the conclusion Freud comes to in his analysis of religion. In *The Future of an Illusion*, the object of his study is the motivation behind religious belief, not the object of that belief. And his conclusion is that such belief is an illusion based on wish fulfillment. Freud is careful to point out that in calling belief in God an illusion he is speaking not of the objective existence or nonexistence of God but only of the psychological motivation which is operative in such belief. In other words, to refer to religious belief as an "illusion" does not necessarily mean that it is a "delusion." A delusion is an error; an illusion may or may not be true.

A more complicated question, however, is the question of the emotional matrix or psychic disposition which might be a factor in the development of Freudian theory. To what extent was Freud's thinking about religion influenced by the perhaps unconscious components of his own psychic structure? What part was played in the development of his thought by his alleged insecurity, megalomania, ambivalence, guilt, and so forth—character traits which represent the residue of his own childhood experiences? Atheism, as well as belief, can be illusory and wish fulfilling. As Jones remarks: "Just as there are neurotic reasons for believing in God, so there are neurotic reasons for refusing belief."[98] Among others, W.W. Meissner has contended that Freud's thinking about religion stems in part from an unresolved ambivalence about religion and particularly about his own Jewish tradition—an ambivalence which "stems from unresolved infantile conflicts."

> Deep in the recesses of his mind, Freud seems to have resolved that his truculent spirit would never yield to the demands of religion for submission and resignation. He would be a Hannibal, a conquistador—and a Moses, a prophet who would find a new religion that would enable him to lead his people to the Promised Land of psychological freedom. But the only way for him to achieve this goal required that he overcome the religion of his fathers and annihilate the very image of the father himself.... Freud was never able to free himself from these deep-seated entanglements and their associated conflicts, and ultimately what he taught us about religion, religious experience and faith must be taken in the context of these unconscious conflicts.[99]

This interpretation of Freud's views on religion is an echo of an earlier (1958) study of David Bakan's entitled *Sigmund Freud and the Jewish Mystical Tradition*. Bakan's thesis suggests that Freud's ambivalence toward his Jewish religious heritage was a reflection of the conflict between two conflicting currents in that tradition: the orthodox, rabbinic tradition with its emphasis on law and tendency toward legalism and the Kabbalistic, mystical tradition within Judaism which seeks, either through reason or emotional experience, the deeper meaning of the law. One of the offshoots of this latter tradition was the large-scale messianic movement known as Sabbatianism beginning in the seventeenth century. Given Freud's understanding of religion as originating in guilt and of God as a projection of the harsh, punishing superego, his rejection of orthodox, rabbinic Judaism would seem appropriate, especially if that tradition were perceived as legalistic and guilt producing. Why then did Freud maintain his Jewish identity? Bakan answers that while rejecting the orthodox, rabbinic tradition, he identified with the opposing mystical tradition within Judaism. Hence his ambivalence and hence the unconscious impact of this form of Judaism on his psychoanalytic work. Freud, he states, "had strong, heretical tendencies, yet he would not relinquish his self identification as a Jew. His quarrel with religion was with the older orthodox forms of Judaism. He felt he could still maintain his Jewish identity despite the violation of orthodoxy."[100]

This ambivalence regarding his religious heritage finds particular expression in Freud's writings about Moses who as the giver of the law is a figure representing orthodox Judaism. As the bearer of a "new law" (psychoanalysis) Freud is seen as both identifying with Moses the lawgiver and usurping his place. As Bakan states, "The identification with Moses turns into its opposite, the destruction of Moses."[101] Freud's opposition to guilt-inducing legalism and the harsh strictures of the superego which puts him in opposition to the Mosaic, orthodox aspect of his religious tradition at the same time identified him with the mystical and messianic tradition within Judaism.

In an attempt to resolve the resulting ambivalence, Freud makes two assertions about Moses for which there is insufficient historical evidence. First, he contends that Moses was an Egyptian and therefore a Gentile. This was an attempt, Bakan argues, "to ward off anti-Semitism" by separating "the Mosaic characteristics from the image of the Jews."[102] Second, Freud suggests that Moses was murdered by the Jews. In this assertion Bakan finds an "allegorical attempt" to destroy the harsh restrictions imposed by rabbinic Judaism—via the superego—on the Jews including Freud himself. In other words, it was an attempt to destroy "the Moses each person carries about with him."[103] Bakan further argues that, in his opposition to rabbinic orthodoxy, Freud carried out the messianic function of relieving guilt and accordingly "conceived of himself as a messiah in the spirit of Jewish mysticism."[104] It should be noted in passing that, in his book *Sigmund Freud's Christian Unconscious* (1988), Paul Vitz uses a combination of factual evidence and speculation to demonstrate a similar ambivalence in Freud's attitude towards Christianity.

What are we to make of this apparent consensus regarding Freud's ambivalence toward religion and consequent emotional and unconscious factors in his thinking about religion? This debate about emotional, unconscious factors in the development of Freud's psychoanalytic concepts in general and in his theory of religion in particular seems to be as self-perpetuating as it is inconclusive. We can offer only the following comments:

First, in Freud's identification with the great figure of Moses as well as in the image of himself as a kind of anti-Mosaic messiah, we can find perhaps a reflection of something we have already observed about Freud's character—namely, a certain megalomania in his leadership of the psychoanalytic movement as reflected in his intolerance of and insecurity about new ideas proposed by his disciples.

Second, when Freud is portrayed as a liberator from the harsh restrictions of the superego, this is not to be taken as meaning that he regarded the development of the superego as such and the resulting guilt as pathological. In *The Future of an Illusion* he speaks of the moral sense represented by the superego as one of the "mental assets" of civilization. It is precisely through this process of internalizing parental and cultural commands which creates the superego, he argues, that external coercion is gradually internalized. It is through this process that we become moral and social beings, and the more successful the process of internalization is, the more culture (including religion) can dispense with external coercion. Hence, for Freud, the strengthening of the superego represents "a most precious cultural asset in the psychological field."[105] The harsh, punishing superego, then, would represent the force of insufficiently internalized commands. In opposition to this, psychoanalysis offers to the patient an analyst who represents—by his accepting and non-judgmental attitude—what Bakan calls a "nonpunishing superego."[106]

Third, though one could argue with Vitz's notion of Freud's "Christian unconscious," it seems clear that Freud's ambivalence about religion extends beyond the confines of orthodox, rabbinic Judaism to include a certain type of Christianity as well. As Bakan remarks, what Freud wanted to destroy was not just Jewish rabbinism but also "the parallels to such rabbinism in Western civilization at large."[107] Foremost among these parallels one would have to place Freud's perception of Western Christianity. This perception, as we have noted earlier, may have been colored by the influence of the Catholic nanny who cared for him until he was two and a half, and who introduced him to her own hell and damnation brand of Catholicism. That Freud's ambivalence extends also to Christianity may be inferred from his juxtaposing (in *Moses and Monotheism*) of the deaths of Moses and Christ as parallel psychological events. Both events trigger the return of the repressed memory of a primeval event.

Fourth, if Freud's attitude to religion was ambivalent, we are forced to qualify his negative assessment of it. Ambivalence refers to a conflict of conscious and unconscious attitudes. Does this mean that Freud's conscious rejection of religion was in conflict with an unconscious attraction to religion? If so, we may perhaps identify that aspect or kind of religion he rejected as legalistic and guilt inducing, a function of the harsh, punishing superego. We have seen that this was his conscious perception of orthodox Judaism and Christianity. But did Freud have an unconscious perception of religion as liberating one from that very guilt—a form of religion which would be a function of the nonpunishing superego? Bakan answers in the affirmative, citing the influence of the Jewish mystical tradition which stood in opposition to legalistic rabbinism.

A similar unconscious link to Christianity might be found in Freud's interest in St. Paul in whom, as Zilboorg suggests, he found "the Jew who created Christian theology."[108] Zilboorg remarks that St. Paul's concept of *caritas* helped Freud clarify the meaning of Eros but that he did not incorporate these concepts into his analysis of religion. If Bakan's analysis of Freud's ambivalence is correct, it is not unreasonable to suspect an unconscious affinity with St. Paul whose God is the source of grace and forgiveness (in psychoanalytic terms, a representation of the "nonpunishing superego") and who proclaimed "freedom from the law." And one is allowed to wonder whether the absence of all this from Freud's analysis of religion is the result of repression.

Is It One-sided?

Freud's theory of human development and therefore of moral and religious development is perceived as inadequate by reason of its one-sided emphasis on the Oedipus (father) complex and its instinctual view of human personality. The one-sidedness of the theory reveals itself, it is argued, in two ways. First, in its instinctual view of the human person, it ignores the relational aspect of human development. Freud's model of human becoming is psychosexual. Development is equated with the development of the sex instinct as the names of the developmental stages suggest (oral, anal, phallic, latency, genital). The focus here is on the inner instinctual dynamics of growth and conflict. Growth takes place through the endless repetition of the instinctual cycle which features the conflict and interplay between the instinctual drives of the id and the controlling forces of the ego and the superego. Other people in one's environment are seen merely as objects for the expenditure of sexual and aggressive energy.

Though Freud defines the ego as the link between the psyche and external reality (it operates on the "reality principle"), it is precisely this relationship between the ego and the environment which is left underdeveloped in his psychosexual model. A second aspect of the perceived one-sidedness of Freudian theory is found in its ignoring of the significance of the pre-oedipal stages and therefore of the role of the mother for moral and religious development. As we have seen, Freud locates the origin of morality and religion in the Oedipus (father) complex and the experience of the male child. In his elaboration of the dynamics of this stage, and of the differing scenarios it posits for the development of the male and the female child, feminist authors in particular have perceived not only a minimizing of the role of the mother but also a devaluation of female personality in general.

Our discussion of Freud's theory of religion will conclude with a brief reference to three developments in post-Freudian psychoanalytic theory which can be seen as responses to these perceived inadequacies of Freudian thought. These three developments are ego psychology, object-relations theory, and the feminist readings of Freudian theory. Clearly, in a more exhaustive work, these lines of thought would constitute at least one separate chapter. Since the focus of our discussion, however, is the seminal theories in psychology of religion, they will be treated here only as elaborations of underdeveloped aspects of Freudian theory.

Ego Psychology. That ego psychology represents an elaboration of something implicit in Freudian theory is emphasized by one of its originators, Heinz Hartmann (1894-1970), who felt that psychoanalytic theory had been guilty of a one-sided focus on the *defensive* functions of the ego—the so-called defense mechanisms of denial, repression, rationalization, and so forth. Hartmann wanted to correct what he perceived as this one-sided interpretation of Freud by emphasizing not those functions of the ego by which it defends against incursions from the unconscious but those functions by which the ego adapts itself to external reality (perception, attention, judgment, etc.). This emphasis on the adaptive function of the ego stresses the idea that human growth and development is not just the outcome of intrapsychic, instinctual conflict but also of the autonomous activity of the ego (i.e., activity beyond its functions of merely acting as a buffer zone between id and external reality) by which it adapts itself to the external environment. In other words, the self is not merely instinctual; it is also relational.

Starting with this understanding of the ego, Erik Erikson proposed a relational model of human development in which, in a total life span, the individual is seen as passing through eight "psychosocial" (as opposed to psychosexual) stages.[109] Development is no longer seen as merely the inner dynamics of sexual development but as a process whereby the ego adapts itself to its environment. It does so by acquiring, at each stage, a particular "virtue" or "ego strength" which represents the successful resolution of a particular psychosocial conflict. Thus, in the first year of life (the oral stage), if the infant, in its relationship with the mother, experiences a predominance of "basic trust" over mistrust, it will begin to develop a rudimentary sense of "hope"— an ego strength which is the foundation of all further development. This view of human development allows for a more positive assessment of the role of religion in human life. Religion is seen not as a defensive reaction to ambivalence and guilt but as potential facilitator of the ego's process of adaptation. Thus, in the developmental process, the infant's feeling of basic trust toward mother is extended to others and to one's total environment. When this fundamental disposition is directed to a transcendent trustworthy object (God), it becomes religious faith. By instilling such faith religion becomes, in Erikson's view, "the institutional safeguard of the child's growing sense of trust." Similarly, in adolescence, religion is seen as providing an "ideology"—a system of beliefs and values—which reinforces the sense of "identity" and "fidelity."

In using Erikson's model for a greater understanding of religious development, Heije Faber stresses the relational aspect of each psychosocial stage.[110] In studying the oral, anal, oedipal, and adolescent stages, Faber focuses on the pattern of relationship with one's environment which emerges in each stage as the result of the ego's attempts to resolve psychosocial conflicts and adapt to its environment. The result, at each of these stages, is a particular pattern of adaptation or relatedness which becomes the prototype for a particular way of relating to God, that is, a particular type or aspect of religion. This hypothesis allows Faber to do two things: First, it makes possible a view of religious development as an ever-maturing kind of relationship with transcendence which parallels human development, which in turn is seen as the natural foundation of religious and spiritual growth. Second, while remaining faithful to the Freudian understanding of religion as projection or transference, Faber is able to go beyond Freud's narrow understanding of religion as having its origin in the ambivalence and guilt of the oedipal stage.

The particular type of relatedness which characterizes each stage is seen as prototypical for and therefore contributing to the development of a particular kind of religious relationship. This allows Faber to locate the psychological roots of different types of religious personality. The patterns, for example, of the oral stage with its emphasis on an all-embracing oneness with mother and of the oedipal stage in which the relationship with the father is established over a distance or separation are seen as prototypical of naturalistic and revealed religions, respectively. An adequate understanding of religion, then, is arrived at only with reference to both the pre-Oedipal mother complex and the Oedipal father complex. In his essay on Leonardo da Vinci, Freud acknowledged but did not develop this idea. "In the parental complex," he states, "we thus recognize that the roots of the need for religion are in the parental complex; the almighty and just God and kindly Nature appear to us as grand sublimations of father and mother, or rather as revivals and restorations of the young child's ideas of them."[111]

Object-Relations Theory. In a 1979 study, Ana-Maria Rizzuto challenges the Freudian contention that one's image of God is based exclusively on the figure of the father—that one's God is a father-substitute or the "exalted father." Rizzuto offers a wealth of clinical evidence to support her thesis that the child's image of God is the projection of his or her experiences with various "significant others" in the child's environment, including both parents, grandparents, or even imaginary figures. All are potential components of one's image of God through the process of "object representation." This refers to the child's internalizing of his or her interactions with his world and those in it and of the sensations, affects, and concepts associated with those interactions. The God representation integrates various aspects of this inner representational world and thereby mirrors the child's own process of integration. This evidence leads Rizzuto to two conclusions. First, it makes it "impossible to accept that the paternal image only is used to form the representation of God" which comes from "varied sources." Second, it means that "formation of the image of God does not depend upon the Oedipal conflict," for "clinical cases show Gods belonging to each level of development from oral to Oedipal."[112]

In speaking of God in terms of object representation, Rizzuto is close to the thrust of object-relations theory, a current in post-Freudian psychoanalytic theory which represents a movement from an instinctual to a relational view of personality and of human development. In object-relations theory the self is seen as structured through the internalization not simply of "objects" but of the whole quality and affective tone of the self's relationships with those objects. The dynamics of personality are therefore primarily the dynamics of interpersonal life rather than instinctual life.

The transition from an instinctual to a relational view of human personality, that is, from strict Freudian instinct theory to object-relations theory, was carried forward by theorists such as Melanie Klein, W.R.D. Fairbairn, Heinz Kohut, and D.W. Winnicott. They represent a more emphatic departure from instinct theory toward a more "person oriented" or relational view of personality. The aim of "libidinal striving" was seen as a relationship with an object and not the gratification of an impulse.

How does this shift in focus suggest a revision of Freud's theory of religion? D.W. Winnicott, perhaps the most influential of the object-relations theorists, is well known for his concepts of transitional objects and transitional phenomena. Winnicott interprets the debate within psychoanalysis between the instinctual and the relational views of personality—personality as driven by inner instinctual drives versus personality as determined by external interpersonal relations—as the tension between subjectivity and objectivity. But between the worlds of pure subjectivity and pure objectivity, he maintains, there lies "an intermediate area of *experiencing*, to which inner reality and external life both contribute" and which keeps "inner and outer reality separate yet interrelated."[113] The infant, through the use of "transitional objects" (e.g., the blanket, the teddy bear) creates this intermediate space which allows him to move beyond his purely subjective world. Erikson had said that the infant's movement from total dependence to some degree of autonomy and achievement in the external world could be achieved only on the foundation of an attitude of "basic trust" toward the mother or mothering person. Winnicott sees the infant as creating, through this same sense of trust, this intermediate space by the use of transitional objects. The transitional object, as it were, makes the mother present, or, more accurately, makes present and operative the security of that first interpersonal relationship with mother. As James Jones remarks, "Transitional objects carry a certain interpersonal reality and perform a certain developmental function."[114] That function would be to facilitate the transition from subjectivity to objectivity from the inner to the outer world. Between these two worlds, the child creates an intermediate world of play, fantasy, and imagination which continues into adult life in the form of art, culture and religion.

Winnicott's mention of "religious feeling" as one of the transitional phenomena brings us to the question of the possible contribution of object-relations theory to an understanding of religion. One such contribution might be found in Winnicott's understanding of religion as a "transitional phenomenon." We perhaps approach this understanding when we speak of the "religious imagination." To some, this suggests that religion is a product of pure subjective fantasy with no objective validity. This would seem to be the intent of Freud's description of religion as an "illusion." When Winnicott, however, speaks of religion as "illusion" or "illusory experience," he is not referring to pure subjectivity but to the aforementioned intermediate area which is imaginative and yet an area to which the external world contributes. This area of "experiencing" is what Winnicott describes as "the potential space between the individual and the environment" where the individual experiences "creative being."[115] Though it is not the only possible way of interpreting religion, one thing we may say about religion is that religious phenomena belong to this intermediate, imaginative world of *experience* which keeps "separate yet interrelated" the worlds of pure subjectivity and pure objectivity. The escape from this "illusion" which Freud proposed would seem to leave us in a psychotic world of pure subjectivity or in a dehumanized, visionless world of concrete, factual reality.

A second contribution from object-relations theory to our understanding of religion might be found, as James Jones suggests, in its conception of transference. In the Freudian understanding, transference is understood as the instinctually driven displacement of repressed sexual or aggressive drives from a person in the past (usually a parent) to the person of the analyst in the present.

For object-relations theory, as we have seen, transference refers to the projection of the quality and affective tone of a relationship of the past onto one's present relationships so that the original relationship is continually relived. Again, for Freudian psychoanalysis, religion is the result of projecting onto an illusory father-substitute the ambivalent feelings of love and hostility experienced toward the real father in the Oedipus complex and the attempt to atone for the resulting feelings of guilt. Thus it also is a case of transference. Jones suggests that, in the light of the relational emphasis of object-relations theory, religion should be thought of as a relationship with God, the sacred, or the cosmos. The psychoanalytic question would then become the question of how this relationship with the sacred reflects the structure of one's internalized human relationships. The object of this kind of study of religion would be not so much the origin of religion but rather the quality of this "affective bond with the sacred."[116] Object-relations theory, in this way, helps to shed light on the quality of sacredness in religious experience. What is experienced is sacred to the extent that it reflects those relationships by which the self has been constituted. Thus something is experienced as sacred when it touches upon "the primal originating depths of selfhood" and "evokes the matrix out of which the self originates."[117]

Feminist Readings of Freudian Theory. Feminist reaction to Freudian theory focuses largely on his account of the dynamics of the Oedipus complex. As we have seen, the Oedipus complex describes the ambivalence experienced by the male child toward the father—a mixture of love and hostility by reason of the fact that the father is perceived as both a loved and admired ideal and source of protection and as a rival for mother's affection. In normal development, the little boy in time abandons his sexual attachment to mother and identifies with his father, internalizing his commands and prohibitions. This internalizing of the father's authority accounts for the formation of the superego or conscience and thus represents the beginning of moral development. In ideal development, these moral restrictions of the superego, if sufficiently internalized, are gradually detached from and lose their dependence on the person of the father. They become abstract and depersonalized. Thus, in ideal male development, resolution of the Oedipus complex requires renunciation not only of the attachment to mother but also of the attachment to and dependence on the father. When this "longing for the father" is not out-grown but merely repressed, it may return in the form of neurotic symptoms or religious phenomena in which God becomes the father-substitute. This re-nunciation of attachment is, in Freud's view, the result of "castration anxiety." The little boy fears that his sexual attraction to mother will be punished by the removal of his offending sexual organ. The desire for the father—to be loved by him—arouses the same anxiety for it involves taking the place of mother who, because of her lack of the male organ, appears to have already been cas-trated.

In reading this account of the Oedipus complex, one might expect an account of the experience of the little girl which parallels it, that is, an expe-rience of libidinal attachment to the father and rivalry with the mother. But, since the girl cannot experience the threat of castration in the same way as the boy can, Freud proposes a different path of development for her life. In-stead of castration anxiety, the little girl experiences "penis envy" because of her obvious lack of the male organ. Instead of fearing castration she perceives herself as having already been castrated. This is the basis for her identification with the mother. She does not, like the boy, enter into rivalry with the father with the resulting internalizing of commands and prohibitions, but, like the mother, remains passively attached to the father. In her fantasy, the baby she will have from him is compensation for the missing penis. Thus, for Freud, the Oedipus complex does not apply to the experience of the girl or at least is ex-perienced in a different way and has a different outcome. In the boy, the Oedi-pus (father) complex is "dissolved" through the threat of castration and the ideal result is an autonomous moral agent through the process of internaliz-ing and depersonalizing of the father's commands and prohibitions. In the girl, the castration complex takes the form of penis envy and leads not to a dis-solution of the father complex but rather to attachment to and passive de-pendence on the father. As Freud remarks: "As regards the Oedipus and castration complexes there is a fundamental contrast between the two sexes. Whereas in boys the Oedipus complex is destroyed by the castration com-plex, in girls it is made possible and led up to by the castration complex."[118]

Though its significance for an understanding of his theory is debated, Freud then goes on to make a statement which has not gone unnoticed by feminist critics and which seems to imply a biologically rooted inferiority in female development. "Here the feminist demand for equal rights for the sexes," he writes, "does not take us far, for the morphological distinction is bound to find expression in differences of psychical development. 'Anatomy is Destiny' to vary a saying of Napoleon's." To what extent Freud believed that these "psychical" differences between the sexes are biologically rooted and, therefore, as it were, ordained by nature, is debatable, but it certainly seems to be the case that his description of gender development—of the process by which boys become masculine and girls become feminine—ascribes a higher value to masculinity than to femininity. And this because, unlike that of the boy whose ideal development requires renunciation of attachment, the girl's Oedipus complex "seldom goes beyond taking of her mother's place and adopting a feminine attitude towards the father." Because there is no threat of castration, there is no motive for her to outgrow the attachment to the father. Consequently there is not the same kind of internalizing, impersonalising, and consequent moral development as there is with the boy.

While admitting that the majority of men do not achieve this ideal of masculine development, Freud still makes the following unfavorable comparison when speaking of women:

> I cannot evade the notion (though I hesitate to give it expression) that for women the level of what is ethically normal is different from what it is in men. Their superego is never so inexorable, so impersonal, so independent of its emotional origins as we require it to be in men. Character traits which critics of every epoch have brought up against women—that they show less sense of justice than men, that they are less ready to submit to the great exigencies of life, that they are more often influenced in their judgments by feelings of affection or hostility—all this would be amply accounted for by the modification in the formation of their superego which we have inferred above. We must not allow ourselves to be deflected from such conclusions by the denials of the feminists, who are anxious to force us to regard the two sexes completely equal in position and worth.[119]

As Judith Van Herik remarks, in the development of femininity "the father and later paternal figures are objects to which she is passively attached. The father figure remains external instead of being internalized and depersonalized."[120] For Freud, it would appear that the way of masculine development with its emphasis on renunciation of attachment, internalizing, impersonalising, and abstraction is more conducive to intellectual and moral progress and, therefore, to cultural advancement, according to his understanding of culture.

Two aspects in particular of this account of the Oedipus complex have elicited responses from feminist thinkers. The first of these is the preeminence that Freud accords to the role of the father and of the father (Oedipus) complex in human moral and religious development, which leaves undeveloped and devalued the role of the mother and the mother (pre-Oedipal) complex in such development. Eli Sagan, for example, points to this one-sidedness as the weakness of Freud's theory of morality when he states: "The fundamental weakness of Freud's theory of morality and the superego is that it ignores the pre-oedipal life of the child."[121] If morality, it is argued, is explained solely in terms of internalization and the formation of the superego, and if boys achieve this more successfully than girls, then the moral inferiority of women is implied. Moreover, Sagan argues, this narrow view of moral development has two fundamental flaws. First, it is pathological since morality is seen as having its origin in repression through identification with an aggressor—the father who threatens castration. Second, it is fundamentally amoral since the superego is more of an agent of socialization than of moral growth. Its function is that of internalizing society's values whether those values are moral or immoral. In a racist society, for example, a strong superego would represent internalized racist values.

Sagan suggests an "alternative narrative" to explain moral development in which the source of moral action is "conscience" which is differentiated from the Freudian superego. Conscience owes its development more to the pre-oedipal experience of the child than to the Oedipus complex. Its source is the experience of "basic love," that is, of a loving nurturing relationship with the mother, which fosters the capacity to love and nurture in return. This capacity is the foundation of moral behavior. Thus the basis of morality is found in "the longings to reciprocate love." Sagan points out that, while Freud recognized that only love (Eros) could overcome the destructive death instinct, he did not apply this idea to his theory of moral development. This "alternative narrative," on the other hand, points to a recognition of the role of the mother in the origins of conscience and to the early identification with the mother both as the good, nurturing mother and as the aggressive "bad mother," which is seen as the origin of moral and immoral behavior. "Long before the superego comes on the scene," Sagan argues, "the ground is fully prepared for all future moral and immoral behavior."[122] While the identification which is the basis of the superego carries the hazard, as we have seen, of internalizing immoral values, in the identification with the mother, the image of the good, nurturing mother is split off from that of the bad, aggressive mother and idealized. Identification with the aggressive mother is controlled by the experience with "the nurturer and the victim," that is, the experience of compassion for one who is suffering—a compassion of which the child is capable because he was the recipient of it at the hand of the nurturing mother. A healthy conscience, therefore, is the result of internalizing healthy, loving, nurturing values, and this begins, Sagan argues, in the pre-oedipal stage of growth.

The second aspect of Freud's oedipal theory, with its consequences for moral and religious development, which engages the feminist critic is the "asymmetry" of its accounts of masculine and feminine development. We have already noted, the fact that in Freud's account, the female oedipal experience does not parallel the male experience but follows a developmental path which seems to theoretically assign to women an inferior capacity as vehicles of moral and cultural advancement. Reaction to this aspect of Freud's oedipal theory reveals two different readings of Freud. Some critics interpret this theory of the development of masculinity and femininity as *prescriptive* and therefore normative. In this reading, Freud is perceived as linking the inferior position of women in a patriarchal society as rooted in the biological differences between the sexes ("anatomy is destiny"), and, accordingly, as a defender of the patriarchal status quo. Simone de Beauvoir[123] argues that, in Freud's account of masculine and feminine development, the boy becomes the cultural norm and the girl is a deviation from it. Woman, then, becomes representative of that nature which man transcends through his cultural achievements. She thus becomes the "other" against whom man defines himself or, in de Beauvoir's term, "the second sex." Along with de Beauvoir, feminist thinkers such as Betty Friedan,[124] Germaine Greer,[125] and Kate Millett[126] have argued that Freud ignored social and historical factors in his account of feminine development. Friedan stresses that the process described by Freud was not biologically and instinctually rooted but merely characteristic of middle-class European men and women of Freud's era—an era, she claims, in which women envied men not for their penis but for their privileged social position. Greer rejects the notion, which she attributes to Freud, that male sadism and aggression and female masochism and passivity are "divinely ordered by biology." And Kate Millett rejects the concept of penis envy as evidence of "a strong masculine bias, even of a rather gross male-supremacist bias."[127] This concept, she argues is Freud's way of avoiding the social and historical explanation which locates the source of women's perception of themselves as inferior in the conditions of patriarchal society.

Other feminist authors such as Juliet Mitchell and Judith Van Herik reject the notion that Freud's account of feminine development is prescriptive or that it is rooted in biological development and therefore normative. Mitchell argues that the oedipal theory is Freud's description of the psychological process by which a patriarchal society is perpetuated. It describes how a civilization, which Freud saw as inherently patriarchal, is unconsciously transmitted. Thus the theory is not about the determining role of biological differences but rather about the "inheritance and acquisition of the human order." As such it provides "the beginnings of an explanation of the inferiorized and 'alternative' (second sex) psychology of women under patriarchy."[128] Freudian psychoanalysis, therefore, is not seen in this view as a prescriptive justification of the status quo for "however it may have been used, psychoanalysis is not a recommendation *for* a patriarchal society, but an analysis *of* one."[129]

Judith Van Herik argues for a similar *descriptive* reading of Freud when she suggests that the asymmetry of Freud's account of the development of masculinity and femininity reflects "the concrete sociological and historical fact of paternal pre-eminence so that mentally, too, the paternal principle is privileged".[130] Furthermore, for Van Herik, Freud's asymmetrical theory of gender differences is not just a key to an analysis of patriarchal culture; it is also the critical component of his psychology of religion. In her interpretation, Freudian theory is not simply about sexual differences but about the development of *gender*, that is, of masculinity and femininity as they develop in either sex. Masculinity is valued because it represents the renunciation of oedipal attachments, which is a requisite for intellectual, moral, and cultural advancement. Femininity is devalued because it represents "fulfillment," that is, the wish-fulfilling clinging to oedipal attachments of dependency. Fulfillment in this sense is seen as an obstacle to moral and cultural advance. Religion is thus negatively evaluated to the extent that it reflects this kind of wish-fulfilling, oedipal attachment to a God who is a projection of and substitute for an insufficiently internalized father figure.

Suggested Readings

BAKAN, DAVID, *Sigmund Freud and the Jewish Mystical Tradition* (Boston: Beacon Press, 1975).

BETTELHEIM, BRUNO, *Freud and Man's Soul* (New York: Knopf, 1983).

BROME, VINCENT, *Freud and His Disciples: The Struggle for Supremacy* (London: Caliban, 1984).

FREUD, SIGMUND, *An Autobiographical Study* (New York: W.W. Norton, 1989).

FREUD, SIGMUND, *Civilization and Its Discontents* (New York: W.W. Norton, 1989).

FREUD, SIGMUND, *The Future of an Illusion* (New York: W.W. Norton, 1989).

FREUD, SIGMUND, *Moses and Monotheism* (New York: Random House, 1955).

FREUD, SIGMUND, *On the History of the Psychoanalytic Movement* (New York: W.W. Norton, 1990).

FREUD, SIGMUND, *Totem and Taboo* (New York: W.W. Norton, 1990).

ISBISTER, J.N., *Freud: An Introduction to His Life and Work* (Cambridge: Polity Press, 1985).

JONES, ERNEST, *The Life and Work of Sigmund Freud* (London: Hogarth Press, 1953, 1955, 1957).

JONES, JAMES W., *Contemporary Psychoanalysis and Religion: Transference and Transcendence* (New Haven: Yale University Press, 1991).

MEISSNER, W.W., *Psychoanalysis and Religious Experience* (New York: Yale University Press, 1984).

MITCHELL, JULIET, *Psychoanalysis and Feminism* (Harmondsworth, England: Penguin Books, 1975).

SAGAN, ELI, *Freud, Women and Morality: The Psychology of Good and Evil* (New York: Basic Books, 1988).

VAN HERIK, JUDITH, *Freud on Femininity and Faith* (Berkeley: University of California Press, 1982).

Notes

1. Sigmund Freud, "On the History of the Psychoanalytic Movement," *Standard Edition of the Complete Psychological Works of Sigmund Freud*, translated and edited by James Strachey (London: Hogarth Press, 1962-1974), Vol. 14, p. 16. (In all subsequent references referred to as *S.E.*)
2. Sigmund Freud, "An Autobiographical Study," *S.E.*, Vol. 20, p. 30.
3. *Ibid., p. 29.*
4. *Ibid.*, p. 45.
5. *Ibid.*, p. 47.
6. *Ibid.*, p. 72.
7. Sigmund Freud, "The Interpretation of Dreams," *S.E.*, Vol. 4, p. 192.
8. Vincent Brome, *Freud and His Disciples: The Struggle for Supremacy* (London: Caliban, 1984), p. 43.
9. *Ibid.*, p. 3.
10. Letter to Wilhelm Fliess, October 3, 1897, in Jeffrey Masson (ed.), *The Complete Letters of Sigmund Freud to Wilhelm Fliess, 1887-1904* (Cambridge: Harvard University Press, 1985), p. 268.
11. Sigmund Freud, "The Interpretation of Dreams," *S.E.*, Vol. 5, pp. 424 & 483.
12. Letter to Fliess, October 4, 1897.
13. *Ibid.*
14. *Ibid.*
15. J.N. Isbister, *Freud: An Introduction to His Life and Work* (Cambridge: Polity Press, 1985), p. 16.
16. See Paul Vitz, *Sigmund Freud's Christian Unconscious* (New York: Guilford, 1988).
17. Sigmund Freud, "An Autobiographical Study," *S.E.*, Vol. 20, p. 8.
18. *Ibid.*, p. 9.
19. *Ibid.*, p. 8.
20. *Ibid.*, p. 72.
21. *Ibid.*, p. 19.
22. Vincent Brome, *Freud and his Disciples*, p. 40.
23. C.G. Jung, *Memories, Dreams, Reflections* (New York: Vintage Books, 1961), p. 151.
24. *Ibid.*, p. 150.
25. Ernest Jones, *The Life and Work of Sigmund Freud*, abridged version (Harmondsworth, England: Penguin Books, 1964), p. 343.
26. Sigmund Freud, "An Autobiographical Study," *S.E.*, Vol. 20, p. 53.
27. Bruno Bettelheim, *Freud and Man's Soul* (New York: Knopf, 1983), p. 32.
28. Sigmund Freud, "An Outline of Psychoanalysis," *S.E.*, Vol. 23, p. 148.
29. *Ibid.*
30. *Ibid.*, p. 199.
31. Sigmund Freud, "On Narcissism: An Introduction", *S.E.*, Vol. 14, p. 94.
32. Sigmund Freud, "The Instincts and Their Vicissitudes," *Collected Papers* Vol. 4, (London: Hogarth Press, 1925), p. 65.
33. Sigmund Freud, "Civilization and Its Discontents," *S.E.*, Vol. 21, p. 117.
34. Sigmund Freud, "The Instincts and Their Vicissittudes," *Collected Papers*, Vol. 4, pp. 67-68.
35. Sigmund Freud, "Civilization and Its Discontents," *S.E.*, Vol. 21, p. 118.
36. Sigmund Freud, "Beyond the Pleasure Principle," *S.E.*, Vol. 18, p.23.
37. Sigmund Freud, "An Outline of Psychoanalysis," *S.E.*, Vol. 23, p. 148.
38. Sigmund Freud, "Civilization and Its Discontents," *S.E.*, Vol. 21, pp. 118-119.
39. *Ibid.*
40. Sigmund Freud, "An Outline of Psychoanalysis," *S.E.*, Vol. 23, p. 148.

41. Sigmund Freud, "Civilization and Its Discontents," *S.E.*, Vol. 21, p. 122.
42. Freud seems to use the words "civilization" and "culture" synonymously. See "The Future of an Illusion," *S.E.*, Vol. 21, pp. 5-6.
43. Sigmund Freud, "Civilization and Its Discontents", *S.E.*, Vol. 21, p. 89.
44. *Ibid.*, p. 122.
45. *Ibid.*, p. 95.
46. *Ibid.*, p. 96.
47. Bruno Bettelheim, *Freud and Man's Soul*, p. 101.
48. Sigmund Freud, "Civilization and its Discontents," *S.E.*, Vol. 21, p. 124.
49. *Ibid.*, p. 133.
50. *Ibid.*, p. 134.
51. *Ibid.*, p. 122.
52. Paul Ricoeur, *Freud and Philosophy: An Essay on Interpretation* (New Haven: Yale University Press, 1970), pp. 309 & 323.
53. Sigmund Freud, "Civilization and Its Discontents," *S.E.*, Vol. 21, p. 122.
54. *Ibid.*, p. 74.
55. *Ibid.*, p. 112.
56. *Ibid.* p. 96.
57. Sigmund Freud, "The Future of an Illusion," *S.E.*, Vol. 21, pp. 6-8.
58. Sigmund Freud, "Civilization and Its Discontents," *S.E.*, Vol. 21, p. 86.
59. Sigmund Freud, "The Future of an Illusion," *S.E.*, Vol. 21, p. 24.
60. *Ibid.*, pp. 32-33.
61. *Ibid.*, p. 31.
62. *Ibid.*
63. *Ibid.*, p. 41.
64. Sigmund Freud, "Civilization and Its Discontents," *S.E.*, Vol. 21, p. 132.
65. *Ibid.*
66. Sigmund Freud, "Obsessive Acts and Religious Practices," *Collected Papers*, Vol. 2 (London: Hogarth Press, 1924), p. 34.
67. Robert Bocock, *Freud and Modern Society: An Outline and Analysis of Freud's Sociology* (Don Mills, Ont.: Thomas Nelson and Sons, 1976), p. 74.
68. Sigmund Freud, "Moses and Monotheism," *S.E.*, Vol. 21, pp. 118 & 119.
69. *Ibid.*, p. 130.
70. *Ibid.*, p. 131.
71. Sigmund Freud, "Totem and Taboo," *S.E.*, Vol. 13, p. 141.
72. *Ibid.*, p. 145.
73. *Ibid.*
74. *Ibid.*, p. 132.
75. *Ibid.*
76. *Ibid.*, p. 156.
77. Sigmund Freud, "Moses and Monotheism," *S.E.*, Vol. 23, p. 119.
78. *Ibid.*, p. 82.
79. *Ibid.*, p. 101.
80. *Ibid.*, p. 77.
81. *Ibid.*, p. 89.
82. *Ibid.*, p. 59.
83. *Ibid.*, p. 60.
84. *Ibid.*, p. 63.
85. *Ibid.*, p. 88.
86. *Ibid.*, p. 101.
87. Sigmund Freud, "Totem and Taboo," *S.E.*, Vol. 13, p. 100.
88. Sigmund Freud, "Moses and Monotheism," *S.E.*, Vol. 23, p. 58.

89. Sigmund Freud, "An Outline of Psychoanalysis," *S.E.*, Vol. 23, p. 148.

90. Sigmund Freud, "Civilization and Its Discontents", *S.E.*, Vol. 21, p. 118 & 119.

91. Erich Fromm, *The Heart of Man: Its Genius for Good and Evil* (New York: Harper and Row, 1964), ch. 3.

92. Herbert Marcuse, *Eros and Civilization: A Philosophical Inquiry into Freud* (Boston: Beacon Press, 1955).

93. Norman O. Brown, *Life Against Death: The Psychoanalytic Meaning of History* (New York: Random House, 1959).

94. S.G.F. Brandon, in *Dictionary of the History of Ideas* (New York: Scribners, 1973), Vol. 4, p. 97.

95. Eli Sagan, *Freud, Women and Morality: The Psychology of Good and Evil* (New York: Basic Books, 1988), p. 79.

96. Gregory Zilboorg, *Freud and Religion: A Restatement of an Old Controversy* (Westminster, Md.: Newman Press, 1958), pp. 15-16.

97. James W. Jones, *Contemporary Psychoanalysis and Religion: Transference and Transcendence* (New Haven: Yale University Press, 1991), p. 1.

98. *Ibid.*, p. 37.

99. W.W. Meissner, *Psychoanalysis and Religious Experience* (New Haven: Yale University Press, 1984), pp. 55-56.

100. David Bakan, *Freud and the Jewish Mystical Tradition* (Boston: Beacon Press, 1975), p. 116.

101. *Ibid.*, p. 127.

102. *Ibid.*, p. 158.

103. *Ibid.*, p. 167.

104. *Ibid.*, p. 170.

105. Sigmund Freud, "The Future of an Illusion," *S.E.*, Vol. 21, p. 11.

106. David Bakan, *Freud and the Jewish Mystical Tradition*, pp. 158-159.

107. *Ibid.*, p. 166.

108. Gregory Zilboorg, *Freud and Religion*, p. 41.

109. Erik Erikson, *Identity and the Life Cycle* (New York: W.W. Norton, 1980).

110. Heije Faber, *Psychology of Religion* (Philadelphia: Westminster, 1975).

111. Sigmund Freud, "Leonardo da Vinci: A Study in Psychosexuality," *S.E.*, Vol. 11, p. 123.

112. Ana-Maria Rizzuto, *The Birth of the Living God* (Chicago: University of Chicago Press, 1979), p. 44.

113. D.W. Winnicott, *Playing and Reality* (New York: Routledge, 1971), p. 2.

114. James W. Jones, *Contemporary Psychoanalysis and Religion*, p. 59.

115. D.W. Winnicott, *Playing and Reality*, p. 103.

116. James W. Jones, *Contemporary Psychoanalysis and Religion*, p. 65.

117. *Ibid.*, p. 125.

118. Sigmund Freud, "Some Psychical Consequences of the Anatomical Distinctions Between the Sexes," *S.E.*, Vol. 19, p. 256.

119. *Ibid.*, pp. 257-258.

120. Judith Van Herik, *Freud on Femininity and Faith* (Berkeley: University of California Press, 1982), p. 133.

121. Eli Sagan, *Freud, Women and Morality: The Psychology of Good and Evil* (New York: Basic Books, 1988), p. 181.

122. *Ibid.*, p. 174.

123. Simone de Beauvoir, *The Second Sex* (New York: Knopf, 1968, c. 1960).

124. Betty Friedan, *The Feminine Mystique*, (New York: Norton, 1983, c. 1963).

125. Germaine Greer, *The Female Eunuch* (London: Granada, 1981, c. 1970).

126. Kate Millett, *Sexual Politics* (New York: Doubleday, 1970).

127. *Ibid.*, p. 182.
128. Juliet Mitchell, *Psychoanalysis and Feminism* (Harmondsworth, England: Penguin Books, 1975), p. 401-402.
129. *Ibid.*, p. xv.
130. Judith Van Herik, *Freud on Femininity and Faith*, p. 194.

II. C.G. JUNG

Religion and Archetype

Carl Gustav Jung (1875–1961)
National Library of Medicine.

Asked in a 1959 B.B.C. television interview whether he believed in God, Jung replied, "I don't believe: I know." For the hard-headed rationalist, this famous remark confirms the stereotype of Jung as a "mystic" whose work can therefore be dismissed. At the same time, this reply is instructive for it offers insight into Jung's thinking about both religion and psychology. For Jung, God is not known through rational arguments for his existence or through blind faith in the traditional teachings of religion, but only through immediate experience. As a child, Jung was reared in an atmosphere of traditional Christianity—his father was a parson—and was taught what he should believe. As his biographer Barbara Hannah remarks, "he tried very hard [to believe] but, like most honest children who have been much connected with the Church, failed entirely; then he *experienced* God and then of course he *knew*."[1] The experiences here referred to are the childhood dreams and fantasies which carried the intuition of God who was not identical with the God of tradition-al dogma. To his father's injunction, "One ought not to think but believe," Jung's unspoken rejoinder was, "no, one must experience and know."[2] This tension between the traditional–conventional and the personal–mystical modes of experiencing religion would be a decisive factor in his psychology of religion and, in particular, his treatment of Christianity.

Not only Jung's thoughts on God and religion but also his psychological ideas seem to have been grounded in his personal experiences. The period from 1913 (following his break with Freud) to 1917 was a time of intense personal inner experience during which, through dreams and fantasies, he encountered the contents of his own unconscious. This confrontation with the unconscious was, by Jung's own admission, the experiential matrix- the *prima materia*—of all his theoretical work. His theoretical task was "to draw concrete conclusions from the insights the unconscious had given me—and that task was to become a life work."[3] That lifetime of theoretical work represented for him "only supplements and clarifications of the material that burst forth from the unconscious and at first swamped me."[4] All the basic concepts of Jung's analytical psychology—collective unconscious, archetype, individuation, the role of myth and symbol—are the results of his attempts to make sense of these inner experiences. As Peter Homans remarks, "By naming his inner experiences, he created his system of psychological ideas."[5] These psychological ideas, derived from his encounter with the unconscious, represented an experiential type of knowledge which, as Homans has pointed out, could be distinguished from both the experimental knowledge of science and traditional religious knowledge based on faith.[6] Consequently one finds in Jung's writings criticism of both the scientific-rationalistic mentality and the faith-demanding dogmatism of religion. Both are accused of impoverishing human existence: the former by its excessive reliance on rational consciousness, the latter by cutting people off from direct experience of the object of religion—God, the numinous, the sacred. In Jung's psychological theory, the unconscious is a source of wisdom and energy, not simply the repository of repressed memories and impulses, as in Freudian psychoanalysis. In his theory of religion, while God and the unconscious are not synonymous, the experience of the unconscious has a *numinous* quality which makes it indistinguishable from the experience of the divine. Jung believed that religious symbols and dogmas were expressions and embodiments of the archetypal motifs of the unconscious and thus attributed a "religious" function to the psyche.

Life

Carl Gustav Jung was born at Kesswil in Switzerland on July 26, 1875. His father (Paul Jung), a parson in the Swiss Reformed Church, moved his family to Laufen when Jung was six months old and when he was four to Klein-

Huningen near Basel. It was here that Jung spent his school years first at the local school and then at the Gymnasium in Basel. When, in his eighty-third year, Jung collaborated with Aniela Jaffe in writing his autobiography, he referred to his life story, his "personal myth," as "a story of the self-realization of the unconscious." Thus, in the telling of this story, the external events of his life are of secondary importance. It is much more a recounting of the events of his inner psychic life and of contents of his unconscious psyche on the premise that "outward circumstances are no substitute for inner experience."[7]

This is true even of Jung's childhood years, the key events of which, as recalled by Jung, are dreams and fantasies as well as inner feelings and anxieties. A childhood illness, for instance, is related to anxiety over the troubled state of his parents' marriage, which caused his mother to be hospitalized in Basel for several months. Jung remarks: "I was deeply troubled by my mother's being away. From then on, I always felt mistrustful when the word 'love' was spoken."[8] Jung seems to have regarded his mother as strong but unreliable; his father as reliable but weak. In his earliest remembered dream, which seems to have been influential for his subsequent development, he discovers enthroned in an underground chamber an enormous phallus with a single upward-gazing eye at the top. In time, this came to represent "a subterranean God 'not to be named'" and the underground "counterpart" of the loving and kindly "Lord Jesus."[9] This dream represents Jung's first intuition of what he would later call the "dark side" of the Christian God-image.

During his years of intense encounter with the unconscious, Jung experienced the split between conscious and unconscious dimensions of his psyche as a double personality, which he later expressed theoretically as the ego/self axis. This awareness of his double personality was brought home to Jung for the first time by his ambivalent reaction to a scolding administered by the father of one of his playmates for his reckless behavior in a rowboat. On the one hand, he was chastened because he realized that the scolding was quite justified. On the other hand he was enraged that "this fat ignorant boor" should dare to insult him. The person who felt insulted was not the insecure child but a grown-up, authoritative person deserving of respect and awe. Describing this event in his autobiography, Jung remarks:

> Then to my immense confusion, it occurred to me that I was actually two different persons. One of them was the schoolboy who could not grasp algebra and was far from sure of himself; the other was important, a high authority, a man not to be trifled with, as powerful and influential as this manufacturer. This "other was an old man who lived in the eighteenth century, wore buckled shoes and a white wig...."[10]

Thus Jung's image of himself was "of myself living in two ages simultaneously, and being two different persons."[11] It was an image that remained with him throughout his life, and he denied that it could be diagnosed psy-

chiatrically as a "split" personality or as dissociation. On the contrary, he maintains that the interplay of "personalities no. 1 and no. 2"—conscious and unconscious—"is played out in every individual."[12]

Nevertheless, until his tenth year, Jung admits to a "tormenting sense
of being at odds with myself" because he felt that the world of personality no.
1—the world of time and change and progression—was pulling him away
from the "eternal" world of personality no. 2. In an attempt to maintain continuity with this other realm, curious rituals developed: a small fire he lit in
the garden of his home and constantly tended because it "had an unmistak-
able aura of sanctity"; a favorite rock on which he would sit for hours because "there was no doubt whatsoever that this stone stood in some secret
relationship to me"; the tiny manikin which he carved at the end of his school
ruler and hid, together with a painted stone, on a beam in the attic of his
home. This in some way, made him feel safe and provided relief from the
inner tensions he was experiencing.[13] This access to the dark and eternal
world of the unconscious struck the young boy as a kind of secret knowledge—"all this was a great secret," he says of the hidden manikin—which
seemed to be at odds with the teachings of institutional Christianity that he
was expected to embrace. This was confirmed by a fantasy he experienced in
the cathedral square in Basel. Contemplating the beauty of the cathedral
standing under the blue summer sky, he imagined God seated on a throne
above overseeing all this beauty but found he was unable to pursue his fantasy any further. A sense of impending disaster impeded his thoughts. For
three days he tried to ward off the anxiety-producing, obsessive thought before, believing it to be God's will, he allowed his thoughts to proceed. In the
ensuing fantasy, "I saw before me the cathedral, the blue sky. God sits on his
golden throne, high above the world—and from under the throne an enormous turd falls upon the sparkling new roof, shatters it, and breaks the walls
of the cathedral asunder."[14]

Jung's dreams and fantasies were, as we have seen, the seeds of his theoretical formulations. Accordingly, the fantasy of God defecating on his cathedral would appear to be the experiential root of his whole critical yet
therapeutic approach to Christianity, for he took it to be the expression of the
will of a God who is not identical with the God of traditional dogma. He experienced it as the grace of God, that is, as an immediate experience of a God
who stands, omnipotent and free, above His Bible and his Church. The fantasy also suggested through its imagery "that God could be something terrible" and, returning to the theme of secret knowledge, he remarks: "I had
experienced a dark and terrible secret. It overshadowed my whole life, and I
became deeply pensive."[15] As a child, Jung was unsure whether these images
of God—as a naked phallus, as destroying his Church—came from God or
the devil. What he was absolutely certain about was that he had not invented these thoughts and images himself. They came to him as from an autonomous agent, as he would later describe the intrusions of the unconscious

into consciousness. The practical consequence of the childhood experiences was a sense of certainty and security about which Jung remarks, "I did not have this certainty, *it* had me."[16] It was this kind of direct experience of God which Jung saw his father as lacking and which accounted for his father's religious doubts. For Jung himself the knowledge of God could not be proved but this kind of immediate experience meant "that it stood in no more need of proof than the beauty of a sunset or the terrors of the night."[17] This insistence that "in religious matters, only experience counted," as opposed to his father's emphasis on faith contributed to Jung's sense of alienation from both his father and the Christian tradition which his father represented.

In the midst of these feelings of alienation, Jung found support in identifying with his mother in whom he also sensed a double personality, "one innocuous and human, the other uncanny" and whose "no. 2" personality he found supportive "in the conflict then beginning between paternal tradition and the strange, compensatory products which my unconscious had been stimulated to create."[18] Of his relationship with his father, Jung remarks: "Theology had alienated my father and me from one another."[19] In spite of this alienation and tension, one gathers from Jung's words that he desperately wanted to help his father whom, clearly, he perceived as a troubled man. He felt, however, that his father's theology eliminated the possibility of the kind of direct experience of God that his son had undergone. Jung, therefore, saw his father as one betrayed by his Church and its theology. As a result, when the time came to choose a career, Jung had no difficulty in following his father's advice not to study theology. Torn between science and the humanities, a conflict typically described in terms of the tensions between personality no. 1 and no. 2, and again typically resolved by a dream, he decided in favor of science. However, because of his limited resources and the necessity of earning a living, he entered the University of Basel in 1895 as a medical student. When the time came to choose a specialty within the field of medicine, Jung was again torn between surgery and internal medicine. Then something happened which, he writes, "removed all my doubts concerning my future career."[20]

This career choice was inspired by the reading of a textbook on psychiatry by Richard von Krafft-Ebing—a reading undertaken not out of interest but as a required reading for the state medical examination. In the preface of this text Jung was struck by the author's reference to the "subjective character" of psychiatric textbooks and his references to the psychoses as "diseases of the personality." Jung describes his reaction: "My heart suddenly began to pound. I had to stand up and draw a deep breath. My excitement was intense, for it had become clear to me, in a flash of illumination, that for me the only possible goal was psychiatry.... Here was the empirical field common to biological and spiritual facts, which I had everywhere sought and nowhere found."[21] Here was a field in which Jung could resolve the tension within his own personality between the secular, scientific spirit of his age (personality no. 1?)

and the deeper spiritual and religious concerns to which his psychic experiences had led him (personality no. 2?). Colin Wilson suggests that psychiatry, in its then underdeveloped stage, was "a field into which he could pour all his creative energies."[22] The consequences of this merging of scientific and spiritual concerns was a body of scientific and theoretical work which was, in keeping with Krafft-Ebing's description of psychiatry, an elaboration of his own "subjective" experiences of the unconscious; which produced a vision of the psyche as having by nature a "religious" function; and which interpreted the "diseases of the personality" as resulting from frustrated "religious" needs rather than sexual needs.

In 1900—the year in which Freud published *The Interpretation of Dreams*—Jung began his psychiatric career as an assistant to Eugene Bleuler at the Burgholzli psychiatric hospital in Zurich. During the next few years his preoccupation was to rethink the field of psychiatry, which struck him as a rather sterile system of diagnosing and labeling patients and cataloging symptoms with very little attempt at therapy. He felt that little attention was paid to the "psychology" of the patient, that is, to his or her individual symptoms, delusions, and hallucinations, which were considered meaningless. In time, Jung would turn to mythology and the concept of the collective unconscious to find the symbolic meaning of these symptoms of psychiatric illness. In 1903 he married Emma Rauschenbauch with whom he raised a family of five children. In 1905 he became a lecturer in psychiatry at the University of Zurich and senior physician at the Psychiatric Clinic of the university. He resigned his position at the clinic in 1909 because of his growing private practice but continued to lecture until 1913. Jung did not become personally acquainted with Freud until 1907 but had already been exposed to and influenced by his ideas, and Jung's work with the word association test, which brought him considerable recognition, represented a practical application of Freud's theory of repression.

In his autobiography, Jung refers to the fact that he read Freud's *The Interpretation of Dreams* in 1900 without really understanding it. However, when he reread it in 1903 he discovered that it "linked up" with his own ideas because the same mechanism of repression which was operative in dreams, was something he had also encountered in his experiments with word association. Jung was at this time planning an academic career and Freud was *persona non grata* in academic circles. "Therefore," he writes, "the discovery that my association experiments were in agreement with Freud's theories was far from pleasant to me."[23] Nevertheless his continued public defense of Freud's ideas led to an invitation to visit Freud in Vienna. This first meeting took place in February 1907 and, as Jung reports, the two men talked "virtually without pause" for 13 hours. In spite of Jung's misgivings about Freud's insistence on the sexual aetiology of the neuroses, there followed a period of personal friendship and professional collaboration which lasted until their final break in 1913. During these years, Jung was an active member of the psychoanalytic movement.

In our discussion of Freud we have seen something of the theoretical factors which precipitated Jung's break with Freud and the psychoanalytic movement. Jung's initial distrust of Freud's emphasis on sexual motivation in human behavior led eventually to theoretical formulations in which the notion of the repressed sexual impulses of the personal unconscious expressing themselves in neurotic symptoms is seen as less fundamental than that of the deeper, collective unconscious whose contents (archetypes) are expressed in myth and symbol. These reveal the need for individuation, wholeness, or "rebirth" needs which Jung does not hesitate to call "religious." Thus the basic orientation of the psyche, the goal toward which the unconscious archetypes lead us, is more religious than instinctual, and religious needs are more powerful and fundamental than sexual needs.

The personal factors in this dispute, however, are inseparable from the theoretical. We have seen that Freud's ambitious and somewhat megalomaniacal leadership of the psychoanalytic movement was threatened precisely by the new ideas of his followers. Many commentators have suggested that the psychoanalytic movement had all the earmarks of a church or religious movement from which heretics were excommunicated. Asked why so many of his followers eventually left the movement, Freud replied, "precisely because they too wanted to be Popes."[24] All this lends a certain irony to Freud's rejection of Jung's ideas because of their emphasis on the spiritual and religious dimension of the psyche. In a letter to J.J. Putnam on July 8, 1909, Freud writes that at first he found Jung a sympathetic adherent. "Then came his religious ethical crisis with higher morality, rebirth.... It has not been the first or the last experience to reinforce my disgust with saintly converts."[25]

But there seems to have been personal factors on Jung's side as well. Freud refers to "the brutal, sanctimonious Jung" and Wilson suggests that Jung was "undoubtedly a man who liked his own way, no matter what the cost to others."[26] Others have suggested that this was an oedipal relationship in which Jung related to Freud as to a father figure with all the ambivalent feelings that term implies. Whatever the case may be, Jung seems to have been unable to dissociate himself from Freud for some time in spite of their theoretical differences. He seemed reluctant to push his own ideas too vehemently for fear of endangering his personal ties with Freud. Perhaps the relationship of the two men in the latter stages of their collaboration is best illustrated in a 1911 group photograph taken at a psychoanalytic congress at Weimar. The fact that Jung, the taller of the two men, appears considerably shorter in the photo is curious until it is revealed that Freud is in fact standing on a box to enhance his stature and preeminence! That Freud would do this and that Jung would tolerate it tells us much about their relationship.

Jung's 1912 publication, *Symbols of Transformation*, treated subjects such as the unconscious, libido, sexuality, and the meaning of incest in such a way as to constitute a clear theoretical break with Freud's ideas. He was hesitant to publish the work for, as he reports, "I knew in advance that its publication would cost me my friendship with Freud."[27] His hesitation was due to the fact that, although "Freud had lost much of his authority for me," there was still an emotional attachment as to a father figure since "he still meant to me a superior personality, upon whom I projected the father," and "under the impress of Freud's personality I had, as far as possible, cast aside my own judgments and repressed my criticisms."[28] Jung records that this publication not only cost him his friendship with Freud but that "after the break with Freud, all my friends and acquaintances dropped away. My book was declared to be rubbish; I was a mystic, and that settled the matter."[29] This perception of Jung as a mystic has persisted due to the fact that his theoretical formulations were rooted in an experiential type of knowledge, that is, a knowledge of the human psyche derived from the experience of his own unconscious through dreams, visions, and fantasies, most particularly during the years (1913-1917) of professional isolation following his break with Freud. Jung believed that the unconscious (the "soul") had objective reality and was not simply the repository of repressed instinctuality but a deep source of knowledge and vitality. He insisted on the limitations of objective, scientific, rational knowledge which must be complemented by the knowledge that comes from within.

To many, this kind of knowledge may be safely dismissed as "mystical." To Jung, however, psychic realities were empirical facts. Those who do not share this conviction tend to regard Jung's repeated insistence that his conclusions are those of an "empiricist" with reserve, if not suspicion. Colin Wilson suggests that Jung's autobiography reveals "that the scientific psychologist was a public image and, to some extent, a deliberate deception."[30] In retrospect it could be argued that Jung became his own worst enemy by insisting on being ranked among the empirical scientists whose narrow rationalism he otherwise roundly criticized. This has given rise to a false debate in which the "scientific" character of Jung's work becomes the criterion for judging its validity. Instead of insisting on the scientific nature of his work, perhaps Jung would have better served his cause by insisting on the validity of this experiential type of knowledge as complement to scientific knowledge as that term is generally understood. Indeed, this idea runs through all his writings but seems to be obscured by his insistence on being regarded as an "empiricist." Jung's greatness does not depend on his being a "scientist" in the strict sense of the word. It was not by being an "empiricist" that he became—to use Wilson's phrase—the "guru of the Western world."[31]

In the years following his confrontation with the unconscious, Jung turned the dreams and fantasies of those years into theoretical constructs and a psychological theory of the unconscious. In this theory, the archetypal motifs of the collective unconscious are projected onto and find expression in the myths and symbols of the ages. These are all various ways of expressing basic archetypal themes. Hence our fascination with stories of heroic struggle, rebirth, and redemption. It is through these mythical and symbolic projections that we encounter the archetypal contents of the unconscious, which thereby lead us to the goal of psychic wholeness through the incorporation of unconscious contents into consciousness—a process Jung called "individuation." Jung found historical prefigurations of this kind of inner experience in the ancient Gnostic myths and in medieval alchemy, which he studied during the years 1918 to 1926. In the intricate process by which the alchemists tried to bring about chemical transformation, Jung saw an unconscious projection of the psychological process of individuation and of the alchemist's desire for the goal of that process. In alchemy he claimed to have found "the historical counterpart of my psychology of the unconscious" and "the ground which underlay my own experiences of the years 1913 to 1917."[32] The alchemical process helped Jung to understand the unconscious as a *process* of transformation through the action of the unconscious on the conscious ego, a transformation that is revealed in the dreams and fantasies of individuals, and in the symbol systems of the world's religions.[33]

At the age of 68 Jung suffered a serious heart attack, was hospitalized, and in fact was near death. He survived and lived for another 17 years after his recovery. He died in 1961. Wilson suggests that this near-death experience made Jung less insistent upon being regarded as a scientist and accordingly "less defensive about presenting his deepest convictions, less concerned about being accused of stepping beyond the limits of science."[34] While such a change of attitude might be difficult to prove, it is nevertheless true that many of Jung's most intuitive and visionary works such as *Aion, Answer to Job,* and *Mysterium Coniunctionis* belong to this period. Wilson describes Jung as a romantic visionary whose work was based on the fundamentally religious assumption "that the universe is full of meaning, that we are surrounded by unseen powers and forces, and that man can rise above the 'triviality of everydayness' by trying to open his mind and his senses to these meanings and forces."[35] These words are an echo of Jung's own description of his state of mind just before his break with Freud. "My whole being was seeking for something still unknown which might confer meaning upon the banality of life."[36] That unknown something was what Jung, near the end of his life, claimed to "know." But he refused to put a name to or define the archetypal experience to which he was referring. In the words of Aniela Jaffe, "he left the mystery untouched."[37] Jung was among those who see life not as a problem to be solved but as a mystery to be lived.

Theory of Personality

The term "self" is arguably the most frequently used word in the psychological vocabulary. Terms such as "self-esteem," "self-realization," "self-actualization," and a "healthy sense of self" have become so commonplace as to be household words. It may seem surprising then that, as late as 1955, Gordon

Allport was asking, "Is a concept of self necessary?" and proposing a way of using the term which would be acceptable in psychological theory.[38] Allport was responding to those who, to preserve the "scientific" character of psychology, rejected the notion of self which, like the concept of soul, appeared to be a philosophical or religious postulate. Humanistic and existentialist theories, however, reject the notion of human personality as a "product" of heredity and environment and advance the concept of an autonomous self which, by its decisions and commitments, becomes a third determinant in its own development. This self is the center of conscious identity, values, ideals, and goals which give the personality unity and uniqueness. As such it represents an elaboration of the psychoanalytic concept of the ego by stressing, over and above the ego's defensive and repressive functions, its function of adaptation to reality and the self-determining creation of conscious goals and values.

This understanding of the self, however, as the locus of uniqueness and individuality conveys the notion of an integrating and unifying center of *consciousness*. For Jung, as we shall see, the achievement of conscious uniqueness and individuality is only part of the process of human becoming. Beyond the development of consciousness to this point there lay the task of going beyond individuality and rediscovering one's unity with humanity and all reality. This is accomplished through the incorporation into consciousness of the contents of the collective unconscious. This is the process of individuation, which is not the same as individualization. Growth, Jung believes, follows a three-stage pattern of unconscious unity—conscious polarity—conscious unity. Unconscious unity suggests the infant's state before the development of consciousness. Out of this original oneness consciousness develops, bringing with it the ability to consciously differentiate between self and others, male and female, good and evil, and so on. Conscious life, then, is characterized by polarity or the tension of opposites, but it is only in this way that conscious identity and individuality can be established. The task of "the second half of life," Jung suggests, is to reunite those opposites which consciousness has differentiated and thus restore a state of unity or oneness.

The unity of this stage, however, unlike that of infancy, is a *conscious* unity which is achieved by incorporating unconscious contents into our conscious thought and attitudes. In this way, one transcends the feelings of isolation and alienation which accompany consciousness and regains a feeling of being part of the whole or of a greater reality. The self, as Jung uses the term, is the theoretical construct which expresses the goal of this process. It represents the midpoint of personality, the center of the total personality, including conscious and unconscious elements, whereas the ego is the center of consciousness. The process of individuation, then, involves an expansion of consciousness through the incorporation of unconscious elements so that the center of personality shifts from the ego to the self. Two departures from Freudian psychoanalytic theory become immediately obvious. First, Jung views the goal of human growth not as the reduction of instinctual tension through an endless repetition of the instinctual cycle, but as the realization of the self, which signifies psychic wholeness or completeness. Beacause this goal is not fully attained, growth is linear and ongoing. Yes, there is tension, but it is not primarily instinctual tension, which must be reduced through the discharge of instinctual energy, but the tension of opposites, which must be reconciled and harmonized in a higher state of consciousness. Second, in Jungian theory religion is not seen as an illusion or an obsessional neurosis but as a symbolic expression, through myth, ritual, and doctrine, of the archetypal contents of the unconscious which seek conscious expression.

Structure of Personality

Jung's view of the structure of human personality includes the psychic systems (ego, personal unconscious, collective unconscious), functions (thinking, feeling, sensing, intuition), and attitudes (introversion, extraversion). The goal of psychological growth is a kind of wholeness which is experienced as a state of balance or equilibrium among these dimensions of personality. Lack of development or repression of one of the systems, functions, or attitudes creates an imbalance or "psychic disequilibrium" which is felt as tension and which is revealed in psychological and/or physical symptoms.

Systems. The *ego* is the center of consciousness—the conscious, thinking aspect of personality, the locus of conscious identity, and the agent of the psyche's adaptation to external reality. In Jungian theory, the ego as the center of consciousness must be distinguished from the self which is the center of the total personality, including its unconscious dimension. Jung is critical of the mentality of the Western world which mistakes the ego for the center of personality because it identifies personality with consciousness. In reality, he argues, consciousness is like a small island in the ocean (of the unconscious). By comparison, the "ocean" of the unconscious psyche "is immensely wide and deep and contains a life infinitely surpassing, in kind and degree, anything known on the island."[39] The defensive function of the ego creates the *personal unconscious*, that is, the unconscious in the Freudian sense—the reservoir of repressed memories, thoughts, impulses, feelings, and so forth which are connected to traumas in one's personal life experience. The trauma and the resultant repression create a *complex*. Complexes are constellations of thoughts and feelings around some dominating idea. We may speak of someone as having a "hang-up" by which we mean that he or she overreacts or exhibits uncharacteristic behavior in a particular area of life (e.g., in relating to authority figures). The source of the hang-up is the psychic complex, and Jung's word association test was a method of discovering complexes.

If complexes are the structural components of the personal unconscious, the archetypes are the structural components of the *collective unconscious*, that dimension of the unconscious which is not unique to each individual but, in some sense, the common possession of humanity. The collective unconscious is a reservoir of latent images, the residue in the individual psyche of humanity's typical and repeated experiences (e.g., motherhood, childhood, good versus evil, heroic struggle, God, and religion). This means that each individual is born with a predisposition to see reality in a certain way, to relive these typical experiences, and to find meaning in the myths and symbols in which they are given expression. At this collective level the unconscious contains "the whole spiritual heritage of mankind's evolution, born anew in the brain structure of every individual."[40] The traces left by humanity's typical experiences on the individual psyche are the *archetypes*. As such, they are agents which tend toward the repetition of these same experiences. The archetypes are neither specific ideas nor concrete images; they are inherited channels or pathways—potentialities for finding and expressing meaning in myth and symbol through which the archetypes find concrete, conscious expression. Hence Jung refers to the collective unconscious as "the ancestral heritage of possibilities of representation."[41] These "possibilities" are the archetypes.

They represent form without content; they are given concrete content in those symbols, myths, rituals, and so on, onto which they are projected. To speak of something, therefore, as a myth is not to denigrate it as being untrue or unhistorical, for the value of myth does not lie in its historical or ontological truth or untruth but in what it says about human nature. Thus my fascination and identification with a particular myth is due to the fact that I recognize it as "my myth" because it represents a concrete expression of an archetypal motif of my own psyche. Thus Jung refers to the story of his life as "my personal myth" because it is "a story of the self-realization of the unconscious."[42] Myth and symbol, Jung believes, give meaning to life in a direct, experiential way that the operations of rational consciousness— words and concepts—cannot. Those only protect us from direct experience. "Words," he says, "butter no parsnips."[43]

In this view of the structure of personality, consciousness stands between the objective reality of the external world and the equally objective (because transpersonal) world of the collective unconscious. The function, therefore, of consciousness is not only to assimilate external reality but also "to translate into visible reality the world within us."[44] Jung pays special attention to the following archetypes. The *persona* represents one's public personality, the image one tries to project in the attempt to live up to one's ideals and society's expectations, in view of the role one plays in society. Overidentification with the persona results in a sense of alienation from one's true self. The persona is a necessary "concession to the external world" and "a genuine self-sacrifice" but, when it results in the ego's identification with the persona, it produces individuals "who believe they are what they pretend to be."[45] This "shifting of the center of gravity," which involves not only the masking but also the repression of one's true individuality, evokes a compensatory reaction from the unconscious in which one's private moods or behavior betray the public image for "a man cannot get rid of himself in favour of an artificial personality without punishment."[46] Thus a highly rational, controlled, and even-tempered persona could be the mask hiding dark moods, phobias, and compulsions, and outstanding public virtue can exist side by side with private bad temper and irritability. "Whoever builds up too good a persona for himself," Jung writes, "naturally has to pay for it with irritability."[47] He found this to be true of his own father about whom he commented: "He did a great deal of good—far too much—and, as a result, was usually irritable."[48]

Why does the unconscious act in this compensatory fashion? Because the goal of psychic wholeness or selfhood requires that the opposites within personality be held in some kind of creative tension. The investing of too much energy in the persona involves the suppression of those aspects of one's true self which make up the *shadow*, the dark side of one's personality comprising all those aspects which are incompatible with the projected persona. "To be whole," writes Frieda Fordham, "means to become reconciled with those sides of personality which have not been taken into account."[49] The shadow archetype represents this dark, unacknowledged, neglected, or repressed side of one's personality to which one needs to be reconciled in the interest of wholeness and totality. It is the aspect of one's psychic totality which the conscious mind disowns, a rejection which directs the personality along a one-sided path of development because an aspect of one's total personality is denied. By its compensatory activity, the unconscious redirects this development toward the proper goal of wholeness.

Jung defines the shadow as "the 'negative' side of the personality, the sum of all those unpleasant qualities we like to hide, together with the insufficiently developed functions and the contents of the personal unconscious."[50] It is the dark, earthy side of personality. It includes one's capacity for evil and destructiveness—a capacity which is greatly magnified by our tendency to ignore and repress it. In the interest of completeness and totality this dark side must be acknowledged and assimilated into consciousness not only because rational control over its destructive aspect must be exercised but also because it is the source of one's vital, instinctual energies. That which is the source of our destructive capacities is also that which helps us to live with passion. Our repression of it, however, results in the projection of these dark qualities onto others in whom we then encounter our own shadow.

In the course of its development consciousness makes various differentiations including the differentiation between masculine and feminine. As gender is one aspect of identity, the individual consciously identifies with one of these opposites. The contrasexual side of one's personality—a man's "feminine" side or a woman's "masculine" side—is relegated to the unconscious. No longer a component of one's conscious identity, it is projected onto the opposite sex. This then would be the unconscious root of our feelings of affinity with and attraction to the opposite sex in whom we discover the neglected and undeveloped part of ourselves. In Jungian theory this unconscious contrasexual side of personality is represented by the *anima/animus* archetype. Like the shadow, this archetypal content of the unconscious is encountered outwardly through projection. The withdrawal of this projection and the recognition of it as an aspect of one's own psyche is seen by Jung as the mediating function between the ego and the inner world of the unconscious, just as the persona mediates between the ego and the outer world. Because it often represents qualities which one would rather not reveal to the world, it is, like the shadow, the opposite of the persona. Since the anima/animus archetype is the unconscious opposite of one's gender-based conscious attitudes, it follows, Jung argues, that "a very feminine woman has a masculine soul, and a very masculine man has a feminine soul." And on the premise that the masculine consciousness is dominated (at least as ideals) by logic, objectivity, and rationality and the female consciousness by feeling, he concludes that "inwardly it is the man who feels and the woman who reflects."[51]

The goal of the individuation process is represented by the archetype of the *self*. It is the archetype of wholeness, unity, and totality. Jung sometimes refers to it as the "God archetype" because it most typically finds conscious expression in the various God-images which appear in the history of the world's religions. We shall return to this point later. For now, we should simply note that, in Jung's psychology of religion, it is the presence of the inner archetype which makes the outer God-image meaningful for human existence. As with all powerful symbols, the outer image resonates with the deep inner psychic reality. Speaking of the figure of Christ as an expression of the "God-man" archetype, Jung writes, "Had there not been an affinity—magnet!—between the figure of the Redeemer and certain contents of the unconscious, the human mind would never have been able to perceive the light shining in Christ and seize upon it so passionately."[52]

Functions. In addition to these systems of personality structure, Jung distinguishes four psychological functions which form the basis of the typology found in *Psychological Types*. The four functions are thinking, feeling, sensing, and intuition. Thinking, which has to do with the perception of meaning, and its opposite, feeling, which refers to the perception of value, are called "rational functions" by Jung because they both involve some kind of rational judgment. To think is to judge something as true or false; to feel is to judge something as agreeable or disagreeable. On the other hand, sensing, which refers to the immediate perception of reality through sense perception, and its opposite, intuition, which describes an immediate nonrational way of arriving at a truth or a conclusion, are categorized as "irrational" since they are based on immediate perception rather than rational judgment. Jung believed that in each individual personality, one of these functions would be the dominant one, and that this was the basis of personality type. Since, moreover, the four functions are two pairs of opposites, the dominance of one function implies the repression of its opposite. Thus a highly rational, thinking type tends to repress his feeling side. The ideal of wholeness is approached to the extent that all four functions are allowed to play their proper roles.

Attitudes. Finally, in the psychological *attitudes* of extraversion and introversion, Jung describes two basic personality types. The extravert's basic orientation is toward the external, objective world experienced as "responsiveness and a ready acceptance of external happenings, a desire to influence and be influenced by events."[53] The extravert looks outside of himself for the source of all happiness and fulfillment and the solution of all problems. The negative side of all this is a lack of an inner sense of self, inner convictions, and inner direction. The extreme extravert is dependent on and at the mercy of the environment. The introvert, on the other hand, is oriented toward the inner subjective world. His relationship to objective, external reality is more negative than that of the extravert, wanting to protect his integrity and autonomy against the demands of external reality, which is perceived to some extent as a threat. Happiness and fulfillment are perceived as coming from within, not from without. Paradoxically, the boisterous involvement of the extravert reveals the predominance of dependency strivings, while the shy, withdrawn introvert seeks autonomy and does so by "barricading himself against influences from outside," for "he feels at home in his world, where the only changes are made by himself."[54]

Since each of these two basic types may experience any one of the four psychic functions as dominant, there would then be eight basic personality types: the extroverted thinking type, the introverted thinking type, and so forth.

Dynamics of Personality

Jung identifies certain principles of growth according to which the psyche operates.

Compensation. The principle of compensation refers to the self-regulating nature of the psyche. In the interests of balance, equilibrium, or wholeness the unconscious compensates for what is lacking in our conscious attitudes. This is especially true when the conscious mind follows a one-sided path of development (e.g., thinking at the expense of feeling). This creates a state of "psychic disequilibrium" and tension which the unconscious tries to resolve by breaking through into consciousness by way of dreams and fantasies in order to reinstate the unadapted, repressed aspects of personality and redirect its growth toward the goal of wholeness. Thus an extraverted unconscious compensates for an introverted consciousness (e.g., grandiose dreams or fantasies). An emotional intuitive unconscious compensates for an overly rational consciousness. An unconscious shadow compensates for a too strenuous conscious striving after moral goodness. Historically Jung interpreted esoteric movements such as Gnosticism and alchemy with their emphasis on inner experience as compensating for the one-sided, orthodox understanding of God as an objective, external reality. In the same vein he sees the religious wars and atrocities which mar the history of Christianity as the dark side of its pursuit of moral goodness. "Whenever life proceeds one-sidedly in any given direction," Jung argues, "the self-regulation of the organism produces in the unconscious an accumulation of all those factors which play too small a part in the individuals conscious existence."[55]

Projection. The psyche also operates according to the principle of projection by which the unconscious, unadapted side of personality is projected onto and attributed to external realities. The shadow, for instance, with its propensity toward evil, may be projected, with all its undesirable qualities, onto other individuals or groups who are then regarded with dislike and/or fear. Because the process is unconscious, the subject is unaware that, in reality, he is reacting to aspects of himself. The unconscious may assist in the withdrawing of this projection by representing the shadow symbolically in a dream as a "dark stranger" with whom the subject is in conflict. In this case, the projection seems to act as an unconscious defense mechanism which is an obstacle to self-knowledge, and yet it is precisely through such projections that unconscious contents become accessible to observation. Myths, fairy tales, religious ritual, and dogma are seen as having symbolic power in that they represent projections of the inner, archetypal life of the psyche. Jung uses the ancient sun myth as an example. The "movement" of the sun is described as the journey of the sun god across the heavens in his fiery chariot, who finally plunges into the sea, only to be reborn the next day after a night journey through the depths of the sea. For Jung, the appeal of this myth lies in the fact that it gives symbolic expression to the unconscious archetype of rebirth. The same may be said of the story of the death and resurrection of Christ. The fact that millions of Christians believe this latter event to be historically true underlines the fact that the mythical quality of an event is independent of the question of its literal or historical truth. Whether factually true or not, it still represents a symbolic expression of the archetype.

Projections which are not withdrawn prove to be an obstacle to true self-knowledge. The individual remains unrelated to the inner world of the psyche and his relatedness to the external world becomes illusory and false since he relates with only part of his total self by identifying only with his conscious knowledge of himself. In the case of the shadow archetype, its repression interferes with one's ability to deal with evil since the tendency toward and capacity for evil which cannot be acknowledged in oneself are projected onto others and attacked in them as objects of hatred or fear. In this way, human relationships are poisoned. "It is often tragic," Jung writes, "to see how blatantly a man bungles his own life and the lives of others and yet remains totally incapable of seeing how much the whole tragedy originates in himself and how he continually fuels it and keeps it going."[56] In speaking of projection he writes: "This principle is of such alarming general validity that everyone would do well, before railing at others, to sit down and consider very carefully whether the brick should not be thrown at his own head."[57] And the longer and more deeply some aspect of the total self is repressed, the more it tends to erupt into consciousness in its most primitive, childish, and destructive forms, so that one acts in a manner completely at odds with his or her normal, characteristic behavior. This illustrates the law of opposites or *enantiodromia* according to which everything turns into its opposite at one time or another.

Transcendent Function. Our contact, therefore, with the unconscious is by way of its symbolic expression in dreams, fantasies, and religious ritual. Jung believes that the symbols which confront us in this way possess a healing power in that they bring about a union of conscious and unconscious elements. This function of the unconscious of bringing opposites together in a uniting symbol is what Jung calls the *transcendent function*. In a situation of tension and conflict of opposites, the symbol acts as a mediator which unites and reconciles the opposites. The problem or conflict is not resolved in a rational way; it is "transcended." A new conscious attitude emerges in which the opposites are somehow seen as belonging together because the symbol unites them in itself. In this way, though the problem is not solved rationally, it loses its urgency. The transcendent function then is the symbol-forming function of the psyche which has a unifying and transforming effect on the personality— a transformation which is beyond the ability of reason, logic, or willpower. The symbols which emerge from the collective unconscious are frequently mythological and therefore universal in nature. Jung points out that this raises the individual's experience of suffering and tension and conflict to a whole new level in which she sees herself not as an isolated victim but in solidarity with all of humanity. "Not as my sorrow," he writes, "but as the sorrow of the world; not a personal, isolating pain, but a pain without bitterness that unites all humanity. The healing effect of this needs no proof."[58]

These principles of growth are operative in what Jung calls the process of "individuation" and which he defines as "the process by which a person becomes a psychological 'individual,' that is, a separate, indivisible unity or whole."[59] Its goal, therefore, is not conscious individuality but the union of conscious and unconscious for the sake of the psychic wholeness. Since it involves the incorporation of unconscious contents into consciousness and the shift from ego to self as the center of personality, it could be described as the realization of the self, or, as Jung describes it in reference to his own life, "the self-realization of the unconscious." The concept of individuation brings us to Jung's ideas on religion, for it is in the context of the individuation process that Jung speaks of the "religious" function of the psyche.

Theory of Religion

If the experience of the realization of the self is one of wholeness, complete-ness, a sense of being part of a greater reality, then it is analogous to what is usually understood as religious experience, which involves a similar tran-scending of one's isolated individuality. It is not surprising then that the reli-gious and mystical ideal of union with God is seen by Jung as symbolic of the goal of selfhood or wholeness. Nor is it surprising that his writings are sprin-kled with terms such as "reconciliation", "rebirth," and "crucifixion of the ego," which have religious connotations. On occasion he uses the word "soul" as a synonym for the unconscious, especially when emphasizing the "numi-nous" quality of its impact on consciousness. Thus what Jung considers the task of the second half of life—to reconnect with one's unconscious roots—is seen as the task of recovering one's soul. And when Jung speaks of the loss of the religious outlook as a cause of illness, he is referring less to the neglect of traditional religious practices than to the loss of connectedness with the heal-ing and energizing forces of one's own psyche. It is in this sense that the psy-che, through the process of individuation, fulfills a "religious" function. The individuation process is a key to an understanding of Jung's psychology of re-ligion for it is the basis of both his understanding of the psyche as "naturally religious" and of his evaluation of traditional religious symbolism.

Individuation as a "Religious Quest"

Jung maintains that (1) psychological health in the "second half of life" de-pends to some extent on maintaining a "religious outlook" and that (2) such a religious outlook is not necessarily related to orthodox, traditional religion. The individuation process itself is seen as having a religious quality because awareness and acceptance of the archetypal forces of the unconscious are anal-ogous to the religious surrender and obedience to a higher power. In the case of individuation, the higher power is a power beyond the conscious ego. Jung describes the religious attitude as "a careful consideration and observation of certain dynamic factors, understood to be 'powers.'"[60] These "powers" may be understood as religious realities or as archetypes of the collective unconscious. Religious images, including the God-image, are in fact projections of the ar-chetypes, and it is this "archetypal" quality which gives religious imagery—myth, symbols, ritual, and dogma—its peculiar power and meaning for human existence. For this reason they are "psychologically real." Religion, for Jung, is the experience of such powers, and traditional religious symbol-ism is of value insofar as it promotes this type of archetypal experience in which, as Edward Edinger remarks, the ego "acknowledges a supraordinate authority and experiences itself *sub specie aeternitatis.*"[61]

   In Jung's understanding, religion and individuation point to the same goal because the religious desire for rebirth is identical with the desire for psychic wholeness or selfhood. These psychological terms are seen as analogous to the religious language of rebirth and salvation. Religious images of rebirth are symbols which relate meaningfully to the archetype of the self in the collective unconscious for they express the goal of individuation—rebirth or wholeness—in a symbolic way. Both religion and the individuation process are based on the premise that we live in a state of lost unity and harmony which we strive to recover on a higher level of consciousness. Charles Hanna remarks that the recovery of this lost unity "is the primary concern of both religion and psychology." Juxtaposing religious and psychological language, he describes the goal of this recovery as "salvation, health and wholeness."[62] In Jung's view, then, the primary goal of religion is that inner rebirth or transformation which results in the experience of wholeness. At least two consequences follow from this. First, it is an understanding of religion which differentiates him from Freud, whose concern was with the ethical, social, and cultural functions of religion. Second, this emphasis on religion as inner, personal experience leads him to regard the historical or metaphysical truth of religion as less important than its psychological truth. Thus the objective truth of religious dogma is less important than its symbolic function in relation to unconscious archetypes. Christ as a symbol of the self, for instance, is more important than the historical Chtist. Underlying all this is the Jungian premise that experience is more important than faith. For Jung it was sufficient that a religious dogma or symbol be "psychologically" true.

The religious character of the individuation process consists of not only its striving for the same goal as religion but also the "numinous" quality of the archetypal experience. David Cox, a Christian theologian, has suggested a point of comparison between the thought of Jung and of St. Paul. Both believe that healing or salvation takes place when we cease to rely on our own will and conscious effort. When we do this, something *happens* to us, and we come to a way of living which is directed by a "center" which is not identical with the conscious ego.[63] This center is what Jung would call the self, which directs the process of individuation in an autonomous way. The collective unconscious is seen as an objective reality with a life of its own. Its incursions into consciousness are by way of dreams, fantasies, moods, obsessions and inspirations which seem to be beyond the control of one's conscious will. In spite of this, most of us persist in the idea that we create our own mental and emotional states and are therefore responsible for them. Commenting on the case of a patient with an imaginary cancer, Jung argues that this prejudice that we are "the makers of our psychical conditions … is of relatively recent date." But the fact that we frequently cannot rise above a bad mood or dispel an obsessive thought indicates to Jung that it originates "in that part of the psyche which is not identical with consciousness" and therefore must be regarded as "an autonomous development intruding upon consciousness."[64]

The primitive's understanding of the soul as an objective reality which acts independently and sometimes capriciously upon our conscious life is closer to the truth, he maintains, than the modern mentality which sees everything psychic as subjective. In dreams also this "objective psyche" may confront the individual with images drawn from mythology which, therefore, may be unrelated to the personal experience and knowledge of the dreamer. The archetypal experience, therefore, which characterizes the individuation process, shares with religious experience the "numinous" quality by which "it seizes and controls the human subject, which is always rather its victim than its creator."[65]

Individuation is a highly personal experience which suffers when the individual is swallowed up in the mass. Scientific, statistical views of reality which reduce the individual to a statistical unit; mass movements and ideologies and public opinion which reduce the moral responsibility of the individual; abstract definitions which ignore the uniqueness of the individual—all these tend to obliterate individuality and therefore obstruct the process of individuation. In this respect also individuation is like religion, which Jung also understands as personal and experiential. For Jung, the essence of religion is the inner, archetypal experience. For this reason he distinguishes it from "creeds," which he regards as "codified and dogmatized forms of original religious experience."[66] A creed or religious doctrine "gives expression to a definite collective belief, whereas the word *religion* expresses a subjective relationship to certain metaphysical extramundane factors."[67] Insofar as a creed is an expression of a collective mentality—an objective truth to be believed by all or a moral law to be obeyed by all—to that extent it represents that kind of mass-mindedness which is an obstacle to the very personal and individual experience of both religion and individuation. The personal religious relationship of each believer with God parallels the unique relationship of each individual ego with its unconscious depths, and both represent a necessary counterbalance to mass-mindedness.

To summarize, religion and individuation may be linked to each other in three ways: (1) They both seek the same goal of psychological wholeness, which involves the recovery of a lost unity and harmony and is therefore experienced as "rebirth." (2) Both represent a "numinous" type of experience involving the acceptance of the "supraordinate authority" of God or the unconscious. (3) Both are inner, personal, individual experiences whose spontaneous, experiential character is a counterbalance to all forms of mass-mindedness.

Religious Symbolism

When we say that Jung had a more positive attitude toward religion than did Freud, this does not refer to religion in the traditional, orthodox sense. We have seen that he felt alienated from the orthodox Christianity in which he was raised because he felt that its insistence on faith was a hindrance to the kind of direct experiential knowledge of the divine mystery which had come to

him in his boyhood dreams and fantasies. This substitution of faith for experience was a tragedy which he saw lived out in the life of his father. It was true,
nevertheless, that Jung regarded religious and spiritual desires as more fundamental than the instinctual drives which Freud regarded as primary. For
Jung, *libido* was not simply sexual energy but a kind of undifferentiated psychic energy which could be transformed through the power of symbols. Freud,
for instance, had interpreted the little boy's oedipal attachment to his mother as purely sexual. The incest taboo in this case has the function of turning
the child's sexual libido away from the parental figure and toward other objects. These other objects, including religious objects, are then seen as substi-
tutes for the original sexual object. They are, in effect, symbols of unfulfilled
desire.

Jung, on the other hand, maintained that the incestuous wish is not that
which is symbolized by other desires, but was itself symbolic of a more fundamental desire for spiritual rebirth. Such a desire represents, for Jung, a desire for psychic wholeness or selfhood. Victor White, who tried to interpret
Jung's ideas for the Christian world, puts it this way:

> Impregnation of the mother for its own sake, or motivated by the pleas-
> ure principle, was not the ultimate object of the libido at all; what was
> really desired was to return to the womb—rebirth. The incest wish is no
> longer the ultimate "thing symbolised"; it is itself the symbol of a yet
> more fundamental need and desire. Hence it could be that manifest sex-
> uality is itself symbolic; it is in fact only one form of life-urge bigger than
> itself.[68]

In the light of this, the function of the incest taboo is not simply to deflect sexual libido away from the parental figure and toward other objects, but, as Jung
sees it, to create the possibility of transforming psychic energy from a "lower"
to a "higher" form, that is, to redirect it toward the spiritual goal of rebirth.
This transformation is brought about through symbols which redirect the libido toward the goal of spiritual and psychological rebirth.

Herein lies the value of religious myth and symbol. Through images of
the mother and rebirth they canalize psychic energy away from the physical
mother and onto "mother analogies" so that the aim of the libido is "spiritu-
alized."

> Moreover it must be pointed out that the basis of the "incestuous" de-
> sire is not cohabitation, but, as every sun myth shows, the strange idea
> of becoming a child again, of returning to the parental shelter, and of
> entering into the mother in order to be reborn through her. But the way
> to this goal lies through incest, i.e., the necessity of finding some way into
> the mother's body. One of the simplest ways would be to impregnate the
> mother and beget oneself in identical form all over again. But here the

incest prohibition intervenes; consequently the sun myths and rebirth myths devise every conceivable kind of mother-analogy for the purpose of canalizing the libido into new forms and effectively preventing it from regressing to actual incest.... It is not incestuous cohabitation that is desired but rebirth.[69]

Incest then is symbolic of the deeper human desire for rebirth which, in psychological terms, means reunion with the lost part of one's personality—its unconscious depths. Religions, Jung suggests, "exalt this procedure into a system."[70] Thus the sun myth, with its imagery of a dying and rising sun, the death and resurrection of Christ, and the Christian ritual of baptism through immersion in water are all symbols of rebirth—"mother analogies"—which redirect the libido toward this goal of spiritual and psychological rebirth that cannot be accomplished by a mere return to the womb.

Jung's positive attitude towards religion, therefore, would seem to focus on the psychological value of religious myth and symbol, that is, on the power of the symbol to bring about real change and transformation within the individual. It does so by "canalizing" psychic energy toward the goal of spiritual and psychological rebirth for the sake of wholeness or completeness. The Christian believer, for example, is taught to see in his or her baptism a ritual of identification with the death and resurrection of Christ. Jung would see the connecting link between the baptismal rite and the Christ event in the fact that both are symbols of rebirth. Psychological rebirth is by way of reimmersion into the unconscious so as to assimilate its contents into consciousness and thus be "reborn." The baptismal rite of immersion in water (a symbol of mother and of the unconscious) symbolizes this. The death of Christ followed by his resurrection symbolizes the sacrifice of the narrow ego consciousness implied in the notion of reimmersion in the unconscious for the sake of psychic rebirth. For Jung, then, the value of religious symbolism lies in the transforming power of the symbol. The symbol redirects psychic energy toward the goal of wholeness in a way that is beyond the power of reason or willpower. "No man," Jung argues, "can change himself into anything from sheer reason: he can only change into what he potentially is."[71] The archetypes of the collective unconscious represent this potentiality because they represent everything that we have not yet actualized in our conscious life and attitudes. The value of religious symbols lies in their power to effect personal transformation by actualizing (making conscious) these unconscious potentialities.

Jung's interest in religion, therefore, seems to be limited to religion's symbolic or psychological function. This is also seen as the source of its value. Religion has value to the extent that its dogmas, rituals, and symbols correlate with the archetypal motifs and energies of the unconscious and direct our growth toward the assimilation of this archetypal material into our conscious life and, therefore, toward greater psychic wholeness. Like Freud, Jung was interested in the psychological *function* of religion, that is, its function in relation to the human psyche. For Freud, religion operated as a neurotic symptom, the locus for the projection of unconscious hostility and guilt. For Jung, its function was symbolic, the locus for the projection of archetypal material. As a psychologist of religion, Jung was concerned with this religious/archetypal experience and with specific religious doctrines only in their symbolic function, that is, as symbolic expressions of that experience. Because psychology cannot deal with that which transcends human experience, Jung claims that, in speaking of the symbolic function of religious doctrines, he abstracts from their theological or metaphysical truth claims. It has been suggested that he oversteps this methodological limitation at times and speaks as a metaphysician or theologian. Jung insists, however, that when he uses the term "God" he means the God-image or God archetype—realities which are accessible to psychological study. One has to admit that his juggling of these terms makes such a clarification necessary.

Jung states that, in his psychological study of religion, he wants to go beyond the study of the religious personality and include "religious contents." Religious dogmas are among these contents and Jung is interested in them as "symbols of transformation," that is, as meaningfully related to and expressions of the archetypes of the collective unconscious. The relevance of religious dogmas to human existence is related to their transforming power as symbols, their power to bring about real change in human personality. The human basis of religion—that which makes religion meaningful for human existence—is the archetypal structure of the psyche. Jung's criticism of institutional religion points to the fact that religious dogmas tend to lose their connection with this inner archetypal life of the psyche and thus lose their impact on and relevance to the life of the believer. Dogmas should function as the modern substitute for ancient myths, that is, as expressions of archetypal themes and motifs. Unfortunately, Jung argues, "dogma no longer formulates anything, no longer expresses anything; it has become a tenet to be accepted in and for itself, with no basis in any experience that would demonstrate its truth."[72]

When, in religious doctrine, the language of myth and symbol is replaced by rational, logical discourse, then dogmas lose their connection with the inner psychic life of the believer and become statements about objective realities, but realities beyond reason and therefore to be accepted on faith, without being rooted in experience. When dogma is merely this, it has a difficult time holding its own against the scientific worldview. It appears to the modern mind as "a language and outlook that have become alien to our present way of thinking."[73] When religious dogmas have thus become mere statements of fact (e.g., the existence of God) and lose their symbolic connection with the archetypes of the unconscious, then, Jung says, "we have stripped all things of their mystery and numinosity; nothing is holy any longer," because dogmas as expressions of the holy have lost their contact with "the numinous psychic powers that forever control man's fate."[74] They have become logic-defying objects of faith rather than "mysteries" which give life meaning. It is the symbolic, mythical character of dogma which puts everyday life into a larger context of meaning.

Christianity

While Jung's psychology of religion deals with the phenomenon of religion in general and although, in his writings, he displays a profound knowledge of world religions, when it came to the study of "religious contents," his major focus was the symbols and dogmas of Christianity. One reason for this focus was the fact that, in his work as a therapist, he was attempting to correct the imbalances and one-sidedness of the mentality of the Western world, and Christianity was seen as a major contributor to the archetypal structure of the Western psyche. There is also a degree of personal involvement. Jung's father was a parson, and in his father's life he perceived what he considered the failure and one-sidedness of Christianity with its emphasis on faith rather than direct religious experience. With this in mind, we shall now briefly review Jung's study of three Christian dogmas: God, the Trinity, and the Incarnation.

God and the God-Image. As we have seen, the archetype is form without content. It represents a capacity to find and express meaning in myth and symbol onto which it is projected. These approximate the meaning of the archetype, but the essence of the archetype cannot be represented. The basis of Jung's psychology of religion is the correspondence between, on the one hand, the psychological distinction between the essentially irrepresentable archetype of the self and the archetypal images in which its meaning is approximated in a conscious way and, on the other hand, the theological distinction between God as essentially unknowable as He is in Himself and the various images by which He is represented in human consciousness. God and the self archetype are essentially unknowable. Aniela Jaffe states: "The unfathomability of God and the unfathomability of the self account for the synonymity, not the identity, of the two concepts."[75] God and self are not identical, but, because they both represent the experience of wholeness or totality, they are indistinguishable at this experiential level. As a psychologist of religion, Jung could not discuss the essential nature of God, but only the human experience of God. Since "knowledge of God is a transcendental problem,"[76] Jung can explain such an experience only in terms of the inner dynamics of the psyche, not with reference to a reality which transcends the psyche.

The religious point of view would maintain that human beings are created in the image of God and carry this God-image imprinted on the soul. This accounts for the continuity between the human and the divine and the meaningfulness of the concept of God for human existence. Jung too believes that there is an imprint on the soul which makes concepts and images of God meaningful. This imprint is what he calls the unconscious archetype of the self. This is the archetype of wholeness or totality—"the highest point on the scale of objective values"—and it is this archetype which is projected onto human, conscious conceptions of God and makes them meaningful. When it is projected onto a God-image it may be called the "God archetype." Since this term, however, implies the existence of a transcendent source of the archetype—an "imprinter" behind the imprint—Jung prefers the more neutral term "self" to describe the archetype corresponding to the outer God-image. "The religious point of view," he states, "understandably enough, puts the accent on the imprinter, whereas scientific psychology emphasizes the *typos*, the imprint—the only thing it can understand."[77] In this way he preserves the "archetypal indefiniteness" of this psychic content and avoids linking it with any of the particular conscious conceptions of God found in the history of religions. The self, as the archetype of totality, can be projected onto and invest with meaning any number of religious conceptions and images of God as well as onto natural, nonreligious symbols of wholeness.

Nevertheless, the archetype does have a certain God-like, numinous quality in the sense that it is a "superior power," that is, a power transcending the conscious limits of the ego. Consequently, the ego should relate to it as to a superior power. When, therefore, Jung says that God is "psychologically real," he is pointing to the psychic reality of the archetype of totality, which for him is an "empirical" fact. In doing so, he is establishing not the existence of a transcendent God but of the structural component of the psyche which is the human basis for belief in God. The theologian relativizes all human, anthropomorphic images of God by pointing out that they are metaphors for an essentially unknowable God. He distinguishes between God as He is in Himself and our conscious images of God. Jung, as a psychologist, performs a similar function when he points out that the various God-images are projections of the essentially unknowable self archetype. The essence of both God and the archetype remains a mystery which cannot be reduced to a rational formula but which offers life and wisdom to those who are open to its influence.

The notion that the God of one's conscious belief is a projection of an unconscious archetype may serve to shed some light on Jung's belief that God is "within" rather than an objective, external reality. Within the epistemological limits of psychology God is within because the God-image "out there" is known only through projection of the God or self archetype from within. Since what is within is the archetype, Jung is not denying the objective reality of God but is insisting on the fact that God can be truly known only in an experiential way, through an archetypal experience from within rather than through faith in the objective truth of a doctrine. When the theologian Paul Tillich speaks of God as the infinite ground of being and awareness of him as "independent of any encounter with our world," he is echoing Jung's concepts of the collective unconscious and the God within. This difference, however, remains. The infinite ground of being is still a metaphysical reality which transcends the psyche while Jung's "God within"—the archetype—is an intrapsychic reality. The analogy consists of the fact that the archetype—while remaining a depth dimension of the psyche—is experienced, like God, as an objective reality standing over against and transcending the ego. For this reason, Jung proposes that while God and the self archetype are not identical realities, nevertheless, on the level of experience, they and the symbols through which they are experienced are indistinguishable. God and the self are unknowable realities which nevertheless can be experienced. Faith divorced from this inner experience, Jung believed, had no humanly transforming effect.

The Trinity. The psyche, Jung maintained, was "naturally religious" by reason of its archetypal structure which, through projection, invests religious symbols, myth, and dogma with human meaning. The psychological value of religious dogmas lies in their symbolic function, that is, in their connection with the numinous, archetypal powers of the unconscious psyche. As we have seen, when dogmas lose their connection with the inner, archetypal experience of the believer, they become mere statements about objective realities such as the existence and nature of God. In this way they lose their numinous power to effect change and growth within the human personality. They become objects of rational debate or blind faith but, in either case, they are divorced, as Jung points out, from any experience that would give them meaning. Real conviction about God, he argues, does not come from rational arguments or blind faith, but from immediate, inner experience. "Science," he claims, "has never discovered any 'God,' epistemological criticism proves the impossibility of knowing God, but the psyche comes forth with the assertion of the experience of God. God is a psychic fact of immediate experience, otherwise there would never have been any talk of God."[78] Perhaps no Christian dogma has suffered this fate of becoming divorced from human life and experience more than the dogma of the Trinity. Jung recounts that, as a boy, he eagerly looked forward, in his instruction for Confirmation, to the section on the Trinity which intrigued him. His father, however, passed over the topic claiming not to understand it himself.[79] Such is the fate of dogma which has become the object of intellectual "understanding."

In later years, as if by way of compensation, Jung published, at age 67, a lengthy essay in which he discussed the psychological meaning of this dogma. The Trinity is a specifically Christian God-image which for many has lost its connection with the inner, archetypal experience to which it gives conscious expression. "The Trinity," Jung remarks, "and its inner life process appears as a closed circle, a self-contained divine drama in which man plays, at most, a passive part." Consequently, it is "difficult to see what the Trinity could possibly mean for us, either practically, morally or symbolically."[80] When a dogma is stripped of its symbolic meaning in this way, it plays no psychological role since it no longer confronts the believer with the archetypal contents of the unconscious. Jung argues that theology ignores the archetypal meaning of dogmas with the result that it "proclaims doctrines which nobody understands, and demands a faith which nobody can manufacture."[81]

Symbols such as the Trinity are the means by which the conscious mind encounters the archetype of the self, which is, in itself, irrepresentable since it denotes a wholeness or completeness that is beyond rational formulation. In the Trinity Jung finds a twofold symbolism. First, it is a symbolic expression of the "process of unconscious maturation taking place within the individual."[82] As a symbol of the self it represents, in the three divine persons, the three-stage process of growth: original unconscious unity conscious differentiation and polarity and higher conscious unity through the "union of opposites." Second, the Trinity "denotes a process of conscious realization continuing over the centuries."[83] This refers to humanity's growth in consciousness, which parallels the progressive development of the image of God in human consciousness or the human understanding of God. In Jung's words, "God becomes manifest in the human act of reflection."[84]

The significance of each of the three persons of the Trinity, then, must be seen in the light of this twofold symbolism. God the father—the first person of the Trinity—represents God as one and indivisible and, accordingly, reflects the first stage of human growth—infancy—which, because it is anterior to the growth of consciousness, is characterized as a state of unconscious unity. This is a state of identification with parental figures and lack of self-consciousness. Since one has not yet made those differentiations—masculine and feminine, good and evil and so on, which characterize consciousness, this stage corresponds to primitive conceptions of the deity in which God is both good and evil and unconscious of the differentiation. God is therefore perceived as autocratic and punitive.

In *Answer to Job*, Jung attributes these characteristics to the God with whom Job has to deal. Yahweh is "too unconscious to be moral. Morality presupposes consciousness.... He is everything in its totality; therefore, among other things, he is total justice and also its total opposite."[85] His behavior is that of "an unconscious being who cannot be judged morally. Yahweh is a *phenomenon* and, as Job says, 'not a man.'"[86] It is precisely his becoming man—his incarnation in a human consciousness—which constitutes, in Jung's view, God's "answer" to Job who protests against his unjust, autocratic behavior. Before this coming to consciousness, however, the one and indivisible God is like the child who has not yet differentiated good and evil. "The father," Jung states, "denotes the earlier stage of consciousness when one was still a child, still dependent on a definite, ready-made pattern of existence which is habitual and has the character of law. It is a passive, unreflecting condition, a mere awareness of what is given, without intellectual or moral judgement."[87]

God the son—the second person of the Trinity—represents the second stage of growth in both individual human development and the development of the God-image. With the growth of consciousness and self-awareness, conscious choice and decision replace habit. The growing child learns to differ-entiate himself from and become gradually independent of parents. With this development of individuality he or she begins to make conscious differenti-ations between self and others, masculine and feminine, good and evil. Con-sciousness tends to identify with one pole of each of these dichotomies. The result is a one-sided course of development since those aspects of the total personality which are incompatible with this conscious identity are relegated to the dark, unadapted, unconscious side of personality. The development of a moral conscience, for instance, which results in adherence to what Jung calls collective moral norms, calls for the repression of those aspects of personali-ty that are incompatible with the morally good persona. This repression of the shadow is, for Jung, a major part of the modern crisis of humanity. It is an aspect of that one-sidedness which results in a sense of dissatisfaction, in-completeness, and alienation from the self, a sense of something missing—because a part of one's total self has been denied.

This kind of conscious differentiation which take place in individual de-velopment also takes place in the development of the God-image. In Christ, the son of God becomes man, God becomes masculine as distinct from femi-nine and good as distinct from evil. As in individual development, that which is not admitted as part of one's conscious identity (but still part of one's to-tality) is projected onto other objects. In ancient mythology the differentia-tion of the masculine and the feminine aspects of the deity is consciously represented in images of the "syzygy" or divine pair (e.g., Adonis and Aphrodite, Osiris and Isis). The Judaeo-Christian God-image, however, is es-sentially masculine and the feminine aspect is projected onto Sophia, the Old Testament embodiment of wisdom, or—particularly in the Catholic tradi-tion—onto the Virgin Mary or "mother Church."

Jung contends that the inclusion of the feminine symbol makes the God-image a more adequate symbol of totality since a one-sidedly masculine God represents the ideal of perfection rather than completeness. "Perfection," he argues, "is a masculine desideratum, while woman inclines by nature to com-pleteness."[88] For this reason he considered Pope Pius XII's proclamation of the dogma of the bodily assumption of the Virgin Mary into heaven to be "the most important religious event since the Reformation."[89] For Jung, this dogma symbolically restored the feminine aspect of the deity. Mary's symbolic func-tion, then, is to supply the missing feminine principle in the Godhead and thus help to transform it into a symbol of completeness rather than perfec-tion. This function, however, is somewhat vitiated, Jung believes, by the Church's insistence on Mary's sinlessness. This tends to make her, like Christ, a symbol of perfection, for completeness implies imperfection and "the more the feminine ideal is bent in the direction of the masculine, the more the woman loses her power to compensate the masculine striving for perfection."[90]

As the Christ/Mary symbolism differentiates the masculine and femi-nine aspects of the Godhead, so the Christ/Antichrist symbolism differenti-

ates the good and evil, light and dark, aspects of that same totality. The figure of Christ, Jung argues, like that of Mary, is perceived and dogmatically
defined as sinless. It therefore lacks something which is necessary for wholeness or completeness, namely, the "dark side" of human personality, including the human propensity for evil. Job's God has this dark, unconscious side
which is dogmatically excluded from the sinless personality of Christ and
projected onto that of Satan or Antichrist. Thus Christ incarnates only the
light or good side of God. In Christian teaching, God is identified with this
good and light aspect and becomes the good and loving father. By way of
compensation, Satan appears as the incarnation of the "dark side" of God, the
inevitable shadow cast by the light of Christ. In this way the human psyche
turns the three-sided symbol of the Trinity into a quaternity by adding a
fourth "missing" element onto which the dark side of personality is projected. The figures of Sophia and Mary serve the same compensatory function of
supplying a missing fourth element in the Trinity—in this case the feminine
principle. By turning the Trinity symbol into a quaternity, Jung argues, the
psyche transforms it into a more adequate representation of wholeness since
natural symbols of the self archetype which appear in mythology and in
dreams appear as mandala and quaternity or fourfold symbols (representing
the four elements of creation or the four functions of the psyche and therefore wholeness).

From the psychological perspective, it is the self archetype which is projected onto any God-image, including the Trinity, thus making it meaningful
for human existence as a symbol of wholeness. The God-image should therefore include both masculine and feminine elements and what is humanly perceived as good and evil as components of the human totality. If the Trinity is,
as Jung suggests, a symbol of the process of individuation, then it should represent some kind of assimilation or coming to terms with the "dark side" of
personality, and it should reflect the conflict engendered by the conscious differentiations associated with the growth of consciousness, including the conflict of good and evil. Hence the psyche perceives not only "the light shining
in Christ" but its conflict with the dark figure of Satan. In the figure of Christ
one sees not only the goodness of God but also the shadow cast by that goodness and, therefore, the conflict of good and evil which must be undergone by
those in whom the image of God is to be realized. The evil or dark side of
God, then, is not to be understood in a metaphysical way. It refers to the fact
that our human understanding of God or God-image must reflect the fact that
God transcends one's human conceptions of good and evil and therefore one's
image of Him must include both, which the image in some way reconciles.

This concept of the reconciliation of opposites is evident in Jung's remarks about the symbolism associated with the Holy Spirit—the third person
of the Trinity. As a symbol of individuation, the Holy Spirit represents that
higher state of consciousness brought about through the uniting and reconciling of those opposites which consciousness had differentiated. This repre-

sents a higher unity, a unity without the loss of consciousness. It also represents the transcending of a sense of individuality which is one-sided since it assimilates those unconscious aspects of one's totality that the one-sided consciousness had not acknowledged. In *Answer to Job*, this third stage of development is represented by the coming of the Holy Spirit whose function is to continue the incarnation in "empirical man," that is, in ordinary human beings. The effect of this is to create a new humanity characterized by completeness rather than perfection. In the Trinity symbolism the Holy Spirit puts an end to the duality caused by the conscious differentiation and conflict of good and evil in the Godhead, that is, between Christ and Satan. By reconciling these opposites, the Spirit restores the unity lost through the differentiation of Christ and Satan, but at a higher level. In the same way, in the individuation process, the reconciling symbol brings about a union of the opposites created by the growth of consciousness and leads to a higher state of consciousness.

This analysis of the dogma of the Trinity reveals a twofold process: the progressive development and refinement of the image of God and the development of human consciousness in which that image is "incarnated" as an actualization of the archetype of the self. Aniela Jaffe points to these as two sides of the same process, which she calls "the individuation of mankind."[91] The goal of this process is the incarnation of the divine in the human or, as Jung sees it, the actualization of the God archetype in human consciousness. Concerning this process the following points must be kept in mind. First, the actualization of the God archetype is synonymous with the actualization of the self archetype. For this reason, Jung maintains, symbols of the God archetype (God-images) are indistinguishable from symbols of the self. Second, it is an ongoing process that is never completed and therefore continues without end. What is transcendent can never fulfill itself in that which it transcends.

Theologically, this means that all human, finite expressions of the divine and infinite are necessarily partial and fragmentary. Psychologically, it means that the archetype of the self which transcends consciousness can likewise be given conscious expression in only a partial and fragmentary way. All conscious expressions and experiences of wholeness or totality are necessarily limited. Third, the goal of this process is not a God-like perfection but a God-like completeness. Translated into moral terms this means that the goal of moral development is not simply the triumph of good over evil, but, in some sense, the reconciliation of good and evil, just as selfhood in general means the reconciliation of consciously perceived opposites. Such a morality which is "beyond good and evil" is symbolized by the Holy Spirit who represents a reconciliation of the Christ-Satan duality. In terms of practical moral decision making, this means that our conscious, black and white, and often legalistic distinctions between good and evil are relativized in the light of a more ultimate moral criterion. We acknowledge this in a practical way when we admit that what is apparently evil is, in reality, sometimes good and vice versa and that an apparently "evil" act sometimes has good consequences and vice versa. As the old adage has it, "God writes straight on crooked lines." This progressive realization of the self or God archetype is what Jung calls the continuing incarnation in "empirical man."

Incarnation and Redemption. In Jung's psychological interpretation of the Trinity as, in actuality, a quaternity symbol of the self, the original unity of the Father is an unconscious unity of good and evil. Christ and Satan, as incarnations of the "light" and "dark" sides of the Father, represent the differentiation and conflict of good and evil. The Holy Spirit, as the life common to the Father and the Son, is the reconciling principle which resolves this conflict. "Looked at from the quaternity standpoint," Jung states, "the Holy Ghost is a reconciliation of opposites and hence the answer to the suffering in the Godhead which Christ personifies."[92] The suffering of Christ recalls the image of the cross which signifies Christ's redemptive function. For Jung, the image of Christ, crucified between two thieves, symbolizes the conflict of opposites, which is a necessary part of the process of individuation. The cross, with its four points, is also a quaternity symbol of the self. The psychological significance of the figure of Christ consists, for Jung, in the fact that he is a symbol of the self. It is this affinity of the outer figure of Christ with the contents of humanity's unconscious which makes him, from psychological point of view, an object of religious faith. In the first place his humanity adds a fourth, human, material element to the Trinity, thus turning it into a quaternity and, therefore, a symbol of wholeness. He is the God-man who thus signifies the actualization of the divine in the human or the self archetype in consciousness.

There is a sense, however, in which Jung considers the Christ figure to be an incomplete symbol of the self. Christ, as we have seen, incarnates only the "light" side of God, thus becoming a symbol of perfection rather than completeness since the dark side of the human totality is excluded. But since, according to the law of enantiodromia, everything tends to become its opposite, the coming of the sinless Christ leads inevitably, by way of compensation, to the appearance of the Antichrist or Satan. The dark side of the human totality is dogmatically excluded from the figure of Christ and projected onto Satan. Although Christ is "an embodiment of the self," nevertheless,

> looked at from the psychological angle he corresponds to only one half of the archetype. The other half appears in the Antichrist. The latter is just as much a manifestation of the self, except that he consists of its dark aspect. Both are Christian symbols, and they have the same meaning as the image of the Saviour crucified between two thieves. This great symbol tells us that the progressive development and differentiation of con-

sciousness leads to an ever more menacing awareness of the conflict and involves nothing less than a crucifixion of the ego, its agonizing suspension between irreconcilable opposites.[93]

As the crucifixion of Christ is the necessary prelude to his resurrection, so the "crucifixion of the ego" (the conflict of opposites) is the necessary prelude to rebirth or wholeness (the union of opposites).

The complete symbol of selfhood, then, is not merely the figure of the sinless Christ (which suggests an incomplete perfection) but the Christ who is crucified and who rises from the dead. This death and rebirth is a symbol of the "death" of consciousness—its "crucifixion" by the conflict of opposites and its rebirth through re-immersion in the unconscious. The crucifixion of Christ represents the crucifixion of the ego seeking completeness and torn between the goals of perfection and completeness. Those who would achieve selfhood must undergo this crucifixion of the ego. "The whole world is God's suffering," Jung maintains, "and every individual man who wants to get anywhere near his own wholeness knows that this is the way of the cross."[94] For Jung, the death and resurrection of Christ is a variation of the mythical theme of the dying and rising God. As such it represents an actualization of the archetype of rebirth or selfhood and herein, from the psychological perspective, lies its power. Seen in this light—as an historical expression of an inner human experience—the figure of Jesus, who in Christian theological language is the incarnate son of God, becomes, psychologically, the incarnation of the archetypal theme of rebirth to wholeness existing in humanity's collective unconscious. In his analysis of the Catholic ritual of the mass,[95] Jung interprets the mass as a symbolic expression of this theme of rebirth and transformation. The rite is seen as expressing the theme of sacrifice and rebirth which characterizes the individuation process, thereby making that process accessible to the ordinary person.

Eastern Religions

Jung's interest in "religious contents" was certainly not confined to Christian symbols and dogmas. Volume 11 of his collected works, which contains most of his writings directly concerned with religion, is entitled *Psychology and Religion: West and East*. The contents of this volume reveal an interest in Eastern religions and philosophy, from Yoga to Buddhism to Eastern meditation.

Jung's reflections on Eastern religions seem to be guided by two major preoccupations. The first of these is the great stress he places on the differences between Eastern and Western mentalities. In these differences he sees a major obstacle to the uncritical adoption of Eastern spiritual disciplines by people of the West. Second—and precisely because of these differences in mentality—Jung attempts to explain Eastern thought and practices to the Western mind by pointing out the analogies and parallels to the major concepts in his own analytic psychology, that is, the psychology of the unconscious.

He considered his own psychological system to be the closest Western analogue to and the most useful vehicle for understanding Eastern thought.

East and West. In his "Psychological Commentary on the 'Tibetan Book
of the Great Liberation,'" Jung describes the difference between Eastern and
Western thinking in these words: "With us, man is incommensurably small
and the grace of God is everything; but in the East, man is God and he re-
deems himself."[96] The Western attitude is marked by an extraverted obsession with objective facts. Everything god, including God, is outside. This
attitude carries with it a corresponding devaluing of the mind or psyche which
represents the "unreal" world of subjectivity. (The expression "It's all in your
head" means, in effect, that it doesn't "really" exist.) The Eastern attitude, on
the other hand, finds what is real in the subjective realm of mind or psyche.
The external world is one of illusion (maya). Human higher development or
liberation from this illusion comes from within. For Jung, these two attitudes
are irreconcilable: "You cannot be a good Christian and redeem yourself, nor
can you be a Buddha and worship God."[97]

Though these differing attitudes cannot be merged, they can learn from
each other. From the East the Western mentality can learn something of the
healing power that comes from within, that is—in Western language—the unconscious. As already noted, in Jungian theory the unconscious acts in an autonomous way to compensate for one's conscious one-sidedness and thereby
lead one to a state of greater psychological wholeness. It is precisely this state
of wholeness that Jung sees as analogous to the Eastern goal of "enlightenment" or participation in "Universal Mind"—in Jungian terms, the collective
unconscious. The Western mentality, however, tends to shun the unconscious
world of fantasy, just as the Eastern mentality shuns the external world. For
this very reason Jung also believes that the East has something to learn from
the West. Just as Western extraversion devalues the unconscious psyche, so
Eastern introversion seems to devalue ego consciousness. Consequently it
seems to aim at a kind of ego-transcending spiritual transformation that
amounts to a state of consciousness without an ego. For Jung, this seems like
a contradiction in terms. As a result, he is not enthusiastic about the uncritical appropriation by Westerners of practices such as yoga, the goal of which
(samadhi) seems to be "a mental condition in which the ego is practically dissolved."[98] He cautions that spiritual transformation cannot be produced at
will; it must rely on the autonomous activity of the unconscious. The Western
dependence on God is a projection of this attitude.

Another problem that Jung finds with the practice of yoga in the West
is the fact that it encounters among Westerners a condition of mind in which
there is a strict line of division between science, philosophy, and religion. The
result is that, when yoga was imported to the West, it became either an object
of scientific study or a way of salvation. Some religious movements, however—Jung mentions Christian Science and Theosophy—tried to combine reli-

gion and science. These found in yoga a "religious" method that was also "scientific." It was seen as a combination of the physical and the spiritual, in which physical exercises are put into a cosmic context. Jung's argument, however, is that the Western mind is split; it does not naturally combine the physical and the spiritual, the religious and the scientific in this way. "The Indian," he writes, "can forget neither the body nor the mind, while the European is always forgetting either the one or the other."[99]

Elaborating on the difference between the outward-looking attitude of the West and the inward-looking attitude of the East, Jung points to the fact that the Western mentality is always seeking to "uplift," that is, to raise oneself above the world. This seems to be a reference to the religious attitude commonly described as "other worldly" as well as the scientific attempt to transcend and control nature. By contrast, the Eastern attitude involves a sinking or deepening, a tendency to turn back into the maternal depths of nature. For Jung, this means to seek "rebirth" through immersion in the contents of the unconscious. He argues, however, that Westerners are averse to encountering the "darkness" of their own unconscious. "Many people," he writes, "think it morbid to glance into our own interiors—it makes you melancholic, a theologian once assured me."[100]

Eastern Thought and Jungian Psychology. By way of explaining Eastern thought to the Western world, Jung published in 1939 his "Psychological Commentary on the 'Tibetan Book of the Great Liberation.'" Liberation here refers to the Buddhist goal of enlightenment, which involves an experience of "Universal Mind" or the "seeing of reality." This turning inward toward Universal Mind, which is the ground of individual consciousness, is a liberation from the strife and suffering that accompany the desires and cravings for external fulfillment. These desires of individual consciousness are obstacles to the experience of "one mind". Now in Jung's view all this is analogous to the kind of human transformation which is the goal of the individuation process. The experience of Universal Mind becomes the experience of the collective unconscious. Both experiences involve a transcending of the conflict of opposites that characterizes the conscious mind and an experience of that dimension of personality which is one, indefinite, and timeless. Being chained to the world of consciousness is to be unaware of unconscious contents.

As noted earlier, however, Jung does not believe that this process of liberation/individuation can be simply willed to happen through conscious teaching.

> Unless one is prepared to turn away from the world and to disappear into the unconscious for good, mere teaching has no effect, or at least not the desired one. For this the union of opposites is necessary and in particular the difficult task of reconciling extraversion and introversion by means of the transcendent function.[101]

In other words, in order to realize a valid kind of spiritual transformation in which consciousness and the unconscious are truly *integrated*, one is dependent on the spontaneous compensation which the unconscious provides in an autonomous way. This is what Jung calls the "transcendent function" of the unconscious. When the Western mentality attributes this function to God through words such as "grace" or the "will of God," it acknowledges one's dependence on some autonomous power. When Eastern thought uses the term "dharma" (law, truth, guidance) which is "nowhere save in the mind," it acknowledges that this transforming power comes from within.

A similar parallel is drawn in Jung's "Psychological Commentary on 'The Tibetan Book of the Dead.'" The Book of the Dead (Bardo Thodol) is a book of instructions which were read to the dead or dying. It offers guidance to the dead person during the period of "Bardo" existence, that is, the intermediate period of 49 days between death and rebirth. The moment of death is seen as having the greatest potential for the realization of enlightenment. Then the soul falls prey to the illusions which estrange consciousness from this liberating truth and, therefore, lead to rebirth or reincarnation. These instructions try to recall the dead person from the world of things to the primacy of the soul or psyche which is identified with the Godhead or giver of all those things. The dead person falls into a state of "karmic illusion" due to the psychic residue of previous existences. The law of karma is thus a matter of "psychic heredity."

Jung relates this to his own theory of psychic inheritance, that is, the theory of the archetypes of the collective unconscious which are the residue in the individual psyche of human history and experience. Jung refers to the "psychological need of the living to do something for the departed" and sees the only evidence of this in Western culture in the Catholic practice of masses for the dead. Overall, however, the instructions in the Book of the Dead represent "the highest application of spiritual effort on behalf of the departed."[102] Its premise is the idea of the "supratemporality" of the soul or psyche which, for Jung, is analogous to the idea of the collective unconscious. Whether we call it soul or collective unconscious, its full realization (enlightenment/individuation) requires "a whole human lifetime, perhaps even many lifetimes, of increasing completeness."[103] (Jung reminds us that the goal is completeness, not perfection.) The words "perhaps many lifetimes" suggests a consistency of reincarnation with Jung's concept of the individuation process.

Jung is at pains to caution his Western readers about what he perceives as the one-sided goal of Eastern spirituality which seems to call for a loss of ego consciousness—its complete absorption in Universal Mind. This is contrasted with the West's one-sided emphasis on ego consciousness. In Zen Buddhism, however, he seems to find a more complete parallel to his own psychological theory. This seems to be attributed to the fact that the goal of Zen (satori or enlightenment) is—like the individuation process—a natural occurrence. Jung sees both satori and individuation as emancipation from illusion—the illusion of confusing self with ego. The experience of the self is the experience of a broader or higher ego, but in the form of a "non-ego," that is, the aspect of the psyche which transcends the ego. Both satori and individuation involve the emptying of consciousness of external things so that it is open to another influence. That "other influence" is not the result of one's activity but that of the "non-ego". It is not an intellectually controlled process but a "religious" transformation to which one submits as in mystical experience.

When consciousness is emptied of its contents, energy is withdrawn from them and transferred to the conception of emptiness or to the koan (a paradoxical riddle such as the famous "What is the sound of one hand clapping?"). In Jung's terms, energy is thus transferred to the unconscious so that unconscious contents can break through into consciousness. This is not a process whose goal is predetermined, but the creation of readiness for transformation. In this sense it is similar to psychotherapy. The goal is transformation, but one can create a readiness only for that transformation which takes place spontaneously. As Jung notes, "No effort on the part of the doctor can compel this experience."[104]

One of the difficulties for the Western mind on encountering Eastern spirituality is the prejudice that its subjective approach ignores what is "real." The inward quest for absorption in Universal Mind seems to the Western mind to be a "purely psychological" process. This is not a problem for Jung for whom it is sufficient for something to be "psychologically real." Furthermore, to the Eastern mentality, these concepts are not purely psychological but metaphysical. The self—to use Jung's term—is God (or what corresponds to God in Western thinking) and the ego-self tension corresponds to the man-God tension in the West. The terms "ego" and "self," Jung argues, are just as metaphysical as "man" and "God." A parallel is seen here between Eastern religious practice and Western mysticism. The goal in each case is the "shifting of the centre of gravity from the ego to the self, from man to God. This means that the ego disappears in the self and man into God."[105]

A further excursion into Eastern thought by Jung (this time Taoism) is contained in his "Foreword to the 'I Ching'"—a Chinese text in which Jung found "uncommon significance as a method of exploring the unconscious."[106] We know that consciousness relates us to external reality. One of the rational principles consciousness employs as a means of understanding the external world and the relationship between things and events in that world is the principle of cause and effect. The unconscious, however, is not restricted by this principle. Consequently, Jung looked to the unconscious for an explanation of those events that happen simultaneously "by chance" and yet have a meaningful connection which cannot be explained in terms of cause and effect. His term for this is "synchronicity," which can be defined as an "acausal connecting principle." The principle of synchronicity posits that coincidences of events in space and time mean something more than chance. It posits "a peculiar interdependence of objective events among themselves as well as with the subjective (psychic) state of the observer or observers."[107] (Astrology, for example, tries to establish such an interdependence.) For Jung, the *I Ching* was a clear expression and application of the principle of synchronicity. The method outlined in the *I Ching* involves the creation of a "hexagram" (a series of six broken or unbroken lines) by the throwing of yarrow stalks (in its original form) or, in its modern adaptation, coins. The combination of heads and tails of these thrown coins adds up to a number. This translates into a broken or unbroken line depending on whether the number is even or odd. When this is done six times the hexagram is complete. The subject then locates the passage in the *I Ching* corresponding to this hexagram, that is, the particular combination of broken and unbroken lines. Jung found an uncanny connection between the passage in the *I Ching* and the subject's life situation or problem he or she was confronting at that point in time. Here was a way of finding meaning that clearly had nothing to do with cause and effect. It was an expression of the principle of synchronicity and, therefore, explainable only in terms of unconscious forces.

Jung's interest in Eastern religions and forms of spirituality was deeper and more far-reaching than that of any of the other theorists we are reviewing in this book. It remains true, nevertheless, that the primary focus of his psychology of religion is Western Christianity. Why is this so? Murray Stein has suggested that Jung saw himself as a healer of Christianity, a tradition which he saw as ailing and in need of psychotherapeutic help. His concern was with Christianity's psychological health and wholeness. His personal relationship to Christianity, Stein argues, involved a "powerful impulse" to heal it. This impulse was first directed toward his father, whom Jung saw as exemplifying the spiritual plight of those for whom Christianity was not supplying an adequate spiritual answer to the scientific rationalism of the age. Jung rejects his father's traditional, dogmatic form of Christianity but at the same time wants to heal his father's suffering. These feelings—both rebellious and therapeutic—are later transferred onto Freud, who is seen as another father figure. Here again he rejects Freud's dogmatism but wants to heal what he perceives as the one-sidedness of psychoanalysis, that is, the primacy of sexuality in psychological life.

This rebellious yet therapeutic attitude is transferred finally to Christianity. In Christianity, Jung perceived a similar kind of dogmatism that demands faith in place of the direct, intuitive experience of God and a similar kind of one-sidedness in its image of God which, as a symbol of selfhood, excluded the dark side of the human totality. For Jung, as we have seen, the encounter with God is not through blind faith but through a direct experiential kind of knowledge. Even in his writings on alchemy, he finds a confirmation of this approach and thus a corrective to and unconscious compensation for Christianity's one-sided preoccupations. Stein concludes: "Jung's early wish to heal his father... passed over ("transferred") first to Freud and psychoanalysis and finally came to rest on Christianity. If the physician was born of an ailing Swiss pastor, he went on until he found his true patient in the original source of his father's disease—modern Christianity."[108]

Evaluation

The issues raised by Jung's psychology of religion might be organized around the same four questions we asked of Freud's theory of religion, though, admittedly, the questions are somewhat overlapping.

Is It Reductionist?

The reductionist attitude is an attitude of "nothing but." For Freud religion was "nothing but" an illusion which was symptomatic of an obsessional neurosis. He did not differentiate this as descriptive only of pathological expressions of religion. This illusion was the religion of the "man in the street," which, he argued, was the only religion deserving of the name. In this view, religion is a purely psychological phenomenon, entirely explainable in terms of the dynamics of an obsessional neurosis. Can Jung's treatment of religion be accused of the same kind of reductionism? The popular view is that Freud held a negative view and Jung a positive view of religion. Freud saw religion as neurotic and regressive and, therefore, an impediment to full human development. Jung saw religion as potentially conducive to human growth and maturity because the symbolic character of religion correlates with the archetypal structure of the psyche. There are, however, dissenters to this popular view. Erich Fromm sees in Freudian theory an attempt to preserve the "ethical core" of religion and maintains that Jung "reduces religion to a psychological phenomenon and at the same time elevates the unconscious to a religious phenomenon."[109] As a humanist, Fromm seems uncomfortable with the notion of "surrender" to a superior power, whether that power be God or the unconscious. One may legitimately argue, however, that it is just such a surrender to a superior power rather than ethics which constitutes the "core" of religion.

Fromm also believes that, in reducing all religions to a common experiential, archetypal root, Jung is guilty of a certain relativism regarding truth which is contrary to the spirit of religions such as Christianity, Judaism, and Buddhism. In this he is echoing an earlier—and much more polemical—attack by Edward Glover who accuses Jung of putting experience ahead of truth. "Nobody is to care," he writes, "whether God exists, Jung least of all. All that is necessary is to 'experience' an 'attitude' because it 'helps one to live.'"[110] These criticisms amount to charges of reductionism for both are accusing Jung of reducing religion to a psychological phenomenon and limiting the value of religion to its psychological value. It is true that in his study of "religious contents"—the symbols and dogmas of religion—he stresses their symbolic or psychological value, that is, their correlation with the archetypal contents of the unconscious. Dogmas perform the function of myth and are thus conducive to the pursuit of psychic wholeness. It must be admitted that Jung, in stressing the psychological value of religious dogmas, gives the impression that their historical or metaphysical truth is relatively unimportant. For the religious believer, however, it may be important that God be more than "psychologically real," or that the divine-human nature of Christ be more than a mythical expression of the God-man archetype, or that his death and resurrection be more than a symbol of rebirth.

On the other hand, it must be pointed out in Jung's defense that, in focusing on the psychological reality and values of religious contents, he is observing the methodological limits of the psychology of religion which can study religion only as a psychological phenomenon. It seems entirely appropriate, therefore, that he should locate the value of religion in its human basis—the archetypal structure of the psyche. It is also difficult to disagree with Jung's fundamental position that the objective truth of religious dogmas is psychologically inconsequential unless they are, at the same time, humanly transforming. The source of the apparent reductionism, seems to be twofold. First, there is Jung's manner of expression. While he makes the necessary distinction between God as He is in Himself and the God-image by which He is represented in consciousness and claims to speak psychologically only of the God-image, this distinction is not always clear in his writing. Furthermore, he expresses himself in such a way as to give the impression that the metaphysical or historical truth of a dogma is *less important* than its psychological truth. At times the objective truth of a dogma (e.g., the reality of the "historical Christ") is perceived as of such secondary importance to its symbolic function as to be almost irrelevant. Second, this relativizing of the objective, metaphysical truth claims of religion seems to be rooted in Jung's belief that the inner archetypal experience is the essential core of religion. Some would see this as an overemphasis on the personal and experiential aspect of religion at the expense of the ethical, social, and communal.

Is it Unscientific?

This question arises primarily from the fact that Jung's theoretical formulations were derived, as we have seen, less from scientific testing or clinical observation, and more from the critical encounter with the contents of his own unconscious during the years 1913 to 1917. This has led to the charge that he was more of a mystic than a scientist. Were Jung's psychological ideas scientific conclusions or mystical vision?

Colin Wilson believes that Jung was an artist, visionary, and romantic passing as a scientist and that his greatness lies not in scientific achievement—as that term is generally used—but in being the "guru of the Western world."

As a romantic, he was "possessed by a sense of the boundless mystery of the universe," a mystery which is traditionally expressed in myth. His psychological theory, therefore, is fashioned out of the need to find some connection between myth and depth psychology. Hence the theoretical construct of the collective unconscious, which finds conscious expression in myth and symbol. In contrast to Freud who saw the unconscious as having no positive function, Jung saw the unconscious as "full of mysterious, life-giving forces." This is the view, in Wilson's opinion, of a "romantic optimist" as distinct from that of Freud, the "realist pessimist."[111] It is also a fundamentally religious point of view since the unconscious, due to its archetypal structure, is seen as healing and saving.

In trying to answer the question "Was C.G. Jung a mystic?" Aniela Jaffe describes the mystical experience as an "immediate experience of the numinous" or "the perceiving of an originally hidden transcendent reality, the 'other side.'" This type of experience, she acknowledges, "plays a central role in Jung's approach to analytical psychology," which is based on "the consideration of images and contents which enter into consciousness from the hidden background of the psyche, the collective unconscious." Jung's psychology, then, not only is an inquiry into but also is derived from Jung's own experience of a kind of archetypal experience of the unconscious which may be called mystical in the sense that it shares with mystical experience the quality of numinosity associated with the direct experience of a superior, transcendent power. In such an experience of something which is incomprehensible but nevertheless effective, there is conveyed "the sense of a *mysterium* that transcends the human and simultaneously encompasses him." It remains, however, an intrapsychic experience—the experience of one's own unconscious depths—and "may not be taken to be objective knowledge about... the metaphysical."[112] On these grounds, Jaffe proposes that Jung was not a mystic in the usual (religious) sense since he acknowledged this "epistemological limitation." Although the autonomy and numinous quality of the archetypes make them, at the level of experience, indistinguishable from that "compelling numinosity" which has traditionally been called God, Jung stops short of naming the ultimate source of archetypal experiences.[113]

But if Jung was not a mystic in the usual sense, neither was he a scientist in the usual sense. The archetypal experience represents a direct, intuitive, experiential kind of knowledge which put Jung at odds with both the scientific rationalism and the religious dogmatism of his age. As Homans has pointed out, Jung was caught between "the old world, organized by religion, and the new world, organized by modernity or secularity."[114] Religion here refers to traditional orthodox Christianity and "modernity" includes the spirit of scientific rationalism. Jung's psychological thinking, as we have seen, served as a bridge which enabled him to relate to both worlds. It was neither wholly experimental or wholly religious in the traditional sense and offered a critique of both. It was, in a word, "psychological." As such, it was a way of thinking which was distinct from traditional religious thinking, with its emphasis on the objective truth of its dogmas and traditional scientific thinking, with its emphasis on the observation of objective data. Jung's new way of thinking—introspective and intuitive—led to a kind of experiential knowledge which provided a critical perspective on both science and religion.

We may wonder, nevertheless, whether Jung was fully appreciative of this. His writings abound in criticism of both religious dogmatism and scientific rationalism. Nevertheless, when he directly addresses the epistemological question, he seems to muddy the waters by insisting on being regarded as a scientist in the strictly "empirical" sense. Jung regards himself as an empiricist because he deals, not with ultimate, transcendent realities, but with human experiences, and these psychological experiences he regards as objective and factual. To most of his readers, however, it may not be so easy to regard such psychological realities and experiences as "empirical data" as that phrase is generally used. While Jung is clear on the need for a deeper understanding of religion, it is unfortunate that he is not as explicit as, for instance, Abraham Maslow on the need to expand the horizons of science. Maslow, who seems curiously unaware of Jung's work, is nevertheless preoccupied, in much of his writing, with the same problem—the need to go beyond the limitations of scientific rationalism, or what Maslow calls a "narrowly conceived" science. However their theoretical formulations may differ, he is one with Jung in calling for a greater openness to those intuitive experiential sources of knowledge which are excluded from a science that deals with empirical facts to the exclusion of values. This same appeal runs through Jung's writings side by side with his claims to be an "empirical" scientist. In this context, David Wulff suggests that, more than theoretical concepts, Jung was intent on communicating "an attitude and a challenge." This refers to an attitude of openness to "the nonrational and the mysterious, to what lies beyond the logic of the philosopher and the instruments of the scientist" and a recognition of "the powers that lie outside our comprehension and control."[115]

Is It Prejudiced?

In the case of Freud, the question of bias or prejudice revolves around his overt atheism. Are his negative conclusions about religion the result of an atheism which is maintained on other grounds? And is that atheism, in turn, the consequence of his scientific rationalism and/or his negative or ambivalent personal experiences of religion? Of any theorist it must be asked what kind of preformed emotional attitudes inform his or her theoretical formulations. Do we find in Jung anything corresponding to Freud's ambivalence in regard to religion? In this regard we may note that while Jung rejected religion in its traditional orthodox expression, particularly its dogmatism and the faith it demanded, he was nevertheless attracted to religion in its mystical, experiential expression. It was this kind of religious expression he found in Gnosticism and alchemy and hence viewed them as historical movements which compensated for the one-sidedness of orthodox Christianity—its "dark side"—and as historical links to his own psychology of the unconscious. For Jung, religion was a matter of direct, personal, inner experience rather than faith in traditional dogmas.

This rejection of religion in the traditional, orthodox sense, coexists in Jung's thought with an affirmation of its mythical/symbolic value by reason of the correlation of its symbol system with the archetypal structure of the psyche. We have seen that, even as a child, be experienced a tension between his own inner experience of God and the religious tradition in which he was being raised. Both Freud and Jung reject a certain dogmatic and legalistic type of religion, which they identify as traditional and orthodox. Freud, on the premise that this is the only form of religion, rejects it on scientific-rational grounds and opts for an "unrepentant" atheism. Jung rejects it as an obstacle to authentic, archetypal, religious experience. If it is legitimate to ask whether Freud's view of religion is prejudiced in favor of his scientific-rational world-view, it may also be legitimate to ask whether Jung's view of religion is prejudiced in favor of his "romantic" worldview. In comparing Freud and Jung, Erich Fromm suggests that Freud, the rationalist, arrived at an understanding of the unconscious which "was based on his wish to control and subdue it," while Jung, the romantic antirationalist, saw the nonrational unconscious as "the deepest source of wisdom." He concludes: "Jung's interest in the unconscious was the admiring one of the romantic; Freud's the critical one of the rationalist."[116] This is reflected in their differing views of religion, for both locate the human source of religion in the unconscious. For Freud, religion is the result of the neurosis-producing projection of unconscious repressed contents which must be brought to the light of conscious, rational reevaluation. For Jung, religious "contents" represent the projection of unconscious archetypes which are sources of life and wisdom. As such, they represent a type of inner experience which is life-giving and healing.

This differing view of the unconscious clearly leads Jung to a more positive view of religion than that of Freud. It means, further, that his critique of traditional, orthodox religion proceeds not from a position of atheism as with Freud, but from a perception of the meaning of authentic religious experience. While Freud rejects religion as such, Jung rejects what he perceives to be a distortion of authentic religion. If Stein's assessment is correct, Jung wanted to heal the religion of his father; Freud wanted to replace it with science. The question remains: Does Jung's admittedly more positive view of religion and religious experience devalue some aspects of traditional, orthodox religion? Does its one-sided emphasis on the personal, mystical, experiential dimension of religion give it an elitist quality which excludes those masses of religious believers whose God is more without than within and whose religion is more ethical than mystical and more communal than individual? This bring us to our final question.

Is It One-sided?

We have already touched upon some aspects of the alleged one-sidedness of Jung's theory of religion: that it emphasizes the personal dimension of religion at the expense of the communal, the mystical at the expense of the ethical, the inner, experiential meaning of religion at the expense of objective meaning, and an elitist understanding of religion at the expense of an egalitarian one. It remains to discuss briefly the types of one-sidedness which are perceived in Jungian theory by that development of Jung's analytical psychology described as "archetypal" psychology and by the feminist critique of Jungian theory.

Archetypal Psychology. According to James Hillman, the preeminent exponent of archetypal psychology, the perceived one-sidedness of Jungian theory is its "monotheism." This theological term serves as a model for the ideal of unity and wholeness which characterizes Jung's analytical psychology. In Jung's archetypal theory, the various archetypes are subsumed under the supra-ordinate authority of the self archetype and our experience of them is perceived as stages in the process of individuation, the goal of which is the realization of the self in which all opposites are harmonized and unified. In other words, a correlation exists between the psychological ideal of integration, wholeness and unity as the highest expression of psychological health, and the theological ideal of monotheism as the highest expression of religion. Hillman challenges the notion of the superiority of monotheism, attributing it to the "psychological bias of the historians of religion who put monotheism on top in the name of integration."[117] He argues that Jung's monotheistic model of the psyche with its notion of a superior, unifying self, attained through the progressive stages of individuation, reflects this theological attitude which sees polytheism as inferior to and a preliminary stage to monotheism. In this view, the duality of the anima/animus experience and the multiplicity of archetypal experiences are preliminary to the unifying and integrating experience of the self. He concludes: "As the Self seems a further integration than anima/animus, so seems monotheism superior to polytheism."[118]

Over against this monotheistic view, Hillman proposes a "polytheistic" model of the psyche which, he believes, does justice to the multiplicity of human experiences. Jung's concept of a supra-ordinate, unifying self is seen as a reflection of a theological bias in favor of monotheism and as accounting for the appeal of Jungian theory among the Christian community. If, however, it is legitimate to question the theological superiority of monotheism, "so the superiority of monotheistic models for the self should as well be questioned."[119] Hillman wants a model of the psyche which does justice to its "inherent polytheism" and to the "innate diversity" of human existence. Archetypal psychology, then, derives its name from its emphasis on the multiplicity of the archetypes and complexes which constitute the psyche without assigning a supra-ordinate or unifying role to any one. Hillman argues that such a view of the psyche is rooted in Jungian theory and quotes Jung's words, "The anima/animus stage is correlated with polytheism, the self with monotheism."[120] The preeminence and centering role of the self archetype is seen as an expression of Jung's "theological temperament." As this unifying archetype is given expression, in Jungian theory, in the image of a monotheistic God whose archetype is indistinguishable from that of the self, so, in archetypal psychology, the multiplicity of archetypes is given expression in "the traditional language of our civilization, i.e., classical mythology" which provides "a divine background of personages and powers for each complex."[121]

In this view of the psyche, the archetypal patterns of existence coexist in all their multiplicity and diversity and find expression in the language of myth, most preeminently in the stories of the Greek gods and goddesses. The ideal is no longer to integrate all these "possibilities of existence" into a unified pattern through the agency of one centering archetype but to allow each one its proper expression within the diversity which constitutes human existence, "since in polytheism the possibilities of existence are not jealous to the point of excluding each other."[122] This bringing to expression of various archetypal possibilities through identification with mythical motifs is what Hillman calls "soul-making," and archetypal psychology is thus a "psychology of soul." Soul is not given a precise definition, but at least two aspects are stressed. First, the soul represents the multiplicity and diversity of archetypes and hence is "polytheistic." "If a psychology," Hillman contends, "wants to represent faithfully the soul's actual diversity, then it may not beg the question from the beginning by insisting, with monotheistic prejudgment, upon unity of personality. The idea of unity is, after all, only one of many archetypal perspectives."[123] Second, the soul is perceived as the locus of imaginative life. "To live psychologically," Hillman states, "means to imagine things; to be in touch with soul means to live in sensuous connection with fantasy."[124] Archetypes are seen as giving structure to our fantasy images by directing them along mythical patterns.

Myth then becomes the imaginative, metaphorical language of the soul. For this reason, Hillman proposes that we have a natural tendency to personalize the archetypes for "these basic structures are always imagined to be partial personalities "and one's life is the result of these components of personality "playing through their archetypal scenes" so that "psychodynamics becomes psychodramatics."[125] Classical mythology provides one avenue of personifying personality components for "our descriptions of the archetypes and the classical descriptions of the Gods, heroes and daemons have to be analogous."[126] Since such archetypal images are the language of the soul, archetypal psychology resists the temptation to translate the image or the god into the rational language of either theology or science, which "depersonifies" the language of imagination thus rendering it psychologically ineffective.

Mythical, poetic language, on the other hand, personifies rational concepts, as when, for instance, we speak of being "stalked" by terror, "hounded" by anxiety, or "enslaved" by love. We assimilate archetypes, therefore, by relating to them in this personified form. Archetypal psychology desires "to save the phenomena of the imaginal psyche" by focusing on the image itself and relating it to mythical motifs. In this way it aims to give full expression to the many "partial personalities" that make up one's psychic totality and to avoid reducing them to various "roles" played by one unified personality, which may well experience such roles as being in fundamental conflict. In this view, such conflict is the result of pursuing the false goal of unity, order, and hierarchy and refusing to accept the diversity, multiplicity, and complexity of the psyche. As Thomas Moore remarks, the soul's complexities "are not to be simply ironed out, because they are the stuff of human complexity." In a polytheistic view of the psyche, "conflicts no longer seem so decisive."[127]

Both Jungian theory and archetypal psychology recognize the fundamentally religious nature of the psyche in its archetypal structure. While Jung recognizes the multiplicity and diversity of this structure, he sees it as corresponding to a polytheistic stage of human cultural development while the concept of a centering, integrating archetype of the self corresponds to the stage of monotheism. Hillman, however, sees this monotheistic model as responsible for "the repression of a psychological diversity that then appears as psychopathology."[128] In other words, when order, hierarchy, integration, and unity are the criteria of psychological health, then diversity and multiplicity are experienced as fragmentation and dissociation. In Jungian theory there is an implicit critique of traditional, orthodox, monotheistic religion, which is seen as running counter to the psyche's natural, archetypal experience of religion. In Hillman's archetypal psychology there is an implicit critique of monotheistic religion as such which is seen as running counter to the psyche's "inherent multiplicity." At the same time, we may note in both theorists an affirmation, as the natural ground of religion, of the validity of an imaginative area of human experience which bears some analogy to Winnicott's notion of religion as a "transitional phenomenon" of an imaginative world of experience which occupies an intermediate space between the worlds of pure subjectivity and objective, factual reality.

Feminist Critique. In a recent radio interview, a father complained about the sexual stereotyping which marked his little girl's "graduation" from kindergarten. Awards were presented, it appears, with all the awards for intelligence and achievement going to the boys while the girls were rewarded for charm and social skills. It was agreed that the implicit message to these little girls was that "their minds didn't count." No one seemed concerned about the possible negative message being delivered to the boys, namely, that their capacity for being friendly, cooperative, and easy to get along with didn't matter; all that mattered was brainpower and achievement. Sexual stereotyping is a two-way street. The fact, however, that we tend to see, in this instance, the little girls as more victimized may be an indication of that very "patriarchal" bias which is the object of feminist criticism. Do we value the so-called "masculine" virtues of rationality, assertiveness, and achievement more highly than the "feminine" virtues of relatedness, receptivity, and feeling? And if so, how does one redress the balance? By insisting that "the feminine" includes those qualities traditionally ascribed to men, or by rediscovering the value of those feminine qualities which patriarchy has devalued? This question may be one way of categorizing feminist responses to Jungian theory. One type of feminist response is to see in Jung's theory of sexual complementarity a validation of the feminine principle and of women and, therefore, a critique of the one-sidedness of patriarchy. Others see Jung's good intentions as flawed by his own androcentric attitudes and his treatment of the feminine principle as reinforcing a patriarchal view of women as passive and submissive.

Ann B. Ulanov may be taken as exemplifying the first type of response. What is positive for Ulanov in Jung's approach is the fact that it "pays serious attention to the feminine as an original psychic mode of being rather than as a deficient masculinity."[129] She lists the distinctive features of Jung's approach to the feminine as the fact that the feminine is not confined to females since the male personality has a contrasexual, feminine side; his description of the feminine in the language of symbol and myth; and his theory that personal wholeness involves the assimilation of one's contrasexual side.[130] In Jungian theory the feminine is an archetypal aspect of the human psyche and, as such, represents one pole of the masculine-feminine polarity. Ulanov accepts the masculine and feminine principles—which Jung named logos and eros respectively—as inherent structures of the psyche. Logos, as characterizing the masculine consciousness, represents rationality, logic, intellect, achievement, assertiveness, and objective interest, that is, interest in nonpersonal truth. Its unconscious, contrasexual complement is the anima, the feminine dimension of the masculine psyche. Eros, the symbol of feminine consciousness, represents relatedness, feeling, receptivity, passivity, and an interest in personal rather than impersonal truth. Its contrasexual counterpart in the unconscious is the animus, the masculine dimension of the feminine psyche.

Ulanov finds value in this aspect of Jungian theory on at least three scores. First, it represents a validation of the feminine, for receptivity, feeling, and passivity are regarded as qualities badly needed by a society dominated by scientific rationalism. Second, the complementarity of logos and eros implies that the masculine and feminine principles are components of each psyche, and either principle may theoretically dominate the consciousness of either men or women and complement each other. This complementarity suggests to some that women need not become "masculine" in order to compete with men. Finally, Ulanov finds in the receptivity and passivity the essence of the religious attitude. Demaris Wehr notes that, for Jung, receptivity "is the sine qua non of religious experience,"[131] and further notes two differing reactions to this. Some feminists feel that this is another instance of stereotyping women and depriving them of being agents in their own right. Others feel that receptivity is a quality that needs to be affirmed.

Ulanov is representative of this latter position. The feminine ego, she writes, is inclined "to let things happen as they will," and achieves transformation largely through passivity and surrender. A woman, she argues, "orients herself to the changes which happen to her rather than initiating those changes." When we fail to see the connection between such passivity and spiritual transformation, then we regard women as "seeming to have no independent will or judgment, and seeming always to be seeking pain."[132] Ulanov's view seems to be consistent with Jung's understanding of spiritual transformation as demanding a kind of "surrender" to a "higher power" (the unconscious) and therefore with his view of the "religious" function of the psyche. Jung's critique of the Christian God-image as lacking completeness because of the lack of—among other things—a feminine component also seems to support the view of Jung as affirming the value of the feminine.

Other feminists thinkers do not find in Jungian theory such an unqualified validation of the feminine and have questioned its value for women's authentic self-understanding. The question they have raised might be stated as follows: *Do Jung's androcentric attitudes distort his discussion of women, the feminine, anima, and animus?* Jung promises us that when he speaks of God he is speaking of the archetypal God-image, but seems, on many occasions, not to keep his promise. In the same way, he speaks of eros and logos as archetypal principles, but speaks of them, at times, in such a way as to appear to be discussing the differences between men and women. Andrew Samuels remarks: "Because Jung never specifically made the distinction, he was often unaware that at times he was speaking of sex and sex differences (male and female) and at other times of gender differences (masculine and feminine)."[133] In the view of some feminist thinkers, this confusion allows Jung's own patriarchal and androcentric views of women to creep into his descriptions of the feminine. The result appears to be an unequal evaluation of anima and animus. "There is no doubt," writes Samuels, "that Jung saw the anima as a more pleasant figure than the animus." And although he theoretically ascribed eros and logs to both men and women"he seemed surprised and concerned that women should think rather than feel, work rather than mother—and even, or so it has been rumoured, wear trousers rather than skirts."[134]

In reference to this "inequity of the anima-animus model," Naomi Goldenberg remarks: "It is true that Jung genuinely values woman for her remarkable and all too often overlooked Eros, but it is equally true that he confines her to this sphere."[135] This refers to the fact that, while Jung speaks so positively of the benefits of integrating the anima into the masculine consciousness, the irruptions of the animus into the feminine consciousness seem to be described in almost exclusively negative terms, that is, as exaggerated assertiveness, argumentativeness, irrational opinions, and so forth. It is as if

Jung wants men to become more feminine but women to remain feminine. The result, as Goldenberg notes, is that women are thought of as handicapped in all "Logos arenas," which militates against change in the social sphere.

In the same vein, Jung is charged with locating the feminine, and therefore women's self-understanding, in the unchanging archetypal structure of the psyche rather than in changing social and cultural patterns. Wehr, for instance, charges that Jung derives his understanding of the feminine from the masculine anima and, in so doing, ignores the "context of patriarchy's influence on men's (including Jung's) anima images and women's sense of self," including the notion that "woman's identity is found in the service of a man."[136] The result is that the feminine as a conscious model of behavior is seen as "cosmic," symbolic, and archetypal to the exclusion of social factors. Similarly, while Jung can describe the male anima from his own experience, his treatment of the animus remains "a step removed from women's lived experience."[137] Consequently, descriptions of the negative animus predominate, which reinforce women's "internalized oppression." Jung's sometimes blistering descriptions of the "animus-possessed" woman portray someone incapable of a healthy integration of her contrasexual side. All this seems to raise a question about Jung's theory of religion. If the goal of the religious quest is the same as that of the individuation process—a kind of "rebirth" which is synonymous with wholeness or selfhood—is that quest beneficial and meaningful only to men? In spite of Jung's efforts to the contrary, is his view of religion "patriarchal"?

Jung is reported to have said that he did not want anyone to become a Jungian. His theory, he maintained, was not a fixed doctrine but views presented for discussion. We can only surmise that he would regard this ongoing critique and revision of his work as a positive development.

Suggested Readings

CLIFT, WALLACE, *Jung and Christianity: The Challenge of Reconciliation* (New York: Crossroad, 1982).

DOURLEY, JOHN, *The Illness That We Are; A Jungian Critique of Christianity* (Toronto: Inner City Books, 1984).

HALL CALVIN S. and NORDBY, VERNON J., *A Primer of Jungian Psychology* (New York: New American Library, 1973).

HANNA, CHARLES, *The Face of the Deep: The Religious Ideas of C.G. Jung* (Philadelphia: Westminster, 1967).

HANNAH, BARBARA, *Jung: His Life and Work* (New York: C.P. Putnam's Sons, 1976).

HOMANS, PETER, *Jung in Context: Modernity and the Making of a Psychology* (Chicago: University of Chicago Press, 1979).

JAFFE, ANIELA, *Was C.G. Jung a Mystic? And Other Essays* (Einsiedeln, Switzerland: Daimon, 1989).

JUNG, C.G., *Memories, Dreams, Reflections* (New York: Random House, 1961).

JUNG, C.G., *Modern Man in Search of a Soul* (New York: Harcourt, Brace and World, 1933).

JUNG, C.G., *Psyche and Symbol: A Selection from the Writings of C.G. Jung*, ed. by Violet S. de Laszlo (Garden City, N.Y.: Doubleday, 1958).

JUNG, C.G., *Psychology and Religion* (New Haven: Yale University Press, 1938).

STEIN, MURRAY, *Jung's Treatment of Christianity* (Wilmette, Ill.: Chiron, 1986).

STORR, ANTHONY (ED.), *The Essential Jung* (Princeton, N.J: Princeton University Press, 1983).

WEHR, DEMARIS, *Jung and Feminism: Liberating Archetypes* (Boston: Beacon Press, 1987).

WHITE, VICTOR O.P., *God and the Unconscious* (London: Fontana Books, 1960).

WILSON, COLIN, *C.G. Jung: Lord of the Underworld* (Wellingborough, England: Aquarian Press, 1984).

Notes

1. Barbara Hannah, *Jung: His Life and Work* (New York: C.P. Putnam's Sons, 1976), p. 124.
2. C.G. Jung, *Memories, Dreams, Reflections* (New York: Random House, 1961), p. 43.
3. *Ibid.*, p. 188.
4. *Ibid.*, p. 199.
5. Peter Homans, *Jung in Context: Modernity and the Making of a Psychology* (Chicago: University of Chicago Press, 1979), p. 83.
6. *Ibid.*, p. 157.
7. C.G. Jung, *Memories, Dreams, Reflections*, pp. 3, 5.
8. *Ibid.*, p. 8.
9. *Ibid.*, p. 13.
10. *Ibid.*, pp. 33-34.
11. *Ibid.*, p. 35.
12. *Ibid.*, p. 45.
13. *Ibid.*, pp. 19-23.
14. *Ibid.*, p. 39.
15. *Ibid.*, p. 40.
16. *Ibid.*, p. 48.
17. *Ibid.*, p. 92.
18. *Ibid.*, pp. 48, 90-91.
19. *Ibid.*, p. 93.
20. *Ibid.*, p. 107.
21. *Ibid.*, pp. 108-109.
22. Colin Wilson, *C.G. Jung: Lord of the Underworld* (Wellingborough, England: Aquarian Press, 1984), p. 76.
23. C.G. Jung, *Memories, Dreams, Reflections*, p. 148.
24. See Ludwig Binswanger, *Sigmund Freud: Reminiscences of a Friendship* (New York: Grune and Stratton, 1959), p. 9.

25. N.G. Nole (ed.), *James Jackson Putnam and Psychoanalysis: Letters Between Putnam and Sigmund Freud, Ernest Jones, William James, Sandor Ferenczi and Morton Price* (Cambridge: Harvard University Press, 1971), p. 189.
26. Colin Wilson, *C.G. Jung: Lord of the Underworld*, p. 71.
27. C.G. Jung, *Memories, Dreams, Reflections*, p. 167.
28. *Ibid.*, pp. 163, 164.
29. *Ibid.*, p. 167.
30. Colin Wilson, *C.G. Jung: Lord of the Underworld*, p. 121.
31. *Ibid.*, p. 9.
32. C.G. Jung, *Memories, Dreams, Reflections*, pp.205, 209.
33. *Ibid.*, p. 209.
34. Colin Wilson, *C.G. Jung: Lord of the Underworld*, p. 8.
35. *Ibid.*, p. 136.
36. C.G. Jung, *Memories, Dreams, Reflections*, p. 165.
37. Aniela Jaffe, *Was C.G. Jung a Mystic? And other Essays* (Einsiedeln, Switzerland: Daimon, 1989), p. 102.
38. Gordon Allport, *Becoming: Basic Considerations for a Psychology of Personality* (New Haven: Yale University Press, 1955).
39. C.G. Jung, "Psychology and Religion", *Collected Works of C.G. Jung* (Bollingen Series XX), 20 volumes, translated by R.F.C. Hull (Princeton, NJ: Princeton University Press, 1953-1979) Vol. 11, paragraph 142. (Referred to in all subsequent references as *C.W.X:Y*, where X is the volume and Y is the paragraph number.)
40. C.G. Jung, "The Structure of the Psyche," *C.W.8:342.*
41. *Ibid.,8:321.*
42. C.G. Jung, *Memories, Dreams, Reflections*, p. 3.
43. *Ibid.*, p.144.
44. C.G. Jung, "The Structure of the Psyche," *C.W.8:342.*
45. C.G. Jung, "Two Essays in Analytical Psychology," *C.W.7:306.*
46. *Ibid.* 7:307.
47. *Ibid.*, 7:306.
48. C.G. Jung, *Memories, Dreams, Reflections*, p. 91.
49. Frieda Fordham, *An Introduction to Jung's Psychology* (Harmondsworth, England: Penguin Books, 1966), p.77.
50. C.G. Jung, "On the Psychology of the Unconscious," *C.W.7:103.*
51. C.G. Jung, "Psychological Types," *C.W.6:884 & 805.*
52. C.G. Jung, "Aion," *C.W.9(2):283n.*
53. C.G. Jung, "Psychological Types," *C.W.6:71.*
54. *Ibid.*, 6:75 & 76.
55. C.G. Jung, "The Role of the Unconscious," *C.W.10:20.*
56. C.G. Jung, "Aion," *C.W.9(2):18.*
57. C.G. Jung, "The Role of the Unconscious," *C.W.10:39.*
58. C.G. Jung, "The Structure of the Psyche," *C.W.8:316.*
59. C.G. Jung, "The Archetypes and the Collective Unconscious," *C.W.9(1):490.*
60. C.G. Jung, "Psychology and Religion," *C.W.11:8.*
61. Edward Edinger, *The Christian Archetype: A Jungian Commentary on the Life of Christ* (Toronto: Inner City Books, 1978), p. 112.
62. Charles Hanna, *The Face of the Deep: The Religious Ideas of C.G. Jung* (Philadelphia: Westminster, 1967), p. 85.
63. David Cox, *Jung and St. Paul* (London: Longmans Green and Co., 1959).
64. C.G. Jung, "Psychology and Religion," *C.W.11:20.*
65. *Ibid.*, 11:6.
66. *Ibid.*, 11:10.

67. C.G. Jung, "The Undiscovered Self," *C.W.*10:507.
68. Victor White O.P., *God and the Unconscious* (London: Fontana Books, 1960), p. 77.
69. C.G. Jung, "Symbols of Transformation," *C.W.*5:332.
70. *Ibid.*
71. *Ibid.*, 5:351.
72. C.G. Jung, "Aion," *C.W.*9(2):276.
73. *Ibid.*, 9(2):271.
74. C.G. Jung, "Symbols and the Interpretation of Dreams," *C.W.*18:582.
75. Aniela Jaffe, *The Myth of Meaning* (New York: Penguin Books, 1975), p. 113.
76. C.G. Jung, "The Undiscovered Self," *C.W.*10:565.
77. C.G. Jung, "Psychology and Alchemy," *C.W.*12:20.
78. C.G. Jung, "Spirit and Life," *C.W.*8:625.
79. C.G. Jung, *Memories, Dreams, Reflections*, pp. 52-53.
80. C.G. Jung, "A Psychological Approach to the Dogma of the Trinity," *C.W.*11:226.
81. *Ibid.*, 11:285.
82. *Ibid.*, 11:287.
83. *Ibid.*, 11:288.
84. *Ibid.*, 11:238.
85. C.G. Jung, "Answer to Job," *C.W.*11:574.
86. *Ibid.*, 11:600.
87. C.G. Jung, "A Psychological Approach to the Dogma of the Trinity," *C.W.*11:270.
88. C.G. Jung, "Answer to Job," *C.W.*11:620.
89. *Ibid.*, 11:752.
90. *Ibid.*, 11:627.
91. Aniela Jaffe, *Was C.G. Jung a Mystic?*, p.70. The term was first used in the text of an honorary doctorate awarded to Jung in 1955 by the Federal Institute of Technology in Zurich.
92. C.G. Jung, "A Psychological Approach to the Dogma of the Trinity," *C.W.*11:260.
93. C.G. Jung, "Aion," *C.W.*9(2):79.
94. C.G. Jung, "A Psychological Approach to the Dogma of the Trinity," *C.W.*11:265.
95. C.G. Jung, "Transformation Symbolism in the Mass," *C.W.*11.
96. C.G.Jung, "Psychological Commentary on 'The Tibetan Book of the Great Liberation'," *C.W.*11:768.
97. *Ibid.*,11:772.
98. *Ibid.*,11:775.
99. C.G.Jung, "Yoga and the West," *C.W.*11:867.
100. C.G.Jung, "The Psychology of Eastern Meditation," *C.W.*11:940.
101. C.G.Jung, "Psychological Commentary on 'The Tibetan Book of the Great Liberation,'" *C.W.*11:803.
102. *Ibid.*, 11:855.
103. *Ibid.*, 11:857.
104. C.G.Jung, "Foreword to Suzuki's 'Introduction to Zen Buddhism'," *C.W.*11:904.
105. C.G.Jung, "The Holy Men of India," *C.W.* 11:958.
106. C.G.Jung, "Foreword to the 'I Ching,'" *C.W.* 11:966.
107. *Ibid.*,11:972.
108. Murray Stein, *Jung's Treatment of Christianity* (Wilmette, Ill.:Chiron, 1986), p.108.
109. Erich Fromm, *Psychoanalysis and Religion* (New Haven: Yale University Press, 1950), p. 20.
110. Edward Glover, *Freud or Jung?* (Cleveland: World Publishing Co., 1956), p.163.
111. Colin Wilson, *C.G. Jung: Lord of the Underworld*, pp. 75-79.
112. Aniela Jaffe, *Was C.G. Jung a Mystic?* pp. 1-5.
113. *Ibid.*, p. 27.

114. Peter Homans, *Jung in Context*, p. 157.
115. David M. Wulff, *Psychology of Religion: Classic and Contemporary Views* (New York: John Wiley and Sons, 1991), p. 465.
116. Erich Fromm, *Sigmund Freud's Mission* (New York: Harper, 1959), pp.53-54.
117. James Hillman, "Psychology: Monotheistic or Polytheistic," *Spring*, 1971, p.195.
118. *Ibid.*
119. *Ibid.*, p. 196.
120. C.G. Jung, "Aion," *C.W.*9(2):427.
121. James Hillman, "Psychology: Monotheistic or Polytheistic," p. 197.
122. *Ibid.*, p. 201.
123. James Hillman, *Re-visioning Psychology* (New York: Harper and Row, 1975), p.xiv.
124. *Ibid.*, p. 23.
125. *Ibid.*, p. 22.
126. *Ibid.*, p. 36.
127. Thomas Moore (ed.), *A Blue Fire: Selected Writings by James Hillman* (New York: Harper and Row, 1989), p. 38.
128. James Hillman, *Archetypal Psychology: A Brief Account* (Dallas: Spring Publications, 1985), p. 33.
129. Ann B. Ulanov, *The Feminine in Jungian Psychology and Christian Theology* (Evanston, IL: Northwestern University Press, 1971), p. 154.
130. *Ibid.*, p. 141.
131. Demaris Wehr, *Jung and Feminism: Liberating Archetypes* (Boston: Beacon Press, 1987), p. 6.
132. Ann B. Ulanov, *The Feminine in Jungian Psychology and Christian Theology*, p.183.
133. Andrew Samuels, *Jung and the Post-Jungians* (London: Routledge and Kegan Paul, 1985), p. 207.
134. *Ibid.*, pp. 214-216.
135. Naomi Goldenberg "A Feminist Critique of Jung," *Signs: Journal of Women in Culture and Society*, vol. 2, no. 2, 1976, p. 445.
136. Demaris Wehr, *Jung and Feminism*, pp. 104-105.
137. *Ibid.*, p.118.

III. WILLIAM JAMES

Religion and Temperament

William James (1842–1910)
Library of Congress.

William James (1842-1910), who was successively a professor of physiology, psychology and philosophy, at Harvard University, believed that one's philosophy was a reflection of one's temperament. Our philosophy, he argued, is not "a technical matter." It is rather "our more or less dumb sense of what life honestly and deeply means."[1] Thus the history of philosophy becomes, to a great extent, a clash of human temperaments. Assuming, for the moment, the truth of James' contention, at least two corollaries would follow from this principle. First, what is said of one's philosophy might also be said of one's religion: It too is, to some extent, a product of one's temperament. We shall see this principle illustrated in James' psychology of religion. Second, it must follow that James' own philosophical and religious convictions are to a large extent a reflection of his own temperament. Temperaments have been subjected to various classifications. In trying to assess the peculiar quality of

James' own psychic temperament—his habitual mode of emotional response to life—it is helpful to consult his own classification of temperaments. In keeping with the notion that one's philosophy is a reflection of one's temperament, James suggests that there are two basic philosophical approaches which reflect two basic temperaments: "the tender-minded" and the "tough-minded." Among the characteristics he attributes to these two types, James mentions that the tender-minded tend to be rationalistic (going by "principles"), monistic (believing in the unity of things), and religious (believing in a principle of unity). The tough minded, on the other hand, tend to be empiricist (relying on "facts"), pluralistic (believing that reality is many rather than one), and irreligious and skeptical.[2]

As a philosopher James was an empiricist and a pluralist. This would seem to identify him as "tough-minded." At the same time he appears to have searched throughout his life for a faith that would sustain him. Hence the term "irreligious" does not seem to apply. In his book *Pragmatism* he speaks of the ideal of combining the tough-minded "scientific loyalty to facts" with the tender-minded religious sensibilities and commitment to human values. In practice however, he complains, we find scientific tough-mindedness linked with "inhumanism and irreligion" and tender-mindedness with a kind of religious monistic philosophy which "keeps out of all definite touch with concrete facts and joys and sorrows."[3] While the tough-minded scientist may lose touch with human and religious values, the abstract philosophy of the tender-minded religionist may in fact lose touch with the concrete realities of everyday life.

For the pluralist, those concrete realities are diverse and frequently in conflict. Thus, for example, good and evil are in conflict and not reconciled by any unifying principle. Reality is many (plural) and evil is alien to good, not part of the same reality. Monism, on the other hand, ascribes some kind of meaning or purpose to life's negative experiences so that, together with the good, they contribute to some unified, comprehensive system of meaning. Such a philosophy appeals to the type of temperament which feels the need for comfort and reassurance while pluralism, with its emphasis on the conflict of good and evil as alien realities and, therefore, on the imperfection and incompleteness of the world, appeals to that temperament which responds to the challenge of working toward the world's perfection. James, though a philosophical pluralist, was sympathetic toward monism because he recognized its religious value in offering comfort and reassurance. In the *Varieties of Religious Experience* James describes the religious experience which emphasizes comfort, assurance, and saving grace as (somewhat misleadingly) the religion of the "sick soul." "Healthy-minded" religion, on the other hand, with its emphasis on active moral effort toward the betterment of the world—what James called the "strenuous life"—was more compatible with the tough-minded, pluralistic outlook.

The philosophical contrast, then, between pluralism and monism is paralleled by the religious contrast between the "healthy-minded" and the "sick soul." And both contrasts, James would argue, are rooted in differences of temperament. J.S. Bixler has proposed that if James experienced the conflict of these contrasting philosophical and religious tendencies to an unusually high degree it was because of the personal conflict within himself of his own active and passive tendencies. Throughout his life James had difficulty reconciling and harmonizing his active "will to survive, to believe and to achieve" with "the more passive desire for assurance, stability and comfort."[4] Our nature, Bixler argues, demands both active effort and the assurance of safety. If we fail to integrate and harmonize these two tendencies, then we shall experience them—as James did—as "alternating moods". We have seen that James, though a philosophical pluralist, was sympathetic toward monism because of its religious value. This was so, in part, because he frequently experienced the helplessness and despair of the "sick soul" in need of assurance and redemption. James was alternately active and passive, pluralistic and monistic, healthy-minded and sick-minded. One is tempted to add, manic and depressive.

Pluralism along with the kind of healthy-minded religion and strenuous moral effort it inspired was, for James, the human ideal. But in his own personality the healthy-minded, strenuous mood alternated with feelings of helplessness, depression, and at times despair. Hence his recognition of the need for divine help and assurance, for a God who is comforter and savior as well as a challenge to moral effort, and therefore of the value of sick-soul religion. In the *Varieties* this type of religion is in fact given a higher value than the kind of shallow healthy-mindedness that ignores evil and the dark side of life. It could be argued that it was this inner conflict and turmoil which in large measure led James to an appreciation not only of the "varieties" of religious experience, but also of the connection between temperament and philosophical and religious convictions. And herein lie what are perhaps his two major insights and contributions to the psychological study of religion: the primacy of "experience" in religious life and the typology or "varieties" of religious experience. His work enjoys the most enduring significance of any of the pioneer psychologists of religion who made up what might be called the "American School" at the turn of the twentieth century.

Life

It has been frequently remarked that William James was a philosopher who wrote like a novelist while his brother Henry was a novelist who wrote like a philosopher. However it may have manifested itself in their writing, it certainly seems true that William was the more temperamental, volatile, and impetuous of the two famous brothers. William was born January 11, 1842, in New York City, the eldest of five children born to Henry James Sr. and Mary Robertson Walsh. William's father, Henry James Sr., was the son of William

James, who had emigrated from Ireland at age 18 and eventually, through a variety of business ventures, became one of the wealthiest men in America. Three aspects of Henry's upbringing were particularly significant for his adult life. First, he was raised in an atmosphere of rigid Calvinist piety and frugality, both of which he eventually rejected (as did his siblings). In adult life he found an alternative to this strict Presbyterianism in the teachings of the Swedish mystic Emanuel Swedenborg. Second, he was injured in a boyhood accident and his right leg had to be amputated above the knee. The accident seems to have turned Henry from an active lover of the outdoors into a more introspective lover of reading. Third, Henry inherited sufficient wealth from his father that it was not necessary for him to earn a living.

All of these circumstances seem to have impacted on the life and personality of his son William. Throughout his life William seemed to have been unable to adopt either the strict Calvinism of his grandfather or the Swedenborgian mysticism of his father. This lack of faith seems to have been the source of much inner turmoil and desperation throughout his life. Moreover, the combination of physical disability and inherited wealth had turned Henry Sr. into something of a dilettante, a professional student, who spent his life studying and writing. Freed from the distractions of a career of his own, he became a "hands on" supervisor of his children's education. William and his brother Henry were both the beneficiaries and the victims of his indecision in this area, being shuttled back and forth across the Atlantic as their father's enthusiasm alternated between American and European schools. As schoolboys William and Henry Jr. found to their embarrassment that they had no answer when asked by other children what their father did for a living. When they confronted their father with this problem he replied: "Say I'm a philosopher, say I'm a seeker for truth, say I'm a lover of my kind, say I'm an author of books if you like; or best of all, just say I'm a student."[5]

The combination of the example of such an unfocused role model and a disrupted and chaotic school experience seems to have left William with a chronic inability to decide upon a career for himself. This indecision in turn seems to have been one of the roots of the mental and spiritual turmoil expressed in apparently psychosomatic symptoms (backaches, headaches, eyestrain) which began during his university student years and continued off and on throughout his life. His eventual decision to study medicine seems to have functioned as what Erik Erikson would call a "moratorium"—an unconscious marking of time until one can discover one's real purpose in life. In James' case, though he studied medicine and received his M.D. from Harvard in 1869, he never entered medical practice. Though he was sustained in his medical studies by his interest in physiology because of its relation to mental processes, his dissatisfaction with medicine as such was revealed in the restlessness and inner turmoil which afflicted him during his medical studies. The James biographer Gay Wilson Allen remarks: "What he needed, above all else, was a personal faith such as his father had—faith in himself, in some power outside himself, and in a goal growing out of such a faith; but medicine did not provide it."[6]

After completing his studies at the Lawrence Scientific School at Harvard and the Harvard Medical School, James' emotional turmoil and depression reached a critical point. In the year following his graduation from medical school he underwent a traumatic emotional experience. An account of this experience—triggered apparently by the death of his cousin Minny Temple—is reported in Lectures 6 & 7 of the *Varieties* ("The Sick Soul"). It is attributed to a fictitious Frenchman but it is in fact James' own experience. James claims to "translate freely" as follows:

> Whilst in this state of philosophic pessimism and general depression, I went one evening into a dressing-room in the twilight to procure some article that was there; when suddenly there fell upon me without any warning, just as if it came out of the darkness, a horrible fear of my own existence. Simultaneously there arose in my mind the image of an epileptic patient whom I had seen in the asylum, a black haired youth with greenish skin, entirely idiotic, who used to sit all day on one of the benches, or rather shelves against the wall, with his knees drawn up against his chin, and the coarse grey undershirt, which was his only garment, drawn over them enclosing his entire figure. He sat there like a sort of sculptured Egyptian cat or Peruvian mummy, moving nothing but his black eyes and looking absolutely non-human. This image and my fear entered into a species of combination with each other. *That shape am I*, I felt, potentially. Nothing that I possess can defend me against that fate, if the hour for it should strike for me as it struck for him. There was such a horror of him, and such a perception of my own merely momentary discrepancy from him, that it was as if something hitherto solid within my breast gave way entirely, and I became a mass of quivering fear. After this the universe changed for me altogether. I awoke morning after morning with a horrible dread at the pit of my stomach, and with a sense of the insecurity of life that I never knew before, and that I have never felt since. It was like a revelation; and although the immediate feelings passed away, the experience has made me sympathetic with the morbid feelings of others ever since. It gradually faded, but for months I was unable to go out into the dark alone.[7]

This incident in James' life is significant for at least three reasons. In the first place, it takes place in the year following his graduation from medical school and one may, therefore, legitimately speculate that the profound insecurity he felt on this occasion may have had something to do with his dissatisfaction with medicine and anxiety about a life headed in the wrong direction, exacerbated perhaps by his decision in 1861, to reject a promising future in painting in favor of science (perhaps because of his father's objections). Second, this experience bears an uncanny resemblance to an equally traumatic "panic attack" suffered by his father 26 years earlier when William was an infant. Sitting at the dinner table one evening after the rest of the family had left, his feelings of contentment were suddenly interrupted by a similar feeling of fear and terror, which reduced him to a state of "helpless infancy." Like his son, Henry Sr. was left in an ongoing state of "doubt, anxiety and despair." In his case, however, relief from this deep-seated fear and insecurity was found in the teachings of Emanuel Swedenborg. William later referred to these teachings as his father's "bundle of truth." James himself, however, never seems to have found the "bundle of truth" that would give him relief from his emotional and spiritual turmoil. In spite of this—and to come to our third point of significance—James recognized the religious quality of the crisis. Later in the passage quoted, the fictitious subject concludes: "I have always thought that this experience of melancholia of mine had a religious bearing." He further explains that he clung to his sanity only by repeating certain biblical texts. This experience seems to have had much to do not only with his sympathy for "the morbid feelings of others" but also with his recognition of the religious value of monism and the validity of the religion of the sick soul.

The melancholy which James experienced so traumatically on this occasion was to remain beneath the surface of his personality throughout his life and to erupt occasionally in bouts of depression. His public persona—active, outgoing, witty - did not always successfully mask a fragile, insecure ego in need of support and assurance. In 1915 a former student would recall James as a combination of playfulness and sadness. "There was," he wrote, "in spite of his playfulness, a deep sadness about James. You felt that he had just stepped out of this sadness in order to meet you, and was to go back into it the moment you left him."[8] Though he remained a man of alternating moods, two events helped James to get beyond this immediate crisis. The first was his reading of the French philosopher Charles Renouvier. Influenced by Renouvier's definition of free will—"the sustaining of a thought because I choose to when I might have other thoughts"—he wrote in his diary: "My first act of free will shall be to believe in free will."[9] By assuming the truth of free will he would liberate his own creative powers and escape from the prison of his depression.

The other circumstance that helped to restore some equilibrium to James' emotional life was the offer of a teaching position at Harvard. In the spring of 1872 Charles Eliot, president of Harvard and James' former chemistry teacher, offered him the position of instructor in anatomy and physiology, which would begin in January of the following year. The effect of this teaching experience seems to have been to bring him out of his introspective brooding. In March of 1873 his father, in a letter to Henry Jr., reported William as saying to him: "Dear me! What a difference there is between me now and me last spring this time: then so hypochondriacal ... and now feeling my mind so cleared and restored to sanity. It is the difference between death and life."[10]

This sense of renewal of life was clearly the result of doing something he obviously enjoyed and which at the same time gave purpose and direction to his life. This was the beginning of a career at Harvard that was to last until 1907. One can surmise however, that, in the beginning, it was teaching as such that sustained him, since physiology was not his first choice of subject matter. As Allen remarks, James found himself at age 30 as a teacher of physiology "simply because his first offer to teach happened to be in this field."[11]

James' interest in physiology was primarily the question of the relationship of physiological processes to mental processes. It was not long therefore before he moved on to psychology, giving his first course in psychology in 1875 and to philosophy in 1879 for his ultimate interest was in philosophical and moral questions. In the meantime he had married Alice Howe Gibbens in 1878. With Alice, William would raise a family of four sons and one daughter—just as his own father had. In that same year he contracted with the publisher Henry Holt and Company to write a book on psychology for that publisher's "American Science Series." The publisher wanted the book completed within a year. James asked for two years and then took twelve years to complete *Principles of Psychology*, a two-volume work published in 1890. It became a classic in the field; and when, two years later, he published the more concise *Psychology: Briefer Course,* it became, in the words of biographer Ralph Barton Perry, "the most widely used English text in the subject."[12] The combination of a temperament that was easily bored and a physical constitution that was easily fatigued rendered James wary of long-term tasks, as the writing of the *Principles* bears out. It was for this reason also that physiology did not sustain his interest, impatient as he was with the tedium and repetition of laboratory work. Like Freud, who considered his early preoccupation with medicine, the natural sciences, and even psychotherapy as a "detour" on the way to his more fundamental concern with cultural and religious questions, James also would come to the philosophical and religious questions which most fundamentally concerned him by way of physiology and psychology.

In the course of this intellectual journey he published in 1902 *The Varieties of Religious Experience.* Though this work is seen as James' enduring contribution to the psychology of religion, it is sometimes described as a philosophy of religion. There is no doubt that what James says here about God, religion, and morality is informed by his philosophical positions—his pragmatism and pluralism. At the same time it is also an expression of what James called his "radical empiricism," which stressed the value of experiential, intuitive knowing over conceptual or representational knowing. It is this focus on direct religious experience as distinct from religious thought and behavior which makes the *Varieties* a pioneer work in the psychology of religion. This work consists of a series of lectures (the Gifford Lectures) given at the University of Edinburgh in 1901-1902. In the spring of 1900, while preparing the lectures, James wrote to a friend explaining the main point of emphasis in the lectures.

The problem I have set myself is a hard one; first, to defend (against all the prejudices of my "class") "experience" against "philosophy" as being the real backbone of the world's religious life—I mean prayer, guidance and all that sort of thing immediately and privately felt, as against high and noble general views of our destiny and the world's meaning; and second, to make the hearer or reader believe, what I myself invincibly do believe, that, although all the special manifestations of religion may have been absurd (I mean its creed and theories), yet the life of it as a whole is mankind's most important function. A task well-nigh impossible, I fear, and in which I shall fail; but to attempt it is my religious act.[13]

This emphasis on the primacy of experience in religious life is repeated in a letter written in June of 1901 toward the end of the first series of lectures. Here James refers to "the mystical experience of the individual" as "the mother sea and fountain-head of all religions," adding that "all theologies and all ecclesiasticisms are secondary growths superimposed."[14] It should be noted that James prepared and delivered these lectures under considerable duress, still recuperating as he was from straining his heart while hiking in the Adironack Mountains in 1898. This event left him with a chronic heart condition, and in the succeeding years his health was in decline until his death in 1910. Nevertheless, in the final years of his life, he completed two of his most significant works in philosophy: *Pragmatism* (1907) and *A Pluralistic Universe* (1909). In addition, a series of essays which appeared between 1905 and 1907 was published posthumously in 1912 under the title *Essays in Radical Empiricism*. These works represent the mature statement of a set of philosophical ideas, which provides the background for James' psychology of religion. Unlike the other theories we are reviewing, James' psychology of religion is not directly related to a psychological theory of personality. His focus, to be sure, was religious *experience* and, therefore, what he presents can be considered a psychology of religion. At this point in his career, however, he is a philosopher and his ideas are rooted in philosophical premises. These philosophical ideas are the context for understanding his psychology of religion.

Philosophical Context

J.S. Bixler summarizes James' career as follows: "James began his professional life as a physiologist, then turned to psychology asking what possible use there could be in spending all one's time over 'bones.' Later he dropped psychology as decisively as physiology, its interest for him having been superseded by that of philosophy. And the culmination of philosophy for him lay … in the philosophy of religion."[15] Indeed, the underlying concern in all of James' thought seems to have been an understanding of religious phenomena—God, religious experience, morality—and philosophical positions were seemingly embraced for their pragmatic value for human and religious life. Three terms are particularly associated with James as a philosopher: pragmatism, pluralism, and radical empiricism. We shall look briefly at the implication of each of these for his views on religion.

Pragmatism

The James biographer G.W. Allen quotes the words of Heinrich Straumann on pragmatism: "The pragmatic view of life more commonly and also more honestly adopted in the United States than anywhere in the Western World had its firm grip on the majority of Americans long before anyone attempted to describe it in terms of abstract thought."[16] To this it must be added that James was foremost among those who attempted to translate this way of thinking and living into a theory of truth and meaning. What is pragmatism? James describes it as a method of settling metaphysical disputes. It asks the question: "What difference would it practically make to anyone if this notion rather than that notion were true?"[17] If it makes no practical difference, then the alternative ideas mean, in practical terms, the same thing. Thus when two ideas are in apparent conflict—for example, whether the world is one or many or whether the human being is free or determined—the pragmatic method tries to interpret each notion in terms of its practical consequences. Practical consequences here means the impact of an idea on one's concrete existence. An idea, James argued, is a part of our overall experience and it "becomes true" to the extent that it helps us to deal satisfactorily with other parts of our experience. We have seen, for instance, that for James the notion of free will became "true" when he believed in it and acted upon it, for, in doing so, he was able to deal more effectively with his mechancholy and anxiety.

But what makes dealing more effectively with one's psychological problems a desirable goal? Or, to put it more generally—what is the criterion for deciding what constitutes dealing more satisfactorily with our human experiences? Here James reminds us that pragmatism is only a method; it does not propose what results should be looked for. The popular version of pragmatism — what is true is what "works"—leaves open the question "Works toward what end or goal?" Pragmatism does not answer this question. That answer must come from another source. That source will probably be our deepest human convictions, which, James would argue, are rooted in something deeper than reason alone. This is not to say that pragmatism does not offer a theory of truth, but it is a theory in which rational truth is relative to our more absolute convictions about the meaning and purpose of human existence. Such a theory accepts the traditional definition of truth—the agreement of an idea with reality—but reinterprets the term "agreement." Thus truth does not mean an idea's ability accurately to reflect or represent reality but its ability to help us to assimilate and deal with reality more effectively. This is the verification which renders an idea true. As James states: "The truth of an idea is not a stagnant property inherent in it. Truth *happens* to an idea. It *becomes* true, is *made* true by events."[18]

James hoped that this pragmatic view of truth would help to reconcile the religious view of life with the empirical view, which tended to be irreligious. To this end, pragmatism judges religious and theological ideas in the light of their value for concrete life. It does not choose the concrete over the abstract as a matter of principle. Thus, if religious ideas are rejected, it is not simply because they are abstract as opposed to concrete but because of the negative consequences for human life. At the same time, James suggests that pragmatism is more compatible with a pluralistic/healthy-minded religion than with a monistic/sick-soul religion. As already noted, the monistic view of the world as an ultimate unity in which opposites including good and evil are reconciled offers peace and reassurance to the sick soul. The healthy-minded religious person, for whom this ideal of unity is not an assured reality, sees himself as an ally of God in working for the world's betterment and ultimate salvation.

This struggle for a better world and belief in the world's perfectibility is what James calls "meliorism," and it is this melioristic aspect of pluralism which makes it more compatible with pragmatism. For this reason he concludes that pragmatism can be called religious "if you allow that religion can be pluralistic or merely melioristic in type."[19] In the *Varieties* James brings a kind of pragmatic judgment to bear on religious experiences, the value of which is to be found in their practical results, the fruits they bear for human existence.

Pluralism

James is reported to have said once to one of his classes: "If at the last day all creation was shouting hallelujah and there remained one cockroach with unrequited love, *that* would spoil the universal harmony."[20] In this example the unfortunate cockroach represents one of the many "paradoxes and perplexities" of monism. Philosophical monism or absolutism proposes that reality is one; that the apparent diversity of the world as we perceive it really masks an underlying unity and that there is an ultimate harmony beyond the apparent conflict of opposites. James was sympathetic to this point of view because of its religious value, that is, because of the comfort and assurance it gives to the "sick soul." But what assurance does it provide? The assurance which accompanies the belief that if all of reality makes up a meaningful whole, then the negative, evil, or dark aspects of life have some meaning attached to them and serve some positive purpose in the grand scheme of things. Thus, while the evil aspects of life are not overcome, they are assigned a meaning or purpose. This carries with it the suggestion that everything is as it ought to be and the reassurance that goes with such a suggestion.

As an overarching philosophy of life, however, James saw monism as inadequate in terms of its pragmatic consequences for human life. While it provided the "moral holiday" from the strenuous life which we all need occasionally, it nevertheless failed to arouse our human and moral energies to work toward the world's perfection and completion, which should be our more habitual mode. As a pragmatist James felt that the "problem of evil" was not the speculative question of how evil arose or what its purpose might be, but the practical question of how to overcome it. As a philosopher, therefore, James rejected the monistic view of the world's underlying unity and harmony and adopted the pluralistic view that the world is in reality as we perceive it to be—diverse and contradictory. If indeed the world's ideal state is one of unity and harmony, this state represents a goal which the world has not yet achieved. Therefore, the world is as yet imperfectly unified, incomplete, and in the process of becoming what it was meant to be. And this last point seems to be the point of emphasis in James' pluralism, that is, the growing, changing quality of the world rather than simple diversity. As Bixler suggests, the pluralist points to "the only kind of unity which life as we experience it offers, the unity of an unfolding process rich in undetermined possibility."[21]

This pluralistic view of reality underlies several recurring themes in James' thought. First there is a stress on freedom, creativity, and individuality. If the world is imperfect and incomplete then the free, creative activity of the individual does make a difference to the world's becoming. Second, in James' pluralistic universe God is not the all-embracing totality which is coextensive with all of reality. God is not the unifying principle from which all of reality proceeds. Only that which is good proceeds from God. Evil is a foreign reality proceeding from some other principle. Moreover, as James argues, each of us, in our individual consciousness, is continuous with the divine consciousness or "a wider spiritual environment," but only by way of our own subconscious "wider self." In our everyday conscious life we are shut off from this "larger soul." All of this suggests to James the notion of a "finite God" who is not responsible for evil, since it suggests that this "superhuman consciousness" (God) "has an external environment and consequently is finite."[22] Finally, this pluralistic view with its finite God promotes, in James' view, a greater sense of "intimacy" with the divine. Of such a God James says: "Having an environment, being in time, and working out a history just like ourselves, he escapes from the foreignness from all that is human, of the static, timeless, perfect absolute."[23] Such a God also needs the cooperation of our moral energies in completing and perfecting a world that is not yet complete or, in religious terms, not yet saved. Thus for James, the pluralistic view is more conducive to the stimulation of our moral energies and the living of the strenuous life.

Radical Empiricism

We have already noted James' distinction between the rationalist thinking of the monist and the empirical approach of the pluralist. Rationalism, James explains, is the habit of explaining the diverse parts of reality as parts of an all-encompassing whole. For example, monistic religious systems see the diverse parts of reality as inhering in a God who represents the totality of things. Empiricism is the habit of explaining the whole by its parts. For James, the objectionable feature of rationalism was that it created unity by introducing some unifying principle from beyond the realm of our immediate, perceptual experience. This unifying principle would be a religious concept such as God or a philosophical category such as existence or substance. This results in conceptual knowledge which he describes as derived from and secondary to direct experiential knowledge. James was an empiricist who believed that the subject matter of philosophy was all things experienced or experienceable and that knowing things by direct experience was superior to knowing *about* things. This principle is evident in the *Varieties* in which the primacy of religious experience as a way of understanding religion is affirmed. Religious doctrine and organization are seen as outgrowths of an original direct experience and therefore of secondary importance.

James distinguishes his brand of empiricism from ordinary empiricism by describing it as "radical," and he explains: "To be radical, an empiricism must neither admit into its constructions any element that is not directly experienced, nor exclude from them any element that is directly experienced."[24] The element of direct experience, he believed, which ordinary empiricism excluded from its constructions, was the element of connectedness or conjunction. Its tendency, he argued, was "to do away with the connections of things, and to insist on the disjunctions."[25] James' empiricism is radical in that it insists that we take the objects of our immediate experience *as they are experienced*, and in many instances this means *as related to each other*. An example would be the contents of consciousness which, James argued, are experienced as a "stream" in which "one experience passes into another when both belong to the same self."[26] He insists that these states of consciousness are not merely experienced as discrete, separate entities, but as connected, continuous, related. In other words the continuity of experience is an object of direct experience. Radical empiricism does justice to these "conjunctive relations." It does not keep the successive content of consciousness as separate and discrete units; nor does it unify them by appealing to a philosophical or religious construct such as a substantive self or soul as a unifying, integrating principle. The units are *experienced* as continuous or related.

We shall see that in the *Varieties* James posits the idea of religious experience as a specific type of experience which has the quality of being the direct experience of connectedness and relatedness. "I think it may be asserted," he says, "that there *are* religious experiences of a specific nature, not deducible by analogy or psychological reasoning from our other parts of experience. I think that they point with reasonable probability to the continuity of our consciousness with a wider spiritual environment from which the ordinary prudential man is shut off."[27]

James' Psychology of Religion

God and Religious Belief

The ongoing conflict which James experienced throughout his life could be described temperamentally as the conflict between the active and passive sides of his nature and philosophically as the conflict between pluralism and monism. Correspondingly, we find in his writings an ongoing effort to balance two conflicting conceptions of God and of the function of religious belief. On the one hand, there is the conception of God found in his writings on pluralism, the "strenuous life," and in his 1877 essay "The Will to Believe." Here God is portrayed as one who challenges human beings to moral action and stimulates their latent capacities for the strenuous life and their moral energies. This is the God of James' "pluralistic universe," a finite God who engages and depends on his human agents in the task of completing and perfecting the world. It is also the God of the "healthy minded" whose need for challenge and action is greater than their need for comfort and assurance. Bixler correlates this understanding of God with James' early conception of pragmatism in which the meaning of an idea is equated with its consequences.[28] God is here defined in terms of his function, that is, as one who releases our moral energies. The fact that this form of pragmatism emphasizes the meaning rather than the truth of a concept is reminiscent of Immanuel Kant's moral argument for the existence of God. James' God, in this instance, seems to be a postulate reflecting a subjective human need, a God who is necessary to give meaning to our moral life.

On the other hand, the conception of God found in the *Varieties* is that of a saving power—a God who comforts the "sick soul," heals the divided self, and brings about conversion. This God is not so much the stimulator of our moral energies, but the source and author of saving experiences. It is also a conception of God which appeals to the passive dimension of human nature, that dimension which experiences the need for comfort and assurance and which is more passively receptive to saving and mystical experiences. In the *Varieties* James recognizes this side of human nature (and of himself). He recognizes the need for assurance and peace and not just for a challenge to action. For the most part, the *Varieties* is a study of the "sick soul" and the type of saving and transforming religious experience to which it is receptive. Furthermore, James here seems to be interested not only in describing and classifying these experiences but in hypothesizing a God as the probable cause of such religious experiences. Bixler correlates this understanding of God found in the *Varieties* with a later form of James' pragmatism in which not just the meaning but the truth of a concept is equated with its consequences, that is, its value for human existence. In the *Varieties* the suggestion is that God and religious experience are *true* by reason of their practical consequences.[29] Value thus becomes a criterion of truth. It is no longer a question of a human need (the moral life) justifying a postulate. Rather, it is argued that the empirical value of religious experience points to an ultimate truth—"the continuity of our consciousness with a wider spiritual environment." Though this aspect is underdeveloped in the *Varieties*, James clearly wanted to argue that religion could claim some kind of objective truth over and above its subjective value.

Religious Experience

One of James' stated purposes in writing the *Varieties* was to show that experience rather than philosophy was "the real backbone of the world's religious life." Accordingly, after a preliminary discussion of religion and neurology, he makes it clear in Lecture 2 that his emphasis throughout will be on religious experience rather than religious thought and behavior. One hundred years later, it is perhaps difficult for us to appreciate what a radical departure this represents from the doctrinal and moral emphasis which, until that time, had prevailed in the study of religion. At the outset James distinguishes two aspects of religion, "institutional" and "personal," and announces his intention "to ignore the institutional branch entirely, to say nothing of the ecclesiastical organization, to consider as little as possible the systematic theology and the ideas about the gods themselves, and to confine myself as far as I can to personal religion pure and simple."[30] What is to be studied then is not religion as expressed in theologies, moral teachings, or the organization of church life but religion as it is experienced by the individual. This emphasis on personal experience leads James to propose the following definition of religion: "the feelings, acts and experiences of individual men in their solitude, so far as they apprehend themselves to stand in relation to whatever they may consider the divine."[31]

Why does James choose this point of departure? Why is religion best understood by examining the personal, individual experience of religion? In answer, James argues that personal experience is the most fundamental aspect of religion. Religious experience is the primary phenomenon in the religious life in at least two senses. First, every religious tradition begins with the personal religious experience of its founder. The tradition or church exists for the purpose of initiating its believers into the experience of the tradition's founder—Christ, Mohammed, and so on. Theology, moral teachings, and what James calls "ecclesiasticisms" are merely means to that end. The churches, James argues, are expressions of the tradition, "but the *founders* of every church owed their power originally to the fact of their direct personal communion with the divine."[32] Second, James argues that the religious life of each individual is rooted in personal experience. Believers are not believers because of the rational appeal of religious doctrines. Their faith is rooted in something deeper than reason—in the experiential, emotional, and intuitive depths of the person. Consequently, rational arguments against his or her belief in God are ineffective and, conversely, the deeply rooted convictions of the atheist are not dispelled by rational arguments in favor of faith. Our deepest convictions are not derived from reason and are not susceptible to rational proof. Rational arguments serve only to reinforce what we already believe on other grounds. "The unreasoned and immediate assurance," James argues, "is the deep thing in us, the reasoned argument is but a surface exhibition. Instinct leads, intelligence does but follow."[33]

Types of Religious Experience

For James, there are two fundamental types of religious experience and of religious personality: healthy-minded religion and the religion of the sick soul. As we have seen, these correspond respectively to philosophical pluralism and monism. The religion of the pluralist who accepts the apparent diversity and imperfection of reality, tends to take the form of responding to the moral challenge of working for the world's completion and perfection. This is healthy-minded religion. The monist, on the other hand, takes comfort in his or her belief that beyond the apparent diversity and incompleteness of reality, there is an underlying unity. This means that there is a sense in which the world is "as it should be" since even its darker aspects have a role to play in the ultimate meaning of things. The religion of the monist then tends to be experienced more as a source of comfort and assurance than as a challenge to one's moral energies. Religious experience in this case is more of a saving experience than a moral challenge—a remedy for the sick soul. While James was philosophically a pluralist, his emphasis in the *Varieties* is on God as a saving power and consequently on the value of this sick-soul type of religious experience and its superiority to the more shallow forms of healthy-mindedness.

The basis of James' distinctions between healthy-minded and sick-soul religion is the attitude of each toward the obvious evil which is part and parcel of the world's diversity. The type of healthy-mindedness he has in mind in this context represents a failure to recognize evil or account for it. Nature, including human nature, is seen as good and its evil aspects are ignored. To such healthy-minded types James attributes "a certain authoritativeness in their feeling that Nature, if you will only trust her sufficiently, is absolutely good."[34] To describe such believers in the absolute goodness of nature and of human beings, James borrows from Francis W. Newman the term "once-born." This implies that for the healthy-minded, religious growth is not a matter of sudden conversion or rebirth but rather the gradual unfolding of one's natural powers and development of one's natural goodness. The healthy-minded person does not experience the tragic sense of separation from God which makes the sick soul feel the need to be reborn and to become a new creature. There is a sense of continuity with the divine. This healthy-minded attitude represents, for James, a type of pantheism whereby "we are already one with the Divine without any miracle of grace, or abrupt creation of a new inner man."[35]

James distinguishes two types of healthy-mindedness. "Involuntary" healthy-mindedness is described as "a way of feeling happy about things immediately."[36] It describes one who is spontaneously and temperamentally disposed to be optimistic, to view his or her human nature as naturally good, and to see the goodness of the world to the exclusion of evil. Such people are in James' phrase, "animally happy." By contrast, "systematic" healthy-mindedness is "an abstract way of conceiving things as good." This type of healthy-mindedness refers to any system of thought (philosophical theological, etc.) which sees good as "the essential and universal aspect of being" and therefore "deliberately excludes evil from its field of vision."[37] James points to the writings of the poet Walt Whitman as an example of this kind of deliberate exclusion of evil from one's field of vision. Another example is the studied optimism of what James calls the "mind-cure movement," that is, all those trends in the popular literature of his time which were marked by "an intuitive belief in the all-saving power of healthy-minded attitudes" and a corresponding "contempt for doubt, fear, worry, and all nervously precautionary states of mind."[38] One could safely assume that James would find in today's plethora of "self-help" literature the same basic premise of systematic healthy-mindedness, a belief in the natural goodness and therefore the perfectibility of human nature.

While the healthy-minded person "looks on all things and sees that they are good,"[39] the sick soul looks upon all things with painful awareness of their evil aspects, a sensitivity to life's dark side and nature's potential for evil. Because this applies to human nature as well, the sick soul is painfully aware of her incompleteness and inadequacy, of the evil that is part and parcel of her humanity. In religious terms, this becomes a sense of sinfulness and alienation from God. Religious growth, therefore, is seen not as a natural unfolding of one's innate goodness (for one feels alienated from that goodness) but rather a matter of conversion or rebirth. Rather than becoming more of what one already is (as in the case of the healthy-minded), the sick soul feels the need to become something new, to overcome or transcend one's present state of incompleteness and lack of integrity, in order to feel one with the divine. Such "maximizing of evil," James suggests, is based on the conviction that the evil aspects of life are essential, not accidental features of life and that in order to find meaning in life one must attribute some meaning to its darker side instead of simply ignoring it. It also reveals a pantheistic or monistic point of view which considers all of reality as one reality. Evil, therefore, as an essential part of this one reality, "must have its foundation in God."[40] As an aspect of the reality of the world it must be a part of the world's meaning; it must be "penned in and kept and consecrated and have a function awarded to it in the final system of truth."[41]

James distinguishes two levels of "morbid-mindedness" on the basis of how evil is seen to originate. There are those for whom evil is a maladjustment between one's self and one's environment. This kind of evil is "curable in principle" because it can be remedied by adjustment to the self and/or the environment. Others see evil as rooted in individual human nature. The problems which afflict human existence are seen as having their origin in human nature and therefore, reforms to the social or political environment, necessary though they may be, cannot fully eradicate evil. Again, if the problem is in the individual rather than the environment, then it can be overcome only by some kind of religious experience which transforms the individual. It requires what James calls a "supernatural remedy." In other words, evil consists ultimately in a duality within individual human nature rather than a subject-object (self-environment) duality. Such a view invests human existence with a tragic quality. It means that each of us has a built-in obstacle to the actualization of our essential goodness. This is the contradiction, James argues, which limits our natural happiness and which the healthy-minded tendency to ignore evil cannot eradicate.

For the sick soul, the problem of evil does not admit of a healthy-minded cure because the evil lies within oneself. What is required, therefore, is a new self, a rebirth. The sick soul feels the need of the healing action of a saving power. When evil is thus perceived as being within oneself—when it is the self that is seen as fundamentally flawed—then one cannot simply return to a healthy-minded state of ignorance of evil. As James asserts, "One has tasted of the fruit of the tree, and the happiness of Eden never comes again .... The process is one of redemption, not of mere reversion to natural health, and the sufferer when saved is saved by what seems to him a second birth, a deeper kind of conscious being than he could enjoy before."[42]

In comparing these two types of religious experience, James makes three points. First he suggests that there is a natural antagonism between the two types. To the sick soul the optimism of the healthy-minded seems "unspeakably blind and shallow." On the other hand, the healthy-minded regard the sick soul as excessively morbid, "unmanly and diseased," and preoccupied with misery.[43] Second, as a sort of corollary to the above, he suggests that the healthy-minded tend to be less tolerant and compassionate than the "morbid-minded." Since James does not elaborate on this point, we can only speculate that he is referring to the healthy-minded belief in the goodness and therefore perfectibility of human beings and human society. To such a mentality the sick soul's appreciation and acceptance of the essentially tragic quality of life may be seen as complacency and an obstacle to "reform." Finally, James concludes that, "since the evil facts are as genuine parts of nature as the good ones," then the religion of the sick soul which takes them into account and tries to assign some meaning to them is the more complete and profound religious experience because it "ranges over a wider scale of experience." In other words, a religion which tries to give meaning to all aspects of life—light and dark, good and evil—is more complete than a religion which fails "to accord to sorrow, pain and death any positive and active attention." The completest religions therefore are the redemptive "religions of deliverance" whose basic premise is that "man must die to an unreal life before he can be born into the real life."[44] Though James theoretically links healthy-minded religion with philosophical pluralism, the kind of healthy-mindedness he describes in the *Varieties* seems to lack the "tough-mindedness" of the thoroughgoing pluralist. The pluralist recognizes the duality of good and evil. The healthy-minded, as James describes them, respond to this duality by largely ignoring evil. For this reason, James finds the sick soul's monism, with its sensitivity to the dark side of reality, a more complete religious attitude.

Essence of Religious Experience

In the *Varieties*, James' emphasis is on the religion of the sick soul whose religious experience is one of comfort and assurance and whose God is primarily conceived of as a saving power. But from what is the sick soul saved? What exactly is the sick soul's sickness? In Lecture 8 of the *Varieties* James identifies it as an inner dividedness and, therefore, the saving religious experience as the unification or integration of a divided self. Such integration is, of course, as James points out, the goal of "the normal evolution of character." It should be pointed out that, in the process of psychological growth, two complementary processes take place. The first is the differentiation of all the objects of experience in one's ever-expanding environment and of the various physical, emotional, and cognitive ways of experiencing them. This process is what Gordon Allport called "self-expansion." This process would result in a fragmented self were it not for the parallel process of integration by which all of these differentiated modes of relating to one's world are assigned their proper function and priority within a unified self. The result is what James calls "a stable system of functions in right subordination."

For the morally and religiously sensitive, the lack of such integrated wholeness is experienced as what James calls the "conviction of sin" and which he describes as an inner experience of "two deadly, hostile selves, one actual, the other ideal."[45]

For the sick soul, however, this painful gap between the ideal self and the actual self—between what I ought to be and potentially am and what I actually am—is not merely due to a failure of development but is an existential type of anxiety. Such anxiety and the dividedness which is its source is part and parcel of the human condition. If this be the case, then the desired integration and wholeness from which the sick soul feels alienated can be brought about only by the inner transformation which accompanies the religious experience of "conversion." In Lecture 9 James defines conversion as "the process, gradual or sudden, by which a self hitherto divided, and consciously wrong, inferior and unhappy, becomes unified and consciously right, superior and happy, in consequence of its firmer hold upon religious realities."[46]

According to James, therefore, two things happen in the religious experience of conversion: A divided self is unified and this happens because of the self's "firmer hold on religious realities." This means, as James goes on to explain, that one's religious convictions and commitments become "central" rather than "peripheral" to one's life and consciousness. For James, the set of ideas which are central or occupy "the hot place in a man's consciousness"—the group of ideas to which he devotes himself and from which he works—constitute "the habitual centre of his personal energy." Such a set of ideas is clearly integrating since it unifies the self by providing a central and ultimate source of motivation which influences and unifies all aspects of the self and all areas of life. James concludes: "To say that a man is 'converted' means, in these terms, that religious ideas, previously peripheral in his consciousness, now take a central place, and that religious aims form the habitual centre of his energy."[47]

To this point James has emphasized the unification of *consciousness* as the consequence of religious conversion. When reflecting, however, on the element of surrender to the divine in religious experience, he points to a deeper level of unification which results from the opening of oneself to what lies beyond consciousness. Whether the "higher power" to which one surrenders is the deity or the subconscious or "subliminal" self, in attributing saving power to a force beyond consciousness, James suggests, "psychology and theology are thus in perfect harmony up to this point."[48] Whether, therefore, one calls this experience salvation or wholeness, it is an experience of self-transcendence, of going beyond the limitations of one's ordinary consciousness. Consequently James refers to it as an experience of the "wider self."

One's everyday conscious life is limited in every way, by physical limitations, by fate and destiny, by the limitations we experience in knowledge, understanding, and our ability to relate to others. The desire for self-transcendence is the desire to transcend the limitations of one's present, conscious life. Religion speaks to this desire when it speaks of a reality (the divine) and a life which transcends the limits of one's present, conscious life. The desire for self-transcendence may, therefore, be described simply as the desire for "more." Consequently, James uses the term "the more" to describe that reality beyond consciousness to which one feels united in religious experience. In religious experience, he argues, a person become conscious that the "higher part" of himself is "coterminous and continuous with a *more* of the same quality, which is operative in the universe outside of him, and which he can keep in working touch with, and in a fashion get on board of and save himself when all his lower being has gone to pieces in the wreck."[49]

"The more"—that which is experienced in religious experience—is what religion calls God or the sacred or the numinous and what psychology calls the deeper, unconscious, or subliminal aspect of the self. To accommodate both points of view, James describes the more as having a "hither side" and a "farther side." The hither side is the subliminal self and James proposes that "whatever it may be on its *farther* side, the 'more' with which in religious experience we feel ourselves connected is on its *hither* side the subconscious continuation of our conscious life."[50] This experience of the subliminal self represents the positive content of religious experience, the only content which James, as a psychologist can deal with. But even at this level, he argues, we can speak of the experience of a higher or transcendent power since what we are experiencing transcends consciousness. As for the more ultimate content of religious experience, we might say that, for James, the farther side of the more represents a "God-shaped blank." The subliminal or wider self is described as the link between one's conscious life and whatever the more might be on its farther side (God?, the sacred?). If there are more ultimate sources of religious experience, he suggests, which can directly influence us, "the psychological condition of their doing so *might* be our possession of a subconscious region which alone should yield access to them."[51] The question of whether religious experience is an experience of the subliminal self only or of a more transcendent reality through the medium of the subliminal self is left open.

Elements of the Religious Life

In Lecture 11 of the *Varieties* James turns his attention from the nature of religious experience to what he calls the "fruits of the religious state."

Saintliness. To these positive consequences of religion he gives the collective name "saintliness" and defines the saintly character as one "for which spiritual emotions are the habitual centre of the personal energy."[52] James suggests that certain basic feature of saintliness are universal and the same in all religions. These are an immediate experience—"sensible" as well as "intellectual"—of a higher power and a corresponding sense of living in a wider world; self-surrender to this higher power; a consequent sense of freedom and liberation from the narrow confines of the self; a shift in one's emotional life toward "loving and harmonious affections." These inner states of mind are then said to have certain practical consequences. James points first of all to the well-known *asceticism* of the saint. Self-surrender tends to become self-immolation, self-sacrifice, and forgetfulness of the self. This deliberate seeking of the heroic life is seen as an expression of the "twice-born philosophy" according to which the "element of real wrongness in this world" must be "neutralized and cleansed away by suffering."[53] As with all religious phenomena James offers a pragmatic evaluation of asceticism. The extreme mortifications of some of the saints—fasting, sleep deprivation, flagellation, and other forms of corporal punishment—are judged to be of little value beyond the personal realm of the saint, that is, for human existence and human society in general.

Nevertheless, James argues, one should not, therefore, reject outright this "cultivation of hardship" for it represents "a spontaneous need of character."[54] Self-denial and the "strenuous life" are necessary for the development of the heroic side of character by which self-interest and self-indulgence are transcended. What is necessary, he suggests, is to find more socially useful channels for the kind of heroism which inspired the older, monastic forms of privation and hardship, which James labels "pathetic futilities," aimed as they were at a narrow pursuit of self-perfection. War, of course, calls forth the same kind of self-sacrificing heroism, but James looks for a kind of heroism more conducive to saintliness—"the moral equivalent of war: something heroic that will speak to men as universally as war does, and yet will be as compatible with their spiritual selves as war had proved itself to be incompatible." And James suggests that, in an increasingly materialistic world, the old monastic ideal of poverty might be that alternative. He concludes: "May not voluntarily accepted poverty be the "strenuous life," without the need of crushing weaker peoples?"[55]

Saintliness further expresses itself in a certain *strength of soul* by which personal motives and interests are transcended and become insignificant in the light of the greater object of one's devotion. When such "devoutness" is found in a masterful and aggressive personality it may, when unbalanced, become fanaticism. One's enemies become God's enemies. In a personality that is more gentle and passive the same kind of devotion may become "an imaginative absorption in the love of God to the exclusion of all practical human interest" especially "where devoutness is intense and the intellect feeble." James' prime example of the latter is St. Margaret Mary Alacoque, a seventeenth-century nun so inwardly absorbed as to render her completely inept in her duties in the convent. Such devotion he concludes "though innocent enough, is too one-sided to be admirable."[56] Applying the same pragmatic yardstick to such "professional sainthood of former centuries," he finds it too narrow, narcissistic, and shallow to be of value to the larger human community.

A third expression of saintliness consists of a certain *purity of life*. The "shifting of the emotional centre" to things spiritual requires a certain "cleansing of existence from brutal and sensual elements,"[57] that is, those elements inconsistent with one's spiritual commitment. Again, James points to the excess to which such a tendency can go when it requires such a simplification of one's life and one's world that "the love of God must not be mixed with any other love."[58] Hence the phenomena of the hermit, the cloistered monastic life, and so forth, which James describes as "renunciation of complication," a withdrawal from contact with "the world" so as to preserve the purity of one's love of God. James refers to such focus on the love of God to the exclusion of other loves as "theopathic." Again James illustrates with reference to St. Aloysius Gonzaga, a young sxteenth-century Jesuit whose obsessive fear of contact with the opposite sex bordered on misogyny. This kind of saintliness, he suggests, creates a simplified world by avoiding contact with most parts of it, but at the cost of rendering oneself of no value to the world. Contrasting Gonzaga's flight from the world with the active involvement of other Jesuits such as Francis Xavier, John de Brebeuf, and Isaac Jogues, James concludes: "It is better that a life should contract many a dirt-mark, than forfeit usefulness in its efforts to remain unspotted."[59]

Finally, saintliness finds expression in *tenderness and charity* toward others. Here James considers the commonsense objection that the heroic charity of the saints, which extends even to enemies, does not resist evil and makes no distinction between the deserving and the undeserving, opens the saint to the possibility of being manipulated and taken advantage of, and therefore contributes to the increase of evil and injustice in society. Of these heroes of charity he remarks: "the powers of darkness have systematically taken advantage of them."[60] This point of view, however, is too pragmatic even for James. The "excess" of charity, he points out, which we find in some saints can be a "creative social force." They represent a moral plateau which the world has not yet attained; they are charismatic figures exhibiting a not yet attained stage of humanity's moral development. They seem preposterous, James argues, precisely because they are "forerunners" and "the world is not yet with them."[61]

Mysticism. Given James' understanding of religion as the feelings and experiences of individuals "in their solitude" in relation to the divine, it is not surprising that he considers mystical states of consciousness to be the root of personal religious experience. In speaking of mysticism, James clearly wants to go beyond the popular understanding which equates the term "mystical" with the irrational, the illogical, or the occult. Consequently, he clarifies his own meaning of the term by listing four qualities which characterize the mystical state of consciousness. A mystical experience is *ineffable*, that is, its content cannot be rationally expressed. It is something directly experienced—"more like states of feeling than like states of intellect"[62]—and as such cannot be communicated verbally to others. Second, the mystical experience, even though it is a feeling state, nevertheless has a *noetic quality*. It is a communication which is directly experienced rather than the result of a rational argument. It is a state of authoritative insight into "depths of truth unplumbed by the discursive intellect."[63] To these two essential features of the mystical, James adds two other less essential characteristics but which are "usually found." These are the *transiency* of the experience (it cannot be sustained for long) and the *passivity* of the experiencer who feels that he is not the author of the experience but that he is being acted upon by a higher power.

James distinguishes two modes of experiencing mystical states of consciousness. The spontaneous type of mystical experience includes the sudden insight into the deeper meaning and significance of a familiar truth, the *déjà vu* experience, intoxication, and, in the more religious subject, the immediate experience of the presence of God. In most religious traditions there are also systematic meditative methods for cultivating mystical consciousness.

As with saintliness, James applies a pragmatic criterion in evaluating mystical states of consciousness. What are their "fruits for life"? He rejects the medical-scientific tendency to classify such states as necessarily pathological. If pathology is present, he insists, it is not in the experience itself, but in those experiencers "in whom the character is naturally passive and the intellect feeble."[64] In such mystics "other worldliness" takes the form of withdrawal from and ineptitude in the practical matters of life. Those with strong minds and characters, on the other hand, seem to be spurred by their mystical experiences to greater effort and accomplishment in the practical realm by the formation of a new center of spiritual energy. But to say that the mystic is thus inspired raises the further question of the truth or value of the inspiration. While some mystics have claimed insight into the meaning of specific religious doctrines as a result of their experiences, James suggests that, in general, the mystical experience moves the subject in two theoretical or philosophical directions—optimism and monism. The optimism would seem to be the result of a widening of the context of the subject's life. The passing from the ordinary state of consciousness to the mystical state is a passing "from a less into a more" and "from a smallness into a vastness." Such states "appeal to the yes-function more than to the no-function in us."[65] The monistic direction of the mystical experience refers to the fact that it is a unitive and unifying experience, that is, an experience of the underlying oneness of all things. It is therefore a way of experiencing reality as if "the opposites of the world, whose contradictoriness and conflict make all our difficulties and troubles, were melted into a unity."[66]

As for the truth of any theological or philosophical implications of the mystical experience, James offers a threefold conclusion. (1) Mystical states have absolute authority for those who experience them. The direct experiences of the mystic are for him or her as much "perceptions of fact" as those which provide the basis of the more "rational" beliefs of others, and therefore equally able provide the faith by which one lives. (2) Mystical states have no authority over those who are outside the experience. They are what the Catholic Church would classify as "private revelations," intended only for the individual experiencer and having no particular authority over those who do not share the experience. Moreover, James argues, there is not sufficient unanimity among the experiences of the mystics to establish a consensus about any kind of general truth to be derived from mystical sources. (3) Though mystical states cannot be used to establish authoritative general truths, they do suggest that truth cannot be restricted to its rational sources. Mystical states, James suggests, break down the authority of nonmystical or rational consciousness, showing it to be only one kind of consciousness and not the only criterion of what is to be believed. Here James returns to the starting point of his psychology of religion, the primacy of experience in the phenomenon of religion. It is this other, nonrational criterion—personal experience—which is the basis for personal religion. Philosophical and theological reason can neither prove nor disprove beliefs rooted in such experience.

Belief. What is the basis of religious belief? We have seen that, in James' view, religious belief is rooted in something other than reason and that rational arguments can neither prove nor disprove such convictions. If we say that the religious person believes on the strength of divine revelation, the further question is raised as to why the believer accepts certain truths as divinely revealed. In the end he finds the source of religious belief in the kind of nonrational intuitive convictions of which the mystical experience is the example *par excellence.* Another contributing factor is the pragmatic value of the belief in question. A belief which is consistent with one's human experience of life, which helps one to deal more effectively with the problems of life, and which is consistent with our deepest human aspirations, is true in this pragmatic sense. As James asserts, "the gods we stand by are the gods we need and can use, the gods whose demands on us are reinforcements of our demands on ourselves and on one another."[67]

All of this suggests that religious beliefs are not cold, abstract propositions to be argued on purely rational and speculative grounds, but matters of vital importance for the believer. This being the case, the believer cannot suspend judgment until there is rational proof for his or her beliefs. When the truth of a proposition cannot be established on rational grounds one is forced to make a "leap of faith," that is, to decide on nonrational grounds. In his 1896 essay *The Will to Believe* James quotes the words of FitzJames Stephens: "In all important transactions of life we have to take a leap in the dark."[68] The leap, however, while it is not a rational conclusion, is not irrational. What James is talking about is a proposition the truth of which cannot be decided on intellectual grounds, that is, an hypothesis. When one is faced with conflicting propositions (e.g., the existence or nonexistence of God) which cannot be resolved rationally, one is free, James argues, to choose one of the options voluntarily rather that rationally under certain conditions. It must be a *living* option, a real or credible possibility with practical consequences, that is, it leads one to act on it. Second, it must be a *forced* option—a proposition that must be accepted or rejected. Because of its vital importance for life, one cannot remain indifferent to the question. Finally, it must be a *momentous* rather than a trivial option. It represents, that is, a unique opportunity in which not to choose is to refuse, not to affirm is to deny. Given these conditions, James argues, to simply suspend judgment "is itself a passional decision—just like deciding yes or not—and is attended with the same risk of losing the truth."[69]

Evaluation

Religious Experience as "Feeling"

There can be little doubt about the historical significance of William James for the psychological study of religion. His emphasis on the religious experience of the individual in the study of the religious phenomenon was not only a corrective to the doctrinal, historical, and moral emphasis in previous studies of religion, but served also to define the subject matter of the psychology of religion. It is also true that James' analysis, from this experiential point of view, of such phenomena as religious types, conversion, saintliness, and mysticism still represents a major contribution to the study of religion. Nevertheless, James has been criticized for adopting a too narrow or one-sided view of religious experience. In the first place, though he describes the essence of religion as the *feelings, acts, and experiences* of individuals in relation to the divine, there is a tendency in the *Varieties* to emphasize *feeling* as the essential quality of religious experience. This is reinforced by his choice of traumatic emotional experiences as examples to illustrate the nature of religious experience. The implication seems to be that the degree of emotionality is the criterion for an experience to be religious. It could be argued that James emphasizes the role of feeling in religion at the expense of its voluntary and intellectual aspects.

Religious Experience as Individual

It could be further argued that James' emphasis on the experiences of individuals *in their solitude* neglects the collective or communal aspect of religion. While most would agree with James that the study of "ecclesiasticisms" (church laws, structures, and organization) does not get to the heart of religion, it is also true that such structures represent the crystallization of a genuine experience of community. And for most religious people, their individual religious experience does not take place within a vacuum but in the context of some authentically religious community.

Religious Experience as a Separate Category of Experience

A further qualification must be applied to James' understanding of religious experience in the light of theological developments since the time of James. One's understanding of religious experience is inevitably linked to one's understanding of God. The prevailing theological temperament of today would probably find James' understanding of religious experience inadequate. For James, religious experience was a separate category of experience which could be differentiated from our ordinary everyday experience. The prototype of this kind of religious experience was the experience of conversion. As Peter Homans has observed, religious experience as viewed in this way is seen as "a psychic event with a beginning, a middle and an end."[70] Religious experience, thus, becomes a special kind of experience given over and above one's everyday "secular" experience and clearly distinct from it. James reinforces this concept in the *Varieties* by focusing on examples of religious experience which are extreme and pronounced enough to be clearly labeled "religious" and thereby differentiated from any other kind of experience.

Such an understanding of religious experience reflects a theological view in which reality is made up of two separate realms, the sacred and the secular. In this dichotomous view of reality, God inhabits the realm of the sacred and is therefore experienced by way of incursions into secular reality. Religious experience, then, becomes an experience of this "other" reality which intrudes into one's everyday, secular world. Theological reflection, however, since the time of James has been increasingly informed by a unified worldview which tends to obliterate any dichotomous distinction between the sacred and the secular. Contemporary theology does not speak of the "otherness" or transcendence of God in terms of a supranaturalistic two-tiered view of reality in which God is relegated to another realm "up there" and thereby divorced from human life and experience. God is still seen as a transcendent mystery, but a mystery present within human experience and human relationships. God is not, therefore, to be discovered by looking outside of one's human experience but as the ultimate, depth dimension of that experience. If God, for example, is Love, then the human experience of love will be in some sense an experience of the divine, theologically conceived of as the ultimate ground and dimension of that human experience. The sacred, in other words, is the ultimate depth dimension and meaning of the secular.

But if God is no longer thought of as the Supreme Being standing over against the human—as separate and distinct from one's human, secular experience—but rather as the ultimate depth or dimension of all human experience, then a new understanding of religious experience emerges. It is no longer seen as a separate category of experience, distinct from "secular" experience; rather, all human experience is seen as potentially religious. For the psychology of religion, whose traditional subject matter is religious experience, this means a shift in focus. Thus, Paul Pruyser has suggested a reformulation of the basic question in psychology of religion: "The old question was: *Which are the significant data of religious experiences?* The new question is: *Which data of experience are of religious significance?*"[71] In other words, the focus of the psychology of religion is no longer a type of experience which can be labeled "religious" as distinct from "secular" but rather the religious quality or dimension of human experience in general.

Religious Experience and Theology

In the light of the previous discussion, we could argue that James' study of religious experience suffers from what Pruyser calls a "too narrowly conceived" understanding of religious experience which diminishes its relevance for contemporary psychology of religion. On the other hand, it is perhaps possible to locate James' relevance to contemporary psychology of religion in the current dialogue between psychology and religion/theology. This dialogue has been facilitated by the very shift in focus in the subject matter of the discipline mentioned previously. If that subject matter is no longer a separate category of experience but a dimension of all experience, then a dialogue becomes possible between the psychological and theological interpretations of human experience. This type of experience, which can be interpreted psychologically or theologically, theistically or nontheistically, is what Erich Fromm has called the "X-experience." It is the "experiential substratum" that underlies both psychological and religious language.[72] It could be argued that, in analyzing religious experience as an experience of "the more" of reality, James is speaking of just such an experience which can be described psychologically as an experience of the "subliminal self" (that is, in terms of its "hither side") or theologically as an experience of the divine or the sacred (that is, in terms of its "farther side").

It is clear that James does not approach religious experience in a reductionist spirit. In distinguishing between the hither and farther side of "the more" he makes it clear that there is a kind of experience which is not to be described *either* psychologically *or* theologically in some mutually exclusive sense, but *both* psychologically *and* theologically. By insisting that the subliminal self is merely the hither side of "the more," he leaves room for another interpretation of the experience in term of one's theological "over-beliefs," which are never regarded by James as peripheral and secondary. He seems to treat the over-beliefs as essential to the experience and insists that "the most interesting and valuable things about a man are usually his over-beliefs."[73] In this context, therefore, this subliminal self is seen not only as the psychological explanation of religious experience but also as the psychological condition for the theological explanation or over-belief. If we can experience the direct influence of "higher spiritual agencies," he argues, then the precondition of such an experience "*might* be our possession of a subconscious region which alone should yield access to them."[74]

For James, the positive content of religious experience—the content accessible to psychological analysis—is the experience of the "wider self." This is described as an experience of one's "subliminal self" and therefore represents an experience in which the limitations of one's ordinary consciousness are transcended. Whether this comes about through an encounter with the farther reaches of the self (the subliminal self) or with a reality transcending the self (the divine) will again depend on whether the experience is interpreted psychologically or theologically. The important point would seem to be that, in speaking of the "hither" and "farther" sides of this kind of self-transcending experience, James has offered us a methodological paradigm for the dialogue between psychology and theology. It is precisely this self-transcending experience of the "wider self" which can be understood psychologically as wholeness or integrity and theologically as salvation or redemption. As the goal of both human and religious growth it becomes the common subject matter of psychology and theology.

Religious Experience and Pragmatism

In our review of the seminal psychological theories of religion we have placed James between the depth psychologists (Freud and Jung) and the more humanistically oriented psychologists (Fromm, Allport, Maslow). At the risk of oversimplifying, we might differentiate these two groups by suggesting that, while the depth psychologists are primarily concerned with the origin of religious thought and behavior, the humanists are more concerned with evaluating religion by applying psychological criteria of health and maturity to it. James shares both preoccupations. He theorizes about the source of religious experience in the concepts of "the more" and the "wider self." At the same time, he is concerned with the value of religion for human life and, to that end, applies a pragmatic criterion.

A religious person, however, reading James' pragmatic evaluation of saintliness and mysticism, might—even while nodding his head in agreement—experience certain misgivings. At the root of those misgivings is the nagging question of whether such a pragmatic criterion can adequately evaluate religious phenomena. Pragmatism tends to take a short-term view of what "works" or is of value for human life. Thus, for saintliness to be pragmatically valuable, it must produce practical, beneficial results within the person and lifetime of the saint. According to such a criterion, a St. Margaret Mary may be dismissed as useless and incompetent and a St. Aloysius Gonzaga as a neurotic simpleton. And within that pragmatic context one could hardly disagree. At the same time, the suspicion that this should not be an absolute judgment is based not merely on a pious feeling that saints are not to be judged by ordinary standards, but also on the inherent limitation of all pragmatic and psychological criteria of value or health. James' pragmatism equates truth with what is of value for human existence. This surely means what is of value relative to the goal of human existence but it does not answer the question of the goal of human existence. Thus, when James describes St. Ignatius Loyola as "one of the most powerfully practical human engines that ever lived," he merely reflects history's judgment of the usefulness of Ignatius' achievements, but does not offer us any absolute standard by which to judge this "machine's" usefulness.

Religion, on the other hand, takes a long-term and sometimes paradoxical view of what "works." If it sees human destiny as eternal, it judges all human achievement not in terms of their immediate practical consequences but *sub specie aeternitatis* (under the aspect of eternity). Its judgment as to what constitutes success and of value for human life may also be paradoxical. Only a criterion which transcends the narrow short-term view of pragmatism could offer equal reverence to the bumbling Margaret Mary Alacocque and the dynamic Ignatius Loyola. This, of course, does not mean that the religious criteria are true and pragmatic or psychological criteria are invalid. It does mean that, in the psychological study of religion, one must recognize the limitation of any psychological criterion of health and value as applied to religion. Religion is a many-faceted phenomenon. It is indeed a psychological phenomenon, but this is only one of its many aspects and therefore cannot be evaluated according to an exclusively psychological criterion.

Suggested Readings

ALLEN, GAY WILSON, *William James: A Biography* (New York: Viking Press, 1967).

BIXLER, JULIUS SEELYE, *Religion in the Philosophy of William James* (New York: A.M.S. Press, 1979).

JAMES, WILLIAM, *The Letters of William James*, edited by his son Henry James (Boston: Atlantic Monthly Press, 1920), 2 vols.

JAMES, WILLIAM, *Pragmatism and Four Essays from the Meaning of Truth* (New York: New American Library, 1974).

JAMES, WILLIAM, *Radical Empiricism and a Pluralistic Universe* (New York: E.P. Dutton, 1971).

JAMES, WILLIAM, *The Varieties of Religious Experience* (New York: Macmillan, 1961).

JAMES, WILLIAM, "The Will to Believe" and "The Moral Equivalent of War," in *Essays on Faith and Morals*, edited by Ralph Barton Perry (New York: World Publishing Co., 1962).

LEWIS, R.W.B., *The Jameses: A Family Narrative* (New York: Farrar, Straus and Giroux, 1991).

PERRY, RALPH BARTON, *The Thought and Character of William James* (New York: Harper and Row, 1964).

VANDEN BURGT, ROBERT J., *The Religious Philosophy of William James* (Chicago: Nelson-Hall, 1981).

Notes

1. William James, *Pragmatism and four Essays from the Meaning of Truth* (New York: New American Library, 1974, 1907), pp. 17-18.
2. *Ibid.*, pp. 26-27.
3. *Ibid.*

4. Julius Seelye Bixler, *Religion in the Philosophy of William James* (New York: A.M.S. Press, 1979), p. 3.
5. Quoted in Gay Wilson Allen, *William James: A Biography* (New York: Viking Press, 1967), p. 27.

6. *Ibid.*, p. 121.
7. William James, *The Varieties of Religious Experience* (New York: Macmillan, 1961) p. 138.
8. John Jay Chapman, *Memories and Milestones*, 1915, quoted in G.W. Allen, *William James: A Biography*, p. 302.
9. William James, *Diary*, April 30, 1870, quoted in G.W. Allen, *William James: A Biography*, p. 168.
10. Quoted in G.W. Allen, *William James: A Biography*, pp. 179-180.
11. *Ibid.*, p. 175.
12. Ralph Barton Perry, *The Thought and Character of William James* (New York: Harper and Row, 1964), p. 200.
13. Letter to Frances Morse, April 1900, quoted in G.W. Allen, *William James: A Biography*, p. 415.
14. Letter to Henry W. Rankin, June 1901, *Ibid.*, p. 425.
15. J.S. Bixler, *Religion in the Philosophy of William James*, p. 198.
16. Heinrich Straumann, *American Literature in the Twentieth Century*, quoted in G.W. Allen, *William James: A Biography*, p. 458.
17. William James, *Pragmatism*, p. 42.
18. *Ibid.*, p. 133.
19. *Ibid.*, p. 193.
20. Quoted in J.S. Bixler, *Religion in the Philosophy of William James*, p. 59.
21. *Ibid.*, p. 66.
22. William James, *A Pluralistic Universe* (New York: E.P. Dutton, 1971), p. 269.
23. *Ibid.*, p. 272.
24. William James, *Essays in Radical Empiricism* (New York: E.P. Dutton, 1971), p. 25.
25. *Ibid.*, p. 25.
26. *Ibid.*, p. 27.
27. William James, *A Pluralistic Universe*, p. 264.
28. J.S. Bixler, *Religion in the Philosophy of William James*, ch. 7.
29. *Ibid.*, ch. 7.
30. William James, *Varieties*, p. 41.
31. *Ibid.*, p. 42.
32. *Ibid.*
33. *Ibid.*, p. 75.
34. *Ibid.*, p. 79.
35. *Ibid.*, p. 94.
36. *Ibid.*, p. 85.
37. *Ibid.*
38. *Ibid.*, p. 90.
39. *Ibid.*, p. 85.
40. *Ibid.*, pp. 116-117.
41. *Ibid.*, p. 118.
42. *Ibid.*, p. 135.
43. *Ibid.*, pp. 139-40.
44. *Ibid.*, pp. 140-42.
45. *Ibid.*, p. 146.
46. *Ibid.*, p. 160.

47. *Ibid.*, p. 165.
48. *Ibid.*, p. 176.
49. *Ibid.*, pp. 393-94.
50. *Ibid.*, p. 396.
51. *Ibid.*, p. 198.
52. *Ibid.*, p. 220.
53. *Ibid.*, p. 287.
54. *Ibid.*, p. 241.
55. *Ibid.*, p. 290.
56. *Ibid.*, p. 273.
57. *Ibid.*, p. 221.
58. *Ibid.*, p. 277.
59. *Ibid.*, p. 281.
60. *Ibid.*, p. 282.
61. *Ibid.*, p. 283.
62. *Ibid.*, p. 300.
63. *Ibid.*
64. *Ibid.*, p. 324.
65. *Ibid.*, p. 326.
66. *Ibid.*, p. 306.
67. *Ibid.*, p. 264.
68. Quoted in "The Will to Believe" in Ralph Barton Perry (ed.), *Essays on Faith and Morals* (New York: World Publishing Co., 1962), p. 62.
69. *Ibid.*, p. 42.
70. Peter Homans, "Toward a Psychology of Religion: By Way of Freud and Tillich," *Zygon*, 2, no. 1, 1967, p. 100.
71. Paul Pruyser, *A Dynamic Psychology of Religion* (New York: Harper and Row, 1968), p. 12.
72. Erich Fromm, *You Shall Be as Gods* (New York: Holt, Rinehart and Winston, 1966), ch. 2.
73. William James, *Varieties*, p. 398.
74. *Ibid.*, p. 198.

IV. ERICH FROMM

Religion and Humanism

Erich Fromm (1900–1980)
Lisa Goldering/American Psychological Association.

E rich Fromm (1900-1980) has been variously described as a neo-Freudian psychoanalyst and a social psychologist, but it is his fundamental humanism which informs and defines both of these roles. In these pages we shall think of him primarily as—in Gerhard Knapp's words—"one of the most influential humanists of this century."[1] As such, his concern, in the psychological study of religion, is not so much with discovering the origin of religious phenomena as with establishing psychological criteria for evaluating religious experience. As Fromm himself remarks, the critical question is not whether a person is religious or not but what kind of religion a person practices. Whereas Freud was described as an "unrepentant atheist," Fromm might more accurately be described as a "non-theist." His writings on religion suggest that this term could be used to describe someone who, while not believing in God as an ontological reality, nevertheless finds value in the concept of God as long as it acts as a symbol of and promotes the growth of one's specifically human powers (reason and love) and enhances one's freedom and autonomy. A religion centered on such an understanding of God is termed "humanistic."

Fromm attempts to study religion in the light of what he describes as a "humanistic psychoanalysis." As it turns out, this term has at least a twofold significance for the psychological study of religion. In the first place, it tends to define in what sense Fromm may be considered a neo-Freudian since it suggests a revision of strict Freudian theory along humanistic lines. This can be seen in his reinterpretation of Freudian terminology in which terms having a strictly sexual meaning for Freud are given a broader emotional meaning. Thus "incest" becomes not sexual drive for, but emotional dependence on parent, family, and so forth. "Necrophilia" becomes an attachment to all that is "dead" such as the past or the mechanical; it is an attempt to remove from life all elements of risk and uncertainty so that life is turned into death, which is life's only certainty. This kind of humanistic revision can also be seen in the shift from the inner dynamics of instinctual motivation to an emphasis on the dynamics of the individual's relationship to the environment. One may therefore categorize Fromm as a social psychologist, but one whose social psychology is rooted in the humanistic belief in the natural goodness of individual human nature. In such a view, negative, pathological behavior results not from an innate flaw in human nature but from harmful environmental influences. Consequently, what Freud called the life instinct and death instinct become in Fromm's theory, biophilia (the love of life) and necrophilia (the love of death). These terms do not represent inner drives or instincts but "character orientations" or learned ways of relating to one's environment.

Fromm, however, was not a revisionist from the outset. He was an orthodox Freudian analyst for the first 10 years of his professional practice. In a conversation with Richard Evans he remarks:

> I was an orthodox analyst then, and for about ten years I practised what I had been taught. Slowly, however, I became more and more dissatisfied with both the theory and the technique, and gradually I began to look for elements other than those I had been taught to see. My technique and a good many of my views changed as a result of this critical appraisal of psychoanalytic theory. [2]

In spite of this "critical appraisal," Fromm never seems to have thought of himself as a rebel or a revisionist. Rather, he saw himself as a "pupil and translator of Freud" whose aim was "to translate Freud into philosophical and sociological categories" which were more in accord with contemporary thought. In this way he hoped to "enrich and deepen" Freud's discoveries "by liberating them from the somewhat narrow libido theory."[3]

A second consequence of Fromm's humanistic revision of psychoanalysis is to be found in his functional understanding of religion. In a postscript to Rainer Funk's *Erich Fromm: The Courage to Be Human*, Fromm defines religion as "a system of ideas, norms and rites that satisfy a need that is rooted in human existence, the need for a system of orientation and an object of devotion."[4] As Funk points out, religion is thereby "understood wholly in terms of its significance as a response to a need."[5] Both Freud's psychopathology of religion and Jung's archetypal theory of religion deal with the psychological roots of religious phenomena and this implies some evaluation of the truth or validity of religion. In Fromm's humanistic view what matters is that one should become "productive," that is come to the full realization of his human powers of reason and love. Religion is evaluated in terms of its function in relation to this humanistic goal. As John H. Schaar puts it: "What matters to productive man is not whether his religion is true in some sense but whether it is useful. Does it liberate your powers and help you grow?"[6] If so, it is judged to be "humanistic" as opposed to "authoritarian" religion, which alienates the individual from his or her own productive human powers.

Fromm's humanistic approach was informed by a number of influences in his personal and professional formation. He was first of all, raised in the Rabbinic tradition of Judaism. Though he rejected his orthodox Jewish faith as a young man of 26, he retained throughout his life the deeply humanistic and ethical aspects of that tradition. There is, moreover, in Fromm's works of social criticism a certain utopianism—a hope for a better world—which reflects to some extent the messianic hopes of Judaism. This student of Freud brought to his training in psychoanalysis the deeply rooted humanism of his religious tradition. The result was a "humanistic psychoanalysis." Two other influences of Fromm's thought are worth mentioning. In Marxist socialism he seemed to find the social and political values which best correlated with his humanistic values. In Fromm's view, Marx was essentially a humanist who saw liberation from oppressive economic conditions as a prerequisite for one's liberation from self-alienation and for one's full human development. Finally, in Buddhism, a spiritual system without a personal God, he found perhaps the fullest expression of humanistic religion. For Fromm, the optimal development of one's human powers (reason and love) makes possible a "full, productive response to the world." In its highest form this kind of "productiveness" correlates with the Buddhist goal of enlightenment.

Life

"I was an only child and I had very neurotic parents. I was probably a rather unbearably neurotic child."[7] In these probably unduly harsh words Fromm sums up his childhood. Born March 23, 1900, at Frankfurt, Germany, he was the only child of Naphtali Fromm and Rosa Krause. Naphtali's father had been a rabbi and Talmud scholar and Naphtali himself, a succesful fruit-wine merchant, seems to have been a frustrated rabbi. As Fromm himself has recalled, his father was ashamed of the way in which he made his living and would rather have become a rabbi. As a young boy, Fromm seems to have absorbed this attitude that there was something shameful about being a businessman and spending one's life earning money. A remnant of this attitude can perhaps be seen in the mature Fromm's scathing critique of modern consumer society and the "having" mode of existence in general. Gerhard Knapp further suggests that Naphtali's vocational conflict reflected a conflict of opposing worldviews, the precapitalist, medieval world of religious orthodoxy and the modern consumer society. These two opposing value systems would be expressed theoretically in Fromm's 1976 work *To Have or to Be*.[8]

Fromm's mother, Rosa, did not share her husband's religious and political conservatism and wanted her son to become a famous pianist. In response to the dreams of both parents Fromm pursued both piano and Talmud studies. When he speaks of his parents as "neurotic" he perhaps has in mind the memory of parents obsessed with the success of their only child and vicariously living out their dreams in him. In spite of this, young Erich seems to have managed to steer his own course. Piano lessons were abandoned at the end of high school. Talmud studies, however, would continue until the age of 26, at which point Fromm rejected his orthodox Jewish faith. However, what Fromm considered the humanistic and ethical core of that faith continued to influence his personal and professional life.

During Fromm's adolescence, two incidents in particular made a deep impression on him, confronting him with the irrationalities and inner conflicts of human existence and perhaps influencing his ultimate career choice and later writings. The first was the suicide, when Fromm was 12 years old, of a young girl who was a friend of the family, and whose suicide was occasioned by the death of her elderly father. Thirty-eight years later this case would be recalled in his book *Psychoanalysis and Religion* as an example of neurotic fixation to a parent which Fromm classifies as a modern form of ancestor worship.[9] An even deeper impression was made by the events of World War I, which roughly coincided with Fromm's high school years. The beginning of this war awakened the adolescent Fromm to the "irrationalities of human behaviour." In conversation with Richard Evans he refers to it as "perhaps the most decisive event in my youth." The irrational destructiveness of this war, the "anti-British hysteria" in his native Germany, and the enthusiasm people developed for a war which he viewed a madness prompted him to ask: "How is it possible that men stand in the trenches for years and live like animals—and for what?" It was this introduction to the irrationality of human behavior, he states, which turned him in the direction of his eventual work. "So I studied psychology, philosophy and sociology, learned about psychoanalysis and decided that I would become a psychoanalyst."[10] Again, 50 years later, Fromm, in distinguishing biophilia (the love of life) and necrophilia (the love of death), would give the following answer to his boyhood questions: "People are not afraid of total destruction because they do not love life; or because they are indifferent to life, or even because many are attracted to death."[11]

At 18 Fromm entered the University of Frankfurt to study law. The following year (1919) he transferred to Heidelberg and changed his field of study to psychology, sociology, and philosophy. By 1925 he had completed his doctorate in sociology at Heidelberg. In the meantime, on his return visits to Frankfurt, he became more deeply involved in the life of the Jewish community there. He helped to found the Society for the Education of Jewish People in 1920 and lectured there frequently. In the same year the Free Jewish Academy was founded. Fromm, during the years of his continuing interest in Talmud studies, seems to have been deeply influenced by the humanistic approach to the Talmud of the Academy's director, Franz Rosenzweig. Knapp remarks: "It is safe to say that [Fromm's] own life-long unorthodox relationship to Judaism is owed to a certain extent to Rosenzweig."[12] Another contact at the Academy, Leo Lowenthal, introduced Fromm to the Frankfurt Institute of Social Research. It would be in the context of this group of scholars, which would eventually be identified as the "Frankfurt School," that Fromm would refine his sociopsychological approach to the study of religion and society. By 1930 he was the Institute's consultant for psychoanalysis. In 1926 Fromm had married Frieda Reichmann, a psychoanalyst with whom he had undergone analysis and who was ten years his senior. The marriage was an unhappy one and lasted only four years. They separated in 1930 and both eventually had successful careers in America, where they were divorced. From 1926 to 1929 Fromm studied psychology and psychiatry at Munich and Frankfurt and in 1929-1930 completed his training at the Psychoanalytical Institute of Berlin. This year marked the beginning of his friendship and collaboration with Karen Horney, which would continue in America, as well as his contact with Wilhelm Reich, who influenced Fromm toward the study of Marxism.

Fromm remained a member of the Institute for Social Research from 1930 to 1939. He had opened a private psychoanalytic practice in Berlin in 1930 and was, during these years, a more or less orthodox Freudian analyst. But these were also the years of his "critical appraisal" of strict Freudian theory as well as the development of his sociopsychological method and the humanistic psychoanalysis that would inform his later, more popular writings. The Institute, in Knapp's description, "was predominantly dedicated to the study and application of Marxist theory to practically all areas of social life and interaction."[13] For Fromm the psychologist, this meant an application of Marxist analysis of social and economic forces to an understanding of individual consciousness and character. The result was a more social psychology which placed more emphasis on the social determinants of individual characters. In this view, the development of character is less the result of inner instinctual development, that is, the development of the libido and the erogenous zones, and more the result of the ways in which one relates to the world. This happens in two ways: by assimilation (receiving from the world) and by social-ization (actively relating to and acting upon the world).

From this kind of social psychology Fromm derived a definition of char-acter as "the (relatively permanent) form in which human energy is canalized in the process of assimilation and socialization."[14] On this premise of the so-cial and cultural determinants of character, Fromm developed the concept of "social character," which he defines as "the nucleus of the character structure which is shared by most members of the same culture in contradistinction to the individual character in which people belonging to the same culture differ from each other."[15] Social structures, in other words, mold the character struc-ture of individuals within that society. In this way, human energy is chan-neled toward society's function and goals in such a way that "we are what we have to be, in accordance with the necessities of the society in which we live."[16] Whereas Freud, on the basis of a more pessimistic view of human nature, found society's repression of the individual's destructive instinctual impuls-es an inevitable necessity, Fromm saw in the need to conform to society's ex-pectations a possible source of self-alienation. This would be the case when social structures, ideals, and patterns are inimical to the full development of the individual's potentiality for reason, love, freedom, and responsibility, that is, for the full development of one's essential humanity. In this case "social character" replaces and represses the individual's essential humanity. Thus the psychoanalytic process of making the unconscious conscious is no longer for the purpose of gaining conscious control over destructive unconscious im-pulses but for the purpose of giving conscious expression to one's specifical-ly human powers of reason and love.

In 1931-1932 Fromm spent more than a year being treated for tubercu-losis in Davos, Switzerland. It has been suggested[17] that this illness was psy-chosomatic, coinciding as it did, with the breakup of his marriage in 1930. In 1933 he gave a series of guest lectures at the Chicago Institute of Psycho-analysis. In the meantime the Institute of Social Research was closed down in 1933 by the National Socialist government of Germany. Its director, Max Horkheimer, relocated the Institute in New York in 1934. In the same year Fromm moved to New York City and opened a private practice there. Here he rejoined his colleagues at the Institute and remained an active member until 1937, by which time his neo-Freudian views had become unpopular with some members of the Institute, in particular Theodor Adorno and Herbert Marcuse. After returning to the Davos Sanatorium for further treatment for tuberculo-sis in 1938, he formally resigned from the Institute in 1939. In 1940 Fromm became an American citizen and in 1941 he published *Escape from Freedom*, the first of his many immensely popular English-language publications over the next 40 years.

In addition to his private psychoanalytic practice, Fromm served as vis-iting assistant professor at the American Institute for Psychoanalysis at Co-lumbia University in 1940-1941 and taught psychoanalysis at Bennington

College in Vermont from 1941 to 1950. It was Karen Horney, whose friendship with Fromm began in 1930 in Berlin, who was instrumental in bringing him to Chicago in 1933. In New York, it was through Horney that he became acquainted with and accepted by Harry Stack Sullivan and other prominent members of the American psychoanalytic community. Knapp suggests that "Karen Horney gradually assumed the role of a strong, motherly figure in Fromm's life, especially in the years after the disintegration of his first marriage."[18] The presence in Fromm's life of such strong mother figures as Karen Horney and Frieda Reichmann throws some light, perhaps, on the experiential root of his later theoretical interest in matriarchical social structures and the significance of the mother complex in psychological development as a corrective to Freud's overemphasis on the father complex. For Fromm, the attachments to mother and father each have positive and negative aspects and thereby complement each other. Both mother and father complexes, therefore, have a role to play in the development of conscience, in religious conceptions of God, and in political and social ideologies.[19]

Fromm's friendship with Karen Horney began to dissolve in 1941 when they were both members of the New York Psychoanalytic Society. A disagreement with some fellow members led to Horney's resignation from the Society. With some sympathetic colleagues she established the American Institute for Psychoanalysis. Fromm was a member of the Institute, but he in turn was caught in another power struggle and his status as a faculty member and analyst was questioned on the grounds that he did not hold a medical degree. Fromm resigned from the Institute in 1943 rather than receive a reduction of his faculty status. Knapp suggests that the impetus for reducing Fromm's faculty status came from Karen Horney herself. Two reasons are given. First Horney felt threatened by "Fromm's steadily increasing influence on her own thought, and by his ever-growing popularity in student circles" especially after the publication of *Escape from Freedom* in 1941. Second, Horney's daughter Marianne had undergone analysis with Fromm in 1939 and as a result, had begun to rebel against her mother.[20]

In 1944 Fromm married for the second time. His second wife, Henny Gurland (1902-1952), had escaped from Nazi-occupied France. It was she who was credited with encouraging Fromm's interest in religious, ethical, and mystical questions and even toward an interest in Zen Buddhism. The years of his marriage to Henny Gurland were productive ones for Fromm during which he solidifed his reputation as both an academic and a popular writer. Between 1940 and 1950 he taught at the University of Michigan as well as New York University and published the first three of his major works: *Escape from Freedom, Man for Himself,* and *Psychoanalysis and Religion.* The latter was a publication of the Terry Lectures he gave at Yale University in 1948-1949. Because of Henny Fromm's deteriorating health, however, the couple moved to Mexico, where Henny died in 1952. Fromm remained in Mexico and served as director of the Psychoanalytic Institute of Mexico. In 1953, while still in

Mexico, he married Annis Freeman, an American. The couple continued to live in Mexico until 1969. Fromm had suffered a heart attack in 1968 and, after recuperating, he and Annis moved, in 1969, to Locarno, Switzerland, where they spent the summer months for the next five years, finally taking up permanent residence in Switzerland in 1974 in the town of Muralto. It was here that Fromm died of heart failure on March 17, 1980.

Erich Fromm was plagued by failing health during the last years of his life. Gerhard Knapp reports that to the end of his life he remained a devoted Buddhist, practicing daily meditation and concentration exercises.[21] It could be added that he remained a devoted humanist. His interest in social, ethical, and religious questions was ultimately an interest in individual human character and the full realization of the individual's essential humanity and of his or her specifically human powers, reason, love, freedom, and responsibility. For Fromm, the axiom "man is the measure of all things" means that the ultimate criterion for judging both religious and ethical systems is the realization of one's essential humanity. This kind of self-realization—and the escape from self-alienation and powerlessness that it implies—is the aim of "humanistic religion." While it is possible to dispute Fromm's tendency to reduce God to a symbol of the human and his interpretation of traditional theistic religions, it is also true that the average person would have little use for a religion that was not "humanistic" in this fundamental sense; if not in its conscious aim, at least in its human effects.

Theory of Personality

Basic to Fromm's theory of personality is the distinction between the non-alienated and the alienated personalities. The nonalienated person is one who experiences himself as the subject of his specifically human powers, who experiences the full development of his powers of reason and love toward the realization of, as Rainer Funk puts it, "his own perfect form." This requires becoming free of all "external heteronomous determinations."[22] Only in this way can one experience one's true identity and therefore authentic relatedness to the world. By contrast, the alienated person is one who, unable to experience himself as the subject of his own human powers, fails to overcome his own sense of separateness and powerlessness and relates to the world in an authoritarian, destructive, or conformist manner.

As a psychotherapist, Fromm believed that the traditional Freudian model of therapy was inadequate to the needs of the patients with whom he had to deal and whose basic problem was a sense of "alienation from oneself, one's fellow man and from nature." Such patients could not be helped by merely removing symptoms: "For those who suffer from alienation, cure does not consist in the absence of illness but in the presence of well-being." Well-being is further defined as "being in accord with the nature of man."[23] For

Fromm, to live in accord with one's essential humanity means to find a "productive" answer to the question which life poses to each one of us. This question is: "How can we overcome the suffering, the imprisonment, the shame which the experience of separateness creates; how can we find union within ourselves, with our fellowman, with nature?" For Fromm, the only "productive" or "progressive" answer to this question is "to be fully born, to develop one's awareness, one's reason, one's capacity to love, to such a point that one transcends one's own egocentric involvement, and arrives at a new harmony, at a new oneness with the world."[24]

It is clear from the previous discussion that Fromm considers "relatedness" to be the fundamental problem of human existence. Why is this so? The answer lies in the very nature of human existence which Fromm defines as "life aware of itself." At a certain point in the evolutionary process a new species emerges which is capable of self-consciousness or self-awareness. This means that, while still part of nature, the human animal "transcends" nature in the sense of no longer adapting to its environment in an instinctually determined way but through the exercise of the specifically human powers of self-awareness, reason, and love. As Fromm puts it, the human animal "has to live his life, he is not lived by it. He is in nature, yet he transcends nature."[25] This transcending of nature involves a breaking of what Fromm calls the "primary ties" or "original harmony" with nature, a state which is incompatible with human self-awareness. For Fromm, the emergence of a creature capable of self-awareness means that "man is born."

Two assertions are made about this birth in both its phylogenetic sense (birth of the human species) and its ontogenetic sense (birth of the individual human being). First, it is an ongoing event. Both the species and the individual must continue to transcend nature and grow in self-awareness, reason, and love so as to be "fully born." "The whole life of the individual is nothing but the process of giving birth to himself: indeed, we should be fully born when we die, although it is the tragic fate of most individuals to die before they are born."[26] Second, birth in this sense is perceived as a negative event in the sense that the rupture of the original harmony with nature and the necessity of finding a new *human* form of relatedness to the world is a giving up of security for insecurity and dependence for independence. One is cast out of a paradise, a return to which is impossible.

The fact that the human person transcends nature while remaining a part of nature constitutes, for Fromm, the basic conflict or dichotomy of human existence. As a result, to be human means to experience two conflicting tendencies which Fromm calls progression and regression. The progressive tendency refers to the ongoing process of "birth" or the transcending of nature. This involves the continued growth of self-awareness, the ongoing development of one's human powers of reason and love, as well as growth in freedom and independence and acceptance of the risk and insecurity implied in human freedom. The regressive tendency is the tendency to return to the original harmony with nature. In individual human existence it refers to the tendency to give up reason and freedom for the sake of security and dependence. Among the examples of this that Fromm cites are "incestuous ties" (e.g., remaining dependent on mother or a mother figure) and social conformity, both of which inhibit independent thought, judgment, and action. All human striving, Fromm argues, is an attempt to find answers to this basic problem of human existence. "We are never free from two conflicting tendencies: one to emerge from the womb, from the animal form of existence into a more human existence, from bondage to freedom; another, to return to the womb, to nature, to certainty and security."[27]

It could be argued that Fromm's writings are, for the most part, attempts to elaborate the various ways in which this basic dichotomy of human existence is experienced. In terms of character structure this basic dichotomy is experienced as the conflict of *productive* versus *nonproductive* character orientations. In Fromm's analysis, this basic conflict is experienced in a variety of ways, specifically in five particular conflicts which he calls "existential dichotomies." Each of these existential dichotomies gives rise to an "existential need," that character trait which resolves the dichotomy in the direction of "productive" living. The five existential dichotomies with the corresponding existential needs are as follows: (1) relatedness versus narcissism (productive relatedness); (2) creativeness versus destructivenss (transcendence); (3) brotherliness versus incest (rootedness); (4) individuality versus conformity (identity); and (5) reason versus irrationality (a frame of orientation and an object of devotion). In all of these distinctions it is clear that Fromm, as a psychoanalyst, has maintained Freud's conflictual model of human existence. As a "humanistic" psychoanalyst, however, his focus, unlike Freud, is not on instinctual conflicts but on what he terms "existential dichotomies." These refer to conflicts which are not symptoms of pathology (neurosis) but part and parcel of normal human existence.

Relatedness versus Narcissism (Productive Relatedness)

The self-awareness which characterizes human existence is a mixed blessing. On the one hand, it is the basis for that sense of unique identity by which I differentiate myself from others. On the other hand, that very sense of uniqueness and individuality creates, in turn, a feeling of isolation and separateness. If I am different from everyone else, that very difference makes me separate from everyone else. In Fromm's view, the most fundamental human need is to overcome this sense of isolation, separateness, and, therefore, powerlessness through relatedness to others and to one's world. Failure to do so results in a regression to infantile narcissism. "The necessity to unite with other human beings, to be related to them, is an imperative need on the fulfillment of which man's sanity depends."[28] So fundamental is this need for relatedness that it may be achieved by sacrificing that sense of individuality which accompanies self-awareness. Relatedness which involves the loss of one's individuality is what Fromm calls "non-productive" relatedness. Nonproductive ways of overcoming individual separateness include submission to another person or group (masochism) domination of or control over others (sadism), destructiveness and hatred or gaining the acceptance of others by trying to be like everyone else (conformity). All these forms of relatedness involve the loss of individuality, integrity, and independence. The masochist is dependent on those to whom he submits as is the sadist on those he dominates and the conformist on the group to which he wants to belong. In every case the need to belong obliterates the need to be truly oneself, and one's identity is ultimately defined only in reference to another person or group.

In contrast, "productive" relatedness is the type of relatedness in which one's individuality, integrity, and independence are preserved and which, therefore, allows for the full development of one's human powers. Productiveness in this sense may characterize the different ways in which we relate to our world—through thought, action, and feeling. Productive thought refers to "the proper grasp of the world through reason." It is objective thought in the sense of being free of prejudice or dependency, but it is also concerned in the sense that it is not knowledge for its own sake but motivated by concern for human welfare. Productive action refers to work which is planned and carried out by the subject (Fromm cites art and craftsmanship as examples) so that it is truly an act of self-expression. Productive love refers to the experience of union with another or others in which each party retains his or her sense of individuality and independence. "In the experience of love," Fromm concludes, "the paradox happens that two people become one, and remain two at the same time."[29] Productive love, he suggests has four characteristics: *care* for the growth and fulfillment of the other; *responsibility* in the sense of a freely made response to another; *respect,* which in its root meaning refers to seeing the other as he or she is, not as a projection of one's own fears or desires; *knowledge* of the other without which respect is not possible.[30] It can be seen that all of these forms of productiveness involve self-expression or the expression of what is truly one's own. This ability to think one's own thoughts, do one's own deeds, and feel one's own feelings is what Fromm calls "spontaneity." Productiveness is the experience of oneself as the true subject of one's thought, action, and feeling. The opposite is self-alienation.

> The inability to act spontaneously, to express what one genuinely feels and thinks, and the resulting necessity to present a pseudo self to others and oneself, are the root of the feeling of inferiority and weakness. Whether or not we are aware of it, there is nothing of which we are more ashamed than of not being ourselves, and there is nothing that gives us greater pride and happiness than to think, to feel, and to say what is ours.[31]

Creativeness versus Destructiveness
(Transcendence)

If the acquisition of self-awareness means the breaking of the primary ties and original harmony with nature, it also means that the human animal "cannot be content with the passive role of the creature."[32] The human person is driven by the need to transcend the passivity of being totally a part of nature. He must live his own life rather than have nature live through him, be active rather than passive, and take control of and responsibility for his life. The passive, creaturely condition can be transcended, however, in a positive or negative way, through creativeness or destructiveness. Creativeness means transcending the passive condition of the creature by becoming in some sense, a "creator." This can be achieved through the procreation of new life, through material and artistic creativity, but also through love in the sense that care and nurture of the loved one are creative acts fostering the loved one's self-realization.

The need for transcendence can also be answered by destructiveness seen as a way of transcending life. "If I cannot create life," Fromm argues, "I can destroy it. To destroy life makes me also transcend it."[33] Destructiveness is an alternative to creativeness, a "secondary potentiality" which asserts itself when the capacity for love and creativity are frustrated. It includes not only the physical destruction of life but also the emotional destructiveness of hatred. In Fromm's view the existential conflict between creativeness and destructiveness, love and hate, points to an existential need for transcendence. "Creation and destruction, love and hate, are not two instincts which exist independently. They are both answers to the same need for transcendence, and the will to destroy must rise when the will to create cannot be satisfied."[34]

Brotherliness versus Incest
(Rootedness)

To transcend the original harmony with nature is to be expelled from one's natural prehuman home with all the certainty, security, and sense of belonging it provided. What is required is to find a new home, a new way of belonging in the world based not on instinctual adaptation but upon the exercise of those specifically human powers which accompany self-awareness. As Fromm contends:

> Man's evolution is based on the fact that he has lost his orginal home, nature, and that he can never return to it, can never become an animal again. There is only one way he can take: to emerge fully from his natural home, to find a new home—one which he creates, by making the world a human one and by becoming truly human himself.[35]

This sense of belonging, of being "at home" in the world, is an existential need that Fromm calls "rootedness," the experience of having "roots." Deprived of natural roots, the human person must find new human roots in order to feel at home in the world again. This is true not only of the evolution of the human species but also of the development of the individual. For the infant, the primary tie and original harmony is with the all-loving, all-protective, all-nourishing mother. In this dependent relationship the infant finds her sense of belonging, her rootedness. Growing up means trading the security of the dependent relationship for the insecurity and uncertainty of independence. Fromm concludes: "Just as birth means to leave the enveloping protection of the womb, growing up means to leave the protective orbit of the mother."[36]

Because of the regressive tendency of human nature, however, there is "a deep craving in man not to sever the natural ties, to fight against being torn away from nature, from mother, blood and soil."[37] These are what Fromm refers to as "incestuous ties," ties of dependence and conformity to mother, mother figures, family, nature, race, and social group. Clinging to such ties represents the negative or "non-productive" way of satisfying the need for rootedness in that they inhibit the development of self-awareness, reason, love, and independence. "Productive" rootedness consists in establishing bonds of brotherliness and productive relatedness with others. A truly human form of rootedness can be found only in genuine human community based on reason, love, and individual integrity, not in dependence and conformity. This concept of rootedness offers an insight into Fromm's interpretation of the Oedipus complex, which differs from that of Freud. For Freud the little boy's *sexual* attachment to mother brings him into conflict with the father and must be abandoned because of the presence of this bigger, stronger rival. For Fromm, both boys and girls experience an *emotional* attachment to mother (the source of rootedness). This regressive attachment, in normal development, is abandoned, not because of the threatening father but because the progressive tendency toward independence is stronger.

Individuality versus Conformity
(Identity)

The fact that self-awareness is an ambiguous experience involving feelings of both individuality and separateness points to the need for a strong sense of identity. Only on this basis can one overcome separatenes and powerlessness in a way that preserves one's individuality, that is, in a productive way. Failure to develop a strong sense of individual identity creates the possibility of overcoming existential separation and isolation through what Fromm calls "herd conformity." In this case an individual finds his identity as a member of a group, whether social, economic, religious, or racial. He tries to be like everyone else in the group by conforming to the group's typical modes of thought, actions, attitudes, cultural tastes, and so on. In this way he overcomes his separateness and aloneness by "becoming part of somebody or something bigger than himself,"[38] but at the same time forfeits his sense of personal identity and integrity. Fromm points out that the development of Western culture in the direction of political and economic freedom created the basis for the experience of personal identity as distinct from clan identity of the primitives. Most people, however, because of the regressive tendency, failed to develop a strong sense of personal identity and retreated to a pseudo or herd identity in which one's identity was found in the nation, religion, or social or economic class to which one belonged or the occupation one pursued.[39]

Reason versus Irrationality
(Frame of Orientation and Object of Devotion)

The conflict of reason versus irrationality follows from the need for relatedness with and rootedness within one's world. In discussing this existential dichotomy and the existential need to which it points, Fromm is underlining the fact that one can relate to one's world in a rational or an irrational way. The need for a frame of orientation arises from the need to relate to one's world intellectually. A frame of orientation is thus a consistent way of viewing and understanding one's world. Such a consistent view of the world is rational, Fromm argues, if it satisfies reason, that is, it approximates reality by being consistent with available objective evidence. An irrational frame of orientation is one that, while not objectively valid, and in some cases quite nonsensical, nevertheless satisfies the emotional need to belong in that the thought system in question is shared by a group. "Even the most irrational orientation," Fromm argues, "if it is shared by a considerable body of men, gives the individual the feeling of oneness with others, a certain amount of security and stability which the neurotic person lacks."[40]

The need for a frame of orientation is coupled with the need for an "object of devotion" since one must relate oneself to the world not only intellectually but also with the emotional, affective, and revolutionary aspects of his being; not only with thought but also with feeling and action. Not only is there a need for understanding but also a need for commitment which gives purpose and direction to one's life. A rational object of devotion is one which satisfies this need for the exercise of responsibility through a freely made commitment to a person, a group, a cause, or a god. An irrational object of devotion, by contrast, does not involve an opportunity for the exercise of freedom and responsibility; it provides an "escape from freedom" through submission to an authoritarian person, group, or deity.

The need for a frame of orientation and an object of devotion provides Fromm with the context for his discussion of religion which he defines as: "any system of thought and action shared by a group which gives the individual a frame of orientation and an object of devotion."[41] The distinction, therefore, between humanistic and authoritarian religion reflects the distinction between a rational and an irrational frame of orientation and object of devotion.

Fromm's discussion of the various productive and nonproductive character orientations is relevant to the question of character structure. Thus the various nonproductive orientations are related to certain character types. Masochism is characteristic of the "receptive" character who is essentially dependent, looks outside of herself for the source of happiness and fulfillment, and wants to receive it. Sadism is the character of the "exploitative" character who also sees the nonself as the source of everything good, but by contrast, actively seizes it. Destructiveness is the mark of the "hoarding" character who sees the world as a threat, resists new experiences or ideas, and clings to what he already has. Finally, conformity defines the "marketing" character who sees himself as a product and must conform to make himself acceptable or "marketable" to the group of which he wants to be part.[42]

Fromm also applies the basic dichotomy of progression versus regression to the question of human growth and development. In *The Heart of Man*, he describes this dichotomy developmentally as the conflict of the *syndrome of growth* versus the *syndrome of decay*. Here the conflict is between productive orientations, which represent a progressive movement toward the fullness of growth, and nonproductive orientations which foster a regressive movement toward psychological "decay." In this context Fromm speaks of three existential dichotomies: necrophilia (the love of death) versus biophilia (the love of life) narcissism versus relatedness and "incestuous fixation" versus independence. Again, in *To Have or to Be?* he describes this same dichotomy ethically as the conflict between the *being* and *having* modes of existence. The differentiation here is between two types of *ethical* character and implies an ethical distinction between those who find their sense of identity in what they possess and those who experience themselves as the active subject of their own thoughts, feelings, and actions. Finally, in *Psychoanalysis and Religion*, the dichotomy is seen as experienced religiously in the conflict between *humanistic* and *authoritarian* religion.

Theory of Religion

Fromm's theory of religion is rooted in his view of the fundamental dichotomy of human existence. The fact that the human person transcends nature while remaining a part of nature gives rise, as we have seen, to two conflicting tendencies: progression and regression. The progressive tendency is toward ever greater transcendence, self-awareness and independence, the ongoing development of one's specifically human powers of reason and love as well as toward productive relatedness and a human form of rootedness. The regressive tendency represents a restoration of the prehuman state of harmony with nature, a state of dependence on incestuous ties to mother or mother figures, and a craving for the certainty and security which accompanies such dependence. In Fromm's humanistic view these conflicting tendencies represent innate potential and character is oriented along progressive or regressive lines largely through environmental influences. One of those influences is religion. Hence, for Fromm, the psychological question about religion is not about its origin but about its value. Is it progressive or regressive? Does it contribute towards the full development of one's human powers or stunt the growth of those powers? Since religion may do either, Fromm distinguishes between authoritarian and humanistic types of religious experience.

Authoritarian Religion

This is Fromm's term for a religion or religious experience which orients character development along regressive lines and therefore blocks the development of reason, love, and independence. As the name suggests, it involves irrational submission to authority—to a deity who must be obeyed—not by reason of any moral qualities which God exhibits, such as justice, and love, but simply because of the power and control He exercises over humanity. Therefore, the main virtue of authoritarian religion is obedience while its cardinal sin is disobedience. "In authoritarian relgion," Fromm states, "God is a symbol of power and force. He is supreme because He has supreme power, and man in juxtaposition is utterly powerless."[43] The relative positions of the human and the divine in this description suggest that in this type of religon the human subject finds a regressive or nonproductive answer to the fundamental human problem which Fromm has identified as separateness, aloneness, and powerlessness. In authoritarian religion one tries to overcome these feelings through surrender to a power transcending human existence. Through this kind of submission to a powerful authority, one escapes from the feelings of separateness and powerlessness but at the price of one's independence. Fromm describes it as a kind of nonproductive trade-off: "In the act of surrender he loses his independence and integrity as an individual but he gains the feeling of being protected by an awe-inspiring power of which, as it were, he becomes a part."[44]

In authoritarian religion, then, the human subject is powerless and insignificant and can feel strength only through surrender and submission to a powerful God or religious authority figure. About those who in this way surrender all power of independent thought, action, and love to a power outside themselves, Fromm concludes: "There is nothing they do, feel, or think which is not somehow related to this power. They expect protection from 'him,' make 'him' also responsible for whatever may be the outcome of their own action."[45] Thus the price of such surrender is *alienation* from one's true self. The psychological dynamic at work in such a religion is *projection*. The human subject projects his human powers of reason and love onto God, thereby turning God into an idol, and can therefore get back in touch with his own essential humanity only through submission to this idol. In discussing this point with Richard Evans, Fromm remarks: "This often happens in religion. God or some idol in a pagan image is endowed with a human power. The individual impoverishes himself, gives all his power to the figure outside, and then is in touch with himself only by submitting to and worshipping that figure."[46] Fromm's point (to which we shall return later) is that such idol worship is contrary to the spirit of Judaeo-Christian monotheism. Therefore, those who turn the God of the Bible into an idol through projection betray that tradition.

In thus identifying authoritarian religion with the mechanism of projection Fromm aligns himself with the philosopher Ludwig Feuerbach (1804-1872), who explained religion as resulting from the projection of humanity's essential powers—reason, will, and love—onto a divine figure who is then worshiped as infinite reason, infinite will, and infinite love. In the process, however, the human subject is stripped of these very powers and is reduced to a state of emptiness and powerlessness, which in religious terms translates into "sinfulness." Whereas Hegel had said that human nature was God in alienated form, Feuerbach argued that God was really human nature in alienated form. To study the divine nature is therefore to study human nature. Or, in Feuerbach's famous dictum, theology is really anthropology. In the following key passage from *Psychoanalysis and Religion*, Fromm describes authoritarian religion in terms of such projection and the resulting alienation.

> In authoritarian religion God becomes the sole possessor of what was originally man's: of his reason and love. The more perfect God becomes, the more imperfect becomes man. He *projects* the best he has onto God and thus impoverishes himself. Now God has all love, all wisdom, all justice—and man is deprived of these qualities, he is empty and poor. He had begun with the feeling of smallness, but he now has become completely powerless and without strength; all his powers have been projected onto God. When man has thus projected his own most valuable powers onto God, what of his relationship to his own powers? They have become separated from him and in this process he has become *alienated* from himself. Everything he has is now God's and nothing is left in him. *His only access to himself is through God.* In worshipping God he tries to get in touch with that part of himself which he has lost through projection. After having given God all he has, he begs God to return to him some of what was originally his own. But having lost his own he is completely at God's mercy. He necessarily feels like a "sinner" since he has deprived himself of everything that is good, and it is only through God's mercy or grace that he can regain that which alone makes him human. And in order to persuade God to give him some of his love, he must prove to him how utterly deprived he is of love; in order to per-

suade God to guide him by his superior wisdom he must prove to him how deprived he is of wisdom when he is left to himself.[47]

In Fromm's view, the projection and the resulting alienation feed each other so that the individual "is caught in a painful dilemma. The more he praises God, the emptier he becomes. The emptier he becomes, the more sinful he feels. The more sinful he feels, the more he praises his God—and the less able he is to regain himself."[48]

Humanistic Religion

As the name suggests, this refers to a kind of religion the aim of which is not submission and obedience to an authoritarian God but human self-realization, that is, the actualization of one's human powers of reason and love. It is through the exercise of thought and love, Fromm argues, that one achieves relatedness with one's world. In its highest form that relatedness becomes a mystical sense of "oneness with the all." This core religious experience of humanistic religion is what Rainer Funk refers to as a nontheistic kind of mysticism, which involves "the optimal realization of the experience of man's oneness with himself, his life, and his world."[49] The notion of faith is similarly secularized. Faith is not to be understood as "assent to propositions on the credit of the proposer," that is, not on the basis of divine revelation but rather as "certainty of conviction based on one's experience of thought and feeling."[50]

Apart from Fromm's severely intellectualized understanding of faith ("assent to propositions"), a further question arises: What, if any is the place of a deity in this kind of humanistic religion if not the object of mystical experience or of faith? Can humanistic religion be theistic? Fromm's answer defines a theism in which God becomes a symbol of the human reality: "Inasmuch as humanistic religions are theistic, God is a symbol of *man's own powers* which he tries to realize in his life, and is not a symbol of force and domination, having *power over man.*"[51] A God who is anything more than a symbol of essential humanity suggests to Fromm notions such as revelation and external authority, which conflict with his humanistic understanding of faith. A similar kind of incompatibility is attributed to the Lutheran and Calvinist concepts of human sinfulness and the need for divine grace and forgiveness (as Fromm understands them) as well as the Catholic doctrine of papal infallibility. These represent, for Fromm, a craving for certainty and security at the expense of individual integrity and independence.

Humanistic religion further involves a rejection of what Fromm sees as two basic fallacies of authoritarian religion. The first is the idea that dependence on a power transcending the human subject is natural since dependence is part and parcel of human existence. In reply, Fromm distinguishes between humility and self-humiliation. Humility is a realistic recognition of one's limitations and dependence on forces outside of oneself. Self-humiliation, on the other hand, is a masochistic and self-destructive worship of those forces.[52] The second is the more fundamental concept of the need for transcendence, that is, the human longing to relate oneself to something beyond the self, to something transcendent. It is reasonable, the theist argues, to assume the existence of a transcendent being who corresponds to this human need. Fromm dismisses this argument as a "fallacy of theological thought" and argues in response that such a human need simply proves his own premise that God is a creation of human projection and therefore a symbol of the deep-seated human need for love and relatedness. Such a need, however, does not prove that there is a transcendent being who corresponds to this need.[53]

Fromm's evaluation of authoritarian and humanistic forms of religion is so black and white that one could scarcely disagree with it. What is problematic in this comparison, however, is the implied classification of all theistic religions—those involving a relationship with a transcendent God—as authoritarian. He seems to be suggesting that where God is seen as something more than a symbol of some human value, religion cannot be truly humanistic. He is clearly evaluating religion in the light of his own humanistic version of psychoanalysis. Hence religion is found to be authentic (that is, humanistic) when it has the same goals as humanistic psychoanalysis, that is, the development of our specifically human powers of reason and love. The development of both of these human powers requires that one be liberated from "incestuous ties" of dependency. Growth from incest to freedom and independence is a precondition for both the ability to think for oneself and make independent value judgments as well as the ability to love others as similarly independent persons rather than as functions in one's life. Only those who are free of incestuous ties have sufficient inner freedom to think and love independently.[54]

Fromm states: "Analytic therapy is essentially an attempt to help the patient gain or regain his capacity for love."[55] This aim, he argues, is consistent with the aim of humanistic religions in which the human subject's love of God is a symbol of "productive" love. "The human reality behind the concept of man's love for God in humanistic religion is man's ability to love productively, to love without greed, without submission and domination, to love from the fullness of his personality, just as God's love is a symbol for love out of strength and not out of weakness."[56] The theist could certainly agree with Fromm on at least three points: that the emphasis on love of one's neighbor is common to both religion and humanistic psychoanalysis; that there is often a need for analytic therapy if one is to gain the capacity for love; that the great religions often undermine that very inner freedom which is the prerequisite for love when they become bureaucratic mass organizations. On the other hand, the theist might insist that the ability to love along with the inner freedom which makes it possible is not the human achievement that Fromm describes but something that one is rendered capable of through some kind of redemptive experience. As a humanistic thinker Fromm reveals both the close affinities between humanistic and religious thought and the deep division that separates them.

The Concept of God

In Fromm's understanding of humanistic religion God is not conceived of as a power dominating human existence but as a symbol of human powers of reason and love which the human subject is trying to actualize in his life. This emphasis on the *symbolic* meaning of God is consistent with Fromm's emphasis on the *psychological* meaning or value of religion. While most religious believers would agree that their concept or image of God is a symbolic/ metaphorical representation of a transcendent reality which ultimately cannot be comprehended, they nevertheless believe in the objective reality of that transcendent being. In other words, there is a "God beyond God," that is, beyond the various conceptions of that ultimate reality. For Fromm, however, what is conceptualized in the various concepts of God is a human experience. This is true, he maintains, of all concepts which are therefore valuable only insofar as they faithfully express the human experience to which they refer.[57] While this may be clearly true of a concept such as "love" (Fromm's primary example), which clearly refers to an inner feeling or experience, a concept such as "God" may not so easily be taken as symbolic only of an inner experience. It is nevertheless true that a concept such as God correlates with certain subjective feelings and attitudes in the mind of the one who uses it, and it is this "psychological" meaning of the concept of God that interests Fromm. What does the idea of God mean subjectively to the believer? Freedom or dependence? Love or fear? Integrity or submission? This psychological meaning of the concept of God might also be called the "existential" question ("What does God mean for human existence?") as distinct from the ontological question ("What is God in himself?").

The "question of God" then, for Fromm, is the psychological question, the question of the human experience or attitude behind the human use of the concept. The question becomes: Is God a concept referring to genuine, that is, "productive" human values (freedom, reason, love) or an "idol" which alienates the human subject from her true self? A God who is a symbol of one's productive human powers fosters the development of those powers. A God who demands submission and obedience alienates the believer from his or her human powers since one projects them onto God. Those very powers which are expressions of one's essential humanity are seen now as exclusively divine powers of which the human subject is therefore bereft. This is what Fromm means by an "idol," a figure onto whom one's productive human powers have been projected, resulting in a sense of alienation from one's true self. Accordingly, he interprets the Judeo-Christian tradition of monotheism as liberation from idolatry. "The acknowledgment of God is, fundamentally, the negation of idols."[58] Moreover, in Fromm's interpretation of the Old Testament, the God who forbids idolatry becomes himself less of an idol and more of a humanistic symbol, less arbitrary in his judgments, more subject himself to the principles of justice and, finally, a "nameless" God who, unlike an idol, is not a "thing." In Fromm's view the optimal development of theism is to the point where God is reduced to a symbol. In this respect it is seen as analogous to the development of a child's relationship to its parents. The child begins in a state of dependence on and submission to parents but matures to the point where "he has established the motherly and fatherly principles in himself. He has become his own father and mother." Similarly, theism develops from a state of helpless dependence on and obedience to an arbitrary God to a point where "God ceases to be an outside power, where man has incorporated the principles of love and justice into himself, where he has become one with God, and eventually to a point where he speaks of God only in a poetic, symbolic sense."[59]

Nontheistic Religious Experience

When Fromm concludes that God is to be spoken of "only in a poetic, symbolic sense," he does not mean, as we have seen, that our human conceptions of God are images and metaphors for a more ultimate reality. He means, rather, that the concept of God is symbolic of a certain kind of human experience. In humanistic religion, this human experience is the fullness of human growth and "productiveness." This represents a thoroughly humanistic understanding not only of God but also of religious experience. If the concept of God does not point to any ontological reality, then what is generally called "religious" experience is deprived of any transcendent point of reference. Fromm rejects the idea that religious experience is necessarily connected with a concept of God. Nevertheless, because this is such a widely held opinion, and to avoid ambiguity, he uses the term "X-experience" to describe that fullness of human productiveness which constitutes the "nontheistic religious experience." The X-experience refers to a kind of experience which can be interpreted or conceptualized theistically or nontheistically, that is, with or without reference to God. A religious believer and an atheist, for example, may both have the same kind of mystical experience but will interpret it differently, one as an experience of God, the other in more naturalistic/humanistic terms. For Fromm, what is important is the "experiential substratum," not the differing conceptualizations of it.[60]

The experience behind the concept of God, therefore, is a purely naturalistic experience which has no necessary connection with God. This opens up the possibility of a "humanistic 'religiosity' without religion, without dogmas and institutions."[61] This experience—the X-experience—is described by Fromm as having the following characteristics: (1) the experience of life as a problem, that is, an awareness of life's dichotomies and the problem of human alienation; (2) the experience of values as hierarchical, the highest value being one's own human self-realization; (3) the experience of one's self as an end rather than a means to some further end (pleasure, money, power, etc.); (4) the experience of self-transcendence. This last aspect of the X-experience is what Fromm refers to as the "letting go of one's ego, one's greed, and with it, of one's fears." This refers to the overcoming of separateness, a transcending of the desire to maintain one's isolated ego for the sake of relatedness. This is what Fromm means by "transcending the ego, leaving the prison of one's selfishness and separateness." Here we have a psychological/humanistic/nontheistic understanding of "transcendence."[62]

It is clear from the above description that the X-experience, in its optimal development, works toward "the disappearance of narcissism" and an attitude of openness to one's world. The overcoming of one's egoism and narcissism is seen as the prerequisite for an attitude of openness to, oneness with, and love for one's world. The optimal realization, therefore, of the X-experience results in a mystical sense of "oneness with the all." The overcoming of narcissism and separateness is the foundation of both the ethical and "religious" aims of humanistic religion. In his conversation with Richard Evans, Fromm maintains that these aims are consistent with the ethical aims of Buddhism, Taoism, prophetic religion, and the New Testament.

> ... the aim of life is to overcome one's narcissism, that is to say, to overcome that hindrance to one's development which is the greed for self and for property, that which sustains within one the illusion of one's indestructibility, that which prevents one's being open to the world. As the mystics say, we must be empty in order to be full with the world. That is a command which follows from the nature of man because it happens that a narcissistic person is very unhappy. He is separated, and he is frightened. If he is extremely narcissistic, he is insane; that is precisely what insanity is.[63]

This is Fromm's version of the concept common to both Judaeo-Christianity and Zen Buddhism of "emptying" oneself in order to become completely open and responsive to the world.

For Fromm, the only fundamental way of overcoming the potential insanity of narcissism is "the full productive response to the world which in its highest form is enlightenment."[64] This enlightenment is the aim of humanistic psychoanalysis and, in Fromm's view, it is analogous to that enlightenment which is the aim of Zen Buddhism. Zen enlightenment is made possible by freedom from illusions, which in turn makes possible an immediate, unreflected grasp of reality, a kind of intuitive apprehension of reality "as it is" without "intellection and reflection."[65] Psychoanalysis seeks a similar type of enlightenment in its attempt to make the unconscious conscious. For Freud, this meant consciousness of repressed instinctual impulses. For Fromm it means "to overcome repressedness and alienation from myself, and hence from the stranger. It means to wake up, to shed illusions, fictions and lies, to see reality as it is."[66] These words imply that because our conscious life is socially conditioned (thus creating a "social character") it is subject to "fictions and illusion" which distort the way we see ourselves and our world. Society, in other words, largely determines what enters consciousness and what remains unconscious because language, logic, and behavior are socially conditioned. Fromm calls this the "threefold filter."[67] What results is alienation from one's true self and one's world. The psychoanalytic analogue to Buddhist enlightenment is "derepression" by which the illusions of socially conditioned conciousness are overcome as well as the state of alienation from one's essential humanity or what Fromm calls "the whole human person." This overcoming of alienation from one's true self and one's world is, in Fromm's view, the consistent aim of Zen Buddhism.

Evaluation

We began our discussion of Erich Fromm with Gerhard Knapp's description of him as "one of the most influential humanists of this century." Of this there can be little doubt. Fromm's contribution to humanistic thought and his work as a humanistic social critic are immense. Since, however, our focus is on his theory of religion, we are bound to ask to what extent both his humanism and his social scientific approach can do justice to the essential meaning of religion. What follows is not an exhaustive critique but a few leading questions designed to stimulate discussion of Fromm's undertanding of what constitutes authentic religious experience. These questions are grouped around three fundamental themes of Fromm's thought: his analysis of the human condition, his understanding of religion and religious experience, and his critique of theism.

The Human Condition

Fromm's analysis of the human condition centers around the basic dichotomy that characterizes it, the fact that the human subject is part of nature and yet transcends nature. This is a consequence of human self-awareness which is the source of both the sense of individuality and also the sense of separation and alienation. The need to overcome separation and alienation through genuine productive human relatedness is seen as the human person's fundamental need. The existential conflicts engendered by this need are conflicts between "productive" and "non-productive" means of satisfying it.

This analysis of the human condition is based on psychoanalytic, sociological, philosophical, and ethical insights. Such an interdisciplinary approach along with Fromm's conviction that psychological well-being does not mean mere adjustment but living in conformity with objectively established laws of human nature have led some to label his work as "unscientific" speculation. Rainer Funk responds to such criticism in the following way:

> Such attacks are the result of Fromm's disputes with positivistic tendencies that have no use for anything but precisely demonstrable, objective insights confined to a single discipline. Fromm believed that responsible scientific work cannot ignore the ends of its activity or refuse to synthesize insights from a variety of disciplines. Neither can it be neutral toward the ethical relevance of its findings. Science therefore requires a frame of orientation that is ultimately not deducible from the insights of any single human discipline.[68]

Or as Fromm himself put it: It is better to deal with problems which are significant but which cannot be rigorously proved than to deal with problems which can be proved but are insignificant.[69]

To be sure, Fromm's broad interdisciplinary approach is more adequate to the task of analyzing the human condition than is a purely positivistic one. Nevertheless one may ask whether questions such as the problem of human alienation and its solution escape Fromm's social-scientific analysis. John H. Schaar suggests that Fromm's "sociological" approach "blinds him to basic dimensions of the problem of alienation." This clearly refers to the analysis of alienation in terms of "social character" which, he argues, bypasses "the hard question of how far social reform can heal the wounds of alienation." Such reforms are described as "utopian solutions for problems which have no sociological solutions at all."[70] To be fair, Fromm goes beyond sociology and locates the source of alienation in the reality of human self-awareness. But, as a humanist, he stops short of an existentialist or religious analysis and, in Schaar's view, any solution to the problems of human finitide and estrangement "must be metaphysical, not sociological."[71] Again, it should be pointed out that Fromm's solution to this problem is also psychological, or, more accurately, psychoanalytic. Alienation is overcome by making the unconscious conscious, thereby overcoming the illusions of consciousness and being reunited with one's essential humanity. This is what religion calls "salvation" (wholeness or healing) and it is seen as coming from an external source of grace and redemption. As J. Stanley Glen points out, for Fromm, alienation comes from without (social influences) and salvation comes from within (the unconcious), while for redemptive religions such as Christianity alienation comes from within (the human condition) and salvation from without (the grace of God).[72]

Religion and Religious Experience

As we have seen, Fromm's humanistic approach evaluates religion and religious experience in purely functional terms. The function of religion is to provide the individual with a "frame of orientation and an object of devotion." Its value lies in the extent to which, in performing this function, it contributes toward a "productive" character orientation, that is, toward the development of one's human powers of reason and love. Religion is here being evaluated purely in terms of its psychological value and by the application of purely psychological criteria. Is it conducive to the development of progressive or regressive character orientation? In the theorists we have studied thus far we have already noted the reductionist hazard in this approach. Does it reduce religion to a purely psychological phenomenon having a purely psychological value? On the other hand, it could be argued that this approach represents a legitimate methodological limitation. The psychologist can study religion only in its psychological aspect, that is, can study questions such as God and religions only *as they are experienced by the human subject*. The field of religious studies is made up of several disciplines each of which studies a different aspect of the religious phenomenon (e.g., psychology of religion, sociology of religion, philosophy of religion, etc.). For any one of those disciplines to pretend to exhaust the meaning of religion would be clearly reductionist.

Whether Fromm is reductionist in this sense is open to debate. The fact that psychological theories of religion are only partial explanations of the total phenomenon of religion does not in itself make them reductionist. The litmus test for reductionism would seem to be the extent to which the theorist understands religion on its own terms and is willing to enter into serious dialogue with the religionist and the theologian. In this context, it is significant that the religion to which Fromm is most sympathetic is Buddhism, largely because of its nontheistic features. One could argue that he too easily dismisses theistic religions as, for the most part, authoritarian in character. Though he speaks of the possibility of a humanistic religion which is theistic, it is clear that "theistic" in this context refers to a God who is merely a symbol of the "X-experience" and not a transcendent reality. We shall return to Fromm's attitude toward theism in the following section. At this point, however, it could be argued that one of the roots of this attitude lies in a fundamental confusion between "religion" and "religious experience."

Fromm's most systematic treatment of the distinction between authoritarian and humanistic religion is found in Chapter 3 of *Psychoanalysis and Religion*. The chapter is entitled "An Analysis of Some Types of Religious Experience." By the end of the chapter, however, it becomes clear that when the author turns his attention to theistic religions, he is no longer differentiating types of religious experience but types of religion. Thus he is able to point to the authoritarian character of Calvinism, Lutheranism, and Catholicism. What is overlooked is the fact that among Calvinist, Lutheran, and Catholic believers there is a variety of religious experiences. Some believers appropriate their religious tradition in such a way that it becomes an authoritarian type of religious experience, which inhibits the full development of their human powers. For others it is a humanizing and liberating experience.

It could be argued that Fromm's psychology of religion fails to acknowledge what William James clearly recognized, that the distinction between types of religious experience transcends the distinction between various religious traditions.

Theism

The use of the terms "authoritarian" and "humanistic" to evaluate different types of religious experience is not only legitimate but would seem to correspond to the way most people would think about religion, even if only implicitly. After all, who would not prefer an experience of God and religion that made one more fully human? However, the above-mentioned confusion between religious experience and religion seems to have led Fromm to the conviction that theistic religions are almost inevitably authoritarian, that is, lead to authoritarian type of experience. Unless, of course, God is understood merely as a symbol of human experience. In which case can it still be properly called theism? It will be recalled that Fromm compares the theist's relationship to God with that of child to parents. In both cases he describes development as a progression from complete dependence and submission to a state of autonomy in which both parental and divine figures are internalized and cease to be outside powers. While it is true that the growing child eventually "becomes his own father and mother," develops a conscience, and becomes capable of value judgments independent of parental authority, it is not true that the parents thereby simply disappear. Is it not rather the case that one develops a more mature relationship with one's parents? In the same way, the growing maturity and independence of the theist does not necessarily mean the reduction of God to a figure that can be spoken of "only in a poetic, symbolic sense," but a more mature relationship with a God who remains real just as one's parents remain real. Fromm seems unable to conceive of a God who allows people to grow up.

We shall conclude this discussion with a brief listing of some further areas of misunderstanding which make it difficult for Fromm to link theistic religions with a humanistic type of religious experience.

1. Fromm seems to make no allowance for the paradoxical character of theistic religion and therefore is unappreciative of the lived experience of many theists that, in J. Stanley Glen's words, "there is a kind of authoritarianism and therefore submission and surrender which ultimately liberates the individual."[73]
2. In *Psychoanalysis and Religion* (pp. 54-55), one of the psychological roots of theism—the need for transcendence—is explained as simply the need for relatedness. Others would see it is much more—as the need for an ultimate depth dimension to life, ultimate meaning, ultimate destiny, and

an ultimate reality which gives unity to the diversity of human experience.

3. Humanistic religion, as Fromm understands it, makes human fulfillment and self-realization the direct goal of religion. In theistic religions, human fulfillment is seen as the by-product or side effect of a larger commitment to something or someone beyond the self. Furthermore, not only the theist but also an existentialist thinker such as Viktor Frankl would suggest that human self-actualizaion of any kind, such as the development of one's powers of reason and love, cannot be the direct object of one's human striving; it is rather the by-product or side effect of self-transcendence, that is, of a commitment to something or someone beyond the self (e.g., to a person, a cause, a God).

4. Fromm betrays a lack of understanding of some basic concepts of theistic religion. His severely intellectualized understanding of faith ("assent to propositions") ignores the affective dimension of trust as well as the notion of faith as a total human response to another. In his critique of Fromm, Glen argues that Fromm has "little or no conception of the meaning of grace," seeing it as creating an authoritarian relationship which robs the recipient of his freedom and a legalistic type of religion. Glen concludes: "Despite the fact that Luther and Calvin were unalterably opposed to salvation by works of law, he [Fromm] sees in their gospel nothing but works of law."[74]

5. Finally, Fromm speaks of the goal of human development as the overcoming of narcissism so that one is able to love "from the fullness of his personality just as God's love is a symbol for love out of strength and not out of weakness."[75] Theistic religion contends that the freedom from self-preoccupation (narcissism), which is the basis for this kind of love, is possible not through some symbolic representation of it but through a real experience of divine love or grace.

Suggested Readings

EVANS, RICHARD, *Dialogue with Erich Fromm* (New York: Praeger, 1981).

FROMM, ERICH, *The Art of Loving* (New York: Bantam Books 1963).

FROMM ERICH, *Escape from Freedom* (New York: Avon Books 1965).

FROMM ERICH, *The Heart of Man: Its Genius for Good and Evil* (New York: Harper and Row, 1964).

FROMM, ERICH, *Man for Himself: An Inquiry into the Psychology of Ethics* (Greenwich, Conn.: Fawcett, 1965).

FROMM, ERICH, *Psychoanalysis and Religion* (New Haven: Yale University Press, 1950).

FROMM, ERICH, *The Sane Society* (Greenwich, Conn.: Fawcett, 1965).

FROMM, ERICH, *To Have or to Be?* (New York, Harper and Row, 1976).

FROMM, ERICH, *You Shall Be as Gods: A Radical Interpretation of the Old Testament and Its Tradition* (New York: Holt, Rinehart and Winston, 1966).

FROMM, ERICH, SUZUKI, D.T., and DEMARTINO, RICHARD, *Zen Buddhism and Psychoanalysis* (New York: Harper and Row, 1970).

FUNK, RAINER, *Erich Fromm: The Courage to Be Human* (New York: Continuum, 1982).

GLEN, J. STANLEY, *Erich Fromm: A Protestant Critique* (Philadelphia: Westminster, 1966).

KNAPP, GERHARD, *The Art of Living: Erich Fromm's Life and Works* (New York: Peter Lang, 1989).

SCHAAR, JOHN H., *Escape from Authority: The Perspectives of Erich Fromm* (New York: Basic Books, 1961).

Notes

1. Gerhard Knapp, *The Art of Living: Erich Fromm's Life and Works* (New York: Peter Lang, 1989), p. 1.
2. Richard Evans, *Dialogue with Erich Fromm* (New York: Praeger, 1981), p. 57.
3. *Ibid.*, pp. 58-59.
4. Rainer Funk, *Erich Fromm: The Courage to Be Human* (New York: Continuum, 1982), p. 294.
5. *Ibid.*, p. 101.
6. John Schaar, *Escape from Authority: The Perspectives of Erich Fromm* (New York: Basic Books, 1961), p. 125.
7. Richard Evans, *Dialogue with Erich Fromm*, p. 56.
8. Gerhard Knapp, *The Art of Living*, pp. 8-10. I am primarily indebted to this work for the details of Fromm's life.
9. Erich Fromm, *Psychoanalysis and Religion* (New Haven: Yale University Press, 1950), p. 29.
10. Richard Evans, *Dialogue with Erich Fromm*, p. 57.
11. Erich Fromm, *The Heart of Man: Its Genius for Good and Evil* (New York: Harper and Row, 1964), p. 56.
12. Gerhard Knapp, *The Art of Living*, p. 14.
13. *Ibid.*, p. 24
14. Erich Fromm, *Man for Himself: An Inquiry into the Psychology of Ethics* (Greenwich, Conn.: Fawcett, 1965), p. 67.
15. Erich Fromm, *The Sane Society* (Greenwich Conn.: Fawcett, 1965), p. 76.
16. Richard Evans, *Dialogue with Erich Fromm*, p. 9.
17. Cf. Gerhard Knapp, *The Art of Living*, p. 24.
18. *Ibid.*, p. 40.
19. Cf. Erich Fromm, *The Sane Society*, pp. 42-61.
20. Gerhard Knapp, *The Art of Living*, p. 42.
21. *Ibid.*, p. 206.
22. Rainer Funk, *Erich Fromm: The Courage to Be Human*, p. 114.
23. Erich Fromm, "Psychoanalysis and Zen-Buddhism," in Erich Fromm, D.T. Suzuki, and Richard De Martino, *Zen Buddhism and Psychoanalysis* (New York: Harper and Row, 1970), p. 86.
24. *Ibid.*, p. 87.
25. *Ibid.*
26. Erich Fromm, *The Sane Society*, p. 32.

27. *Ibid.*, p. 33.
28. *Ibid.*, p. 36.
29. *Ibid.*, p. 37.
30. Cf. Erich Fromm, *Man for Himself*, pp. 104-107.
31. Erich Fromm, *Escape from Freedom* (New York: Avon Books, 1965), p. 288.
32. Erich Fromm, *The Sane Society*, p. 41.
33. *Ibid.*, p. 42.
34. *Ibid.*
35. *Ibid.*, p. 31.
36. *Ibid.*, p. 43.
37. *Ibid.*
38. *Ibid.*, p. 36.
39. *Ibid.*, pp. 62-64.
40. Erich Fromm, *Psychoanalysis and Religion*, pp. 32-33.
41. *Ibid.*, p. 21.
42. For a discussion of these character types, see Erich Fromm, *Man for Himself*, ch. 3.
43. Erich Fromm, *Psychoanalysis and Religion*, p. 36.
44. *Ibid.*, p. 35.
45. Erich Fromm, *Escape from Freedom*, pp. 196-197.
46. Richard Evans, *Dialogue with Erich Fromm*, p. 88.
47. Erich Fromm, *Psychoanalysis and Religion*, pp. 49-51.
48. *Ibid.*, p. 51.
49. Rainer Funk, *Erich Fromm: The Courage to Be Human*, p. 120.
50. Erich Fromm, *Psychoanalysis and Religion*, p. 37.
51. *Ibid.*, p. 37. Cf. also p. 49.
52. *Ibid.*, p. 53.
53. *Ibid.*, pp. 54-55.
54. *Ibid.*, pp. 79-87.
55. *Ibid.*, p. 87.
56. *Ibid.*
57. Erich Fromm, *You Shall Be as Gods: A Radical interpretation of the Old Testament and Its Tradition* (New York, Holt, Rinehart and Winston, 1966), pp. 17-18.
58. *Ibid.*, p. 42.
59. Erich Fromm, *The Art of Loving* (New York, Bantam Books, 1963), p. 68.
60. Erich Fromm, *You Shall Be as Gods*, pp. 56-7.
61. Erich Fromm, *To Have or to Be?* (New York: Harper and Row, 1976), p. 202.
62. Erich Fromm, *You Shall Be as Gods*, pp. 57-60.
63. Richard Evans, *Dialogue with Erich Fromm*, p. 102.
64. Erich Fromm, *Zen Buddhism and Psychoanalysis*, p. 122.
65. *Ibid.*, p. 133.
66. *Ibid.*, p. 129.
67. *Ibid.*, p. 104.
68. Rainer Funk, *Erich Fromm: The Courage to Be Human*, p. 9.
69. Cf. Richard Evans, *Dialogue with Erich Fromm*, p. 84.
70. John H. Schaar, *Escape from Authority*, p. 212.
71. *Ibid.*, p. 232.
72. J. Stanley Glen, *Erich Fromm: A Protestant Critique* (Philadelphia: Westminister, 1966), p. 156.
73. *Ibid.*, p. 153.
74. *Ibid.*, p. 193.
75. Erich Fromm, *Psychoanalysis and Religion*, p. 87.

V. GORDON ALLPORT

Religion and Personality

Gordon Allport (1897–1967)
Dominque.

In an autobiographical essay first published in 1967, Gordon W. Allport (1897-1967) reflects on the significance of his book *Personality: A Psychological Interpretation* published 30 years earlier. In the essay, he states, "I felt that my emphasis should be on normality rather than pathology."[1] This brief statement locates Allport's psychological theory in the vanguard of the humanistic/existential reaction to the perceived incompleteness of psychoanalysis and behaviorist theories of personality. Since every theory of personality is essentially a theory of motivation, these theories were, in Allport's view, one-sided by reason of their overemphasis on pathological motivation in the form of either unconsciously repressed motives (psychoanalysis) or conditioned responses determined by early childhood experiences (behaviorism).

In answering the question "What are the dynamics of human behavior?" or "What is the basic motivating force in human personality?" psychoanalytic theory painted a picture of the human person as driven by instinctual needs and seeking a state of homeostasis, which represents the complete gratification of instinctual needs. Behaviorism, on the other hand, described the individual as controlled by learned responses. So-called stimulus-response theories suggested that the way in which a child learns to respond to a certain stimulus becomes the basis for a determined pattern of response to similar stimuli throughout life. For example, a child's learned way of responding to the parental figures becomes determinative for the way in which he will respond to all future authority figures. The humanist and existentialist reactions to such theories typically point to the fact that they account for human behavior in terms of the subhuman aspects of personality and ignore the dynamic or motivating power of the specifically human dimensions of the person, that is the conscious, rational, and even spiritual dimensions.

In opposition to the one-sidedness of such theories, Allport wanted to construct a comprehensive theory of personality which would do justice to its specifically human phenomena. He wanted to create an "image of man" that would allow for the testing of his "humane potentialities." "I did not think," he states, "of man as innately `good,' but I was convinced that by and large American psychology gave man less than his due by depicting him as a bundle of unrelated reaction tendencies."[2] What Allport specifically reacted against were what he saw as the two basic premises of psychoanalysis and behaviorism, "irrationalism," and "geneticism." Irrationalism refers to the psychoanalytic emphasis on unconscious motivation (as opposed to conscious plans and intentions) while geneticism refers to the determining influence of innate instincts and early childhood experiences on adult behavior. Both concepts imply that the adult subject is unaware of his true motives. His consciously expressed motives, therefore, cannot be accepted at face value and the true motives can be discovered only through projective tests. They further imply that adult motives are, in Allport's words, "conditioned, reinforced, sublimated or otherwise elaborated editions" of innate drives or learned responses.[3]

Allport's response to such theories was that projective tests reveal only unconscious, repressed motivation and were, therefore, less useful in the case of the well-integrated, that is unrepressed, subject. Such a subject, he argued, has the "right to be believed" when he reports his conscious motivation. Theories of motivation based on irrationalism or geneticism tend to interpret current motivation as reaction or response to something in the past and thereby deprive the subject of any kind of proactive "intentionality" and deprive conscious goals, plans, and intentions of any motivational significance, since they cannot be taken at face value. Freud, for example, saw motivation as residing in the id. Therefore, Allport concludes, "the conscious, accessible region of personality that carries on direct transactions with the world—that is, the ego—he regarded as devoid of dynamic power."[4] Allport considered this an inadequate theory of motivation for three reasons:[5] (1) It did not acknowledge the "contemporaneity" of motives. (2) It was not sufficiently "pluralistic," that is did not allow for different kinds of motives. (3) It did not ascribe sufficient dynamic force to cognitive processes, that is, to conscious plans and intentions which were directed toward the future, not reactions to the past. The whole thrust of Allport's theory of personality was to acknowledge the dynamic motivational power of the subject's "ego structure," that is, of conscious, rational, self-determining motivation, of conscious values, intentions, and long-range goals. This would lead him to describe the motivation of both the mature adult and the mature religious personality as "functionally autonomous," that is, as independent of infantile and unconscious needs.

Life

Gordon Willard Allport was born November 11, 1897, at Montezuma, Indiana, the youngest of a family of four boys.[6] His father was a country doctor who had entered medicine after a career in business and after the first three of his four sons had been born. Soon after the birth of his fourth son, Allport's father moved his medical practice first to Streetsboro and to Hudson in Ohio and finally to Glenville (Cleveland). It was here that Allport received his elementary and secondary education. As a child Allport felt somewhat isolated since he was "quick with words" but "poor at games." The quickness with words, however, made him a "star" among a small cluster of friends.

Allport describes his home life as a child and adolescent as "marked by plain Protestant piety and hard work." From his mother, a schoolteacher, he learned "an eager sense of philosophical questing and the importance of searching for ultimate religious answers." His father, on the other hand, trained Allport and his brothers in "the practical urgencies of life" by requiring them to assist him in his medical practice ("tending office, washing bottles and dealing with patients").[7] Allport describes his father as "no believer in vacations." In addition to his medical practice, he found time to set up a co-op drug company, build and rent apartments, as well as build and supervise hospitals. The father's "plain Protestant piety" is revealed in his stated rule of life: "If every person worked as hard as he could and took only the minimum financial return required by his family's needs, then there would be just enough wealth to go around."[8] All of this produced a home environment which Allport describes as "hard work tempered by trust and affection."[9]

Next to his home life, the second great influence in Allport's young life was Harvard University, which he entered as an undergraduate in 1915. It was Harvard's "unspoken expectation of excellence" that drove him to realize his academic potential. The focus of his undergraduate studies was psychology and social ethics, and these remained the focus of his professional work for the rest of his life. His studies in the Department of Social Ethics gave Allport ample opportunity for field training in social work. Among these were the conducting of a boys' club in Boston, volunteer visiting for the Family Society, and working as volunteer probation officer. He found all this social service deeply satisfying in at least two ways. It helped Allport in his search for personal identity by giving him a feeling of competence to counteract what he describes as "a generalized inferiority feeling." In addition, he discovered through this work that he liked to help people with their problems. This attraction to the altruistic nature of the work was in turn helpful to him in his attempts to achieve religious maturity.[10] Allport describes this struggle for religious maturity as an attempt to replace his childhood conceptions of religious doctrine with a humanitarian type of religion: He confesses, however, that after four years he abandoned this position "because it seemed to me that to exalt one's own intellect and affirm only a precarious man-made set of values cheapened the whole quest." This attitude of humility in the face of ultimate questions seems to have been carried over into his chosen world of psychological theorizing in which Allport found intellectual arrogance "antagonizing" and believed that "it is better to be tentative, eclectic and humble."[11]

For Allport, his two lines of study—psychology and social ethics—were interrelated. Effective social service, he believed, required a sound conception of human personality. The title of his eventual doctoral thesis would reflect his concern for integrating the two fields: *An Experimental Study of the Traits of Personality: With Special Reference to the Problem of Social Diagnosis*. After his graduation (1919), Allport taught English and sociology for a year at Robert College in Constantinople, after which he was offered a fellowship for graduate study at Harvard. On the return trip from Constantinople he stopped for a visit with his brother Fayette in Vienna. While there, he arranged, out of curiosity, a visit with Freud, who received him courteously but said nothing. To break the ice, Allport recounted for him the actions of a four year old boy he had observed on the tramcar with an obvious dirt phobia. Freud responded, "And was that little boy you?" This reply impressed upon Allport that Freud's tendency was to see evidence of the pathological and the unconscious in his patients. Assuming that Allport had come as a patient he was anxious to break down his projections. As it turned out, this one and only encounter with Freud helped to strengthen Allport's determination to formulate an alternative theory of human motivation which did not overemphasize its unconscious and pathological roots.[12]

This more humanistic alternative to psychoanalysis and behaviorism has by now so established itself that it is difficult for us to imagine the difficulties and even self-doubts that hindered Allport in this groundbreaking venture. A source of strength in this regard was his mentor at Harvard, H.S. Langfeld, who, while inclined toward behaviorism himself, encouraged Allport's independent line of thought. During his doctoral studies Allport experienced doubts about his fitness for a career in psychology because of his lack of competence in fields such as mathematics, science, biology, and medicine.

It was Langfeld who reminded him that there were many branches of psychology. "I think," Allport recalls, "this casual remark saved me. In effect he was encouraging me to find my own way in the humanistic pastures of psychology."[13] Again, in 1922 as he was finishing his doctoral thesis, he was invited to attend a gathering of experimental psychologists led by Edward Titchener. Each student was given three minutes to describe his own research. Allport reported on his work on traits of personality "and was punished by the rebuke of total silence from the group punctuated by a glare of disapproval from Titchener."[14] A discussion with Langfeld led to the discovery that he really didn't care what Titchener thought. Allport describes this event as something of a turning point: "Never since that time have I ever been troubled by rebukes or professional slights directed at my maverick interests."[15]

After receiving his Ph.D. in 1922 at age 24, he was awarded a Sheldon traveling fellowship, which allowed him to spend two years in Europe. What Allport seems to have valued most in this experience was the exposure to the German tradition in psychology in which he found support for his view of personality as an organized structure. Following these two years abroad he was offered an instructorship in social ethics at Harvard to begin in the fall of 1924. At the same time he was asked to offer a new course in the psychology of personality. This is believed to be the first course in personality offered in an American college. Its further significance lies in the confirmation it gave to Allport's research interest, which was to develop a "full-bodied" or comprehensive theory of personality. It is this interest that differentiates Allport from the other theorists reviewed in this text. Concepts such as "trait" as the structural unit of personality, "functional autonomy" as the quality of mature motivation, and the "proprium" as a psychologically accessible understanding of the self are all the direct result of this attempt to give a comprehensive understanding of the mature adult personality, not the residue of psychotherapeutic work. Allport was an academic psychologist, more of a pure theorist and researcher than a therapist.

In 1925 Allport married Ada Trifkin Gould, a clinical psychologist. Their son, Robert, became a pediatrician. Following his marriage, Allport taught at Dartmouth College, offering courses in social psychology and personality, and returned each summer to teach at Harvard. In 1930 he returned to Harvard where he remained for the rest of his career. By 1937 he had become part of the newly formed and independent Department of Psychology, and in that year published his attempt at a comprehensive theory of personality in *Personality: A Psychological Interpretation*. A revised version appeared in 1961 under the title *Pattern and Growth in Personality*. In the 1937 publication Allport introduced the concept of the "functional autonomy" of motives, which was to become the key concept in his understanding of both human and religious maturity. The term was used to describe the independence of mature adult motivation from infantile, unconscious needs and conditioned responses. For the mature adult the motivating force lay "in the present on-moving structure of personality, not in some anachronistic conditioning of past motives."[16]

The other side of Allport's research interest was social psychology and social ethics. He was particularly active in this field during World War II, conducting, along with his students, studies of such questions as civilian morale, the analysis of Hitler's character, wartime rumor and riots, as well as group conflict and prejudice. Allport, who described himself as "a political liberal and a social reformer," found this work congenial, having been involved since 1936 in the Society for the Psychological Study of Social Issues and serving as its president in 1944. Given his research interest in social issues, it is not surprising that in 1946 Allport became part of the newly formed Department of Social Relations at Harvard. This department was made up of elements from the departments of anthropology, psychology, and sociology. In this environment he was able to conduct graduate seminars in problems of group conflict and prejudice. These studies were the basis for his 1954 book *The Nature of Prejudice*. This new department operated for more than eighteen years in seven separate buildings until it moved, in 1965 into the newly constructed William James Hall, a center for the behavioral sciences. This event, two years before his death in 1967, coincided with Allport's semi-retirement. He had spent all but seven of the previous fifty years at Harvard as student and teacher.

In summarizing his own work Allport describes it as "polemic-eclectic." The polemic was directed at all the closed theories of motivation which he considered inadequate, "an overemphasis on unconscious processes, projective tests and simplified drive theories." These theories, he believed, dealt only with the peripheral or "opportunistic" layers of personality. In place of these he advocated a more open and eclectic system, one that would account for the more "propriate" functions of personality, which are expressive of one's self-image, conscious intentionality, and long-range goals, not merely projective of unconscious drives and conflicts. At the same time he recognized that his theory was a supplement to the exaggerated claims of psychoanalytic and stimulus response theories, not a denial of their valid insights. "Although much of my writing is polemic in tone," he confesses, "I know in my bones that my opponents are partly right."[17]

Linked to this admission is a plea for greater scientific tentativeness and humility in psychological theorizing. "What I dislike in our profession," he writes, "is the strong aura of arrogance found in presently fashionable dogmas. To my mind humility is a virtue appropriate for social and psychological scientists to cultivate."[18] The arrogance here mentioned refers to the claims to comprehensiveness of one-sided theories which try to explain the totality of the human phenomenon with reference only to the "mechanical aspects of reactivity to the neglect of man's wider experiences."[19] His own "personal idea" is described as "the search for a theoretical system—for one that will allow for truth wherever found, one that will encompass the totality of human experience and do full justice to the nature of man."[20] A review of Allport's theoretical system will reveal his efforts to do justice to what is truly human in personality and to encompass the totality of human experience including religious experience.

Theory of Personality

We have seen that, for Allport, a comprehensive theory of personality must attribute dynamic, motivating power not only to innate instinctual drives and infantile conditioning but also to conscious, rational, self-determining motivation, not only to the unconscious id but also to the conscious ego. Moreover, it must be assumed that human behavior is motivated by the conscious ego-structure unless there are clear indications of pathology. In other words, the presumption is that the motives behind a person's behavior are those of which he is consciously aware or, as Allport remarks, "the patient should be assumed insightful until he is proved otherwise."[21] In the case of the mature adult, the reasons one gives for one's behavior may be taken at face value; in the absence of evidence for some kind of pathological condition, it is not necessary to account for behavior in terms of defense mechanisms, reaction formations, conditioned responses, and so on.

Structure of Personality

Allport's belief in unique ego-structure or organization leads him to propose the following definition of personality: "Personality is the dynamic organization within the individual of those psychophysical systems that determine his unique adjustments to his environment."[22] Two points in this definition should be immediately noticed. First, in trying to propose a definition which would describe "what a man really is," Allport uses the term "psychophysical" to refer to the human person as a union of body and mind. Second, the definition implies that the ego-structure of each individual is a unique organization, which in turn accounts for the unique way in which he adapts to his or her environment. This stress on uniqueness is a feature of Allport's theory. Freud had accounted for individual differences in terms of the manner in which each individual sublimates or displaces the instinctual energy of the id under the influence of the ego (the reality principle) and the superego (the principle of right and wrong). These, however, represent partial aim-inhibited fulfillments of the primary aim of the sexual and aggressive instincts. Since these instincts are common to everyone, the uniqueness of the individual is only apparent. Allport, however, posited a true uniqueness of personality by insisting that the aims, goals, and intentions of the ego were primary and not the means to some more ultimate goal such as the gratification of instinctual drives.

Since Allport attributes the uniqueness of the individual personality to the organization of its "psychophysical systems," the question arises: What are the systems thus organized? Allport responds by describing the growth of personality as an ongoing process of organization and integration. At the earliest stage of this process an individual learns to respond in a particular way to a particular stimulus. When a particular response becomes characteristic of an individual, it is referred to as a habit and this represents a further stage of organization. A still higher level is represented by the word "trait," which to Allport represents the basic unit in the structure of personality. For this reason his theory has sometimes been referred to as "trait psychology," though Allport rejects this description.[23] A trait represents an organized system of specific habits. Consider the person who habitually responds to insults or putdowns with anger, to competition with spirit and energy, to challenges with hard work, to failure with renewed effort, and to dark moods with increased activity. In such a person specific habits or modes of response have coalesced to form a personality trait which we could call aggressiveness. This trait is clearly an "attitude," but traits can also be expressed as values such as "honest" or interests such as "artistic."

The raw material or foundation for this process of integration and organization consists of three types of what Allport calls "inborn dispositions."[24] These include all types of instinctual behavior, inherited characteristics as well as certain potential capacities such as the capacity to learn or to develop a conscience. Included among these potentialities is the capacity to develop an ego-structure—a structured organization of traits with the accompanying sense of self. This becomes the primary motivating force in the mature adult. Thus Allport refers to them as "potentialities for attaining adulthood," which means becoming a structured system which is "self-regulating" and "self-maintaining." These words suggest the opposite of being driven by instinct or determined by conditioned responses.

The sense of self which is associated with an individual's ego-structure raises the question of whether psychology is justified in using the concept of the self in a way that is analogous to the philosophical or religious concept of self or soul. Such a concept suggests a supraordinate agent which integrates the systems of personality and directs its behavior. Allport points out that the positivistic trend within psychology had rejected such a concept as a philosophical and religious postulate and had attempted to account for the integration and organization of personality without recourse to a concept of self.[25] Nevertheless, the concept was preserved in Freud's theoretical construct of the ego, though the role of the ego was largely a passive and defensive one. Alfred Adler more closely approximated the notion of a self in his concept of the "creative's self," the evidence for which was to be found in each individual's unique "life-style." This term refers to all those activities, values, attitudes, and goals which belong to an individual in a unique way.

To these phenomena Allport applied the term "propriate," that is, everything that belongs to one individual in a unique way or is "proper" to her. "Propriate striving" would then refer to a person's pursuit of his own unique and conscious goals. This in turn is distinguished from "opportunistic striving," which refers to those habits, skills, and cultural conformities which have become second nature to us and help us to adjust to our cultural environment but are not central to our unique sense of self. Learning to drive an automobile may be an all-consuming obsession for a 16-year-old but, by age 40, it has become routine, mechanical and utilitarian. On the other hand, the 40-year-old's most deeply cherished relationships, most ardently pursued goals, and the fundamental values by which he lives have become "proper" or peculiar to him and part of the ego-structure which accounts for his uniqueness. In the examination of such propriate striving Allport finds evidence for a concept of the self which is not merely a philosophical postulate but one that is accessible to psychological investigation. He suggests that the self which is revealed in one's propriate striving be called the "proprium," a concept which includes "all aspects of personality that make for inward unity."[26]

The proprium then is the self which is revealed in one's unique lifestyle, that is, in one's propriate striving. We may say that the proprium is the sum total of one's propriate functions and thus constitutes a self which is accessible to psychological analysis. Allport sees the growth of personality as the development of propriate striving, that is, of the various aspects of the proprium. These are:[27]

1. *Bodily sense,* the awareness of bodily sensations as one's own.
2. *Self-identity,* the awareness of oneself as a being in one's own right, distinct from others.
3. *Ego enhancement,* which refers to the ego's propensity for self-affirmation and self-seeking.
4. *Ego extension,* the identification of the ego with loved objects.
5. *Rational agent,* refers to the ego's functions of problem solving and carrying out intentions.
6. *Self-image,* one's view of oneself.
7. *Propriate striving,* refers to behavior motivated by the ego-structure, that is, by one's self-image and conscious goals of self-perfection rather than instinctual drives and conditioning.
8. *The knower,* refers to the fullness of self-consciousness in which the individual experiences herself as the subject of her propriate functions.

This concept of the knower or cognizing self "that transcends all other functions of the proprium and holds them in view" is Allport's answer to the question of whether there is a substantive self which is distinguishable from the sum total of mental functions and experiences. The self as knower is still for Allport a postulate but an "inescapable" one.

> We not only know *things*, but we know (i.e. are acquainted with) the empirical features of our own proprium. It is I who have bodily sensations, I who recognize my self-identity from day to day; I who note and reflect upon my self-assertion, self-extension, my own rationalizations, as well as upon my interests and strivings. When I thus think about my own propriate functions I am likely to perceive their essential togetherness, and feel them intimately bound in some way to the knowing function itself.[28]

In short, Allport's position is that while the concept of a substantive self or soul which acts in a "transpsychological" manner and is "inaccessible to psychological analysis" is inadmissible in psychology, nevertheless those functions which are commonly attributed to the self (propriate functions) are the proper subject matter of psychology. It is in this sense that self becomes a necessary concept in psychology. Allport's term for this psychologically accessible self is the proprium, a term which describes the "central interlocking operations of personality."

Dynamics of Personality

Here we refer to the motivating force in human personality, what Allport refers to as the "go" of mental life. We have seen that for Allport the source of dynamic motivation in the mature adult is not the instinctual drives of the unconscious id but the propriate functions of the conscious ego, that is, in one's self-image and visions of self-perfection, in one's conscious goals, plans, values, and intentions. In this, as we have seen, Allport was reacting to the perceived overemphasis on unconscious drives and infantile needs and conditioning to explain adult behavior in the then dominant psychological theories. Such theories, he proposed, posited a "functional continuity" between infantile and adult motivation whereby adult behavior, though different from that of the child, nevertheless served the same *function* as infantile behavior. One of Allport's favorite examples is the case of the young man who chooses the same profession as his father (e.g., law, medicine, etc.). The young man's behavior in the practice of law or medicine is not the same as his behavior as a little boy imitating daddy driving the car or going off to work each morning. In this view, however, both the infantile and the adult behavior satisfy the same infantile need to identify with the father. There is a continuity of function.

   In Allport's view, functional continuity is inadequate on three counts: (1) It does not explain the diversity of adult motivation, which cannot be reduced to a few basic instinctual or infantile needs. (2) It does not do justice to the uniqueness of personality since it explains human behavior with reference to basic instincts common to all and ignores the individual's capacity for self-determining uniqueness. (3) It ignores the "becoming" aspect of personality by describing growth as an endless repetition of the instinctual cycle rather than as a continuous process of becoming; as a tension-reducing pursuit of instinctual gratification rather than a tension-maintaining pursuit of long-range goals.

In countering the notion of functional continuity, Allport lists three requirements for an adequate theory of motivation:[29] (1) It must admit the contemporaneity of motives, that is, look for what actually motivates the person's *present* behavior. Past motives, he insists, mean nothing unless they are also present motives and this cannot be assumed. (2) It must be pluralistic, allowing for motives of many kinds. (3) It must ascribe dynamic force to cognitive processes such as conscious plans, goals, and intentions.

The principle of functional continuity seems to leave little room for outgrowing unconscious and infantile motivation. In other words, at the level of motivation, there is no real transformation in the passage from childhood to adulthood. Behavior changes but the motives behind the behavior do not. Allport, however, insists that "just as we learn new skills, so also we learn new motives."[30] This capacity to learn new motives reverses the principle of functional continuity. Instead of attributing the same motivation to different forms of behavior, the same behavior is seen as potentially proceeding from different kinds of motivation. Thus, it is possible that the young man who follows in the professional footsteps of his father may originally be motivated by an infantile need to identify or compete with his father. Allport insists, however, that it may happen—and, indeed, is usually the case—that in pursuing his career he learns new motives. The chosen career now becomes an end in itself, not a means of satisfying an unconscious infantile need. It has become an expression of his ego-structure, his own values and goals, of what he wants to achieve in his life. He is no longer driven by the past but striving for self-determined, future goals. "The ego," Allport suggests, "in taking command, projects itself forward into the future and recasts its motives largely in terms of intentions and plans."[31]

In the case of the young man in our example, Allport would suggest that his career choice, though historically continuous with his infantile attempts to identify with the father, is not functionally continuous with those attempts, that is, does not serve the same purpose or function as the infantile behavior. This independence of adult motives from infantile and unconscious needs is what Allport calls the *functional autonomy of motives*. It allows for the possibility—indeed the probability—that in the course of maturing a person's behavior becomes "propriate," that is, motivated by conscious goals and intentions which are unique to the individual. Thus Allport states that the principle of functional autonomy "helps to express the uniqueness of motives that confer distinctiveness to a person's characteristic adjustments."[32] The achieving of functional autonomy represents the normal and typical goal of human development. It is possible, of course, that an adult may continue to be motivated by unconscious, infantile needs. Allport insists, however, that the neurotic character of such motivation can be observed in its "compulsive, inappropriate, and not age-related character."[33]

In the light of the dominant psychologies of his era, Allport's theory of personality appears at its most innovative in his insistence on the conscious ego-structure of the individual as the seat of dynamic motivation. This insight carries with it at least three corollaries: (1) It introduces a *comprehensive* view of personality by including conscious goals, intentions, and values in its theory of motivation. Thus psychology becomes a study of the whole person. (2) In stressing the motivating power of conscious, "propriate" functions, it focuses on the uniqueness of personality. (3) In stressing the human capacity to learn new motives in the process of development, it points to the transformation of motives as the main feature of human development. Thus the process of growth from childhood to adulthood is one of genuine transformation and not merely a process of sublimation, displacement, and elaboration. These ideas have become so commonly accepted that one may fail to grasp their innovative character.

Theory of Religion

In our own times an increasing number of people seem to be expressing a desire for a "spiritual" life, but claim not to find it in organized religion. Consequently, they experience a sense of alienation from their religious traditions and look to other sources of spiritual wisdom. In his 1950 publication, *The Individual and His Religion,* Allport observes this same twofold trend. Noting that two-thirds of American adults regard themselves as religious and nine-tenths believe in God, he observes nevertheless that many hold the tenets of their religious tradition "with many mental reservations" and doubts. Though they still "feel" religious, the principles regulating their conduct come less from their religious beliefs and increasingly from psychology and psychiatry. While today we might say that the alternative sources of spiritual guidance includes Jungian psychology, Eastern philosophy, New Age Thinking, and politically correct cultural assumptions, nevertheless the ambiguity about traditional religion is the same. Both the situation observed by Allport and that which occurs today point to the same problem. Both suggest that there is a religious or spiritual need in the human person, which, if not satisfied by the teaching of traditional religions, will look to other sources.

This situation has led some to posit a dichotomy between religion and "spirituality," suggesting that one must look beyond religion for genuine spiritual nourishment. Allport eschews such an arguably false dichotomy and describes this subjective need as the "religious sentiment." As a sentiment it would be categorized by Allport as a trait of personality, and in the deeply religious person it would be described as a "cardinal trait," that is, a master sentiment or ruling passion that exercises a central and pervasive influence on all of a person's thought and behavior. In this sense of a set of beliefs with motivating power, the religious sentiment is similar to what William James called the "habitual centre" of one's personal energy. Allport uses the word "sentiment" to include both the cognitive and dynamic aspects of religion. As a central unit of personality it provides both organization and motivation. A sentiment is described as "an organization of feeling and thought directed toward some definable object of value."[34] In his definition of the mature religious sentiment, he identifies this object of value as ideas and principles which have "ultimate importance" for the believer and which are related to what is regarded as "permanent or central in the nature of things."[35]

Two preliminary points should be made about the religious sentiment. First, it represents the subjective side of religion. It is this subjective sentiment which responds to the system of doctrines, symbols, values, and ritual which constitutes the objective side of religion and accounts for the way in which an individual assimilates and experiences his religion. It is this subjective phenomenon which is the proper object of study for the psychology of religion. Second, as a personality trait, the religious sentiment is unique to each individual. For Allport this rules out any explanation of religious phenomena as proceeding from a separate "religious instinct" or a single mental mechanism which would be common to all individuals. Religion as such, therefore, cannot be simply explained in terms of sublimated sexuality or an obsessional neurosis or a father complex or the operation of collective unconscious. On the contrary, religion provides an answer to several human needs which vary in degree and intensity from one individual to the next.

Origins of the Religious Sentiment

Allport lists those human needs to which religion provides an answer and which therefore lend uniqueness to each individual's religious sentiment as follows:[36]

Organic Desire. This includes basic bodily needs (food, shelter, etc.); fear of the threats to one's existence from enemies, nature, sickness, death, and so on; as well as the need for community or human companionship. One is reminded here of Erich Fromm's contention that the intellectual coherence of a religious belief is secondary to the emotional benefit of sharing it with others, that is, of satisfying the need for human relatedness. Again, Allport's remark that one's approach to God is determined by one's present needs, reminds us of William James' contention that we are more prone to "use" God (to satisfy our human needs) than to believe in him. It is evident, however, that the satisfaction of these basic human needs plays a greater or lesser role in the religious motivation of different individuals—from those for whom it is a primary motive to those medieval hermits for whom religion was the pursuit of austerity, deprivation, and solitude.

Temperament. The above-mentioned individual differences are, in turn, largely due to differences in individual temperament. Here again we are reminded of William James' distinction between the healthy-minded and the sick soul. To a large extent it is this difference in temperament which accounts for theological and ritualistic preferences among religious persons. The choice between a religion of thought and intellect versus a religion of experience and imagination, between the pomp and ceremony of a "high" liturgy versus the "folksiness" and spontaneity of a more informal service, between public worship and private devotion—all of these choices depend, to a great extent, on the temperament or prevailing mood of the individual. Allport suggests two reasons why more attention must be placed on the relationship of religion and temperament. First, a balance has to be found to the overemphasis, particularly in American psychology, on environmental factors in conditioning personality. Equal attention must be paid, he insists, to "the inborn climate of personality," that is, the inherited or constitutional determinants of personality, including temperament. Second, the ecumenical movement among religious denominations must take into account the fact that religious differences are often rooted in differences of temperamental preference.

Psychogenic Desires and Spiritual Values. These are to be distinguished from organic or "viscerogenic" desires. Here Allport notes that we tend to objectify the values we seek in concepts such as truth, goodness, and beauty. The desire for such values represents a distinctively human motive. Human growth is seen here as a process of abstracting and categorizing whereby individual good, beautiful, and true objects are categorized in the abstract concepts of Truth, Beauty, and Goodness. In this way the essential qualities of particular objects are objectified and seen as existing outside of ourselves. For many, religion is a way of preserving these values, and God is seen as the ultimate expression of them. Allport points, by way of illustration, to the development of the value of individuality or selfhood. The infant's bodily sense develops into egoism and then to pride in one's individuality. Eventually one learns to value not only one's own individuality but that of others; this fosters the development of associated values such as charity, tolerance, and equality. The religious person may anchor this belief in the value of personal integrity in the notion of a personal God—"the supreme expression of personality"—in whose image each person is created.

The Pursuit of Meaning. By this phrase Allport wants to suggest that behind all of our viscerogenic and psychogenic desires and pursuit of values there lies a desire for some kind of ultimate meaning that would integrate all our fragmented desires into a network of meaning. "I am saying, " he states, "that all the while we are fretting, desiring, valuing, we are often busily seeking to interpret our own unrest."[37] Religion is one way of pursuing this search for complete knowledge, for a sense of ultimate meaning and destiny. Allport undoubtedly has this function in mind when he describes a person's religion as "his ultimate attempt to enlarge and to complete his own personality by finding the supreme context in which he rightly belongs."[38] In carrying out this function religion goes beyond the realm of science, which only answers the question of "empirical causality." When the physicality of death, for example, has been determined, the question of its meaning still has to be grappled with. It might be an oversimplification to say that such existential questions (death, guilt, anxiety, etc.) are religious questions, but they are certainly the kind of questions that religion deals with. The answers given by religion sometimes "leap far ahead of verifiable evidence" and are seen by some (including Freud) as overly optimistic and illusory. Allport counters with the suggestion that all of us—religious or not—base our lives on working principles and assumptions (e.g., I will be alive next year, I will have a good job after graduation) which are equally unverifiable. There are some indeed whose religion is based on wish fulfillment, but religion's tendency toward hope, meaning, and the conservation of values is not necessarily a sign of illusory wish fulfillment.

Culture and Conformity. The "origins of the religious quest" we have discussed thus far point to the uniqueness of the religious sentiment in each individual. These individual preferences, however, are countered by the pressure exerted by one's culture to conform to the values and precepts of that culture's dominant religion. Religion and culture are intimately connected since religion frequently provides the spiritual and moral values on which social, political, and economic systems are based. This leads Allport to ask whether religion should be defined in terms of the culture it informs, that is, in terms of its social or cultural function. In answer he points out that the place of religion in personal life is different from its place in social life. Religion, he argues, is not simply a means of achieving social stability through conformity. It is also an agent of social change. Such change is usually brought about by charismatic leaders who have assimilated their religion in a unique and revolutionary way. Allport concludes, therefore, that whatever the social function of religion might be, the subjective religious attitude is unique in each individual. In fact, he argues, "there are as many varieties of religious experience as there are religiously inclined mortals upon the earth."[39]

The Mature Religious Sentiment

The religious sentiment may find its origin in any or all of the previously mentioned human needs. It is fair to say, however, that for Allport the measure of the maturity of one's religious sentiment is the degree to which it liberates it-self from the function of satisfying human needs, that is, the degree to which it becomes "functionally autonomous." Even the mature religious sentiment, of course, may be a source of comfort, security, companionship, and so forth, but it is mature precisely to the degree that it has become an end in itself and not primarily a means of satisfying such human needs. Mature religion, for All-port, does not refer to the maturity and, therefore, superiority of one set of religious doctrines over another; it refers to the manner in which those doc-trines are appropriated and assimilated by the individual believer. This sug-gests that religious maturity is rooted in the human or psychological maturity of the religious person. Allport lists three attributes of the mature human per-sonality:

1. self-expansion, that is, a variety of "psychogenic interests, values, and desires beyond the viscerogenic level;"
2. self-objectification or the ability to see oneself objectively—as others see us—including a sense of humor; and
3. unifying philosophy of life (self-unification), which serves to integrate the various aspects and interests and desires of the expanding self.

Such a unifying philosophy of life is not necessarily religious; the uni-fying center of personality may be philosophical, ethical, or political. What is distinctive about the religious sentiment, however, is its comprehensiveness. Where religion is the master sentiment, it must integrate and give meaning to every aspect of life and all human experience. A religious sentiment which is based on fantasy and wish fulfillment "provides an escape clause in one's contract with reality."[40] It is this type of immature religion which is the target of most of the criticism of religion. Allport assigns the following characteris-tics to the mature religious sentiment.

Well Differentiated. The mature religious sentiment is recognized by its richness and complexity. Allport uses the term "uncritical abandon" to de-scribe those who accept their religion in an unthinking, uncritical way. Such people simply accept what they were taught in a superficial way and avoid the hard work of critically examining one's religious beliefs without which those beliefs cannot be properly appropriated, be made one's own, and be-come part of an integrating master sentiment. A differentiated religious sen-timent, on the other hand, can admit doubt as an aspect of faith, can distinguish what is essential and important in its religious beliefs from what is nonessential and less important, and is aware of the failures as well as the successes of its own church or religious tradition.

Derivative yet Dynamic. This characteristic of the mature religious sen-timent refers to the "autonomous character of its motivational power."[41] What is true of human maturity is true also of religious maturity; it is characterized by the functional autonomy of motives. We have seen that this phrase refers to the fact that, as a person matures, the motives behind his or her behavior may change. An activity originally undertaken in order to satisfy some unconscious, infantile needs may in time become an end in itself, pursued for its own sake and not as a means to some further goal. In the same way the religious sentiment may be "derivative," that is, derived from the need for comfort, security, companionship; the need for social status or conformity; or even the need to gratify some unconscious or neurotic drive. What Allport insists upon is the fact that a religious sentiment thus derived originally from one's personal needs may mature to the point that it supplies its own driving power. To become thus independent of its origins is to become functionally autonomous. One's religious life no longer serves the same function of satisfying some human need; it has become an end in itself.

For the religious person this means that the religious sentiment is free to direct itself to God and religious values directly and does not have to serve the purpose of achieving some other human goal extrinsic to religion. As Allport states:

> A religious sentiment that has thus become largely independent of its origins, "functionally autonomous," cannot be regarded as a servant of other desires, even though its initial function may have been of this order. It behaves no longer like an iron filing, twisting to follow the magnet of self-centred motives; it behaves rather as a master-motive, a magnet in its own right by which other cravings are bidden to order their course. Having decided that the religious sentiment is the best instrument for dealing with life, the self, as it were, hands over to it the task of interpreting all that comes within its view, and of providing motive power to live in accordance with an adequate frame of value and meaning, and to enlarge and energize this frame.[42]

This passage emphasizes two things: First, in the achieving of religious maturity a real transformation of motives takes place. Whether this transformation takes place by way of gradual growth or sudden conversion, the result is the same, a movement from self-centered motives to self-transcending motives. Second, the sense of freedom or liberation which is frequently described as a feature of religious experience might be interpreted psychologically as liberation from "the magnet of self-centred motives." The mature religious sentiment is liberated from infantile goals such as comfort and security; from narcissistic needs such as the need for self-justification, approval, or reward; from neurotic goals such as the expiation of guilt feelings.

Consistently Directive. This refers to the fact that the mature religious sentiment is able to bring about real change in a person's character. This is so because when it becomes a master sentiment, it encompasses all of life and permeates the whole personality. Consequently, it offers a steady, persistent influence while the immature sentiment directs behavior in a more fragmentary and sporadic way.

Comprehensive and Integral. This refers to the role of the religious sentiment in providing a comprehensive or all-encompassing philosophy of life and in integrating all of human knowledge and all of human experience within that philosophy of life. The religious sentiment, for example, must incorporate in some way new knowledge and scientific advances within its worldview. Even unchanging moral principles, for example, must be applied to technological advances in human reproduction and artificial means of prolonging life. Religion and science, faith and reason must somehow be reconciled. This enterprise is a continuing one, as reason discovers new historical and scientific truths. These advances in knowledge must be assimilated and integrated into one's religious belief system. This feature of the mature religious sentiment also means that it must try to find meaning in all human experience, the dark, negative side of life as well as the good and beautiful. A religious sentiment which fails to include any aspect of life in its system of meaning fails the test of comprehensiveness and integrity and shares in the escapist character of the immature sentiment.

Heuristic. Allport describes a heuristic belief as "one that is held tentatively until it can be confirmed or until it helps us discover a more valid belief."[43] To understand this attribute of the mature religious sentiment it is helpful to remember that every religious doctrine is, to use Allport's phrase, a "working hypothesis." This is necessarily the case since religious doctrines are attempts to put into human language what is essentially a mystery. As with all human attempts at conceptualization, they are approximations of the truth they are intended to convey. Consider the difference, for example, between the essential nature of God and the various images and concepts by which religions attempt to describe that nature. We are well aware that these images and concepts are metaphors drawn from our human experience and projected on to a reality which is beyond human experience and comprehension. If we consider the difference between the way in which God is imaged by a child and a mature adult, we realize that our conceptualization of the deity—as with all religious realities—is subject to development. Any doctrinal formulation, therefore, must be held tentatively (heuristically) since it is always subject to development and to reformulation in a way that more accurately conveys the truth it symbolizes. The belief of an adult who clings to a childish understanding of his religion would lack this heuristic quality. While a religious truth may remain unchanging, the doctrinal formulation used to express it may be subject to change as new insights into its meaning become available. The believer who thus holds his beliefs heuristically and never with complete certainty is "closer to the agnostic than we think,"[44] but Allport agrees with William James that one may act wholeheartedly even in the absence of complete certainty.

Extrinsic versus Intrinsic Religion

The distinction between extrinsic and intrinsic religion was used by Allport to clarify the relationship between religion and prejudice. He had devoted a considerable amount of study to the psychology of prejudice, the results of which were published in his 1958 work *The Nature of Prejudice*. His research indicated that churchgoers tended to be somewhat more prejudiced than nonchurchgoers. The presence of prejudice and bigotry among those whose overt beliefs aimed at brotherhood pointed to an ambiguity in religion which Allport summarized in this way: "Two contrary sets of threads are woven into the fabric of all religion—the warp of brotherhood and the woof of bigotry."[45] In discussing the relative frequency of prejudice among churchgoers, Allport identifies three different religious contexts which may serve as sources of prejudice: The first is the theological context. Theological systems are seen to contain three "invitations to bigotry." The doctrine of revelation may give rise to claims to exclusive possession of final truth and to be the sole authority for interpreting it. The doctrine of election (God ordains in advance those to be saved) promotes the idea of "God's chosen ones," or "God's chosen people," or when linked to nationalism, "God's country." During certain historical periods the concept of "theocracy"—the notion that kings rule by divine right or that the church had authority over civil rulers—created the possibility of the abuse of either secular or religious authority.

It should be noted that the preiously mentioned doctrines constitute "invitations to bigotry" only to those willing to distort them and use them to achieve social and political goals. Allport further notes that the danger of bigotry resulting from these theological roots has greatly decreased in our times. Harsh interpretations of revelation and election have been mitigated by the ecumenical movement, and theocracy has been replaced by the doctrine of the separation of church and state. Of more significance today are the sociocultural and psychological contexts of prejudice. Religion is, of course, a sociocultural phenomenon. It becomes a bigotry, however, when it becomes a primarily sociocultural reality or identified with a particular sociocultural class. It is difficult, in such situations, to determine whether the resulting conflicts are essentially religious or sociocultural, as the ongoing conflict in Northern Ireland and the recent war in Bosnia attest. Allport suggests that, in this context, many churchgoers appear to be more prejudiced than others precisely because some people, by virtue of their psychological makeup, seem to need both religion and prejudice since both seem to provide answers to the same needs and problems. Both provide a sense of self-esteem to those suffering from self-doubt and insecurity. Prejudice provides a scapegoat and religion provides relief in those who are guilt-ridden. For those suffering from a sense of failure, prejudice provides a menacing group of outsiders to blame, while religion promises a heavenly reward. We can immediately recognize here a religious sentiment that is not "functionally autonomous"; that serves a function extrinsic to religion; that satisfies a set of psychological needs which are the same as those satisfied by prejudice. Allport concludes that for many individuals "the functional significance of prejudice and religion is identical."[46]

It is in the personal-psychological context that Allport finds an explanation for the high incidence of prejudice among churchgoers. Studies revealed that the degree of prejudice decreased among those who attended church more frequently to the point where those who attended eleven or more times a month had a significantly lower level of prejudice than even nonchurchgoers. This indicated the possibility that frequent attenders had a qualitatively different religious sentiment than infrequent attenders. To test this he devised a questionnaire to test the extrinsic versus intrinsic value of religion to churchgoers. The purpose was "to separate churchgoers whose communal type of membership supports and serves other (nonreligious) ends from those for whom religion is an end in itself—a final, not instrumental, good."[47] An extrinsic orientation is indicated in a person who agrees with statements such as "The church is most important as a place to formulate good social relationships." An intrinsic type of religious sentiment is ascribed to one who subscribes to statements such as "I try hard to carry my religion over into all my other dealings in life."[48]

The result of this study indicated that the extrinsic religious attitude correlated with prejudice and the intrinsic attitude correlated with very low prejudice. Extrinsic religion is described as one that finds the value of religion in something extrinsic to religion. Religion is used as a means to achieve some other good such as security, peace of mind, business or social status. It may even be used, as we have seen, to reinforce prejudice. If religion is solely for my own benefit, it need not include those who are perceived to be not for my benefit or even as a threat to my security. Intrinsic religion serves an entirely different function. It is an end in itself rather than a means to an end. In other words it is "functionally autonomous." In this case the person commits himself to his religious beliefs—including, as Allport points out, the doctrine of human brotherhood—and tries to adapt and conform his life to those beliefs. He does not, as in the extrinsic orientation, adapt his beliefs to his own lifestyle, including his ruling prejudices. Regarding the relationship of religion and prejudice, therefore, Allport concludes: "It is not really valid to talk about the relationship of religion and prejudice in any gross way. Rather you've got to make a distinction between two kinds of functions that religion can play in different personalities."[49]

Religion and Mental Health

We began our discussion of Allport's theory of religion by reflecting on his remark that many people were turning from religion to psychology and psychiatry in their search for moral guidance in the conduct of their lives. This observation leads him to a discussion of the relationship of religion and psychotherapy. Both are concerned, he points out, with mental hygiene, that is, with the cure of mental illness and the promotion of mental health. His task, then, is to delineate the respective roles of psychotherapy and religion in promoting mental health. Both do so by trying to lead the individual to greater unification or integration of personality. Integration is seen as a concept analogous to the religious idea of "single-mindedness" or "purity of heart" and is defined by Allport as "the forging of approximate mental unity out of discordant impulses and aspirations."[50] This requires what Allport calls a hierarchical organization of sentiments with one master sentiment being dominant.[51] We have seen that a master sentiment such as the religious sentiment, when it occupies a central place in personality, exerts a pervasive motivating influence on all aspects of one's life and personality. All other sentiments are arranged in some kind of hierarchical order according to their relationship to this master sentiment.

Allport suggests that the mature religious sentiment makes for the integration of personality because it supplies many of those things we need which make for the greater integration of personality and sometimes in a way that is superior to psychotherapy.

First, religion provides a unifying master sentiment. While all strong interests tend to unify personality, religion is seen here as "an integrative agent *par excellence*" because of its comprehensive character (permeating every aspect of one's life) and because of the unifying power of its most basic beliefs and values. Religion deals with ultimate meaning and value and with life's most ultimate goals. Long-range goals have an integrating effect since all other interests are subordinated to and assigned their proper place in one's life in relation to them. Religion's long-range goals are never fully achieved and its tasks never completed. Allport concludes: "Precisely because religious accomplishment is always incomplete, its cementing character in the personal life is therefore all the greater."[52]

Second, religion recognizes the human need for affiliation—to love and be loved—and the healing power of such love. Psychotherapy, Allport argues, recognizes the power of love, but has not been able to incorporate it into the therapeutic process. There almost seems to be a "tenderness tabu" in psychotherapy, perhaps due in part, he suggests, to religion's very insistence on it. A psychology which has rejected the religious approach to healing focuses not on the deep-seated affiliative need of the individual but on the pathological symptoms of the frustration of that need. Religion, on the other hand, "is superior to psychotherapy in the allowance it makes for the affiliative need in human nature,"[53] but in practice often fails to live up to the demands of love, thus frustrating its healing potential. Allport notes the relationship between two basic human desires, to preserve one's self-esteem and self-love and to have warm affiliative relations with others. People want friendly relations with others provided they preserve their own sense of integrity and self-esteem. If one fails in the bid for affiliation the result is "anxious fear" and even hatred due to the blocking of one's self-esteem. The complementary truth is that "in proportion as man's affiliative needs are met, aggression and hostility disappear."[54] Thus a person's ability to forget oneself and enter into loving and cooperative relationships with others depends, to a great extent, on the degree of love and acceptance one receives from others. Acceptance leads to what Allport calls an "inclusionist" attitude and way of life, an openness to others; rejection leads to an "exclusionist" attitude, the exclusion of segments of humanity from one's affiliative tendencies. Prejudice and bigotry are examples of this.

Third, religion plays a role in the formation of conscience. For many people religion provides the basic moral values which are internalized in the formation of conscience. Mental illness, as we know, is a state of inner conflict and, in Allport's view, "the moral sense is almost always involved in any serious conflict."[55] Since conscience is the arbiter of those basic values which are central to one's existence and directive of all behavior, it acts as a master sentiment fostering that kind of integration, which is necessary for mental health. To act in all situations according to a basic set of values makes for that consistency of conduct which we call integrity. To perform this integrating function, however, conscience must grow beyond the level of the childhood superego. In Allport's view, the development of conscience takes place in three stages.[56] First, the externally imposed rules of parents and other authorities are internalized and imposed from within on oneself. This process of internalization results in the formation of the superego. Second, the sense of "must" based on fear and prohibition gives way to a sense of "ought" based on self-image and self-respect. By way of illustration, Allport points to the difference in the type of obligation felt between the statements "I must get some gas for my car" and "I ought to write a letter to my friend." At the same time he points out that not everything that was a "must" of the superego becomes an "ought" of the mature conscience. This implies a change in the content of one's moral obligation, which in turn implies some kind of critical assessment of the enforced rules of childhood in the light of one's own growing value system. This growing sense of self and of personal values introduces the third transformation in the growth of conscience: Habits of obedience to concrete rules give way to more generalized principles and values. To be guided by a set of values rather than to obey concrete rules allows for greater adaptability to changing circumstances and greater autonomy and responsibility on the part of the moral agent.

Fourth, religion promotes those things which Allport calls "aspects of integration". These include the following:

1. *Humour.* This is described as the "principal technique for getting rid of irrelevancies."[57] Religion clearly stands for the proposition that there is something in life which is sacred, ultimate, and absolute. If such terms can be applied only to the deity, then everything else (including religion) is relative and nonultimate and therefore a proper subject for humor. As much as the perversions of religion may fail in this regard, true religion promotes humor through the perspective it provides by relativizing what is nonultimate.

2. *Long-range goals.* We have already discussed the role of long-range goals in establishing priorities and thereby organizing and integrating personality. The ultimate goals and never-ending tasks of religion are therefore seen to have an integrating effect since "that which is ever not quite fulfilled is best able to hold the attention, guide effort and maintain unity."[58]

3. *Relaxation.* Psychotherapy recognizes that one of the obstacles to integration is the individual's "grimly determined effort" to resolve inner conflicts or free himself from compulsive behavior. Such struggles often follow the "law of reversed effect"; the harder one tries the more difficult and tense the struggle becomes. Moral struggles in particular require relaxation which religion offers in the form of surrender. Surrender to a divine source of forgiveness and acceptance is, for many, the first step toward resolving such conflicts since it provides release from the self-preoccupation which characterizes neurotic conflict.

4. *Self-objectification.* Integration requires self-knowledge, a clear and objective picture of oneself, of one's strengths and weaknesses, assets and liabilities. The truly religious person lives an "examined life," measuring himself against objective standards of conduct and the example of role models and honestly confessing his failures. When properly carried out such practices are helpful in the process of self-objectification.

It should be pointed out, in summary, that Allport's theory of religion is fully integrated within his theory of personality. Everything attributed to the mature personality—the motivating power of the ego-structure, the uniqueness of the individual, the functional autonomy of motives, and the integrating effect of master sentiments—is found to be characteristic of the mature religious personality.

Evaluation

However one might evaluate Allport's place in and contribution to the psychological study of religion, the following points should be kept in mind. First we have already located Allport in the vanguard of the humanistic/existential reaction to the perceived inadequacies of psychoanalysis and behaviorism. For Allport, the dynamic source of motivation for the mature adult lies in the traits, sentiments, goals, and intentions of the ego-structure. Religion, in its psychological aspect, is one of those sentiments. Thus a view of religion is promoted which sees it as having its own motivating power and not as a projection of some unconscious need or an elaboration of a conditioned response. Just as in his theory of personality he avoids the reduction of the specifically human to a function of the subhuman (e.g., instinct), so in his theory of religion he avoids the reduction of the religious sentiment to a function of some other mental mechanism.

Second, Allport's psychology of religion is representative of the humanistic preoccupation with the value of religion rather than its psychological source or origin. Though he does speak of the "origins of the religious quest," he makes it clear that the mature, "functionally autonomous" religious sentiment is independent of those human needs which might have acted as its original impetus. His main focus is the distinction between the immature ("extrinsic") and the mature ("intrinsic") religious sentiment.

Third, Allport's psychological assessment of religion demonstrates one of the qualities he ascribes to the mature religious sentiment in that it is "well differentiated." He is neither indiscriminately pro or antireligion. He avoids any simplistic evaluation of religion by distinguishing between the immature and the mature religious sentiment, using the same basic criteria he uses to differentiate immature and mature personality. In Allport's case, this distinction is particularly relevant since the focus of his studies is primarily "churchgoers," that is, participants in organized or institutional religion. His studies of the extrinsic and intrinsic religious orientations applied to those who were already religious in a more or less conventional sense. This represents an obvious limitation in Allport's work (which we shall return to) since it omits the potential religious dimension in the lives of nonchurchgoers. At the same time it is an important distinction to be made in an age when simplistic judgments about organized religion abound.

Allport has been an enormously significant figure in what could be called the "American tradition" in psychology of religion beginning with William James. His theory of religion in general and the distinction between extrinsic and intrinsic religious orientations in particular has provided a conceptual and measurement framework for a great deal of empirical research. To summarize briefly: The extrinsic orientation locates the value of religion in something extrinsic to religion itself. Religion is used as a means to some further goal such as security, wish fulfillment, social contacts, or status. The intrinsic religious orientation sees religion as an end in itself rather than a means to an end. Religious beliefs and values are functionally autonomous, constituting a master sentiment which informs and guides all other aspects of life. In short, extrinsic religion is self-seeking while intrinsic religion is self-transcending.

While a significant amount of empirical research has made use of Allport's psychology of religion, in particular the extrinsic/intrinsic distinction and the Religious Orientation Scale by which he measured these two dimensions of religion, there has, at the same time, been a great deal of critical review and discussion. Much of this discussion centers around the value of extrinsic/intrinsic distinction. In a paper published in 1990,[59] Lee A. Kirkpatrick and Ralph W. Hood Jr. review this discussion. Questions raised about the value of the extrinsic/intrinsic distinction include the following:

First, what does "religious orientation" mean? Does it refer to beliefs and practices or to what motivates one's religious life? The answer appears to be simple enough since Allport clearly refers to motivation, particularly when he refers to the functional autonomy of the mature (intrinsic) religious sentiment. This, however, raises a further question. If these terms refer to motivation, do they represent religious variables or personality variables? The authors point out that one can be extrinsic or intrinsic about other areas of institutional behavior. One is reminded here of William James' distinction between healthy-minded religion and the sick soul. In both cases the same question could be asked: Do these terms describe characteristics of one's religious sentiment or, in broader terms, of one's personality? If the terms "extrinsic" and "intrinsic" as types of motivation refer not just to religion but to basic personality variables, then the distinction transcends the distinction between believers and nonbelievers. This view seems to find support in a study by Martin Bolt published in 1975.[60] Bolt administered two tests to a group of college students, Allport's Religious Orientation Scale and J. Crumbaugh's Purpose-in-Life Test. The results indicated that those students whose religion was intrinsically motivated experienced a greater sense of meaning and purpose in life than did the extrinsically motivated. This seemed to support Allport's claim that mature religion "floods the whole life with motivation and meaning." At the same time it was found that the extrinsically religious students did not generally find a compensating sense of purpose in pursuit of secular goals and values. This suggests that the differences between the two groups were not merely religious but basic personality differences.

Second, what is the meaning of "extrinsic" and "intrinsic"? The authors find that the extrinsic orientation is the more clearly defined ("self-centred religion"). The intrinsic orientation, on the other hand, seems to have diverse meanings. C. Daniel Batson [61] has argued that the term "intrinsic religion" is not co-extensive with the term "mature religious sentiment." The latter term includes characteristics such as the ability to face and live with complexity and ambiguity, the capacity for doubt and self-criticism, and the ability to hold one's beliefs tentatively while continuing to search for more insight into religious questions. It is suggested however, that intrinsic religion refers to a state beyond doubt; that it refers to "single-mindedness" in the sense of rigid adherence to doctrinal orthodoxy. Batson argues that, as measured on the Religious Orientation Scale, intrinsic religion appears as a single-minded commitment to religion as the central and master motive in life but without the critical open-ended approach of the mature religious sentiment. Hence, on this test, one who is rigidly orthodox and inflexible may appear to have an intrinsic orientation. He therefore suggests that a third type of religious orientation be taken into account—the "quest" orientation. This would refer to the religious "seeker" who may not be religious in the conventional sense but whose life is "an endless process of probing and questioning" in the face of the ambiguities, doubts, complexities, and tragedies of life. The quest orientation is characterized by what Paul Tillich has called "ultimate concern." This is in part an attempt to compensate for the previously noted limitation of Allport's studies, since it would allow for the possibility of a Religious Orientation Scale that would not be restricted to those who are already religious in the sense of "churchgoers."

Third, is the extrinsic/intrinsic distinction a "value laden" distinction? Does it try to distinguish between "good religion" and "bad religion"? Is Allport's concept of intrinsic religion, for example, motivated by a desire to save "good" religion from the charge of prejudice? Similarly, is research based on Allport's Religious Orientation Scale motivated by the desire to correlate extrinsic religion with negative personality traits and intrinsic religion with positive ones?

This last point raises the more general question of whether a psychology of religion is normative or value-free. Should it be prescriptive or descriptive? Should it—after the manner of religion and philosophy—engage in an unabashed search for the meaning of authentic religion? Or should it restrict itself to a purely scientific description of religious phenomena? Those who favor the latter option point to the traditional distinction between religion and science: Religion deals with values, science deals with facts. Others might take a more pragmatic view in the spirit of William James and ask, "If it does not help us to differentiate between good and bad, authentic and inauthentic religion, of what use is it?" As we shall see (Chapter 6) Abraham Maslow questions this traditional distinction between science and religion and wants to include the study of values within the scope of science. In a 1978 paper, Robert J. Palma [62] discusses the "normative" character of Allport's psychology of religion especially in his description of "mature religion." He concludes that Allport's theory of mature religion is prescriptive and not merely descriptive: "In both his theory of the mature personality and in his conception of mature religion, Allport is clearly using `mature' not simply to describe but also to prescribe an ideal state of affairs that ought to be realized."[63]

There are, of course, different kinds of "norms" but Allport's concept of maturity and mature religion are regarded here as ideal norms and not merely statistical norms. What criteria does Allport use in defining maturity? We have seen that his criteria of mature religion are derived from the criteria of mature personality. But whence does he derive these criteria of mature personality? When he lists the three hallmarks of maturity—self-expansion, self-objectification, and self-unification—he does not offer an elaborate scientific argument in their support but adds simply: "I doubt that any scientifically supported criteria of maturity would differ substantially from these three."[64] When questioned by Richard Evans about the possibility of establishing objective criteria of good mental health or the good life, Allport admits that while psychology can contribute to answering the question "What is the `Good Life'?" it is ultimately a philosophical and ethical question. He then adds, "Even a doctor can't define health, and I'm not sure that anyone can define maturity; it's a kind of ideal state that we think exists, but everyone sees it according to his own set of values."[65]

In this last phrase Allport seems to point to the fact that even the most scientific theories are rooted in the basic values of the theorist, values that are not scientifically demonstrable but represent assumptions about what is and what ought to be. In the case of religious teachings, these values are quite explicitly proclaimed. They tend to be implicit or hidden, however, to the extent that theorizing lays claim to being "scientific." In identifying the personal values which inform Allport's theoretical thought, one cannot overlook the "plain Protestant piety" which characterized his home life, nor the liberal, social, and democratic values that developed during his student years. At a philosophical level, Allport locates himself in the "Leibnitzian" tradition rather than the "Lockean" tradition. He describes the Lockean tradition as based on John Locke's assumption that the mind of the individual is a *tabula rasa* at birth. It is therefore a passive receptor of stimuli and therefore structured by its environment. In the Leibnitzian tradition the mind is seen not as merely the locus of acts but as the source of acts. It is not simply pushed by internal or external stimuli but acts according to its own purposes. It is not difficult to see how this view of the mind translates into Allport's psychological view of the proactive intentionality of the individual ego structure as source of motivation.

Theodore A. McConnell has suggested that the Lockean/Leibnitzian distinction finds a parallel in Allport's distinction between the extrinsic and intrinsic religious orientations.[66] The extrinsic orientation parallels the Lockean view in that is represents "minimal involvement of the self" with the resulting rigidity of doctrinal beliefs and an inability to deal with ambiguity and complexity. The intrinsic orientation is seen as a parallel to the Leibnitzian view insofar as it represents an "intensive involvement and self-commitment," which in turn is seen as the source of a liberal social outlook and an ability to tolerate the ambiguities of life. Clearly the intrinsic orientation represents "good religion" to Allport and an ideal norm—a norm which, as he readily admits, everyone formulates "according to his own set of values." However, whether this conscious awareness of the personal values which inform his theoretical work makes his theory a "normative" psychology of religion is questionable.

Suggested Readings

ALLPORT, GORDON, *Becoming: Basic Considerations for a Psychology of Personality* (New Haven: Yale University Press, 1955).

ALLPORT, GORDON, *The Individual and His Religion* (New York: Macmillan, 1950).

ALLPORT, GORDON, *Pattern and Growth in Personality* (New York: Holt, Rinehart and Winston, 1961).

ALLPORT, GORDON, *The Person in Psychology* (Boston: Beacon Press, 1968).

KIRKPATRICK, LEE A. and HOOD, RALPH "Intrinsic-Extrinsic Religious Orientation: The Boon or Bane of Contemporary Psychology of Religion," *Journal for the Scientific Study of Religion*, 29, 1990, 442-462.

MADDI, SALVATOR R. and COSTA, PAUL, *Humanism in Personology: Allport, Maslow and Murray* (Chicago: Aldine, Alkerton, 1972).

PALMA, ROBERT J. "The Prospects for a Normative Psychology of Religion: G.W. Allport as a Paradigm," *Journal of Psychology and Theology*, 6, 1978, 110-122.

Notes

1. G.W. Allport, *The Person in Psychology* (Boston: Beacon Press, 1968), p. 394.
2. *Ibid.*
3. G.W. Allport, *Personality and Social Encounter* (Boston: Beacon Press, 1960), p. 96.
4. *Ibid.*, p. 103.
5. Cf. G.W. Allport, *Pattern and Growth in Personality* (New York: Holt, Rinehart and Winston, 1961), ch. 10.
6. Cf. G.W. Allport, *The Person in Psychology*, ch. 21.
7. *Ibid.*, p. 379.
8. *Ibid.*
9. *Ibid.*
10. *Ibid.*, p. 382.
11. *Ibid.*
12. *Ibid.*, pp. 383-384.
13. *Ibid.*, p. 385.
14. *Ibid.*
15. *Ibid.*, p. 386.
16. *Ibid.*, p. 395.
17. *Ibid.*, p. 405.

18. *Ibid.*, p. 406.
19. *Ibid.*
20. *Ibid.*
21. G.W. Allport, *Personality and Social Encounter*, p. 103.
22. G.W. Allport, *Personality: A Psychological Interpretation* (New York: Holt, 1937), p. 48.
23. Cf. Richard Evans, *Gordon Allport: The Man and His Ideas* (New York: E.P. Dutton, 1970), p. 24.
24. Cf. G.W. Allport, *Becoming: Basic Considerations for a Psychology of Personality* (New Haven: Yale University Press, 1955), pp. 24-28.
25. *Ibid.*, pp. 36-41.
26. *Ibid.*, p. 40.
27. *Ibid.*, pp. 41-54.
28. *Ibid.*, p. 53.
29. G.W. Allport, *Pattern and Growth in Personality*, ch. 10.
30. G.W. Allport, *Personality and Social Encounter*, p. 149.
31. *Ibid.*, p. 138.
32. *Ibid.*, p. 146.
33. Richard Evans, *Gordon Allport: The Man and His Ideas*, p. 31.
34. G.W. Allport, *The Individual and His Religion* (New York: Macmillan, 1950), p. 63.
35. *Ibid.*, p. 64.
36. *Ibid.*, pp. 7-30.
37. *Ibid.*, p. 19.
38. *Ibid.*, p. 161.
39. *Ibid.*, p. 30.
40. *Ibid.*, p. 61.
41. *Ibid.*, p. 71.
42. *Ibid.*, pp. 72-73.
43. *Ibid.*, p. 81.
44. *Ibid.*, p. 82.
45. G.W. Allport, *The Person in Psychology*, p. 218.
46. *Ibid.*, p. 225.
47. *Ibid.*, p. 230.
48. *Ibid.*, p. 233.
49. Richard Evans, *Gordon Allport: The Man and His Ideas*, p. 72.
50. G.W. Allport, *The Individual and His Religion*, p. 104.
51. *Ibid.*, p. 90.
52. *Ibid.*, p. 105.
53. *Ibid.*, p. 93.
54. G.W. Allport, *Personality and Social Encounter*, p. 207.
55. G.W. Allport, *The Individual and His Religion*, p. 98.
56. *Ibid.*, pp. 99-101. Cf. also *Becoming*, ch. 16.
57. *Ibid.*, p. 104.
58. *Ibid.*, p. 105.
59. Lee A. Kirkpatrick and Ralph W. Hood,"Intrinsic-Extrinsic Religious Orientation: The Boon or Bane of Contemporary Psychology of Religion," *Journal for the Scientific Study of Religion*, 29, 1990, 442-462.
60. Martin Bolt, "Purpose in Life and Religious Orientation," *Journal of Psychology and Theology*, 3, 1975, 116-118.
61. C. Daniel Batson and Lynn Raynor-Prince, "Religious Orientation and Complexity of Thought about Existential Concerns," *Journal for the Scientific Study of Religion*, 22, 1983, 38-50.

62. Robert J. Palma, "The Prospects for a Normative Psychology of Religion: G.W. Allport as a Paradigm," *Journal of Psychology and Theology*, 6, 1978, 110-122.
63. *Ibid.*, p. 114
64. G.W. Allport, *The Individual and His Religion*, p. 61.
65. Richard Evans, *Gordon Allport: The Man and His Ideas*, p. 75.
66. Theodore A. McConnell, "Gordon Allport and the Quest for Selfhood," *Journal of Religion and Health*, 8, 1969, 375-381.

VI. ABRAHAM MASLOW

Religion and Self-Actualization

Abraham Maslow (1908–1970)
Corbis

I n the work of Abraham H. Maslow (1908-1970) we find both a reflection and an extension of the work of two of his contemporaries, Erich Fromm and Gordon Allport. As with Allport, Maslow's mature theory is in part a reaction to the failure of psychoanalytic and behaviorist theories to provide a comprehensive understanding of human personality. Unlike Allport, however, Maslow's early training at the University of Wisconsin was experimental and behaviorist. He was the first doctoral student of Harry Harlow, who was best known for his work on mother-infant bonding among monkeys. Maslow continued this work in his doctoral research by studying the relationship of sexual behavior in primates to patterns of dominance. He would then go on to pursue this same line of inquiry (the relation of sexual behavior to dominance) in regard to human sexuality. These were the early stepping-stones to the work for which he is best known, the question of human motivation in general and in particular the need for self-actualization. With this emphasis on the need for self-actualization—to become everything one is capable of becoming—a new "humanistic" psychology is created which recognizes the "higher needs" of the human being, which were unrecognized by Freud and the behaviorists.

Maslow's humanistic psychology is offered not as a substitute for psychoanalysis and behaviorism but as a supplement. He saw himself, in fact, as a Freudian in the sense that his theory represented a logical extension of Freudian theory, not as a slavish adherent, but as someone carrying on the *spirit* of Freud. Colin Wilson suggests that what distinguishes Maslow from Freud and the behaviorists is a certain optimism which results from seeing human nature and the world as a whole. Maslow's focus was not on one aspect of personality (e.g., the instinctual) or on isolated stimulus-response mechanisms but on the self-actualizing thrust of the whole organism.[1] In an unpublished note dated August 17, 1955, Maslow summarizes his feelings about psychoanalysis. After acknowledging that psychoanalysis has provided us with the best systems of psychotherapy and psychopathology he adds:

> However, it is quite unsatisfactory as a general psychology of the whole human being, especially in his healthier and more admirable aspects. The picture of man it presents is a lopsided, distorted puffing up of his weaknesses and shortcomings that purports then to describe him fully. This it clearly fails to do. Practically all the activities that man prides himself on, and that give meaning, richness, and value to his life, are either omitted or pathologized by Freud. Work, play, love, art, creativeness, religion in the good sense, ethics, philosophy, science, learning, parenthood, self-sacrifice, heroism, saintliness, goodness—these are all weakly handled, if at all.[2]

Maslow's humanistic psychology regards all of these "activities that man prides himself on" as potentialities of human nature. The human being, he asserts, "*can* solve his problems by his own strength.... He doesn't have to fly to a God. He can look within himself for all sorts of potentialities, strength, and goodness."[3]

Though he never succeeded in developing a close friendship with Erich Fromm, Maslow nevertheless regarded Fromm as a mentor and inspiration for his own work. There seem to be, in fact, many affinities between the work of these two men: (1) Both were secular Jews who, nevertheless, reflect in their social criticism the passion for social justice and the building of a better world, which characterize the Jewish tradition. Maslow suggests that his interest in psychotherapy and social therapy (Utopianism) was "peculiarly Jewish."[4] (2) Fromm's notion of psychotherapy as "cure of the soul" whose goal is the realization of one's authentic humanity is reflected in Maslow's concept of a universal idea and ideal of human nature which transcends all cultural relativism and seeks to be actualized. (3) Maslow's understanding of "peak" or transcendent experiences as purely naturalistic phenomena requiring no religious or theological explanation parallels Fromm's concept of the "non-theistic" religious experience.

Maslow's significance lies not only in the role he played in the development of humanistic psychology but also in the impetus his work gave to the emerging "transpersonal" psychology. In his attempt to go beyond the limitations of Freudian psychopathology and formulate a psychology of the healthy person, Maslow tried to list the characteristics of the healthiest, most evolved, most fully human members of society—those he called "self-actualizers." In doing so he discovered that many such people tend to have transcendent experiences in the sense of transcending the narrow, selfish interests of the ego and becoming one with the world in a self-forgetful way. Such unitive experiences were regarded by Maslow as a potential of human nature. They are thus naturalistic in origin and do not require a religious explanation. This contention lies at the heart of his psychology of religion. At the same time, the study of such "peak experiences" sensitized Maslow to humanistic psychology's lack of a religious or spiritual dimension and the corresponding need for a "fourth force" or "transpersonal" psychology.

Life

Abraham Maslow was born on April 1, 1908, at Brooklyn, New York. His father, Samuel Maslow, was a Russian-Jewish immigrant from Kiev who came to America, married his first cousin Rose, and established a cooperage business. Rose gave birth to seven children, six of whom survived and of whom Abe was the eldest. His three younger brothers followed their father into the cooperage business, which prospered. Abe's interests, however, were academic and he spent much of his childhood in the world of books. This was in part a way of compensating for a lonely and unhappy childhood which he later described in the words: "I was a terribly unhappy boy.... My family was a miserable family and my mother was a horrible creature ... I grew up in libraries and among books, without friends. With my childhood, it's a wonder I'm not psychotic."[5] Though his younger siblings did not seem to have such a negative image of the mother, to Abe the "horrible creature" of his recollections was a harsh disciplinarian who constantly threatened him with God's punishment for misconduct. This was the seed of his youthful atheism and contempt for religion. Incidents recorded by Maslow's biographer—the keeping of a bolted lock on the refrigerator, the smashing of several old 78-RPM records that Abe treasured because he did not gather them up from the floor quickly enough, and the act of smashing the heads of two stray kittens Abe had brought home to care for—all these point to a mother with a cruel sadistic streak.

Paradoxically his mother's harshness and cruelty proved to be an impetus to Maslow's later research and theorizing, his utopianism and humanism. All of this, he later recalled "has its roots in a hatred for and revulsion against everything she stood for."[6] Adding to young Abe's unhappiness was the fact that he considered himself "a very ugly child" because of his scrawny physique and large nose. At the same time he felt alienated from and neglected by his father, whose marriage to Rose was deteriorating and who was, as a consequence, frequently absent from the family. It was only after Abe was away at college that his parents were finally divorced, after which a reconciliation between father and son became possible. Maslow was never reconciled, however, with his mother and even refused to attend her funeral. As a child his only escapes from his unhappy home life seem to have been reading, browsing for hours in the public library and the companionship of his cousin Will Maslow.

At Boys High School in Brooklyn, which he and Will entered in 1922, Maslow was introduced by one of his teachers to the novels of Upton Sinclair. Eight years later he recalled this experience as the beginning of his intellectual life. It also helped to instill in him a democratic socialist political outlook and an idealistic desire to create a better world, which stayed with him throughout his life. In history class he was inspired by the lives of Thomas Jefferson and Abraham Lincoln and later included them in his list of self-actualizing people. After high school Maslow enrolled at City College of New York. His intellectual development at this stage was definitely in the direction of the humanities, particularly philosophy. The following diary entry during his first year at City College reveals a strong sense of intellectual superiority and a desire to be accepted by the scholarly world:

> I am a student at the College of the City of New York. My career through high school was distinguished and now in college promises to be brilliant. I have been given to hope that I might make some progress in philosophy, my chosen favourite. My writing has been commended warmly by my English professor. I flatter myself that my college education has not been wasted on me. Already I have found keen delight in warm discussion with scholars of the highest order, whose esteem I think I have won or shortly will win.[7]

The sheer grandiosity of the language suggests an attitude which is a defense against deeply rooted feelings of inferiority. The same may be said of the striving to maintain what his biographer Edward Hoffman describes as "a fiercely rationalist outlook, with contempt for anything that smacked of the slightest religious sentiment."[8] So overdriven was this hard-headed intellectual stance that Maslow seems to have had trouble reconciling it with his growing attraction to music.

In the winter of 1927 Maslow transferred from City College to Cornell University in Ithaca, New York, joining his cousin Will who was already a student there. Cornell provided him with an escape from the unhappiness of his home life. At the same time he experienced a sense of personal isolation due to the pervasive anti-Semitism he encountered there. Consequently, he lasted only one semester, returning to Brooklyn in June 1927. Here he re-enrolled at City College and was also reunited with his cousin Bertha Goodman. The attraction Abe and Bertha had felt for each other was now openly expressed. Recalling the first time he kissed Bertha, Maslow later remarked, "She kissed back and then life began."[9] They were married on December 31, 1928, while Maslow was a student at University of Wisconsin, and raised a family of two daughters.

Back at City College, Maslow was introduced to the work of sociologist William Sumner and the idea that change in societal mores was brought about by charismatic, superior, enlightened individuals who influence the entire culture. Sumner's ideas had a powerful effect on Maslow's grandiose self-image and he dedicated himself to creating a better world through intellectual endeavor. In the summer of 1928, influenced by his reading of behaviorist John B. Watson, he decided that his area of endeavor would be psychology. At this stage, behaviorism struck Maslow as a psychology committed to social improvement and the possibility of bringing about social change through behavioral conditioning appealed to his idealism. Consequently he decided to transfer to the University of Wisconsin to study psychology and "to change the world." Other factors influenced his move to Wisconsin. It would remove him from family pressures and also from Bertha with whom his romance had become increasingly intense without any immediate possibility of marriage. He was also drawn to the liberal atmosphere of the University of Wisconsin, which also had the advantage of being a state university and, therefore, had affordable tuition.

Maslow arrived at the University of Wisconsin in September of 1928. It was the beginning of a period of intellectual and emotional growth. He came under the tutelage of scholars such as William Sheldon and Harry Harlow and for the first time felt himself to be a fully accepted member of an intellectual community. His psychology professors treated him as a promising scholar, which, as we have seen, was important to him. This in turn was balanced by the increased emotional security he experienced as a result of his marriage to Bertha at the end of his first semester. Bertha returned to Wisconsin with him and was accepted as a special student. Academically, Maslow's training at Wisconsin was decidedly experimental and behaviorist. Even during his later career as a humanistic psychologist concerned with mysticism and peak experiences, he never repudiated or denigrated this kind of training or objective experimental research. He began to be aware of its limitations, however, when for his M.A. thesis, he was assigned a research project on learning, retention, and recall of verbal material, involving lists of words on cards, a stopwatch, and a bell. Maslow considered the resulting thesis (completed in 1931) so trivial that he removed it from the psychology library.

In 1931 Maslow became a research assistant and the first doctoral student of Harry Harlow, whose chief area of research was mother-infant bonding among monkeys, and decided that this would be his chief area of research as well. At the same time he was becoming impatient with the narrow intellectual focus and the lack of a broader vision of behaviorism as practiced by his mentors at Wisconsin. At this time also he discovered Freud and Alfred Adler and was intrigued by their differing emphases on sex and dominance, respectively, in human motivation. He wanted to incorporate this question into his doctoral research with monkeys. The result was a doctoral thesis on the relationship of sexual behavior in primates to patterns of dominance. The thesis advanced the theory that a monkey's dominance or power status determined its expression of sexuality not vice versa. The unwritten corollary to this conclusion (in Maslow's opinion) was that Adler's account of human motivation was more correct than Freud's.

Maslow completed his Ph.D. in 1934 at the height of the great depression. Unable to find employment he enrolled in Wisconsin's medical school and taught an introductory psychology course as a teaching fellow. This venture lasted only one semester as Maslow found himself emotionally unsuited to medicine as he and his fellow medical students were taught to practice it. The man who, in his later career, would insist on the importance of discovering the sacred in the "ordinary" things of life found a completely opposite attitude in the medical profession which seemed intent on eliminating any sense of the sacred—any feelings of awe, respect, or reverence—by the cultivation of a cool, detached, unemotional approach to its work. Thirty years later he recalled his first experience of surgery:

> The first operation I ever saw—I remember it well—was almost paradigmatic in its efforts to desacralize: that is, to remove the sense of awe, privacy, fear, and shyness before the sacred and the forbidden, and of humility before the tremendous, and the like. A woman's cancerous breast was to be amputated with an electrical scalpel. It cuts by burning to prevent metastasis.... Half the kids there got nauseous. The surgeon made carelessly cool and casual remarks about the pattern of his cutting, paying no attention to the [freshman] medical students rushing out in distress. Finally, he cut off the breast, tossing this object off through the air onto a marble counter where it landed with a plop. I have remembered that plop for thirty years. It has changed from a sacred object into a lump of fat, garbage, to be tossed into a pail. There were, of course, no prayers, no rituals or ceremonies of any kind, as there most certainly would be in most preliterate societies.... Here, this was handled in a purely technological fashion: the expert was emotionless, cool, calm, with even a slight tinge of swagger.[10]

Clearly, medical school and a medical career were not the answer for Maslow.

In 1935, when Maslow seemed to be at the dead end of his career options, he received, unexpectedly, the offer of a postdoctoral fellowship from Edward Thorndike at Columbia University in New York. The assignment was to assist Thorndike on a research project—Human Nature and the Social Order—at the Institute of Educational Research. This project dealt primarily with the relative influence of heredity versus environment on human behavior. Bored with this project, Maslow spent more time on his own study of sex and dominance (now applied to human sexual behavior). Thorndike eventually gave him a free hand to pursue his own line of research. This decision seems to have been based on the fact that Maslow had scored an amazing 195 in an I.Q. test administered by Thorndike's Institute. Interestingly, and perhaps as an indication of an underlying insecurity, this score was a source of pride and even an occasion for boasting for the rest of Maslow's life. In pursuing this research Maslow determined to interview men and women concerning their sexual behavior. He soon concluded, however, that women were more open and honest on this subject and decided to concentrate solely on female subjects. His conclusion was that women experience and regard sexuality differently depending on their degree of dominance-feeling, a trait closely related to self-confidence. Those with high dominance-feeling experienced sex more casually and as pleasurable in its own right, and were more sexually active, adventurous, and experimental.

Soon after the United States entered World War II Maslow abandoned this kind of sociological research and turned his attention to the broader questions of human motivation and self-actualization. This may have been due in part to the fact that his return to New York in the thirties had put him in touch with a number of great psychologists, some of whom were German emigres. Among those were Alfred Adler, Erich Fromm, Karen Horney, Kurt Goldstein, Max Wertheimer, and Kurt Kofka. He considered himself fortunate to have these great thinkers as his mentors and learned eagerly from them. At the same time he developed an interest in anthropology through his acquaintances in the anthropology department at Columbia. Among these he was particularly impressed by Ruth Benedict who, along with Max Wertheimer, supplied Maslow with his two primary examples of self-actualizing persons and triggered his interest in that area. It was Benedict who encouraged him to do real fieldwork and experience another culture directly. The result was a summer (1938) spent working among the Blackfoot tribe in Alberta. The experience caused Maslow to abandon the notion of cultural relativism in favor of a concept of universal human nature underlying all cultural diversity. His further research would be aimed at defining the fundamental personality structure, the basic personality traits and motivations that transcend cultural differences. And if such basic, universal motivations could be identified scientifically, then the goals of the ideal personality, that is, values, could be studied scientifically.

In February of 1937 Maslow began teaching at Brooklyn College. He remained there until 1951. This sojourn was interrupted by a two-year leave of absence from 1947 to 1949 due to ill health. During these two years he recuperated by accepting a very undemanding job of managing a branch of his brothers' cooperage corporation in Pleasanton, California. The extreme fatigue he experienced at this time was originally diagnosed as cancer. It was only after suffering a heart attack in December of 1967 that it was suggested to him that this earlier illness may have been a first heart attack. After the 1967 heart attack, Maslow would refer to the remainder of his life as the "post mortem life"—a gift of life, as it were, beyond one's allotted span in which everything previously taken for granted is perceived in a new light. It was during his years at Brooklyn College that Maslow began collecting data on self-actualizing people or, as he called them, "Good Human Beings (GHB)." In 1950 he published the paper "Self-Actualizing People: A Study of Psychological Health" in which he identified 13 common features of self-actualizers. Having found almost a complete dearth of suitable subjects among his students, he based his findings on historical and public figures as well as personal acquaintances who were distinguished by an absence of significant inner problems and the full use of talents, capacities and potentialities.

In the spring of 1951 Maslow was invited to head the psychology program at Brandeis University. Situated in Waltham Massachusetts, 15 miles west of Boston, Brandeis was a nonsectarian, Jewish-sponsored institution which had been founded in 1948. Maslow spent the rest of his career at Brandeis, although he resigned as head of the psychology department in 1961. As a researcher and theorist the years at Brandeis witnessed the full development of his thought in the direction of self-actualization, peak-experiences, and the development of the emerging humanistic or "being" psychology, that is, a psychology of the fully evolved and authentic self. The direction of his research led him to the study of existentialist thought and existential psychology as well as Eastern thought and the great mystics who reported what Maslow called peak-experiences. This latter interest led him to investigate the possibility of a "fourth force" psychology concerned with the spiritual dimension and transcendent experiences of human personality. It was an area he felt was underdeveloped in "third force" or humanistic psychology. During these years Maslow also came to be regarded as the preeminent spokesman for the emerging humanistic trend in psychology. One of the consequences of this was that he was increasingly sought after by corporations and government agencies interested in fostering self-actualization and creativity among their employees.

It should be noted however that all of this was accomplished against the background of a growing sense of personal frustration and isolation. This isolation was experienced on at least three levels: (1) His relations with students at Brandeis were increasingly strained over the years. Compared with the hardworking and eager students he had taught at Brooklyn College, these seemed to lack drive and ambition. During his own student days, and even the early years of his professional career, he had always been eager to learn from his professors and mentors. Small wonder that he found the demands of the student rebels of the 1960s for the freedom and authority to set their own curriculum nonsensical. His response: "When you get older, you'll be nice people. But right now, you're immature jerks."[11] (2) He felt isolated from and unappreciated by his colleagues at Brandeis, particularly after his resignation as head of the psychology department, which was becoming increasingly experimental as he was becoming increasingly humanistic. (3) He was frustrated by the tendency of the leaders of the 1960s counterculture to anoint him as their leader or "father of the revolution." All this in spite of the fact that Maslow criticized them for the shallowness of their "experiential" approach to human transformation and their anti-intellectualism. The counterculture seemed to have appropriated humanistic psychology as its underlying rationale, but totally ignored Maslow's emphasis on the need for hard work, discipline, classical forms of education, and rigorous professional training.

The foregoing should prompt us to add at least two footnotes to the description of Abraham Maslow as one of the founders of humanistic psychology. First, just as Maslow should not be identified with all the features of the 1960s counterculture, we may also assume that he would be dismayed at much of the popularized versions of humanistic psychology which have appeared since his death in 1970. Our inner transformation and self-actualization, he might argue, are tougher nuts to crack than much of today's self-help literature might lead us to believe. Second, it might be overly simplistic to describe Maslow as a stereotypically atheistic, antireligious humanist. His study of the "core" religious or peak experience led him away from his youthful, blanket rejection of all religion to a recognition that, from a humanistic point of view, religion can be good or bad.

Theory of Personality

We have seen that Maslow, who gained his early reputation as a behaviorist, was led, by his study of human motivation, to the conviction that both behaviorism and psychoanalysis were incomplete psychologies. He shares with Allport the conviction that these dominant theories did not provide a comprehensive understanding of human personality. Specifically: (1) They focused on the instinctual dimension of personality or learned behavior patterns to the exclusion of the "higher reaches of human nature," the valuing process, and the pursuit of self-actualization. (2) They offered explanations of the sick, neurotic personality, not the healthy personality. (3) They produced a pessimistic rather than an optimistic view of human nature. By the 1960s Maslow had become the leading spokesperson for a third alternative to psychoanalysis and behaviorism, a "third force" or "humanistic" psychology which would study humanity's higher nature rather than its lower nature, health rather than sickness, and the totality of human personality rather than isolated drives and S-R patterns. Humanistic psychology's agenda was to study what makes people healthy and not only what makes people sick. With Fromm, however, he is quick to point out that the healthy person is not simply the well-adjusted person. The healthy person is not one who merely adjusts to environmental influences, but one who is self-fulfilling and who "fully expresses his intrinsic human nature."[12]

Fromm, Allport, and Maslow can all be seen as participants in the humanistic/existentialist reaction against all systems of thought which dehumanize, which define the human person with reference to something less than what makes him uniquely human. At the beginning of his book *Toward a Psychology of Being*, Maslow enunciates what he believes to be the basic assumptions of humanistic psychology which are part of that reaction. Some of the assumptions are as follows:[13]

1. Each person has an essential, biologically based inner nature which is intrinsic and unchanging.
2. In its most essential features this intrinsic nature is "species wide." We are not simply created by environmental and cultural forces.
3. Our essential human nature can be studied scientifically.
4. Our inner human nature is not intrinsically evil. Evil behavior stems from the frustration of intrinsic human needs.
5. Since human nature is intrinsically good or neutral, it should be expressed rather than repressed.
6. Suppression of one's intrinsic human nature leads to sickness.
7. Our intrinsic human nature can be overpowered by habit, cultural pressure, and wrong attitudes toward it.
8. Even when suppressed, our intrinsic human nature presses toward self-actualization.
9. The actualization of one's inner nature is not inconsistent with the experience of discipline, deprivation, pain, frustration, and tragedy. These experiences have to do with a sense of achievement and ego strength and, therefore, with a sense of healthy self-esteem.

These assumptions are "basic" for at least three reasons: (1) They are the basis of a psychology which studies psychological health rather than sickness. If our intrinsic nature is good, then the norm of psychological health is the full expression of that nature, and knowledge of what constitutes psychological health and maturity is gained through the study of those in whom this inner nature is most fully expressed, that is, "self-actualizing" people. (2) They are, in Maslow's view, the basis of a naturalistic value system or scientific ethics. Good is identified with the full functioning of one's intrinsic human nature; evil with its suppression. Therefore, knowledge of intrinsic human nature becomes the basis for differentiating good and evil and for prescriptions on "how to be good, happy and fruitful, how to love and how to fulfill one's highest potentialities." In other words, the basic ethical imperative is to act in accordance with what we are essentially. (3) They place humanistic psychology within a broader intellectual context by linking it with existential thought. Maslow sees humanistic psychology as sharing with existentialism a radical stress on individual identity as well as an emphasis on "experiential" knowledge. Both begin with subjective experience rather than systems, concepts, and abstract categories. Thus the self, rather than the external sources, becomes the locus of values. The nature of "peak experience," for instance, can be known only by direct experience of it or by the subjective account of the experience. Moreover, its value for the experiencer needs no external confirmation. It is self-validating.

The basic assumptions implicit in any theory usually become explicit only after the theory is fully developed. For convenience sake, we may trace the development of Maslow's theory with reference to three of his areas of research: the study of human motivation, of self-actualizing people, and of peak-experiences.

Human Motivation

Maslow's first area of research was the relationship between dominance and sexual behavior in primates. This led him to the study of the motivation behind human sexual behavior and eventually to the broader question of human motivation in general. His aim now was to scientifically describe these basic, universal motivations. In 1943 he published "A Theory of Human Motivation"[14] in which he advanced the concept of the "hierarchy of needs." This theory proposes that human needs arrange themselves in a hierarchy of "prepotency." A "prepotent" need is one that is more powerful or more fundamental. The experience of any human need, therefore, depends on the satisfaction of other more fundamental needs. In other words, as lower, more fundamental needs are satisfied, higher needs emerge or make their presence felt.

Maslow suggests the following hierarchy of needs listed according to their relative "prepotency."

1. *Hunger needs*. The basic need for food, sustenance, nourishment. One who is starving, for instance, is incapable of experiencing any need higher than his hunger in any real way.
2. *Safety needs*. The basic need for feeling a sense of physical security. This would include freedom from pain and fear and some kind of orderly environment. The psychological damage suffered by a child through a chaotic home or school environment is continued in adult life through such experiences as unemployment and/or marital discord.
3. *Love needs*. The basic need to be loved by others such as family members or friends. These are sometimes referred to as "belongingness

needs" since their satisfaction secures one a place or sense of belonging in one's family or group. One is reminded of Fromm's term "rooted-ness."

4. *Esteem needs.* The basic need for a sense of self-esteem and self-worth, which in turn is dependent on the esteem one receives from others.

5. *The need for self-actualization.* This refers to the need to become every-thing that one is capable of becoming. It is the drive to develop fully, to fulfill the capacities and potentialities of our intrinsic human nature.

The need for self-actualization emerges when one's basic needs (food, safety, love, and esteem) are gratified in some adequate way. Hence the drive toward self-actualization takes one beyond the realm of basic needs and into the realm of higher or "metaneeds." This refers to the pursuit of those values associated with self-actualization—beauty, goodness, truth, and so on—which are sought not because they fulfill a personal need or deficiency but for their own intrinsic worth. Maslow, therefore, refers to them as "being values" or "B-values." One's degree of self-actualization is seen as the measure of psycho-logical health and maturity. Consequently, the higher needs or values associated with self-actualization are regarded by Maslow as equally "in-stinctoid" or fundamental as the lower needs. They are intrinsic to human na-ture and essential to psychological health, not simply sublimations (as Freud would have it) of one's lower needs. If, therefore, self-actualization is the hall-mark of maturity, and if the self-actualized person is one who is no longer motivated by basic needs (which have been met) but rather by metaneeds, we may conclude that the mature individual is distinguished by a certain type of motivation. B-values such as beauty, truth, justice, and creativity are not pursued to satisfy some basic need or deficiency but as needful to one's fur-ther growth. Thus Maslow refers to the self-actualizing person as motivated by metamotivation or "growth motivation." This is contrasted with "defi-ciency motivation," that is, the desire to satisfy basic needs.

Self-Actualization

Humanistic psychology focuses on the study of psychological health rather than sickness. In 1950 Maslow published a paper entitled "Self-Actualizing People: A Study of Psychological Health."[15] The premise of this study is that if one wishes to study psychological health, one should study the most psy-chologically healthy human beings, those who are most fully human and have most fully actualized the potentialities of their intrinsic human nature. Find-ing a suitable number of subjects who fitted this description was a problem for Maslow who, therefore, based his findings on public and historical fig-ures as well as personal acquaintances such as Max Wertheimer and Ruth Benedict. In presenting his findings he emphasized two points: (1) These sub-jects were healthy in the deep sense of self-fulfilling and fully functioning, not in the shallow sense of "well-adjusted." (2) The picture of the self-actual-ized person which emerges from his study is not a set of manufactured norms but a study of real people, but healthy as opposed to sick people.

According to Maslow's findings, growth toward self-actualization is marked by the following clinically observed characteristics.[16]

1. Superior perception of reality (seeing reality as it is, not as related to one's subjective needs).
2. Increased acceptance of self, others, and nature.
3. Increased spontaneity.
4. Increase in problem-centering as opposed to being ego-centered and self-absorbed.
5. Increased detachment and desire for privacy (because of decreased de-pendency on the world for need gratification).
6. Increased autonomy and resistance to enculturation (follows from 5).
7. Greater freshness of appreciation and richness of emotional reaction (less apt to fall into boredom, routine, or become jaded).
8. Higher frequency of peak-experiences.
9. Increased identification with human species—both its good and its evil aspects—rather then with a particular segment of it (a particular race, so-cial class, etc.).
10. Improved interpersonal relations.
11. More democratic character structure (see 9).
12. Increased creativeness.
13. Certain changes in the value system.

Given the definition of a self-actualized person as one whose basic needs are met and who is therefore motivated by metaneeds and pursues B-values, the question arises: How does such growth beyond the satisfaction of basic needs take place? Maslow answers:

> The answer I find satisfactory is a simple one, namely, that growth takes place when the next step forward is subjectively more delightful, more joyous, more intrinsically satisfying than the previous gratification with which we have become familiar and even bored; that the only way we can ever know what is right for us is that it feels better subjectively than any alternative. The new experience validates itself rather than by any outside criterion. It is self-justifying, self-validating.[17]

This answer carries with it two important implication: (1) Growth in self-actualization is a process of self-discovery. With each step forward we learn what we like, what our abilities are, what we are good at. In this way, self-actualization is closely linked to a sense of personal identity. (2) Each step forward is a freely made choice and growth is a series of such choices. This implies that there is always an alternative choice, which is the choice not to move forward but to remain with what is safe and familiar because of the element of risk in what is new. For example, the choice between accepting promotion to a more challenging job or remaining with something one knows is well within one's capabilities. Maslow again echoes Erich Fromm in describing forward growth as a never-ending series of free choices between safety and growth, dependence and independence, regression and progression, immaturity and maturity. Forward growth takes place "when the delights of growth and anxieties of safety are greater than the anxieties of growth and the delights of safety."[18]

The presence of this regressive tendency reminds us that self-actualization is not an ideal, problem-free state. "We must realize," Maslow insists, "not only that [people] try to realize themselves, but that they are also reluctant or afraid or unable to do so."[19] This "dialectic between sickness and health" means that freedom from the "basic needs" does not ensure a life lived "happily ever after." Accordingly, Maslow defines self-actualization as "a development of personality which frees the person from the deficiency problems of youth, and from neurotic (or infantile, or fantasy, or unnecessary, or `unreal') problems of life, so that he is able to face, endure and grapple with the 'real' problems of life."[20] The "real" problems are the human, existential problems to which there are no perfect solutions.

Peak-Experiences

Among Maslow's findings on self-actualized people was the fact that they reported a higher frequency of "peak-experiences." This was Maslow's term for transient experiences of bliss, ecstasy, or joy which tend to evoke emotions of awe, reverence, and wonder and have a transforming effect on the subject of the experience. As we shall see, it is also an umbrella term which includes religious or mystical experiences. Maslow's findings on peak- experiences are based on interviews with about 80 individuals as well as written responses by 190 college students who were asked to describe ecstatic moments in their lives. On the basis of these surveys Maslow concluded that the most defining feature of peak-experience was a transformed way of viewing and knowing reality—the world and the people in it—which he called the "cognition of being" or "B-cognition." The distinction between this and ordinary cognition parallels the distinction between growth and deficiency motivation. B-cognition is the experience of the total being of a person or object or seeing the object as it is in itself. "D-cognition," on the other hand, is organized by the deficiency needs of the subject; the object is perceived in terms of its usefulness to the perceiver. B-cognition, as a feature of peak-experience, will be discussed further in the context of Maslow's theory of religion.

B-cognition also turns the peak-experience into an experience of personal identity. Maslow contends that as one perceives the essential Being of the world, one also becomes closer to one's own being, to one's own perfection, to being more perfectly oneself, and to actualizing one's own "B-values" such as integration, individuality, spontaneity, expressiveness, effortlessness, courage, power, creativity, and the like. In the peak-experience one feels less divided and more unified, more at peace with oneself; more able to fuse with the world and to function in a more effortless and spontaneous way; more at the peak of one's powers and able to use one's capacities more fully; less determined and restricted by fears and inhibitions and more free of the past and future and fully attentive to the present moment. In the language of religion one feels "blessed" or "graced."

Theory of Religion

With Maslow the humanistic approach to the study of religion takes a new turn. Allport's intrinsic/extrinsic distinction represented a criterion for evaluating the psychological value of religious experience. Erich Fromm rejected the notion of religious experience as a separate category of experience and spoke rather of the "X-experience," an ego-transcending kind of experience which could be interpreted religiously or psychologically, theistically or nontheistically. Though the peak-experience is similar to the X-experience, for Maslow it is a purely natural phenomenon which can be explained psychologically, that is, in a purely scientific or naturalistic way. No theological or religious interpretation is necessary. Religious experiences, therefore, are really peak-experiences and religious values are really "B-values." This is the basic premise of Maslow's book, *Religions, Values and Peak-Experiences.* "They are well within the realm of nature," he asserts, "and can be investigated and discussed in an entirely naturalistic way."[21] This line of reasoning challenges the traditional distinction between science and religion.

Science and Religion

The thesis that "religious experiences are natural experiences" and Maslow's single-minded insistence on science as the means of understanding "religious" experience and discovering "religious" values would seem to render religion in the traditional sense irrelevant. He insists, however, that his work is not a rejection of religion but an empirical, scientific validation of the teachings of the great religious mystics. Maslow wants to demonstrate that religious values are in fact human values; that the values the saints lived by are the values of self-actualizing people. Therefore, he concludes, the "more perceptively religious man" should welcome this attempt to put religion on a scientific basis which is aimed at relieving him of the necessity of relying only on "tradition, blind faith, temporal power, exhortation, etc." While it secularizes religion, at the same time it religionizes all that is secular.[22] Maslow argues that this approach to the study of religion is "in a direct line" with that of William James. The reader, however, will recall that James' concept of the "more" of reality allows for the possibility of a more ultimate source and explanation of religious experience which is beyond the capabilities of empirical science.

Maslow states his purpose as follows:

> "I want to demonstrate that spiritual values have naturalistic meaning, that they are not the exclusive possession of organized churches, that they do not need supernatural concepts to validate them, that they are well within the jurisdiction of a suitably enlarged science, and that, therefore, they are the general responsibility of all mankind."[23]

Religious experience and values, therefore, fall within the realm of science, but only if science is "suitably enlarged." Here Maslow rejects the traditional distinction between science and religion which proposed that science dealt with facts, with the actual not the ideal, that it was descriptive rather than normative; that it abstracted from all questions of values, ethics, or spirituality. Religion, on the other hand, dealt with the values, ends, goals, and purposes of life. This working distinction is seen to produce a "dichotomized science" and a "dichotomized religion." In divorcing itself from questions of meaning, purpose, and morality, science becomes "valueless," having nothing to say about ends or ultimate values. Science is thus doomed to be "nothing more than technology," which can be used for any purpose, good or evil. Religion, on the other hand, in cutting itself off from scientific insight and relying solely on revelation and tradition, tends to become rigid, unchanging orthodoxy. This dichotomizing of science and religion, of facts and values, of the actual and the ideal produces, in Maslow's view, "cripple-science and cripple-religion, cripple-facts and cripple-values."[24]

Maslow calls for a "humanistic" science, that is, a science broadened and redefined so as to include questions which were originally the exclusive domain of religion. Humanistic psychology is here regarded as the forerunner in developing a whole new way of looking at science which makes it possible "to accept the basic religious questions as a proper part of the jurisdiction of science, once science is broadened and redefined."[25] A science thus redefined would be a science "with larger powers and methods, a science which is able to study values and to teach mankind about them." This would include "practically everything in religion that can bear naturalistic observation."[26] The religious believer might well object that the essential core of his religion—the transforming power which is the object of his faith—is beyond the "naturalistic observation" of even an expanded science. This, however, merely points out the limitations of science and does not invalidate the attempt to demonstrate that the pursuit of religious values coincides with our intrinsic nature's pursuit of self-actualization. In the end science can study only the observable phenomena of religion—in this case religious experience and religious values—but must abstract from the question of the possible transcendent source of that experience or of those values.

Religious Experience

Maslow seems to observe this methodological limitation without explicitly acknowledging it. Thus when he comes to speak of the "intrinsic core, the essence, the universal nucleus of every known high religion," he identifies that essential nucleus as "the private, lonely, personal illumination, revelation or ecstasy of some acutely sensitive prophet or seer."[27] This private illumination is then identified as a "peak-experience." The essential core and starting point of religion is thus a mystical or peak-experience. Again the religious believer might argue that the essential core of his or her religion is not someone's experience of a revelation but the revelation itself and its transcendent source. Maslow, however, dismisses the possibility of a "supernatural revelation" as an historically and culturally conditioned way of describing the experience. He asserts that "it is very likely, indeed almost certain, that these older reports, phrased in terms of supernatural revelation, were, in fact, perfectly natural, human peak-experiences of the kind that can be easily examined today, which, however, were phrased in terms of whatever conceptual, cultural, and linguistic framework the particular seer had available in his time." Therefore, he concludes, "we can study today what happened in the past and was then explainable in supernatural terms only," and we can do so "in a way that makes [religion] a part of science rather than something outside and exclusive of it."[28]

In his enthusiasm Maslow may well be confusing religion with religious experience and thereby exceeding the methodological limits of the psychology of religion. One is reminded of the way in which Fromm applies the categories "authoritarian" and "humanistic" not just to religious experience but to religion as such. If, however, this distinction is kept in mind, we may profit from Maslow's description of the core religious *experience* as having the characteristics of naturalistically observable peak-experience. This enables us, as Maslow suggests, to identify what is common to all mystical, transcendent, ecstatic experiences, regardless of the varying religious vocabularies in which they might be expressed. It also allows us to bring Maslow's statement about the essential role of religious or peak-experience in the development of religion in line with William James' contention that experience is prior to—in the sense of more fundamental than—intellectual belief. We have seen that, in Maslow's view, the transforming effect of the core religious experience or peak-experience is a radically different way of viewing and knowing reality—what Maslow called "B-cognition." Maslow lists the following characteristics of B-cognition and therefore of peak-experiences:[29]

First, the object is seen as a whole and complete unit detached from any possible usefulness or purpose. This characteristic relates the peak-experience to the traditional meaning of the term "contemplation." Maslow's meaning is reflected in the experience of being "lost" in the contemplation of a work of art, a piece of music, or the beauty of nature. This complete absorption means that the object is perceived as independent or irrelevant to human concern and free of human projections. It is not used, feared, or reacted to but perceived for what it is in itself. For this reason, B-cognition is said to be ego-transcending or "unmotivated" in the sense that no ego needs or concerns are projected on to the object.

Second, B-cognition renders the peak experience self-validating or self-justifying. It has an intrinsic value with no purpose beyond the experience itself. It serves no obvious utilitarian purpose to "take time to smell the flowers," yet very few people would dispute the wisdom of doing so.

Third, B-cognition frequently involves a disorientation in time and space. We forget where we are and how much time has elapsed. We may be so absorbed in an activity that we "forget to eat," but only if we are absorbed in the activity for its own sake apart from any purpose it may serve. In such cases we are "caught up" in the activity itself or the object of the activity. This total absorption and fascination signifies a giving up of control or manipulation of the object (or other person). Hence Maslow describes B-cognition as more passive and receptive than active. The great religious mystics would agree.

Fourth, B-cognition evokes emotional reactions of wonder, awe, reverence, humility, surrender as to something great. What is ordinarily called "religious experience" is essentially a "unitive" experience; it is the experience of one's isolated individuality as part of some greater reality. Maslow includes, as a feature of the peak-experience, this experience of something transcendent or of what religion would call the sacred.

Fifth, B-cognition implies the perception of an object in its essential reality. When perceived in this way reality appears not as evil but as essentially good or neutral. Evil is a partial phenomenon, a product of limited vision. This is because the polarities and conflicts such as good and evil which characterize D-cognition are somehow transcended or resolved in B-cognition. Maslow refers to this kind of perception as "God-like" in the sense of a complete, loving, uncondemning, compassionate, and perhaps amused acceptance of the world or of another person.

A simple example of this last point would be the fact that a human being is capable of loving and accepting another person even though the other is necessarily imperfect. It is not a case of loving the perfections and tolerating the imperfections but of somehow seeing the perfect and imperfect as belonging together, as being necessary aspects of the totality of the other person. This is what Maslow calls "B-love," that is, love for the Being of the other person or object in all its aspects. Such love, he asserts, is rooted in "a particular kind of cognition for which my knowledge of psychology had not prepared me, but which I have since seen well described by certain writers on esthetics, religion and philosophy. This I shall call cognition of Being, or for short, B-cognition."[30] Such love, rooted in the "unmotivated" cognition of the total and essential being of the other, challenges the popular notion that "love is blind" since B-cognition is more preceptive than ordinary cognition. Consequently "the B-lover is able to perceive realities in the beloved to which other are blind, i.e., he can be more acutely and penetratingly perceptive."[31]

Having stated his version of the primacy of experience and identified the essence of religion with the core or peak-experience, Maslow then differentiates between two types of religious personalities: the person whose religion is personally apprehended through peak-experience (the "peaker") and the person—the "non-peaker"—whose religion is rooted in loyalty to the church or organization whose purpose is to communicate the prophet/founder's original revelatory experience to the masses. Maslow illustrates this distinction with reference to the extreme versions of two religious types: the prophet and the priest. The prophet here represents one "who has discovered his truth about the world, the cosmos, ethics, God, and his own identity from within, from his own personal experiences, from what he would consider to be revelation."[32] The priest, on the other hand, is one "who is loyal to the structure of the organization which has been built up on the basis of the prophet's original revelation in order to make the revelation available to the masses."[33] Churches and religious organizations try to communicate the original peak-experience of the prophet/seer to the masses through doctrine, ritual, and ceremonies. In Maslow's view, when this task becomes a case of nonpeakers communicating to other nonpeakers, the doctrines and rituals tend to become "functionally autonomous," that is, ends in themselves—objects of faith—rather than means of communicating religious experience. These then become the "sacred things and sacred activities" in place of the original revelation. The result is that "the essential, original meaning gets so lost in concretizations that these finally become hostile to the original mystical experiences, to mystics, and to prophets in general, that is, to the very people that we might call from our present point of view the truly religious people."[34]

Maslow concludes that the peak-experience may be the model for those incidents of religious experience and illumination which lie at the heart of most religions. It also becomes the hallmark of authentic religion, that is, religion rooted in one's personal experiences. The hazard of organized religion, from this point of view, is that is tends to "dichotomize" life. The reason for this, in Maslow's view, is that religion, in the conventional sense, "religionizes" or makes sacred one part of life while "de-religionizing" or secularizing the rest of life. Religious experiences (the holy, the sacred, awe, reverence, surrender, mystery, piety, gratitude, etc.) are confined to religious activities, to certain times and places and certain prescribed rituals. The hazard is that this creates an attitude in some believers which renders them less open to the possibility of religious experience at any other time or any other place or in any other dimension of their lives. Maslow concludes: "Religionizing only one part of life secularizes the rest of it."[35] For this reason Maslow suggests that "non-theistic religious people," that is, those who are not conventionally religious (nonchurchgoers), may be more open to religious experience in any part of their lives and in any circumstances.

Religious Values

Maslow takes the position that values result from an inner valuing process, that is, they come from within as the result of healthy human growth. Self-actualizing people, he argues, reveal that the highest spiritual values are natural in origin; they evolve as personality grows. Supernatural sanctions for these values are therefore unnecessary; we have no need to learn values and spirituality from a divine source or a church or a religious authority. The values of which Maslow is speaking are the so-called "B-values" such as wholeness, justice, simplicity, beauty, goodness, truth, honesty, aliveness, and so on. These are seen as the innate potentialities of our "higher nature," that intrinsic human nature which seeks to actualize itself. This raises the question: Why was it necessary in the first place to learn spiritual values from a divine or religious source if those values are natural in origin? Maslow's answer suggests that the awareness of our innate human goodness was repressed by doctrines, both religious and secular, which stressed the "innate depravity of man" and the "maligning of his animal nature." Thus, if goodness and virtue are not seen as innate human potentialities, then "they must be explained from outside of human nature."[36] One who is "totally depraved" must obviously be taught how to live virtuously or even coerced into doing so.

In this context Maslow is speaking of the same hazard which Erich Fromm finds in "authoritarian" religion. According to this view, when one projects all his own innate human goodness onto God, he is then left empty and powerless and stands in even greater need of God's goodness and power. Maslow concludes: "The worse man is, the poorer a thing he is conceived to be, the more necessary becomes a god."[37] Belief in "supernatural sanctions," however, is seen to be giving way to faith in the higher possibilities of human nature. The principle involved is that what can be explained naturally, such as spiritual values, does not require a supernatural explanation. For those, however, who cannot separate spiritual values from divine sanctions—among whom Maslow includes the "less sophisticated" and the "more orthodoxly religious"—this represents a risk. "If the only sanction for 'spiritual' values is supernatural," he proposes, "then undermining this sanction undermines *all* higher values."[38]

Having stated this basic premise—that spiritual values do not need supernatural sanction since they are natural in origin—Maslow goes on to broaden the scope of his discussion. If the values by which we are to live are not learned from a supernatural source, how are we to learn them? How are we to construct a value system to guide human existence? Maslow's answer is that, if spiritual values are intrinsic to human nature, then knowledge of them is the result of studying humanity at its best, that is, by studying self-actualizing people. Here Maslow points to the crisis experienced by many as a result of the decline of religion and the resulting weakening of supernaturally or religiously grounded systems of ethics. Without the support of religious faith, many put their faith in science. But, since science was conceived of in a positivistic, valueless way, it was not able to provide an adequate source of ethics or values. A spiritual vacuum was thus created in which the prevailing valuelessness gives rise to a variety of existential anxieties among the symptoms of which Maslow lists "rootlessness, value pathology, meaninglessness, existential boredom, spiritual starvation, other-directedness, the neuroses of success, etc."[39]

Maslow's answer to this crisis is an expanded, humanistic science which would include the study of values and provide the basis of a naturalistic value system. Faith in such a value system would then be a naturalistic kind of faith, or what Erich Fromm calls "humanistic faith." In 1959 Maslow edited a collection of essays under the title *New Knowledge in Human Values*. In the preface to this work he makes his profession of (humanistic) faith in three statements:[40] (1) The ultimate disease of our time is valuelessness. (2) The cure for this disease is "a validated, usable system of human values," values to which humanity can dedicate itself "because they are true rather than because we are exhorted to "believe and have faith." (3) Such a value system, based on valid knowledge of human nature, is possible today. Again, at a 1961 symposium on human values Maslow makes the following comment on the four papers presented.[41]

> There is no appeal in any of these papers to an extrahuman source or locus of values. No supernatural is involved, no sacred book, no hallowed tradition. All the speakers agree that the values which are to guide human action must be found within the nature of human and natural reality itself.[42]

In the articulation of his theory of values Maslow exhibits, in his mature years, the same kind of idealism that characterized his youthful work. Science was to create a better world. Now, however, it is no longer the positivistic, behavioristic science of his youthful enthusiasm but a broadened humanistic science engendering a new humanistic faith which replaces both the religious and scientific/rationalistic faith of the past.

The premise of this scientific approach to values is that the free choices of self-actualizing people can be descriptively studied as a naturalistic value system. In such an enterprise the expectations or hopes of the observer are irrelevant. The question is "What are the values of the best human beings?" not "What should their values be?" But what is a good human being (GHB)? Maslow answers that a good human being is good to the extent that he or she fulfills or satisfies the concept of human being and to the extent that all his or her capacities are well developed and fully functioning.[43] On the further premise that our deepest needs and therefore our *free* choices are not, in themselves, dangerous or evil or bad, Maslow concludes that the main function of a healthy culture is the fostering of universal self-actualization. "The role of the environment," he argues, "is ultimately to permit or help [the individual] to actualize *his own* potentialities not *its* potentialities."[44] As a specific application of this principle Maslow defines the goal of education as follows: "to aid the person to grow to fullest humanness, to the greatest fulfillment and actualization of his highest potentials, to his greatest possible stature ... to become actually what he deeply is potentially."[45] This principle becomes in turn the criterion for discriminating between good and bad education. It also implies the following corollaries: (1) Education is for everyone, the feeble-minded as well as the intelligent; (2) it is a lifelong process; (3) it applies to all human capacities, not just to cognitive ones; (4) it is not confined to the classroom; (5) since everyone's capacities are unique, there can be no rigidly set curriculum.

For Maslow, it seems clear that the task of formulating a naturalistic value system falls to the kind of humanistic psychology which he represents. With the decline of orthodox religion, the direction of human life was left either to orthodox, positivistic, value-free science or to religious liberals and secular, nontheistic humanists. These latter groups, however, tried to build a value system for the most part on the foundation of orthodox science or an impersonal rationalism, on the natural sciences rather than the psychological sciences. In doing so, however, they restricted themselves to the cognitive and impersonal dimensions of human nature to the neglect of emotional, impulsive, and volitional. Such an excessively rational approach leaves people without what Fromm would call an "object of devotion" or, as Maslow puts it, something "to admire, to sacrifice themselves for, to surrender to, to die for."[46] Consequently, they fail to make room for those types of experiences which organized religions tried to make possible: reverence, devotion, humility, awe, and what Maslow refers to as the "Dionysiac experiences, wildness, rejoicing, impulsiveness."[47] Any religion, Maslow argues, including therefore any nontheistic system that takes the place of orthodox religion, must be not only intellectually credible but also emotionally satisfying. Since liberals and nontheists have failed in this latter respect, they have failed to adequately fill the gap left by the decline of orthodox religion. Maslow believes that a larger, more inclusive science, can fill this gap. Such a science would include "the data of transcendence," that is, of transcendent, ecstatic peak-experiences. Humanistic psychology represents Maslow's attempt to create such a science.

Evaluation

Any evaluation of Maslow's work rests on the premise that he was the leading figure in the development of humanistic psychology. It follows, therefore, that one's estimate of Maslow's contribution to the psychology of religion will reflect one's estimate of humanistic psychology and its basic premises. In this regard, even the most critical reader would probably agree that Maslow, along with Fromm and Allport, has provided a needed corrective to the one-sidedness of psychoanalytic and behaviorist theories. Humanistic psychology attempts to give due recognition to the "higher reaches" of human nature, that is, the human potential for self-actualization, self-transcendence, creativity, spirituality, and religious or "peak" experiences. Maslow's particular concern was to demonstrate that these potentialities were just as "instinctoid," just as fundamental to human nature as sex and dominance; they were not to be seen as merely sublimations of instinctual drives. Maslow's immediate influence, particularly among industrial leaders who consulted him with a view to developing self-actualization and creativity among their employees, was considerable.

As for the question of Maslow's wider and more lasting influence, the picture is more muddled. Progressive, permissive, and student-centered trends in education, the primacy of individual rights in social life, and the emphasis on the subjectivity of values: All these trends—rightly or wrongly linked to Maslow's influence in the 1960s—are being rethought amid the educational, social, and moral chaos of the early twenty-first century. It is not always easy, however, to establish a direct link between Maslow's ideas and certain social trends. The waters are muddied by the fact that many who did not thoroughly understand his ideas nevertheless claimed him as their inspiration. We have already alluded to his frustration with the leaders of the 1960s counterculture who saw in him the "father of the revolution." Maslow in fact had little affinity for their emphasis on feeling and experience to the exclusion of hard work, discipline, and rigorous professional training. We have also seen that Maslow—a believer in classical forms of education—was thoroughly disenchanted with students who wanted to set their own curriculum. As we have already noted, Maslow should not be identified in any simplistic way with the 1960s counterculture or with the "pop psychology" versions of his ideas and the "self-help" literature it produced. While this literature is obsessed with the notions of self-actualization and inner transformations, it lacks, for the most part, Maslow's sensitivity to the dark, regressive side of human nature and the self-actualizer's transcending of ego concerns and freedom from self-absorption. There is surely a world of difference between Maslow's idea that we grow when the choice for growth is more "intrinsically satisfying" than the choice for safety and the 1960s slogan "If it feels good, do it!"

At a more fundamental level, however, some of the basic premises of Maslow's humanistic psychology of religion raise questions for both the psychologist and the theologian. As we shall see, Viktor Frankl offers a different perspective on the meaning of self-transcendence and the source of values. Frankl rejects Maslow's emphasis on self-transcendence as resulting from an inner process of growth which expresses the inner potentialities of the organism. He insists rather on the necessity of an "intentional referent" for self-transcendence. Self-transcendence is seen as a relationship to what transcends the individual, a person, a task, a cause, a God, and so forth. Only through commitment to such a relationship does one become self-forgetful. In the same vein, he proposes that values are not the result of an inner valuing process, that they do not come from within the person as a result of healthy human growth. Values and meaning, he suggests, have an objective existence in the form of someone to be loved, a task to be accomplished, and the like. Values are not matters of self-expression but of self-transcendence; not invented but encountered; not products of self-actualization but of self-transcendence.

For the theologian the problem is one of reconciling Maslow's basic premise of the natural goodness of human nature with the religious idea of sin and the necessity of redemption, a fundamental premise of any religion that can be called "redemptive." For Maslow self-actualization represents the full expression of the inner potentialities of human nature. For redemptive religions, self-actualization requires a transforming religious experience of redemption. Maslow appears to confuse the issue somewhat when he refers to religious doctrines of the "innate depravity of man" and the "maligning of his animal nature" as blinding us to the goodness within ourselves. In fact, the issue is more complex than a choice between black and white conceptions of human nature. Nor can the religious view be identified, in a simplistically general way, with notions of the "total depravity" of human nature. Maslow approaches a more nuanced view of human nature when he speaks of its regressive tendencies which limit and impede the process of self-actualization.

Perhaps the most serious question that might be raised about Maslow's psychology of religion is the question of reductionism. If religious experiences are natural experiences which can be studied and explained "in an entirely naturalistic way," then there is no room for a religious or theological explanation. Maslow seems to reject entirely the possibility that transcendent or peak-experiences might indeed have a transcendent source. Moreover, he claims that this approach (the reduction of religion to a purely natural phenomenon) is "in a direct line with William James." The reader will recall however that James' approach is much more nuanced. For James, religious experience is an experience of the "more" of reality, of that which transcends our conscious life and experience. As such, it may be interpreted in terms of the "hither side" (the "subliminal self") or in terms of the "farther side" (the holy, the numinous, or the divine) of the more. James' understanding of religious experience definitely included "whatever the more might be on its farther side." Again, Maslow is at pains to align his humanistic understanding of religion with theologian Paul Tillich's definition of religion as "ultimate concern." In using this term, however, Tillich wants to describe religion as concern for what is ultimate, absolute, and infinite. This of course refers to what is transcendent, understood not as a divine, supreme being but in the more ultimate category of "Being itself." There is a difference between deepening one's understanding of transcendence and simply eliminating it.

It would not be unreasonable to suggest that this reductionist tendency finds its source as much in Maslow's early life experience as in his research. We have seen that his mother's harsh, cruel, and seemingly religiously motivated discipline drove him to an early rejection of all religion and to a rather militant brand of atheism. The combination of this atheistic stance with young Maslow's growing idealism seems to have produced in him a desire to create a better world, not through religion but through science. Hence his early enthusiasm for behaviorism, which struck him as a vehicle for real change in the world. Though his antireligious stance softened with the realization that religion could be both good and bad, he clung to the belief that religion and religious experience could be explained in an "entirely naturalistic," that is, a scientific way. And though his behaviorism gave way to a more humanistic psychology, he still adopted the persona of a rigorous scientist. All of this gives rise to the following questions:

First, is Maslow's atheism the reason for his refusal to take seriously the claims of religion? Does his description of religious experience in purely naturalistic terms represent a personal need as much as the conclusion of his research? It is noteworthy that Maslow's study of self-actualization amounts to a descriptive listing of the characteristics of seemingly self-actualized people. The further question of how they achieved this level of maturity is not addressed. It seems to be assumed that it is the product of healthy growth which includes the satisfaction of basic needs. The questions of whether that healthy growth is due in part to a religious orientation does not seem to be considered relevant.

Second, this raises the further question of how "scientific" Maslow's theory of religion and of spiritual values is. It is an admirable project to use the human sciences—including psychology—to study religious experience and the development of values. However, whereas other theorists remind us that psychology can study only the human side of religion (how religion is experienced humanly), Maslow's was an expanded science that would study all those problems that were once the exclusive domain of religion—"the ends, the goals, the purposes of life." One is tempted to ask: Are there no limitations to the scope of science? Is there anything left for philosophy and theology? Is such an expanded science viable? Maslow's writings seem to be full of tentative conclusions which have to be validated by "further research." But in the end are any of these conclusions validated in any rigorously scientific way? He seems to share with Jung a desperate need to be seen as a scientist, and this straining to be "scientific" almost seems to trivialize his profound insights into the "farther reaches" of human nature. As with Jung, would not this visionary have been better advised to base his conclusions on a different, experiential kind of knowledge—the knowledge derived from humanity's peak-experiences?

Suggested Readings

HOFFMAN, EDWARD, *The Right to Be Human: A Biography of Abraham Maslow* (Los Angeles: Jeremy P. Tarcher Inc., 1988).

MASLOW, ABRAHAM, *The Farther Reaches of Human Nature* (New York: Viking Press, 1971).

MASLOW, ABRAHAM, *The Journals of Abraham Maslow*, edited by Richard J. Lowry (Lexington, Mass.: Lewis Publishing Co., 1982).

MASLOW, ABRAHAM, *Religions, Values and Peak-Experiences* (New York: Penguin Arkana, 1994).

MASLOW, ABRAHAM, *Toward a Psychology of Being* (New York: D. Van Nostrand & Co., 1968).

WILSON, COLIN, *New Pathways in Psychology: Maslow and the Post-Freudian Revolution* (New York: Taplinger Publishing Co., 1972).

Notes

1. Colin Wilson, *New Pathways in Psychology: Maslow and the Post-Freudian Revolution* (New York: Taplinger Publishing Co., 1972), p. 145.
2. International Study Project, Menlo Park, California, *Abraham H. Maslow: A Memorial Volume* (Monterey, Ca.: Brooks/Cole Publishing Co., 1972), p. 71.
3. Ibid., p. 113
4. *Ibid.*, p. 65.
5. Quoted in Edward Hoffman, *The Right to Be Human: A Biography of Abraham Maslow* (Los Angeles: Jeremy P. Tarcher Inc., 1988), p. 1. I am indebted to this work as the principal source of information on Maslow's life.
6. *Ibid.*, p. 9.
7. *Ibid.*, p. 19.
8. *Ibid.*, p. 20.
9. *Ibid.*, p. 29.
10. *Ibid.*, pp. 66-67.
11. *Ibid.*, p. 317.
12. A. Maslow, *Toward a Psychology of Being* (New York: D. Van Nostrand & Co., 1968), p. 5.
13. *Ibid.*, pp. 3-5.
14. *Psychological Review*, 50, 370-396.
15. *Personality Symposia: Symposium #1 on Values* (New York: Grune and Stratton, 1950), pp. 11-34.
16. A. Maslow, *Toward a Psychology of Being*, Ch. 3.
17. *Ibid.*, p. 45.
18. *Ibid.*, p. 47.

19. *Ibid.*, p. 166.
20. *Ibid.*, p. 115.
21. A. Maslow, *Religions, Values and Peak-Experiences* (Columbus: Ohio State University Press, 1964), p. xii.
22. *Ibid.*
23. *Ibid.*, p. 4.
24. *Ibid.*, p. 17.
25. *Ibid.*, p. 11.
26. *Ibid.*, p. 17.
27. *Ibid.*, p. 19.
28. *Ibid.*, p. 20.
29. A. Maslow, *Toward a Psychology of Being*, pp. 73-95.
30. *Ibid.*, p. 73.
31. *Ibid.*
32. A. Maslow, *Religions, Values and Peak-Experiences*, p. 21.
33. *Ibid.*
34. *Ibid.*, pp. 24-25.
35. *Ibid.*, p. 31.
36. *Ibid.*, pp. 36-37.
37. *Ibid.*, p. 37.
38. *Ibid.*
39. *Ibid.*, p. 38.
40. A. Maslow (ed.), *New Knowledge in Human Values* (Chicago: Henry Regnery Co., 1959), pp. vii-viii.
41. Presented by Charlotte Buhler, Herbert Fingarette, Wolfgang Lederer, and Alan Watts.
42. A. Maslow, *The Farther Reaches of Human Nature* (New York: Viking Press), p. 150.
43. A. Maslow, *Toward a Psychology of Being*, pp. 170-171.
44. *Ibid.*, p. 160.
45. A. Maslow, *Religions, Values and Peak-Experiences*, p. 49.
46. *Ibid.*, p. 42.
47. *Ibid.*

VII. VIKTOR FRANKL

Religion and Self-Transcendence

Viktor Frankl (1905–1997)
AP/Wide World Photos

Viktor Frankl (1905-1997) stands, along with Fromm, Allport, and Maslow, in the tradition of the humanistic/existential reaction to psychoanalysis and behaviorism. As we have seen, that reaction, while recognizing the valid contributions of these psychological theories, seeks to correct their neglect of what is perceived to be the truly human dimension of the self—its "productiveness" (Fromm), its "propriate striving" (Allport), or its "self-actualizing" tendencies (Maslow). For Frankl, what is most uniquely human about the self is its "spiritual" dimension, which manifests itself in the "will to meaning." The most basic and fundamental motivating force in human personality is not instinctual drives or learned behavior patterns but the desire to discover the meaning of one's individual existence. The frustration of that drive results in what Frankl calls "noogenic" neurosis, a frustration not of the instinctual level of the self but of the spirit (*nous*) in its pursuit of meaning. The experience of meaninglessness leads to an existential type of anxiety, which is a uniquely human type of anxiety since it is experienced not at the instinctual level but at the spiritual level of human existence.

To treat this type of noogenic neurosis, Frankl devised a new psychotherapeutic system which he called "logotherapy," incorporating the Greek word *Logos,* which he understands as "meaning." This system represents what Frankl liked to call "the third Viennese school of psychotherapy," to differentiate his own theory from those of his fellow Viennese theorists, Freud and Adler. Whereas Freudian psychoanalysis had identified the "will to pleasure" as the basic motivating force in personality and Adler's individual psychology had stressed the "will to power," Frankl points to "will to meaning" as the basic tendency of the unconscious. This emphasis on the spiritual dimension of the self leads William Blair Gould to conclude that Frankl's major achievement was "his challenge to Freudianism in psychotherapy, behaviorism in psychology and positivism in philosophy."[1] Frankl himself believed that to offer a corrective to what is perceived to be the incompleteness of other theories is to necessarily express a bias. Since we do not possess absolute truth, he argues, our biased relative truths have to act as correctives to one another. The bias of logotherapy is against the nihilism and cynicism which debunks, in a reductionist way, what is truly human (the spiritual) in human existence. He writes:

> My own bias, about which I am both aware and outspoken, attacks the cynicism for which nihilism is to blame, and for which cynicism is responsible. This is a vicious cycle of nihilistic indoctrination and cynical motivation. What is needed to break this cycle is for us to *unmask the unmaskers*—those advocates and practitioners of a thoroughly biased "depth psychology," which prided itself on its powers "to unmask" the dark, unconscious mysteries in persons. Freud has taught us how important the unmasking is. But the unmasking has to stop somewhere, and the place to stop is where the "unmasking psychologist" is confronted with something that *cannot be unmasked for the simple reason that it is genuine.*[2]

What is genuine in this context is "what is truly human in human beings," the spirit's will to meaning.

Before formulating his own system, Frankl spent brief periods of time under the successive influences of Freud and Adler. From the outset, however, he was keenly interested in the boundary area between psychology and philosophy and in the question of meaning and values in psychology. At age 20 he published an article on this theme in Adler's *Journal of Individual Psychology.* His youthful insight into the motivating power of the "will to meaning" was confirmed in his more mature thought by his experience as a prisoner in a Nazi concentration camp during World War II. Here he observed in himself and in others that "those who were oriented toward the future, toward a meaning that waited to be fulfilled—these persons were more likely to survive."[3] These were the prisoners who were able, by the attitude they assumed toward their desperate situation, to turn "an apparently meaningless suffering into a genuine human achievement." Frankl concludes: "I am convinced that, in the final analysis, there is no situation that does not contain within it the seed of a meaning. To a great extent, this conviction is the basis of logotherapy."[4]

Life

Viktor Frankl was born March 26, 1905, in Vienna. His father, Gabriel Frankl, was a civil servant in the Austrian Ministry of Social Services. Frankl describes his father's temperament as "Spartan" with "a strong sense of duty." His mother Elsa, on the other hand, is described as "kindhearted and deeply pious." While Elsa was descended from "an old, established Prague patrician family," Gabriel was "the penniless son of a master bookbinder" who had to drop out of medical school for financial reasons. Viktor seems to have had a deep emotional attachment to both parents and describes his own personality as a tension between the rationality of his father and emotionality of his mother. He also had a deep attachment to the parental home, wanting to stay there as often as possible, even in his adult years. Gabriel was the first of the family to be imprisoned by the Nazis and died at the Theresienstadt concentration camp before the rest of the family were imprisoned. One week after Frankl and his first wife Tilly had been deported to the Auschwitz death camp, Elsa herself was deported to Auschwitz and sent directly to the gas chamber. Frankl's older brother Walter died in a mine attached to the Auschwitz camp. Thus, with the exception of his sister Stella, who had emigrated to Australia, Frankl lost his entire family to the death camps.

As a high school student Frankl developed a precocious interest in psychoanalysis and carried on a correspondence with Sigmund Freud. In one of his letters to Freud he enclosed a paper he had written on "the origin of the mimic movements of affirmation and negation." Freud had the paper published in the *International Journal of Psychoanalysis* in 1924. Later, as a university student, he had a chance meeting with Freud. When Frankl introduced himself, Freud not only recognized his name but remembered his exact address! His fascination with Freudian psychoanalysis, however, was not long lasting. While still at university he came under the influence of Alfred Adler and his school, becoming an active member of the Society for Individual Psychology. Under the influence, however, of Rudolf Allers and Oswald Schwarz, Frankl began to deviate from strict Adlerian ideas. In 1927 his relationship with Adler deteriorated to the point that he was formally expelled from the society. At this time Frankl was a medical student and went on to become a neurologist and psychiatrist. A casual remark by a fellow medical student to the effect that he was "gifted for psychiatry" seems to have brought Frankl to the realization that becoming a psychiatrist was somehow linked to his own sense of identity and self-actualization.

During the 1920s Frankl was involved in the Academic Society for Medical Psychology in Vienna. It was in the study group of this Society that he first spoke of "logotherapy." By 1933 he had systematized his ideas and was also using the term "existential analysis." Frankl himself, however, points out that even as early as his teenage years he had developed two of the basic concepts of logotherapy: (1) that meaning is encountered rather than invented; (2) that ultimate meaning exists in the form of "suprameaning," which cannot be comprehended but only believed in. In Frankl's own view, the motivation behind the development of logotherapy was compassion for the victims of the "depersonalizing and dehumanizing" tendencies of psychotherapy.

After his expulsion from the Adlerian society Frankl organized youth counseling centers in Vienna and six other cities. Upon graduation from medical school he worked first under Otto Potzl at the University Psychiatric Clinic and then for four years in the Am Steinhof mental hospital. In 1937 he opened a private practice in neurology and psychiatry. Only a few months later, in March 1938, Hitler's troops invaded Austria. Frankl accepted a position as chief of neurology at Rothschild Hospital, which he believed would afford him and his parents some measure of protection from deportation to the concentration camps. Many of his patients here were Jews who had attempted suicide in the wake of the Nazi takeover. Meanwhile Frankl had applied to emigrate to the United States. In 1941 his quota number came up and he was asked to pick up his visa at the American Consulate. At the last moment, however, he hesitated, concerned about abandoning his parents who would surely be deported to the concentration camps. Unsure of what to do, he went for a walk looking for "some hint from heaven" as a way out of his dilemma. Returning to his parents' home he discovered that his father had retrieved a small piece of marble from the synagogue which had been destroyed. On the marble was inscribed part of the fourth commandment, "Honor thy father and thy mother." This was Frankl's "hint from heaven" and he remained in Vienna with his parents.

In that same year Frankl married Tilly Grasser, a nurse at the Rothschild Hospital. They and another couple were the last of the Viennese Jews to obtain permission to marry before the Jewish registrar's office was closed by the Nazi authorities. When Tilly became pregnant the fetus had to be sacrificed to abortion, since pregnant Jewish women were immediately deported to a concentration camp. Frankl's 1978 book *The Unheard Cry for Meaning* carries the dedication "To Harry or Marion, an unborn child." Nine months after the wedding the couple was imprisoned at the Theresienstadt concentration camp and shortly thereafter deported to Auschwitz. Before his deportation, Frankl had written a first draft of his book *The Doctor and the Soul*. The manuscript, hidden in the lining of his coat, was lost when his coat was taken from him at

Auschwitz. Now separated not only from his wife but also from his life's work, he fell back on what he would later call "the last freedom" one has and which can never be taken away, the freedom to adopt an attitude toward unavoidable suffering. In Frankl's case this meant closing the door completely on his former life and devoting himself to the reconstruction of his life's work. His resolve to reconstruct the lost manuscript became the meaning of his life in the concentration camp and, by his own admission, the reason for his survival. "For my 40th birthday," he writes, "an inmate had given me a pencil stub, and almost miraculously he had pilfered a few small SS forms. On the backs of these forms I scribbled notes that might help me reconstruct *The Doctor and the Soul.*"[5]

The third and last draft of this book was completed in Vienna after his liberation. He seems to have dictated it almost nonstop to a team of three stenographers. It was a way of burying himself in work after learning of the death of his wife in the camps. In the same way, shortly thereafter, he dictated *Man's Search for Meaning* in nine days. At this time Frankl also joined the staff of the Vienna Policlinic Hospital and remained as head of its neurology department for 25 years. In 1947 he married Eleonore (Elly) Schwindt. The translations of his books—in particular, *Man's Search for Meaning*—brought him an international following. As a result, he was for many years in great demand as a guest lecturer throughout the world. In his autobiography he notes that he had lectured at more than 200 universities outside of Europe and had made 92 lecture trips to the United States alone. At age 90 he was still receiving an average of 92 letters a day, mostly from people expressing gratitude for the impact he had made on their lives. Frankl died in 1997 at age 92. His life is best summed up in two quotations. The words of Nietzsche quoted in *Man's Search for Meaning*—"He who has a *why* to live for can bear almost any *how*"—describe the tragedy-filled first half of Frankl's life. The words of an American student to Frankl—"The meaning of your life is to help others find the meaning of theirs"—describe the internationally recognized psychotherapist, author, and lecturer he became in the second half of his life.

Theory of Personality

Sigmund Freud has often been criticized for what his critics perceive as a materialistic, mechanistic, atheistic view of the human person; for reducing the person to an instinctually driven mechanism while ignoring the higher dimensions of personality. All the other theorists we have examined in this survey have tried to correct this perceived one-sidedness of Freudian theory. All have pointed to a level of motivation beyond the instinctual and to the possibility of genuine "religious" or spiritual experience (theistic or nontheistic), which is not only compatible with but also conducive to authentic human growth and self-actualization. Among these theorists, Jung and Frankl speak most explicitly of a religious or spiritual dimension of personality. For Jung, however, human religiousness originates within the psyche—in the autonomous activity of the collective unconscious—and thus is a matter of self-expression, while for Frankl human religiousness is revealed in the freedom and responsibility of the self's response to the world and is therefore more adequately described in terms of self-transcendence. Self-transcendence is here understood in such a way as always to imply an "intentional referent"; it always refers to one's relationship to what transcends the individual, a commitment to someone or something beyond the self—a person to be loved, a task to be completed, a cause or a goal to serve, and so forth.

Because of this emphasis on self-transcendence rather than self-expression, Frankl refers to his psychological theory as "height psychology" rather than depth psychology. Coincidentally, it should be noted that Frankl's interest in height went further than psychological theory. His lifelong hobby was mountain climbing and at age 67 he took up flying lessons! Of his passion for mountain climbing he writes: "I go to the mountains as some go to the desert: to gather my strength on solitary walks.... Every important decision I have made, almost without exception, I have made in the mountains."[6]

The freedom and responsibility by which the human person achieves self-transcendence are, for Frankl, evidence of a spiritual dimension of personality. Human nature is seen as having three dimensions: the physical, the psychological, and the spiritual. The psychological dimension is what Freud called the level of instinctual drives and represents, therefore, what Frankl calls the "will to pleasure." The spiritual dimension is, by contrast, the seat of the "will to meaning." The hypothesis of a spiritual dimension has a threefold significance for Frankl's understanding of human personality: (1) It allows for the formation of the theoretical construct of the "spiritual unconscious" as a dimension of personality structure beyond Freud's instinctual unconscious. (2) The spiritual unconscious is then posited as a distinct source of humanity's "spiritual" activities. These higher activities, which go beyond direct instinctual gratification, are motivated by the human will to meaning; they are not merely sublimations of more basic instinctual needs as Freud had maintained. (3) It makes for a new attitude toward the instinctual renunciations which Freud saw simply as the price one had to pay for the benefits of civilization. In Frankl's view instinctual gratification can be renounced or postponed for the sake of a more fundamental need—the need to give meaning to one's human existence.

In Freud's view, the creative tension in human existence was between the "will to pleasure" (instinctual drives) and the gratification of those drives in either a direct or a sublimated way. If, however, human motivation at its most fundamental level is spiritual, then, for Frankl, this creative tension is experienced as the tension between the will to meaning and the fulfillment of meaning; or, as Frankl phrases it, being versus meaning. Freud's insistence that instinctual energy must be expended on objects in the world of reality is parallelled by Frankl's concept of self-transcendence. This concept suggests that the will to meaning is realized by responding to something transcending the self, that is, to an objective world of meaning and value. Meaning, therefore, is not an expression of one's own being, but rather a challenge from beyond the self to which one responds. There is a sense, therefore, in which meaning has an objective reality. It is not something I create within myself and then impose on my own life; it is encountered as an objective reality in the form of a task to be carried out, a responsibility to be assumed, a suffering to be undergone.

This understanding of meaning puts Frankl out of step with some existential thinkers who claim that human existence has no objective pattern of meaning; it has only the meaning that each individual subjectively creates for himself or herself. Frankl argues that, in neglecting the objective character of meaning, the existentialists are neglecting a basic feature of their own view of human existence: "Though they never weary of repeating *ad nauseam* that man is `being in the world,' they seem to forget that meaning is also `in the world' and thus not merely a subjective factor. It is more than a mere self-expression, or a projection of the self *into* the world."[7] At the same time, the objective character of meaning does not mean that it exists in "ready-made" form after the manner of objective rational knowledge. For this reason Frankl insists that the logotherapist cannot give a meaning to the life of a patient; he can only assist the patient to discover the concrete meaning of his or her own existence. This meaning is objective only in the sense that it is to be discovered not within the individual but in objective realm of responsibilities, opportunities, and challenges presented to and differing with each individual. "This meaning," Frankl concludes, "is to be discovered and not invented."[8]

Frankl maintains that the actualizing of meaning in this self-transcending way is the only authentically human way of achieving self-actualization. In answer to the question of whether or not one's primary motive or ultimate destiny could be described as self-actualization, he replies as follows:

> I would venture a strictly negative response to this question. It appears to me to be quite obvious that self-actualization is an effect and cannot be the object of intention. Mirrored in this fact is the fundamental anthropological truth that self-transcendence is one of the basic features of human existence.[9]

In identifying the self-transcending pursuit of meaning as the master motive in human existence, Frankl distances himself from Maslow's humanistic view, which sees the drive toward self-actualization as basic and fundamental. His critique of Maslow's position seems to be twofold. First, the effect of making self-actualization the ultimate motive of human activity is that it "devaluates the world and its objects to mere means to an end."[10] Here Frankl quotes Maslow's contention that the environment is merely a means to human self-actualization. Second, the primacy of the drive for self-actualization is rejected on the more pragmatic grounds that it does not work. Self-actualization, he argues, cannot be the direct object of intention; it can only be realized as a side effect of the self-transcending pursuit of meaning.

> By declaring that man is a responsible creature and must actualize the potential meaning of his life, I wish to stress that the true meaning of life is to be found in the world rather than within man or his own *psyche*, as though it were a closed system. By the same token, the real aim of human existence cannot be found in what is called self-actualization. Human existence is essentially self-transcendence rather than self-actualization. Self-actualization is not a possible aim at all, for the simple reason that the more a man would strive for it, the more he would miss it. For only to the extent to which a man commits himself to the fulfillment of his life's meaning, to this extent he also actualizes himself. In other words, self-actualization cannot be attained if it is made an end in itself, but only as a side-effect of self-transcendence.[11]

This principle is held to be true also of the various adjuncts of self-actualization such as happiness, health, and a good conscience. None of these can be ends in themselves or objects of direct pursuit. These can be experienced only as the side effects of the true objects of human striving which are their causes. One experiences happiness only when there is a *reason* to be happy (e.g., the successful completion of a task). In the same manner health can only be the side effect of a healthy lifestyle and a good conscience the by-product of a belief in and pursuit of moral values. To pursue such goals as ends in themselves makes for a kind of self-absorption which militates against self-transcendence and is thus self-defeating.[12]

To paraphrase Frankl, we might say that as meaning is not invented but discovered, so also such things as self-actualization and happiness are not pursued but discovered as consequence of the will to meaning. The will to meaning as the basic motivating force in human existence is one of the three basic principles or tenets of logotherapy. The first—the freedom of the will (and the responsibility it implies)—is the prerequisite for the concept of the will to meaning. These in turn presuppose the "third tenet of logotherapy," the meaning of life. Frankl summarizes as follows: "Our contention is that there is a meaning of life, a meaning, that is, for which man has been in search of all along [the will to meaning], and also that man has the freedom to embark on the fulfillment of this meaning [freedom of the will]."[13] As we have seen, the meaning of one's life is discovered through self-transcendence, that is, through commitment to an objective world of meaning and values. It can thus be thought of as the pursuit or actualization of values. Frankl distinguishes three types of values which, in the context of his theory, are seen as three ways of finding meaning. These are creative, experiential, and attitudinal values. One can find meaning in life (1) by what one gives to the world through his or her creations (creative values); (2) by what one takes from the world through encounters and experiences (experiential values); (3) by the stand one takes in the face of unavoidable suffering or adversity (attitudinal values).

Frankl further specifies the meaning of the three types of values by identifying creative values with *work* in the sense of carrying out a task for which one feels responsible; experiential values with *love* as the experience of the essence of another human being; attitudinal values with *suffering* courageously borne. Work, love, and suffering are seen then as the three basic ways of actualizing meaning in a self-transcending way, and for Frankl this is a conclusion based on phenomenological analysis rather than moral or philosophical principles.

> The logotherapist is neither a moralist nor an intellectual. His work is based on empirical, i.e., phenomenological analysis, and a phenomenological analysis of the simple man in the street's experience of the valuing process shows that one can find meaning in life by creating a work or doing a deed or by experiencing goodness, truth, and beauty, by experiencing nature and culture; or, last but not least, by encountering another unique being in the very uniqueness of this human being—in other words, by loving him. However, the noblest appreciation of meaning is reserved to those people who, deprived of the opportunity to find meaning in a deed, in a work, or in love, by the very attitude which they choose to this predicament, rise above it and grow beyond themselves. What matters is the stand they take—a stand which allows for transmuting their predicament into achievement, triumph and heroism.... This is why life never ceases to hold a meaning, for even a person who is deprived of both creative and experiential values is still challenged by a meaning to fulfill, that is, by the meaning inherent in the right, in an upright way of suffering.[14]

Suffering is given meaning, therefore, by the attitude of the sufferer. It goes without saying, however, that this refers only to necessary, unavoidable suffering. As Frankl points out, in the case of avoidable suffering (e.g., a curable cancer), logotherapy shares the aim of traditional psychotherapy to restore the patient's capacity to work and to enjoy life.

Through the actualizing of such values life transcends itself and this self-transcendence has a twofold dimension. The fulfilling of values constitutes what Frankl calls self-transcendence in "height." Since, however, work, love, and suffering have social implications, one may speak of self-transcendence through participation in community, that is, in "breadth." Frankl insists, however, that life can never be an end in itself so that its meaning cannot be found in biological life itself and its continuation through reproduction. In other words, life does not transcend itself in "length" (through reproduction) but only in height and in breadth. As Frankl maintains, "a life whose only meaning lay in its propagation would *eo ipso* be just as meaningless as the propagation."[15] Thus he argues that motherhood cannot be the sole and ultimate meaning of a woman's life for only a life that is already meaningful can give meaning to its reproduction.

The three basic principles of Frankl's theory, then, are freedom of the will, the will to meaning, and the meaning of life. This is what Frankl calls the "first triad" of logotherapy. The second triad consists of three ways in which the meaning of life is to be found—through the actualizing of creative, experiential, and attitudinal values, that is, through work, love, and suffering. A third triad consists of the three sources of human suffering toward which one must take a stand or assume an attitude. These are pain, guilt, and death; they constitute what Frankl calls "the tragic triad." While logotherapy shares with traditional psychotherapy the aim of restoring the capacity to work and enjoy life, it goes further "by having the patient regain his capacity to suffer, if need be, thereby finding meaning even in suffering."[16] Frankl's phenomenological analysis of human existence may then be illustrated schematically.

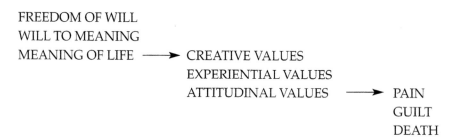

FREEDOM OF WILL
WILL TO MEANING
MEANING OF LIFE ⟶ CREATIVE VALUES
                              EXPERIENTIAL VALUES
                              ATTITUDINAL VALUES ⟶ PAIN
                                                             GUILT
                                                               DEATH

Theory of Religion

We have seen that, in general, the humanistic psychologists were primarily interested in the question of the psychological *value* of religion. With Frankl, we see a return to that which preoccupied Freud and Jung—the question of the psychological *origin* of religious phenomena. For Frankl, however, the source of the religious sentiment is not to be found in the projections of the instinctual unconscious (Freud) or of the archetypal unconscious (Jung) but in the spiritual core of human personality which he calls the spiritual unconscious. At this spiritual core or center there is a self which seeks meaning. This spiritual self is the distinct source of human, spiritual, that is, meaning-seeking activity. Religion and morality, therefore, are ultimately explained in terms of this spiritual core of personality which is essentially unconscious. Frankl maintains that while any human phenomenon—physical, psychological, or spiritual—may be conscious or unconscious, the spiritual core of human existence is ultimately unconscious. This basic proposition is reflected in his understanding of conscience as intuitive and in his concept of "unconscious religiousness." If human spirituality has an ultimately unconscious source, then human existence, at its most fundamental level, cannot reflect upon itself. The human person, in other words, cannot reflect on what he basically is; the unconscious spiritual core of existence can be known only through its activity, the free and responsible pursuit of meaning. Frankl uses the analogy of the eye, which is the source of vision but cannot observe itself. "In its origin," he concludes, "the human spirit is unconscious spirit."[17] This spiritual core is seen as the psychological source of both morality and religion.

Morality

Ethical or moral behavior is, in Frankl's perspective, a consequence of the human search for meaning, which is rooted in the spiritual unconscious. The function of conscience in directing our moral behavior is to discover the unique meaning that is to be actualized in any given situation. This existential understanding of conscience dissociates it from an understanding of morality as duty or obedience to moral rules or principles. Conscience is not seen here as the rational function of applying moral rules or values to particular situations but an "irrational" (in the sense of intuitive) function of discerning unique meanings. William Blair Gould defines Frankl's understanding of conscience as "the human intuitive capacity to find out the unique meanings in each situation."[18]

Why does Frankl consider conscience to be an irrational or intuitive function? First, because it is an aspect of the will to meaning, which is rooted in the spiritual unconscious rather than the rational dimension of personality. Its decisions, therefore, do not proceed from rational reflection but from intuition. Conscience, Frankl argues,

> reaches down into unconscious depths, stems from an unconscious ground; and it is precisely those momentous, authentic—existentially authentic—decisions that take place completely unreflectedly and thus unconsciously. Precisely where it originates, conscience delves down into the unconscious.[19]

Second, conscience is intuitive precisely because it must make such "existentially authentic" decisions. This means that it must discover the unique meaning to be actualized in each situation or what Frankl calls the unique "ought to be" which each situation calls for. Such a unique meaning cannot be rationally discovered through the application of universal moral laws which cannot comprehend unique situations; it must be intuited. This intuitive faculty represents, for Frankl, a "premoral understanding of meaning." This

means that it precedes and operates independently of the logical understanding of values and principles. Consequently it is "prelogical" or intuitive.
Conscience anticipates what ought to be in a given set of circumstances. Such
anticipation is intuitive and, in Frankl's view, cannot be explained rationally
while it is in action. It is only "after the fact" that we can indulge in rational
self-scrutiny.[20]

Conscience then is an intuitive faculty and it deals with what is unique.
In these two respects, Frankl finds it to be analogous to both love and art.
Love too is irrational or intuitive. Just as conscience intuitively anticipates an
ethical possibility, love anticipates a "personal possibility," that is, "potentialities dormant in the loved person, which he still has to make real." Like conscience, love also deals with what is unique. As conscience deals with the
unique meaning of a life situation, so love "enables the loving person to grasp
the uniqueness of the loved person." In a similar way the inspiration behind
the unique creations of the artist, like conscience, is intuitive and dependent
on unconscious sources.[21]

This view of conscience sees it as an expression of that unconscious spirituality which is the source of the "will to meaning," the desire to actualize the
meaning of one's unique human existence. As we have seen, however, it is
Frankl's view that meaning is to be sought in a self-transcending way, that is,
by one's response to an objective world of meaning and value. This leads
Frankl to speak of the "transcendent" quality of conscience. By this he means
that conscience seeks to actualize the meaning of concrete situations in a self-
transcending way. A decision of conscience is an act of responsibleness. Responsibleness, however, must have an "intentional referent." One can only
be responsible not to oneself but to something or someone beyond the self; this
is the essence of the transcendent quality of conscience.

> But just as drives and instinct cannot repress themselves, likewise the self
> cannot be responsible merely to itself. The self cannot be its own law-
> giver. It can never issue any autonomous "categorical imperative" for a
> categorical imperative can receive its credentials only from transcen-
> dence. Its categorical character stands and falls with its transcendent
> quality. It is true that man is responsible for himself, but ultimately he
> is not responsible before himself. Not only man's being free, but also his
> being responsible requires an intentional referent. Just as freedom means
> little, indeed means nothing, without a "to what", likewise responsible-
> ness is incomplete without a "to what."[22]

What, therefore, Frankl says of meaning may also be said of a decision of conscience: What I feel I ought to do, is not invented but discovered.

This transcendent quality is reflected, Frankl argues, in expressions such
as "obedience" to one's conscience or being a "servant" of one's conscience.
Such expressions ring true only when conscience is understood as tran-

scending the self, or, more accurately, when conscience is seen as mediating something other than myself. Obedience to one's conscience then becomes obedience to something which transcends the individual and his conscience. For this reason Frankl finds the expression "the voice of conscience" misleading since conscience cannot be its own voice. It is rather the voice of this transcendent "something" to which the individual feels responsible. This relationship to something transcendent, Frankl argues, must be included in our understanding of our term "person": "Through the conscience of the human person, a trans-human agent *per-sonat*—which literally means, `is sounding through.'"[23] Frankl's phenomenological analysis does not permit him to name this transcendent agent; it is seen as a necessary postulate to explain the observable phenomenon of human responsibleness. Responsibleness implies that one is responsible *to* something or someone. He does point out, however, that what distinguishes the religious person from the irreligious is a willingness "to denote transcendence by the age-old word 'God.'"[24] In other words, conscience is a universal experience of responsibleness to that which transcends the self. In this context, the religious person is someone who *names* that to which he or she feels ultimately responsible.

Religion

Frankl describes his existential analysis of human existence as developing in three stages:[25] (1) Phenomenological analysis reveals the human being as conscious and responsible and his humanity consists of a combination of these, that is, in consciousness of his responsibility. (2) Human responsibleness is found to be rooted in one's unconscious spiritual depths, that is, in the spiritual unconscious. Thus conscience—responsibleness in action—is an intuitive expression of the spiritual unconscious. (3) Since conscience is the human faculty of responding to that which transcends the self and its conscience, it has a transcendent quality. As we have seen, Frankl does not name this intentional referent of human responsibleness; he refers to it simply as "transcendence," that to which we feel responsible. The phenomenon of conscience, however, suggests that we stand in a relationship of responsibleness to this "trans-human agent"—to transcendence. This relationship is a "latent" one since it is rooted in our unconscious spirituality. Frankl calls this latent relationship to transcendence "unconscious religiousness," which he considers as "part and parcel of the spiritual unconscious." This unconscious religiousness becomes conscious for one who recognizes the intentional referent of this relationship as a transcendent God.

For many people this relationship to transcendence, which can be called religiousness, remains unconscious. In Frankl's words, such a person considers conscience the ultimate "to what" of responsibleness, without inquiring into the question of a transcendent intentional referent of responsibleness. Such a decision not to accept a religious point of view must be respected,

Frankl suggests, nor must it be perceived as necessarily having any ill effects on the individual. Frankl allows for the possibility that a patient's religiousness may be unconscious not merely in the sense of latent but because it is repressed. Freud had warned of the neurotic consequences of repressed instinctual drives. Frankl suggests that some neuroses can be the result of repressed spirituality or religiousness. In this view, religion is no longer seen as a regressive illusion with a doubtful future but a timeless reality by reason of humanity's intrinsic religiousness. Since it is rooted, however, in the spiritual unconscious, human religiousness "can remain, or again become, unconscious, or be repressed." In the latter case, the task of the logotherapist is to help the patient unlock the repression and allow unconscious religiousness to enter the conscious mind again.

> After all, it is the business of existential, analytic logotherapy to trace the neurotic mode of being to its ultimate ground. Sometimes the ground of neurotic existence is to be seen in a deficiency, in that a person's relation to transcendence is repressed. But although concealed in "the transcendent unconscious", repressed transcendence shows up and makes itself noticeable as an "unrest of the heart."... So what holds for the unconscious in general is also true of unconscious religiousness in particular: repression winds up in neurosis.[26]

In such cases, Frankl suggests, it may be possible to reverse Freud's statement about religion; it is no longer a question of religion being a symptom of compulsive neurosis derived from the Oedipus complex but rather of the compulsive neurosis being a symptom of "diseased religiousness."

The "unrest of the heart" may express itself in a sense of meaninglessness or even overdriven hostility to religion; or various forms of superstition may provide a substitute for authentic religiousness. On the Freudian premise that dreams reveal the contents of the unconscious, Frankl makes reference to several case histories to illustrate his contention that the analysis of dreams can bring to consciousness not only repressed instinctual drives but also elements of the spiritual unconscious including repressed religiousness. This may occur even in patients who, in their conscious attitudes, are quite irreligious since "there is not only repressed and unconscious *libido*, but also repressed and unconscious *religio*."[27] Frankl suggests that one reason for the repression of religiousness is the fact that sometimes people are ashamed of their religiousness and try to conceal it even from the psychotherapist. At the same time, he makes it clear that, when he uses the term "shame," he is not referring to "neurotic inhibition." It refers to a perfectly natural attitude which protects that which is intimate and personal from the public view. That which is personal such as love cannot be objectified, cannot be turned into a mere object for onlookers. Frankl suggests that "love flees publicness, for man is afraid that what is sacred to him might be profaned by becoming public."[28]

In an analogous way, the intimate and personal quality of religion is protected by a sense of shame. Frankl sees genuine religiousness as being intimate in two senses. First, it is "*intimum* in the sense of innermost"; it is a dimension of one's interior life involving self-knowledge and self-discovery. Second, like love, it is "protected by shame" and "hides from the public." Why is this so? For the same reason that love is protected by shame: because people often "do not want to deliver their intimate experiences into the hands of people who would perhaps lack understanding and thus misinterpret them."[29] This could be particularly true of the psychotherapist who may interpret their religiousness as a manifestation of unconscious conflicts or complexes.

Logotherapy, on the other hand, would interpret such religiousness as a manifestation of the spiritual unconscious and, therefore, an expression of the "will to meaning." If the most basic motivating force in human existence is the pursuit of meaning, then the distinguishing characteristic of religion is the pursuit of *ultimate* meaning usually through a relationship to a transcendent God.

Religion, therefore, is seen as giving an ultimate dimension to the human pursuit of meaning and to the ways in which meaning is actualized. If meaning is actualized through he pursuit of creative values, that is, through work or the performing of a task, then the religious person is one who not only experiences life as a task or assignment but also experiences God as "the authority from which the task comes," or the one who assigns the task. In religious language, the task is perceived as the "will of God." In Frankl's words: "In our opinion, we have here an essential characteristic of the religious man; he is a man who interprets his existence not only in terms of being responsible *for* fulfilling his life tasks, but also as being responsible *to* the taskmaster."[30] Again, if meaning is actualized through the pursuit of experiential values or the love of another person, then the religious person is one for whom the experience of human love is, in its ultimate dimension, an experience of the love of God. Finally, if meaning is actualized through attitudinal values, that is, through suffering, then the religious person is one who accepts suffering with some kind of faith in its ultimate meaning—a meaning which is not rationally obvious. In the case of suffering, Frankl maintains, we are dealing not with thinking but with believing, with faith that what we are experiencing has some ultimate meaning or "suprameaning" which we do not grasp "on intellectual grounds but on existential grounds, out of our whole being, i.e. through faith."[31] Frankl insists that authentic human existence is impossible without faith in the sense of a basic trust in life's ultimate meaning. This is the basis of his contention that the human person is "basically religious."[32]

Does this fact of the human person's unconscious religiousness mean that the logotherapist, acting on this premise, should actively lead the patient toward a conscious religious attitude? In other words, is logotherapy, in effect, pastoral counseling? In rejecting this idea Frankl makes two important points:

First, religion and psychotherapy have separate goals and can be of assistance to each other only if each pursues its own goal independently. The goal of religion is spiritual salvation, that of psychotherapy mental health. The effects of pursuing these goals may overlap so they may indirectly achieve each other's goals, but this happens only indirectly and as a side effect. Religion may indeed promote greater mental health and inner equilibrium. Nevertheless "its aim does not primarily concern psychological solutions but, rather, spiritual salvation."[33] In the same way, he insists that psychotherapy must pursue its goals independently and never be reduced to a function of religion. To make psychotherapy "a handmaid in the service of theology" not only deprives it of its dignity (i.e., the value it has in itself as an independent science), it also takes away the potential indirect value it might have for religion. Frankl insists that "psychotherapy has to refrain from setting any preconceived goals along religious lines" since only independent research "uninfluenced by presuppositions borrowed from religion" can be helpful to religion.

Second, if, in the process of therapy, the patient recovers a previously repressed religiousness, this must occur as a "spontaneous breakthrough"; it cannot be the preconceived aim of the therapist. This is even and especially true for the therapist who is himself personally religious. He, above all, should be able to appreciate the fact that genuine religion has to be "existential", that is, not something we are driven to by an instinct or, as Frankl adds, "pushed by a psychiatrist"; it must be something we commit ourselves to by freely choosing it.

Evaluation

An appreciation of Frankl's thought requires that it be seen in its various contexts: philosophical, psychological, and religious.

Philosophical

As a form of existential analysis, logotherapy is rooted in existentialist thought. In Frankl's view of the human condition, we may observe at least three recurring ideas which seem to be fundamental to existentialism.

The Priority of Existence over Essence. To know a thing or person in its essence is to know it in the essential nature it shares with others of the same species, that is, in a "de-individualized" way (e.g., a human person known as bearer of representative of "human nature"). Existence, on the other hand, refers to a being in its concrete, unique individuality. The existential emphasis is on the individual's own immediate experience of herself as a free, responsible "being in the world." Self-consciousness is thus seen as an awareness of one's unique existence in a concrete time and place and of the "becoming" quality of that existence. One is always in the process of becoming what one is.

Freedom and Responsibility. These concepts are linked because free-dom—a matter of immediate awareness—implies responsibility. One must use one's freedom to give meaning and purpose and direction to one's indi-vidual existence. This responsibility in turn implies that anxiety ("existential" anxiety) is part and parcel of human existence.

Subjectivity. This refers to the knowledge or understanding of one's own existence, which is not a matter of abstract, objective information that is assimilated in a detached impersonal way. Existential truth elicits a personal response from the knower involving the exercise of freedom and responsi-bility in giving meaning to one's existence. Existential knowledge leads to de-cision and commitment.

The term "subjectivity" can be applied to Frankl's thought only with caution since he very explicitly rejects the subjectivism of much existentialist thought. He is critical of existentialists such as Jean-Paul Sartre who reject any idea of an objective meaning of life and insist that each individual must "in-vent" the meaning of his own unique existence. In other words, the only mean-ing one's life has is the meaning one assigns to it. We have seen that Frankl rejects this extreme subjectivism and insists on the "objectivity" of meaning in the sense that the meaning of life "is not invented but discovered" through a self-transcending response to what life asks of the individual. The "subjec-tivity" of Frankl's position is to be found rather in his affirmation that the meaning of life is unique to each individual. Though one may be able to state the meaning of life in general terms, in the context of logotherapy, what mat-ters "is not the meaning of life in general but rather the specific meaning of a person's life at a given moment." Everyone's task or mission in life is unique and "therein he cannot be replaced, nor can his life be repeated."[34] In these statements we find reflected the existentialist emphasis on the value and pri-macy of individual human existence as well as on freedom and responsibili-ty as the defining characteristic of human nature. The meaning of one's existence is discovered, Frankl insists, only by being responsible, that is, by freely responding to life's tasks and challenges. Responsibleness is thus "the very essence of human existence."[35]

Psychological

The uniqueness and significance of Frankl's psychological thought must be located in the concept of the spiritual unconscious, which defines the essential humanness of the person in terms of the spiritual dimension of personality. This emphasis on the spiritual dimension of human existence has, not sur-prisingly, been greeted favorably by most theologians, clergy, and religious believers even though it is used by Frankl in a religiously neutral way. Thus, like Maslow, he is received with equal enthusiasm by that increasing number of people who profess no particular religious affiliation, but seek some form of spiritual fulfillment. In a 1972 article,[36] W.E. O'Connell argued that the attractiveness of Frankl's ideas to the religiously and spiritually inclined was more a matter of vocabulary than substance. O'Connell, an Adlerian, argued that what Frankl meant by the term "spirituality" is implicitly contained in Adler's concept of "social interest." It is certainly true that Adler's mature understanding of social interest goes well beyond Frankl's somewhat reductionist categorization of it as will to power and does suggest a will to meaning and self-transcendence. Nevertheless, it could be argued that Adlerian theory does not go beyond the social dimension of personality and does not relate the person to transcendence as does Frankl's concept of "unconscious religiousness."

It is precisely through concepts such as "spiritual unconscious," "will to meaning," and "unconscious religiousness" that Frankl believes he has reaffirmed what is specifically human in the human person. This understanding of human personality, he asserts, is arrived at through a phenomenological approach to the study of personality. This kind of approach seeks to bypass preconceived categories which explain uniquely human phenomena in terms of subhuman phenomena. In Frankl's case, this means that the free, responsible, and self-transcending pursuit of meaning is an "irreducible" human phenomenon. It is taken at face value and not explained as a sublimation of instinctual drives as in Freudian psychoanalysis. It will be recalled that Allport had sought to reaffirm what was uniquely human in the person by asserting the "functional autonomy" of the conscious ego in the pursuit of its own goals from unconscious needs and drives. Frankl appears to go a step further in stressing the responsibleness of the self toward that which transcends it. This is the specifically human phenomenon.

This fundamental view of human nature and the human condition which emerges from psychological theory may be termed "psychological anthropology." John J. Shea suggests that Frankl's anthropology—with its emphasis on freedom, responsibility, and meaning—has "rehumanized psychoanalytic man." Freud's theory is reversed: The person is no longer an object but a subject; values are not subjective self-expressions but objective realities; religion is a real (and healthy) phenomenon, not a symptom of neurosis. Religion is— at least potentially—"that which realizes in a unique and perhaps incomparable way man's basic will to meaning."[37]

It may be argued further that Frankl not only humanizes "psychoanalytic man" but also spiritualizes "humanistic man." On the premise that self-transcendence is the essence of human existence, the "autonomous self" of humanistic psychology becomes the "responsible self" of logotherapy. If the "will to meaning" differentiates Frankl's thought from that of Freud and Adler, we may also point out that the self-transcending quality of the will to meaning differentiates it from the humanistic ideal of self-actualization. As we have seen, he rejects Maslow's contention that "the environment is no more than means to the person's self-actualizing ends,"[38] on the grounds that self-actualization cannot be an end in itself and therefore one's most basic motive; it can be experienced only as a side effect of self-transcendence. Maslow does make reference to the self-transcendence of the self-actualized person, but attributes it to an inner process of growth; it represents a transformation from self-absorption to self-transcendence, which takes place through the unfolding of the individual's inner potentialities. Frankl questions whether genuine self-transcendence takes place in such a closed system and insists on the necessity of an "intentional referent" for self-transcendence. The self transcends itself by commitment to something beyond the self.

This fundamental difference in regard to the meaning of self-transcendence results in differing approaches to the psychological study of religion. For Maslow, religious experience is a purely naturalistic "peak-experience" and religious or spiritual values are human values. Both are explained as the result of the inner growth toward self-actualization; they do not require an explanation in terms of a supernatural source or sanctions. They can be studied in a purely naturalistic way. For Frankl, on the other hand, it is not sufficient to speak of values as mere self-expression. Values and meanings have an objective existence in the form of a task to be completed, a person to be loved, and so forth. Similarly, he rejects the idea that a naturalistic approach can exhaust the meaning of the "religious" or "peak" or "transcendent" experience. Religion is a phenomenon that can be studied naturalistically or psychologically "but only in its human aspect." Like values, religion is not a matter of self-expression but a relationship to that which transcends the self.

This relationship to transcendence is an aspect of the spiritual unconscious. It is therefore originally an unconscious relationship. It may remain unconscious, become conscious in the form of religious faith or be repressed. Whether conscious or unconscious, it is expressed, Frankl believes, in the phenomenon of human responsibleness. Frankl's view seems to be that whether or not one thinks of transcendence as God, it always remains that to which one is responsible.

Religious

In his emphasis on a transcendent dimension of human existence, Frankl approaches the religious view that human existence is fulfilled only in relation to what transcends it. This raises the question: Is logotherapy a religious system? In pondering this question two points should be noted: First, Frankl was himself a believer and his writings contain a significant number of religious and biblical references. In 1995 at age 90 he was questioned by an interviewer about his own religious convictions and their relevance to logotherapy. When he speaks of God, for instance, did he mean God or did he use this word as signifying some kind of human metaphor, projection, or archetype?

Frankl replied that in his work and writings as a logotherapist, his personal religious stance is irrelevant, since his perspective is purely psychological and medical. At the same time he acknowledges that one who posits the idea of a suprameaning which is rooted in faith rather than reason may be called religious, and religion may be defined as one's longing for ultimate meaning. Although this falls short of positing the existence of an Ultimate Being, nevertheless "a religious person may identify supermeaning as something paralleling a Superbeing, and this Superbeing we would call God."[39] Second, Both logotherapy and religious thought stress self-transcendence as an essential feature of human existence. This basic similarity leads to a number of significant parallels: (1) Both speak of human existence as having a "vertical" and a "horizontal" dimension. Self-transcendence "in height" corresponds to the believers' relationship to a transcendent God. Transcendence "in breadth" corresponds to the communal aspect of religion. (2) Frankl's emphasis on the unique meaning of individual existence as opposed to an abstract meaning of life in general recalls religion's understanding of each believer's unique relationship and responsibility to his or her God. (3) Both logotherapy and religion try to assign meaning to suffering.

It is perhaps in this last point of similarity that we might begin to differentiate between religion and psychotherapy. As we have seen, Frankl contends that a truly human life is impossible without some kind of faith, not only in life's meaning but also in its ultimate meaning. Indeed, the religious quest is described as the search for ultimate meaning. Even the irreligious person, however, when faced with apparently meaningless suffering, must respond with faith in what Frankl calls a "suprameaning." This refers to ultimate or unconditional meaningfulness which "necessarily exceeds and surpasses the finite intellectual capacities of man." In Frankl's view, the intellectual response is not simply to endure the meaninglessness of life but rather to bear one's "incapacity to grasp its unconditional meaningfulness in rational terms. *Logos* is deeper than logic."[40] It would seem that Frankl is here insisting on a religious kind of faith. Yet he does not necessarily link such a faith in what is ultimate in meaning with what is ultimate in being (God). Faith in a suprameaning is a human capacity. For the religious person, God is the "ultimate referent" of this faith. The logotherapist may make use of a patient's faith in God but does not insist on it.

Again, Frankl seems to be speaking the language of religion when he speaks of the "transcendent quality" of conscience. Decisions of conscience are exercises in human responsibleness, which must always have an intentional referent—a "to what." Therefore, conscience does not speak with its own voice but mediates the voice of transcendence, that to which I am responsible and which Frankl refers to as a "trans-human agent." But again he stops short of the theological statement that this trans-human agent is God. The religious person, he suggests, is one who points to God as the ultimate intentional referent of his or her responsibleness, but at the same time, respects the freedom of the irreligious person to stop short of this faith interpretation of transcendence. We have then an undifferentiated term—"transcendence"—understood as the intentional referent of human responsibleness, or that to which I am responsible, or that which speaks through one's conscience, which may or may not be identified with the religious transcendent (God). Rabbi Reuven Bulka concludes that logotherapy "is a secular discipline open to the religious dimension."[41]

Transcendence, therefore, is not simply a characteristic of religious life; it is a fundamental quality of human existence as such. In a 1961 article[42] Frankl uses this principle to delineate the unique theory of motivation proper to logotherapy. He suggests that there are three types of motivation. The psychoanalytic image of the person driven by instinctual necessity suggests a kind of motivation conveyed by the words "I must." The humanistic image of the autonomous self with a capacity for self-actualization suggests an "I can" type of motivation. Frankl offers an understanding of human motivation which represents a third alternative to the "I must" of psychoanalysis and the "I can" of humanistic psychology: He therefore speaks of the "I ought" type of motivation of the person who sees himself responsible for the actualization of those values and meanings which challenge him from beyond the self. In terms of motivation, therefore, being ("I am") may be interpreted in terms of necessity ("I must") or in terms of possibility ("I can"). But, in Frankl's view, we miss the essential quality of human existence unless we interpret the "I am" phenomenon in terms of responsibility ("I ought").

Suggested Readings

FRANKL, VIKTOR, *The Doctor and the Soul* (New York: Bantam Books, 1967).

FRANKL, VIKTOR, *Man's Search for Meaning* (New York: Washington Square Press, 1963).

FRANKL, VIKTOR, *Psychotherapy and Existentialism* (New York: Washington Square Press, 1985).

FRANKL, VIKTOR, *Recollections: An Autobiography* (New York: Plenum Press, 1997).

FRANKL, VIKTOR, *The Unconscious God* (New York: Simon and Schuster, 1975).

FRANKL, VIKTOR, *The Unheard Cry for Meaning* (New York: Washington Square Press, 1985).

FRANKL, VIKTOR, *The Will to Meaning* (New York: New American Library, 1970).

Notes

1. William Blair Gould, *Viktor E. Frankl: Life with Meaning* (Pacific Grove, Ca.: Brooks/Cole Publishing Co., 1993), p. 47.
2. Viktor Frankl, *Recollections: An Autobiography* (New York: Plenum Press, 1997), p. 126.

3. *.Ibid.*, p. 97.
4. *Ibid.*, p. 53.
5. *Ibid.*, p. 98.
6. *Ibid.*, p. 42.
7. Viktor Frankl, *Psychotherapy and Existentialism* (New York: Washington Square Press, 1985), p. 55.
8. *Ibid.*
9. *Ibid.*, p. 56.
10. *Ibid.*
11. Viktor Frankl, *Man's Search for Meaning* (New York: Washington Square Press, 1963), p. 175.
12. Cf. Viktor Frankl, *The Will to Meaning* (New York: New American Library, 1970), pp. 37-41.
13. *Ibid.*, pp. 68-69.
14. *Ibid.*, pp. 69-70.
15. Viktor Frankl, *The Doctor and the Soul* (New York: Bantam Books, 1967), p. 55.
16. Viktor Frankl, *Man's Search for Meaning*, p. 180.
17. Viktor Frankl, *The Unconscious God* (New York: Simon and Schuster, 1975), p. 31.
18. William Blair Gould, *Viktor E. Frankl: Life with Meaning*, p. 55.
19. Viktor Frankl, *The Unconscious God*, p. 33.
20. *Ibid.*, pp. 33-34.
21. *Ibid.*, pp. 34-39.
22. *Ibid.*, p. 57.
23. *Ibid.*, p. 53.
24. *Ibid.*, p. 56.
25. *Ibid.*, ch. 6.
26. *Ibid.*, pp. 67-68.
27. *Ibid.*, p. 48.
28. *Ibid.*, p. 46.
29. *Ibid.*, p. 47.
30. Viktor Frankl, *The Doctor and the Soul*, p. 47.
31. Viktor Frankl, *The Will to Meaning*, p. 145.
32. *Ibid.*, p. 150.
33. Viktor Frankl, *The Unconscious God*, p. 74.
34. Viktor Frankl, *Man's Search for Meaning*, pp. 171-172.
35. *Ibid.*, p. 173.
36. W.E. O'Connell, "Frankl, Adler and Spirituality," *Journal of Religion and Health*, 11, 1972, 134-138.
37. John J. Shea, "On the Place of Religion in the Thought of Viktor Frankl," *Journal of Psychology and Theology*, 3, 1975, 179-186.
38. Viktor Frankl, *Psychotherapy and Existentialism*, p. 56.
39. Matthew Scully, "Viktor Frankl at Ninety," *First Things*, 52, 1995, 39-43.
40. Viktor Frankl, *Man's Search for Meaning*, pp. 187-188.
41. Reuven Bulka, "The Ecumenical Ingredient in Logotherapy," *Journal of Ecumenical Studies*, 11, 1974, 13-23.
42. Viktor Frankl, "Logotherapy and the Challenge of Suffering," *Review of Existential Psychology and Psychiatry*, 1, no.1, 1961, 3-7.

APPENDIX

Questions and Answers

I. What Is Religion?

FREUD: Religious belief is an illusion rooted in the "longing for the father," that is, the desire to have a loving, protecting father even in adulthood and projected onto a divine being. Religious observance and ritual are symptoms of an obsessional neurosis rooted in the ambivalent feelings towards one's human father which are projected onto God as a surrogate father.

JUNG: Religion is a "careful and scrupulous observation" of the "numinosum," that is, God, the sacred, the transcendent, or the unconscious. All these can be described as "a dynamic existence or effect, not caused by an arbitrary act of the will. On the contrary, it seizes and controls the human subject, which is always rather its victim than its creator."

JAMES: Religion is "the feelings, acts, and experiences of individual men in their solitude so far as they apprehend themselves to stand in relation to whatever they may consider the divine."

FROMM: Religion is "any system of thought and action shared by a group which gives the individual a frame of orientation and an object of devotion."

ALLPORT: Religion is a person's "ultimate attempt to enlarge and complete his own personality by finding the supreme context in which he rightly belongs."

MASLOW: Religion is a system of doctrine and ritual which attempts to make a prophet's original revelation ("peak experience") available to "the masses." Religion also attempts to apply supernatural sanctions to values which are purely naturalistic in origin. Religious experience is a natural experience and religious values are human values.

FRANKL: Religion is a function of the "spiritual unconscious" which is the source of the "will to meaning." As a search for ultimate meaning, religion is the conscious expression of an "unconscious religiousness," that is, "a latent relation to transcendence."

II. What Is the Psychological Source or Root of Religion?

FREUD: Religion originates in the dynamics of the Oedipus complex. For men, religion represents a failure to resolve the ambivalent feelings of love and hostility toward one's own father which characterizes the oedipal stage. These feelings, along with the resulting guilt feelings, are then projected onto the surrogate father (God). For women, religion finds its source in the failure to outgrow the "longing for the father" since she does not experience the rivalry with and threat from the father that the boy experiences in the oedipal conflict.

JUNG: Religion is rooted in the archetypal structure of the psyche. The archetypes of the collective unconscious act in an autonomous way to lead a person to psychological wholeness, or to the realization of "the self," or—in religious language—to "rebirth." Religious symbols, ritual, and dogma represent symbols onto which the unconscious archetypes are projected, thus investing them with the power to transform personality in the direction of rebirth or selfhood.

JAMES: "Healthy-minded" religion is rooted in the human desire for the "strenuous life," that is, the desire to actively expend one's moral energy in working toward the world's perfection. The religion of the "sick soul," on the other hand, has its origin in the more passive desire for comfort, reassurance, and redemption from feelings of inner dividedness and incompleteness.

FROMM: The psychological root of religion lies in the human need for relatedness to one's world and those in it. This includes both the need to understand one's world as it is (a frame of orientation) and the need for commitment to what the world should be (an object of devotion). Religion is a way of satisfying this twofold "existential need."

ALLPORT: The mature religious sentiment corresponds to the human need for a "unifying master sentiment" which has an integrating effect on personality by providing ultimate meaning and long range goals that permeate all other aspects of life.

MASLOW: Religion finds its source in the human need for self–actualization. Growth towards self–actualization involves an inner valuing process and is sometimes accompanied by "religious" or "peak" experiences. These are purely naturalistic in origin and require no religious explanation or sanctions. In the past, values and spirituality were considered the domain of religion and not of a "narrowly conceived" science that dealt only with facts.

FRANKL: Religion is rooted in the "spiritual unconscious" which is the source of the "will to meaning." For the religious person, religion is the search for ultimate meaning and God is the ultimate "to whom" one is responsible for the meaning of one's life and the ultimate "intentional referent" for the self-transcending search for meaning.

III. What Is the Psychological Value of Religion?

FREUD: Religion is, from a psychoanalytic perspective, regressive and neurotic—the "universal obsessional neurosis." It is based on wish-fulfillment (God as surrogate father) and represents a failure to successfully resolve the Oedipus complex and a projection of the ambivalence of that experience.

JUNG: The psychological value of religion consists in the power of its symbols to effect change or transformation in human personality. Religion offers a symbol system onto which the archetypes of the collective unconscious are projected. The archetypal structure of the psyche creates the possibility of finding meaning in religious myth, symbol, ritual, and dogma. Both religion and individuation have as their goal the rebirth of the individual or the realization of the self.

JAMES: The value of religion consists in the pragmatic, beneficial results it produces for human life—its "fruits for life." Religion can be a call to the "strenuous life" of effort, achievement, and moral endeavor. "Saintliness" refers collectively to the possible positive consequences of religion: liberation from the narrow confines of the self and "loving and harmonious affections." The "cultivation of hardship" characteristic of saintliness may take neurotic and masochistic forms that are of little value, but may also make possible a kind of heroic self-sacrifice that might be the "moral equivalent of war" as a means of tapping one's heroic potential. Mystical states, while they have no authority over those outside the experience, nevertheless suggest that truth cannot be restricted to its non-mystical, rational sources.

FROMM: Religion has a psychological value insofar as it contributes to the growth of one's specifically human powers of reason, love, freedom and responsibility. "Authoritarian" religion, since it involves irrational submission to authority, alienates the believer from these human powers and causes them to be projected onto the deity. It is, therefore, "non-productive." "Humanistic" religion, the aim of which is not submission and obedience but human self-realization, is "productive" in that it promotes the experience of oneself as subject of one's own human powers. Here God is not a symbol of force and domination but a symbol of one's own powers.

ALLPORT: A mature religious sentiment fosters many of those elements that make for the integration of personality: a unifying master sentiment; a recognition of ones "affiliative needs"; basic moral values to be internalized in the formation of conscience; long range goals that set priorities; a source of forgiveness and acceptance; and self objectification through living an "examined life."

MASLOW: The great religious mystics are examples of a kind of "religious" experience and a set of "religious" values, which are in fact natural human experiences, and natural human values. They are the values of self-actualizing people. As such they can be studied naturalistically by a broadened "humanistic" type of science that studies values as well as facts. The language of divine revelation to account for religious experience and religious values represents an historically and culturally conditioned way of describing them. Organized religion may even have a harmful effect if it "religionizes" or makes sacred one part of life while "dereligionizing" or secularizing the rest of life.

FRANKL: If the essence of human existence is "responsibleness," religion provides an ultimate "intentional referent," that is, a God *to whom* one is ultimately responsible. Religion, however, does not exist primarily to provide "psychological solutions" but rather "spiritual salvation." Any psychological benefits deriving from religion (e.g., greater mental health or inner equilibrium) are experienced as side effects of pursuing the self-transcending goals of religion. A need to express the search for meaning religiously can be repressed. This "diseased religiousness" can express itself in a sense of meaninglessness or an over-driven hostility to religion.

IV. What Is Religious Experience?

FREUD: Religious experience in the sense of the mystical sense of oneness with the universe (the "oceanic feeling") is explained psychoanalytically as the persistence in an individual of the "primary ego-feeling," that is, the experience of the infant who has not yet differentiated the ego from the external world. The source of religious feeling in a more general sense is the infantile feeling of helplessness and the consequent "longing for the father."

JUNG: Religious experience is the experience of the "numinosum" which, as far as psychology can explain it, is the experience of the autonomous activity of the collective unconscious. Since it transcends rational consciousness, the unconscious is experienced as a "supraordinate" reality or superior power, analogous to the religious experience of the divine or the sacred. In either case the goal of the experience is wholeness, or the realization of the self, or what religion would call healing/salvation/rebirth.

JAMES: Religious experience is the experience of the "more" of reality. On its "hither side"—the only aspect that can be analyzed psychologically—it is an experience of the subconscious, or "subliminal" self. Whatever it might be on its "farther side"—the divine? the sacred?—this more ultimate source of religious experience is experienced only through the medium of the subliminal self. The effect of religious experience is the healing of a divided self, or the experience of the "wider self."

FROMM: The concept of religious experience can be subsumed under the more general term "X-experience." This refers to a non-theistic type of experience in the sense that it is not necessarily connected with a concept of God. The X-experience describes the fullness of human productiveness or the full realization of one's humanity and one's human powers. As such, it involves the overcoming of narcissism and the transcending of one's ego, or separateness, for the sake of relatedness. At its optimal level, the X-experience results in a mystical sense of "oneness with the all."

ALLPORT: Authentic religious experience is the experience of a religious sentiment that is "intrinsic." This refers to a religious sentiment that sees religion as an end in itself rather than a means to some other end (comfort, security, social status). Intrinsic religion is "functionally autonomous." It involves adapting one's life to one's religious beliefs, not adapting one's religion to one's lifestyle and prejudices.

MASLOW: The term "religious experience" is a culturally and historically conditioned way of describing what is a purely naturalistic phenomenon.

In calling this kind of experience an ecstatic, mystical, or "peak" experience, we avoid giving the impression that it can happen only in a religious context. Peak experiences are transient experiences of bliss, ecstasy, or joy that evoke emotions of awe and reverence and have a transforming effect on the subject of the experience. As the passive recipient of such an experience, the subject feels—to use the language of religion—blessed or graced.

FRANKL: Religious experience can be described psychologically as the experience of "self-transcendence," that is, the search for meaning through commitment to that which transcends the self—a person, a cause, an ideal, a god. The responsibility one feels to discover and respond to meaning is experienced as responsibility to that which transcends oneself and one's conscience. When this ultimate "to whom" is identified with God, the experience is consciously religious. Apart from this explicit "intentional referent," however, the experience still remains a function of the "spiritual unconscious."

INDEX

A

Adler, Alfred, 6, 7, 172–73
  Frankl and, 224, 225
Adorno, Theodor, 140
Aggression
  death instinct and, 12
  guilt and, 15–16
  repression of, 13–14
Aion (Jung), 59
Alacoque, Margaret Mary, Saint, 123, 131
Allen, Gay Wilson, 106–7, 111
Allport, Gordon W., 10, 59–60, 165–94
  biographical data, 167–71
  personality theory, 171–76
    dynamics in, 174–76
    structure in, 171–74
  religion and. *See* Religion, Allport's theory
Aloysius Gonzaga, Saint, 123–24
Ambivalence, religious belief and, 19, 20–22
Anima/animus archetype, 64
Answer to Job (Jung), 59, 77, 80
Archetypal psychology, 93–95
Archetypes, 61, 62
Atkinson, J.J., 23
Authoritarian religion, 150–52
  obedience/disobedience in, 150
  projection in, 150–51

B

Bakan, David, 34, 36
Basic trust, concept of, 40
Batson, C. Daniel, 189–90

B-cognition, 208–9
  characteristics of, 211–13
Beauvoir, Simone de, 45
Belief, in Jamesian theory, 126
Benedict, Ruth, 201, 206
Bettleheim, Bruno, 8, 14
Beyond the Pleasure Principle (Freud), 11
Bixler, J.S., 105, 110, 113
Bleuler, Eugene, 56
Bocock, Robert, 22
Bolt, Martin, 189
Brandon, S.G.F., 31
Breuer, Josef, 1
Brome, Vincent, 3, 6
Brotherliness *vs.* incest, as existential dichotomy, 146–47
Brown, Norman O., 31
Brucke, Ernst, 5
B-values, 214

C

Castration complex/anxiety, concept of, 42
Christ, in Jungian theory, 78–79,80, 81–82
Civilization, Freudian theory of,13–16
  aim-inhibition and, 15
  totemism and, 25
  tragic aspect of, 14–16
Civilization and Its Discontents (Freud), 13
Collective unconscious, 56, 60,61–62, 90
Compensation principle, 65–66
Complexes, 61
Conscience, as irrational/intuitive function, 233–35
Conscious polarity, 60

Conscious unity, 60
Cox, David, 69
Creativeness *vs.* destructiveness,as existential dichotomy, 146
Crumbaugh, J., 189
Culture, religion and, 179

D

Darwin, Charles, 23
D-cognition, 208
Death instinct
     instinct theory and, 11–13
     theory of civilization and, 13–14,
          15–16
Displacement, 10
Doctor and the Soul, The (Frankl), 226–27
Dogmas, religious, 73–74, 89
Dream interpretation
     Frankl and, 236
     Freud and, 2

E

Eastern religions
     Fromm and, 137, 141, 156–7
     in Jungian theory, 82–87
Edinger, Edward, 68
Ego
     in Freudian theory, 9, 172
     in Jungian theory, 61
Ego psychology, religion and, 37–39
Empiricism, in Jamesian theory, 104
Enantiodromia, 67
Erich Fromm: The Courage to Be Human (Funk), 137
Erikson, Erik, 38, 40, 106
Eros
     death instinct *vs.*, 11–13
     theory of civilization and, 13–14
Escape from Freedom (Fromm), 140, 141
Essays in Radical Empiricism (James), 110
Esteem needs, 206
Evans, Richard, 136, 156, 191
Evil, in Jamesian theory, 118, 119, 120
Extraversion, 65
Extrinsic *vs.* intrinsic religion, 183–85,
          188–89
     critique of concept, 189–90,191–92

F

Faber, Heije, 38–39
Fairbairn, W.R.D., 39
Feeling, as psychological function, 64
Feminist critiques
     of Freudian theory, 41–46
     of Jungian theory, 95–98
Feuerbach, Ludwig, 151
Fliess, Wilhelm, 4
Fordham, Frieda, 63
Frame of orientation, existential need
     for, 148–49
Frankl, Eleanore (Elly) Schwindt (wife
     of Viktor), 227
Frankl, Elsa (mother of Viktor), 225
Frankl, Gabriel (father of Viktor), 225
Frankl, Tilly Grasser (wife of Viktor),
     225, 226
Frankl, Viktor, 10, 223–43
     biographical data, 225–27
     personality theory, 227–32
          basic principles, 230
          critique of Maslow, 229–30
          dimensions of human nature, 228
          human suffering, 231, 232
          self-transcendence, 218, 228, 229
          values and, 230–31
          ways of finding meaning, 230–31
     religion and. *See* Religion, Frankl's
          theory
Freud, Amalie Nathanson (mother of
     Sigmund), 3
Freud, Jacob (father of Sigmund), 3
Freud, Martha Bernays (wife of Sigmund), 5
Freud, Sigmund, 1–50
     biographical data, 3–7
     dream interpretation, 2
     Frankl and, 225
     personality theory, 7–16
          civilization and, 13–16
          instincts and, 8–15
     psychoanalysis, origins of, 1–2
     religion and. *See* Religion, Freud's
          theory
     repression, theory of, 1–2
     sexual theory, 6–7
Friedan, Betty, 45
Fromm, Annis Freeman (wife of Erich),
     142
Fromm, Erich, 12, 14, 30, 31, 88, 135–63

biographical data, 137–42
character types, 149
humanistic approach to religion,
    136–37
Marxism and, 137, 139
Maslow and, 196–97
as non-theist, 135–36
personality theory, 142–49
    brotherliness *vs.* incest, 144,
        146–47
    creativeness *vs.* destructiveness,
        144, 146
    individuality *vs.* conformity, 144,
        147–48
    overview, 142–44
    reason *vs.* irrationality, 144, 148–49
    relatedness *vs.* narcissism, 144–45
    religion and. *See* Religion, Fromm's
        theory
    "social character" concept, 140
    Zen Buddhism and, 137, 141, 156–57
Fromm, Henny Gurland (wife of Erich),
    141
Fromm, Naphtali (father of Erich),
    137–38
Fromm, Rosa Krause (mother of Erich),
    137, 138
Fromm-Reichmann, Frieda (wife of
    Erich), 139, 141
Functional autonomy of motives, 167,
    169, 175–76, 240
Functional continuity of motives,
    175–76
Funk, Rainer, 137, 142, 152, 158
Future of an Illusion, The (Freud), 33

G

Gender differentiation, in Jungian
    theory, 63–64
Glen, J. Stanley, 158
Glover, Edward, 88
God
    in authoritarian religion, 150–52
    in humanistic religion, 153, 154–55
    in Jamesian theory, 115–16
    in Jungian theory
        archetype, 64, 73, 75
        God-image, 73, 74–76
Goldenberg, Naomi, 97–98

Gonzaga, Aloysius, Saint, 123–24
"Good Human Beings (GHB)", 202, 216
Gould, William Blair, 224, 233
Greer, Germaine, 45
Guilt
    internalized aggression and, 15–16
    religion and, 20–22

H

Hanna, Charles, 69
Hannah, Barbara, 51
Harlow, Harry, 195, 199, 200
Hartmann, Heinz, 37
Healthy-minded religion, 104–5, 117–18
    evil and, 119–20
    involuntary and systematic, 118
Heart of Man, The (Fromm), 149
Herik, Judith Van, 43, 45–46
Hierarchy of needs, concept of, 205–6
Hillman, James, 93–95
Hoarding character, 149
Hoffman, Edward, 198
Homans, Peter, 52, 90, 128
Hood, Ralph W., Jr., 189
Horkheimer, Max, 140
Horney, Karen, 139, 141
Humanistic religion. *See* Allport, Gor-
    don W.; Fromm, Erich; Frankl,
    Viktor; Maslow, Abraham
Hunger needs, 205

I

I Ching, Jung on, 86–87
Id, 9
Identity, individuality *vs.* conformity
    and, 147–48
Illusion, religion as, 17–20
Inborn dispositions, concept of, 172
Incarnation, in Jungian theory, 81–82
Incest taboo
    Jungian view of, 71–72
    totemism and, 24
Individual and His Religion, The (Allport),
    176
Individuality *vs.* conformity
    as existential dichotomy, 147–48
    religion and, 179

Individuation, 60, 67
    goal of, 64
    as religious quest, 68–70
Instinct theory, 8–13
    aim-inhibition in, 10
    ego instincts *vs.* sex instincts, 10–11
    Eros *vs.* death instinct, 11–13
    human behavior and, 8–9
    stages in development of, 10–12
Intentional referent, 218
Interpretation of Dreams, The (Freud), 1, 5
Introversion, 65
Intuition, as psychological function, 64
Involuntary healthy-mindedness, 118
Isbister, J.N., 4

J

Jaffe, Aniela, 53, 74, 80, 90
James, Henry, Jr. (brother of William),
    106
James, Henry, Sr. (father of William),
    105–6, 108
James, William, 103–63
    biographical data, 105–10
    philosophical context, 110–15
        pluralism, 112–13
        pragmatism, 111–12
    religion and. *See* Religion, James'
        theory
    temperament and, 103–5
Jones, Ernest, 7
Jones, James, 33, 34, 41
Jung, Carl Gustav, 3, 4, 6, 51–102
    biographical data, 52–59
    experience of God, 51–52, 54–55
    Freud and, 56–58
    personality theory, 59–67
        attitudes, 65
        dynamics, 65–67
        functions, 64–65
        structure, 61–65
        systems, 61–64
    Rauschenbauch, Emma (wife of
        Carl), 56
    religion and. *See* Religion, Jung's
        theory

K

Kirkpatrick, Lee A., 189
Klein, Melanie, 39

Knapp, Gerhard, 135, 138, 139, 141, 142,
    157
Kohut, Heinz, 39

L

Langfeld, H.S., 168, 169
Locke, John, 191
Logotherapy, 224, 225, 231, 236, 237–38,
    241–42
    basic principles, 230–31
Love needs, 205–6

M

Man for Himself (Fromm), 141
Man's Search for Meaning (Frankl), 227
Marcuse, Herbert, 31, 140
Margaret Mary Alacoque, Saint, 123
Marketing character, 149
Maslow, Abraham, 190, 195–221
    biographical data, 197–203
    Fromm and, 196–97
    personality theory, 203–9
        basic assumptions, 204–5
        Frankl's critique of, 229–30, 241
        human motivation, 205–6
        peak-experiences, 208–9
        self-actualization, 195–96, 206–8
    religion and. *See* Religion, Maslow's
        theory
Maslow, Bertha Goodman (wife of
    Abraham), 199
Maslow, Rose (mother of Abraham),
    197–98
Maslow, Samuel (father of Abraham),
    197, 198
Masochistic character, 149
Mature religious sentiment/personality,
    167, 179–83
    characteristics of, 180–83
McConnell, Theodore A., 191
Meaning
    pursuit of, 178–79
    understanding of, 229
Meissner, W.W., 34
Mental health, religion and, 185–87
Millett, Kate, 45
Mitchell, Juliet, 45
Monism, 104, 112–13

Monotheism
    Freudian theory and, 25–27
    Jungian theory and, 93–94
Moore, Thomas, 95
Morality
    Frankl on, 233–35
    in Freudian theory
        feminist critique of, 43–46
        religion and, 18–20
        totemism and, 25
    in Jungian theory, 80–81
Morbid-mindedness, 119
More, the, 121–22
Moses
    in Freudian theory, 26–27, 34–35
    Freud's identification with, 35
Moses and Monotheism (Freud), 22, 23, 25, 29
Motivation, 165–67, 174–76. *See also* specific personality theories
    mature adult, 167, 169–70
    mature religious personality, 167
Mysterium Coniunctionis, 59
Mysticism, 124–26
Myth/mythology, 62
    archetypal psychology and, 94–95

N

Narcissism
    overcoming of, 156
    relatedness *vs.,* 144–45
Nature of Prejudice, The (Allport), 170, 183
New Knowledge in Human Values (Maslow, ed.), 215
Noetic quality of mystic experience, 124
Nonproductive character orientation, 144
Nontheistic religious experience, 155–57, 214
Noogenic neurosis, 223

O

Object of devotion, existential need for, 148–49
Object-relations theory, religion and, 39–41

Obsessional neurosis, religion as, 20–22
O'Connell, W.E., 240
Oedipus complex
    Adler and, 7
    feminist critique of, 41–46
    Jung and, 7
    religion and, 20–21
    totemism and, 24–25
Organic desire, as source of religious sentiment, 177–78

P

Palma, Robert J., 190
Pattern and Growth in Personality (Allport), 169
Peak-experiences, 197, 202, 208–9
    characteristics of, 211–13
Penis envy, concept of, 42, 45
Perry, Ralph Barton, 109
Persona archetype, 62–63
Personality: A Psychological Interpretation (Allport), 165
Personality theories
    Allport, 171–76
    Frankl, 227–32
    Freud, 7–16
    Fromm, 142–49
    Jung, 59–67
    Maslow, 203–9
Personal unconscious, 61
Pleasure principle, 9
Pluralism, 104, 105, 112–13
    melioristic aspect of, 112
Pragmatism, 111–12
    religious experience and, 130–31
Pragmatism (James), 104, 110
Prejudice, religion and, 183–85
Principles of Psychology (James), 109
Productive character orientation, 144
Productive relatedness, 144–45
Progressive tendency, in dichotomy of human existence, 143
    religion and, 149–50
Projection
    in authoritarian religion, 150–51
    principle, in Jungian personality theory, 66–67
Propriate striving, 173
Proprium, 169, 173–74
Pruyser, Paul, 128, 129

Psychoanalysis. *See also* Freud, Sigmund
  dream interpretation, 2
  repression, theory of, 1–2
Psychoanalysis and Religion (Fromm),
  138, 141, 149, 151
Psychogenic desires, as source of religious sentiment, 178
Psychology: Briefer Course (James), 109
Psychology and Religion: West and East
  (Jung), 82
Psychopathology of Everyday Life (Freud),
  5
Purpose-in-Life Test, 189
Pursuit of meaning, as source of religious sentiment, 178–79

R

Radical empiricism, 111, 114–15
Rationalism, in Jamesian theory, 104
Rauschenbauch, Emma, 56
Reality principle, 9
Reason *vs.* irrationality, as existential dichotomy, 148–49
Rebirth, religious/psychological concepts of, 68–69, 71–72
Redemption, in Jungian theory, 81–82
Regressive tendency, in dichotomy of human existence, 143–44
  religion and, 149–50
Religion, Allport's theory, 176–92
  aspects of integration, 187
  extrinsic *vs.* intrinsic religion, 183–85, 188–89
  mental health and, 185–87
  prejudice/bigotry and, 183–85
  prescriptive *vs.* descriptive aspects, 190–91
  religious sentiment, 177
    mature, 167, 179–83
    origins of, 177–79
Religion, Frankl's theory, 232–43
  conscience, 233–35
  morality, 233–35
  philosophical critique, 238–39
  psychological critique, 239–41
  religious critique, 241–43
  religiousness, 235–38
  shame in, 236–37
  spiritual unconscious, 232–33
Religion, Freud's theory, 2–3, 4–5, 16–46
  ego psychology and, 37–39

feminist readings of, 41–46
historical foundation for, 22–28
illusion in, 17–20
object-relations theory and, 39–41
obsessional neurosis and, 20–22
Oedipus complex and, 20–21
one-sided aspect, 36–37
prejudicial aspect, 33–36
reductionist aspect, 28–30
unscientific aspect, 30–32
Religion, Fromm's theory, 149–61
  authoritarian religion, 150–52
  concept of God, 154–55
  dichotomy of human existence and, 149–50
  human condition and, 157–58
  humanistic religion, 152–54
  nontheistic religious experience, 155–57
  reductionistic aspect, 158–60
  theism, 160–61
Religion, James' theory, 115–31
  evil, 118–20
  God and religious belief, 115–16, 126
  monism, 104, 112–13
  pluralism, 104, 105, 112–13
  pragmatism, 111–12, 130–31
  radical empiricism, 111, 114–15
  religious experience, 116–17, 218–19
    essence of, 120–22
    as individual, 127
    pragmatism and, 130–31
    as separate category of experience, 127–28
    theology and, 129–30
    types of, 117–20
  religious life, elements of, 122–26
    belief, 126
    mysticism, 124–26
    saintliness, 122–24
Religion, Jung's theory, 68–98
  Christianity and, 74–82, 87–88
    God and God-image, 74–76
    incarnation and redemption, 81–82
    Trinity dogma, 76–81
  Eastern religions and, 82–87
  individuation and, 68–70
  one-sided aspect, 93–98
    archetypal psychology and, 93–95
    feminist critique, 95–98
    prejudicial aspect, 91–92

reductionist aspect, 88–89
religious symbolism and, 70–74
unscientific aspect, 89–91
Religion, Maslow's theory, 209–20
critique of, 217–20
peak-experience, 211
reductionist aspect, 218–19
religious experience, 211–14
religious personalities, 213
religious values, 214–16
science in, 209–11, 219–20
*Religions, Values and Peak-
Experiences* (Maslow), 209
Religious Orientation Scale, 189, 190
Repression
ego and, 10
theory of, 1–2
Return of the repressed, monotheism
and, 26, 27
Ricoeur, Paul, 16
Right and wrong, principle of, 9
Rizzuto, Ana-Maria, 39
Rootedness, as existential need, 146–47

S

Sadistic character, 149
Safety needs, 205
Sagan, Eli, 32, 43–44
Saintliness, 122–24
asceticism and, 122–23
purity of soul and, 123–24
strength of soul and, 123
tenderness and charity, 124
Samuels, Andrew, 97
Sartre, Jean-Paul, 239
Schaar, John H., 137, 158
Self
archetype of, 60–61, 64, 75, 77, 80
as locus of uniqueness, 60
proprium and, 173–74
Self-actualization, 195–96, 206–8
defined, 208
need for, 206
Self-transcendence, 218, 228, 229
conscience and, 234–35
religion and, 235–36
Sensing, as psychological function, 64
Sentiments, concept of, 177
Shadow archetype, 63
Shea, John J., 240

Sick soul, religion of, 104–5, 115, 117, 118
evil and, 119–20
ideal self *vs.* actual self, 120–21
*Sigmund Freud and the Jewish Mystical
Tradition* (Bakan), 34
Sigmund Freud's Christian Unconscious
(Vitz), 35
Smith, W. Robertson, 23
Spiritual values, as source of religious
sentiment, 178
Stein, Murray, 87–88
Stephens, FitzJames, 126
Straumann, Heinrich, 111
Studies on Hysteria (Freud and Breuer),
1, 5
Sublimation, 10, 15
Suffering, in Frankl's theory, 231, 232,
237
Sullivan, Harry Stack, 141
Sumner, William, 199
Superego
in Allport's theory, 186–87
in Freud's theory, 9, 18–19, 35–36
Swedenborg, Emanuel, 106, 108
Symbols of Transformation (Jung), 57–58
Syndrome of growth *vs.* syndrome of
decay, 149
Systematic healthy-mindedness, 118

T

Temperament
James on, 103–5
as source of religious sentiment, 178
Tender-minded temperament, 104
Thinking, as psychological function, 64
Thorndike, Edward, 201
Tillich, Paul, 219
Titchener, Edward, 169
To Have or to Be (Fromm), 138, 149
Totem and Taboo (Freud), 22, 23
Totemism
incest taboo and, 24
Oedipus complex and, 24–25
as origin of religion, 24–25
Tough-minded temperament, 104
Toward a Psychology of Being (Maslow),
204
Traits, concept of, 169, 172
Transcendence
conscience and, 234–35
human need for, 146

Transcendent function, 67
Transitional objects, 40
Transpersonal psychology, 197
Trinity, dogma of, 76–81
    Christ, 77–79
    God, 77
    Holy Spirit, 79–80
Truth, pragmatic view of, 111–12

U

Ulanov, Ann B., 96, 97
Unconscious unity, in Jungian theory, 60
Unheard Cry for Meaning, The (Frankl),
    226

V

Values, approaches to
    Allport, 178
    Frankl, 230–31
    Maslow, 215–16
Varieties of Religious Experience, The
    (James), 104, 105, 107, 109, 114–15,
    116, 120
Virgin Mary, Jungian symbolism and,
    78–79
Vitz, Paul, 35

W

Watson, John B., 199
Wehr, Demaris, 96–97, 98
Wertheimer, Max, 201, 206
White, Victor, 71
Will to Believe, The (James), 126
Will to meaning, 223, 228
Wilson, Colin, 56, 58, 59, 89–90, 196
Winnicott, D.W., 40
Wish fulfillment, religion and, 19

X

X-experience, 155–56

Y

Yoga, Jung on, 83–84

Z

Zen Buddhism, Fromm and, 137, 141,
    156–57
Zilboorg, Gregory, 33, 36